The covers collected [in these volumes] show exactly what covers are designed to do – stimulate eye and mind – and also act with Pavlovian intensity on the designer/reader's behaviour knowingly or not. They are indeed meant to have IMPACT.

Steven Heller

Impact 1.0

–

Design magazines, journals and periodicals [1922–73]

Unit 27

Contents

Foreword
—
The editors

This book and its companion volume, *Impact 2.0, Design magazines, journals and periodicals [1974–2016]*, have their origins in two visits made by Tony Brook. The first was to the University of the Creative Arts (UCA) archive in Epsom, UK, and the second was to the Herb Lubalin Study Center of Design and Typography in New York, USA. Both locations house a superabundance of design magazines from the early 20th century to the present day. The opportunity to make a book out of these stellar collections was too good to pass up.

At its core, these volume are an attempt to catalogue the excellence of design magazines, journals and periodicals catering for design of all kinds. We've chosen to only show covers – and only covers that exhibit superior design values. Interestingly, this means that the publications we have included here also tend to be the publications that have the most merit. Poor covers usually mean poor content.

We have spread our net wide. Although the covers shown here are mostly from graphic design publications, we have included some from architecture and material design – but again, only when the design is exemplary.

These are also books that seek to acknowledge the contribution that the editors, writers, publishers and designers of journals have made to the evolution of design. Without the design press, we are entitled to wonder if design would have travelled quite so rapidly from a marginal artisanal craft of the industrial era to the sophisticated communication and information discipline that it is in today's information era.

We take them for granted, we even allow them to wither away, but a discipline without its journals of record is hard to conceive.

Reading the design zeitgeist: a graphic design perspective

—

Adrian Shaughnessy

Magazines, journals and periodicals catering for designers of all kinds are like maps for tourists visiting new cities – essential for anyone who doesn't want to get lost. The creative professions, crafts and trades move at a frenzied pace. Today's innovations are tomorrow's redundancies; what is hot now becomes tepid in the blink of an eye. Keeping up is a full-time job.

Design publications allow practitioners to 'keep up' with developments in their respective disciplines. In the pages of the design press it is possible to maintain close contact with stylistic trends, technical developments, ethical issues, commercial legalities and upheavals in the creative disciplines. They also provide a ringside seat from which to view the activities of friends and rivals, and to monitor the work of new talent and old masters. At their best, design publications educate designers in both the practice and theory of design, and occasionally, in the workings of the world beyond design.

The more high-minded and less commercially focused publications offer critique, informed commentary and technical know-how. Other, less rigorous, journals (the so-called 'show and tell' publications, though in truth they are mostly 'show' and not much 'tell'), offer the recycling of PR handouts promoting star designers, hip studios and new products regardless of quality or merit. Yet when viewed retrospectively, the design press – both good and bad – provides an unrivalled opportunity for the ethnographic study of design: where else can the student of past trends and eruptions on the never-ending catwalk of creative endeavour find such a condensed source of material? As Steven Heller puts it, the design press provides 'an invaluable commentary that is simply not available in any other form'.[1]

Successful designers who don't need the leg-up that exposure in a design publication can provide take pleasure in haughtily pointing out that they no longer read the design press ('I'm more interested in *Frieze* or *Artforum*'). On the other hand, many designers at the beginning of their careers, and in mid-career, view the design press as an important platform for self-promotion and exposure. A third group have already abandoned the printed format in favour of the instant sugar hit of online feeds and blogs, with the consequence that printed design magazines are under threat of execution from the world of free, always-available online content. No printed publication can compete with the speed of the Internet, and some, like the UK's *Design Week* and *Grafik*, and *I.D.* in the USA, have already succumbed to the online guillotine, and no longer exist in paper and ink forms.

Yet it's also worth noting that not all printed publications are about to disappear. Some are thriving. And there is good reason for optimism as increasing numbers of magazines abandon their roles as news platforms and promotional vehicles in favour of a more reflective and interrogatory stance. Today, it's not unusual to see design magazines devoting entire issues to a single topic, thus allowing a deeper analysis of subject matter. In this context we might single out *Slanted* (Germany), *Graphic* (South Korea) and *Mas Context* (USA), as three current examples of periodicals that devote individual issues to one theme. Paradoxically, as more and more publications – many established in the great design and media boom of the 1980s – slide inexorably towards the online realm or, in some cases, oblivion, we seem to be entering a period when the printed design journal is actually discovering a new and more meaningful role within design culture. If that is the case, then it feels like an opportune moment to celebrate the tradition of printed publications devoted to the practice of design, and to acknowledge the design profession's debt to printed design journals.

The design of design magazines

For graphic designers – and enlightened designers of all stripes – the design of the magazines themselves is a subject of perennial interest. For most designers, to be asked to design a design magazine is the professional equivalent of winning an Olympic gold medal. Surely here, of all places, designers are free to do the work that most conventional clients would never sanction? In the pages of this book you will find many examples of journals that have taken advantage of the licence afforded them by addressing a design audience: standout examples include *Typographische Monatsblätter* (1932), *Portfolio* (1949), *Neue Grafik* (1958), *Emigre* (1984) and *Dot Dot Dot* (2001). These, and many others, are publications that thumbed their noses at conventional magazine design and produced publications that offered a startling alternative. They took the view that designers don't need to be fed the sort of 'I-Speak-Your-Weight' design that publishers of conventional magazines assume to be unavoidable.

Not all design journals manage this. Some cling to newsstand conventions and produce magazines that are barely distinguishable from other trade publications. Some flare up in moments of modish frenzy, grabbing the vapour trails of the latest fashion, only to look tired and faded a few years later. Yet those that defy convention, and trust their audience to expect 'different', constitute an unofficial guide to design trends and graphic innovation that is unequalled anywhere else – except perhaps in certain strands of avant-garde publishing and the best record covers. They offer a condensed timeline of graphic innovation that allows the student of design to plot trends and to take delight in the graphic design that emerges when the publishers of magazines are also the designers.

Design journals are not a new thing

Design periodicals of one kind or another have been in existence since the beginning of the 20th century. Before then, around the end of the 19th century, there were art journals and publications that catered for the moneyed classes by chronicling the decorative arts, the beaux-arts and architecture. And as the world entered the industrial era, a handful of journals focused on the fast-growing print trade and the cult of the poster.

TM
1932–present
Switzerland

Neue Grafik
1958–65
Switzerland

Industrial Design/I.D
1954–2009
USA

There is no clear consensus on which was the first graphic design journal. The term 'graphic design' didn't come into use until coined by WA Dwiggins in 1922, but prior to this a number of publications were devoted to the print trade and what can safely be described as the beginnings of a professional literature for the embryonic discipline of graphic design. Design historian Paul Shaw (pp. 049) cites *The Inland Printer* (1883), *The American Printer* (1883) and *The Printing Art* (1903), as pioneering American publications in the field.

The Studio (1893, UK) and *Les Maîtres de l'Affiche* (1895, France) covered the applied arts and posters. In Germany, *Das Plakat* (1910) was an early attempt to produce a publication that treated the poster as a serious art form, and an example of a publication dealing with the growing importance of the graphic arts in the newly industrialised Europe.

At the turn of the century, two journals appeared that had typography as their subject matter: *Typographische Mitteilungen* (1903, Germany), and *The Monotype Recorder* (1902, UK). In the 1920s, *Typographische Mitteilungen* was to provide the first indication of graphic design as a maturing discipline. Under the editorship of Jan Tschichold it offered a controversial introduction to the New Typography.

In 1924, HK Frenzel launched *Gebrauchsgraphik*, a German professional magazine dedicated to advertising art. It was edited by Frenzel, and published in English and German. Frenzel believed that advertising was a force for good in the newly established world of mass-produced consumer products. He featured the work of Herbert Bayer and advocated the Bauhaus philosophy of integrating art, design and manufacturing. *Gebrauchsgraphik* was closed by the Nazis, but resurfaced in the post-war era. It exists today in the form of *novum* magazine.

With the rise of advertising as a vital support system for the new consumerism in America, a number of publications took on the role of promoting the discipline of graphic design and its related crafts – art direction, photography and typography – to the American business community. These included *Commercial Art* (1922), *PM* (1934) and *Art and Industry* (1936). The American editor of *Gebrauchsgraphik* was Dr Robert L Leslie, and when the German publication folded in 1934, he created his own version – *PM*

(Production Manager) magazine. *PM* was launched with covers designed by prominent figures such as Lucian Bernhard, Herbert Bayer and Lester Beall. The name was sold in 1940 and the magazine continued under the name *AD* magazine, with covers by Paul Rand, amongst others.

These and other publications were to mark the rise of the art director, a individual described by the great pioneer of magazine design, the Russian-born Mehemed Fehmy Agha (*Vogue, House & Garden, Vanity Fair*) as someone who 'plans, co-ordinates and rehearses, but does not perform; at least not in public'.[2] But it was to be another Russian émigré who was to take the role of art direction to unprecedented heights. Alexey Brodovitch was the art director of *Portfolio* (1949), a publication that only lasted for three issues, but which was to have an enduring impact on publication design. Large format, free of advertising and designed without the normal constraints of an over-zealous publisher, it was to become a blueprint for independent design publishing in the ensuing years.

Another kind of blueprint was established by *Graphis* (1944), which came to represent the publishing model for the 'showcasing' of graphic design. With Walter Herdeg as owner and editor, the showcasing was done with style, eclecticism and good judgment. *Graphis* presented, for the first time, the best design and illustration from Europe, America, Eastern Europe (especially Poland), Japan and South America. To be seen in *Graphis* was to receive a special kind of benediction. Now based in the USA, the magazine continues under the ownership of publisher and design and editorial director Martin M Pedersen. Over 350 issues have been published to date.

Typographica (1949, UK), designed and edited by Herbert Spencer, offered yet another model. Spencer established a publication for designers and typographers that looked beyond professional boundaries and explored the historical, scholarly and cultural context of the craft. Funded by the printer and publisher Lund Humphries, Spencer was given exceptional freedom to explore the outer limits of the typographic universe. For many commentators *Typographica* stands as a paradigm for the independent reflective publication, unconcerned with the need to accommodate commercial imperatives, and free from the requirement to be modish.

Idea magazine appeared in Japan in 1953. Its early editions were remarkable for their sure-footed exploration of the Japanese *and* non-Japanese world of design. When copies began to appear in the West, it gave European and American designers a first sighting of the numerous brilliant Japanese designers who emerged in the post-war years. But it did the reverse too, and brought Western designers – often designers under-valued in their home countries – to a Japanese and Asian audience. To browse through editions from the late-1960s and early-1970s, is to encounter profiles of 'obscure' American designers such as Norma Updyke and Fred Troller (both *Idea* No.118); to find articles on African American designers (*Idea* No.104); and Czech film posters (*Idea* No.124). *Idea* still flourishes today and remains a muscular and respected voice in the graphic design ecosystem. Under the editorship of Kiyonori Muroga it continues to display an aptitude for covering topics of relevance to a discerning and internationally-minded audience.

From the 1970s onwards, the proliferation of the design profession, and the willingness of many of its support services (photography, typesetting, printing and recruitment) to buy advertising, meant that publishing houses realised that producing magazines covering graphic design could be a lucrative activity. During the second half of the 20th century, a great many magazines came to prominence by offering different levels of engagement with the discipline. A good example of this was *U&lc* (1970, USA), owned by ITC (International Typeface Corporation), and edited by designer Herb Lubalin, it had a controlled circulation of over 250,000 and an international readership (according to ITC) of one million. In the 1970s it was a rare studio that didn't have a copy of the magazine on display.

The design magazines of the 1980s thrived on the unspoken promise that you – or your studio – might one day be included in their pages; you might even feature on the front cover. This was a tactic used by, amongst others, the British magazine *Direction* (1980s), which made a feature of modish photographs of the star designers of the moment. These and other publications provided a platform for design to show off its latests models (hip studios, the occasional superstar designer and the latest work destined for the supermarket shelves). Subscriptions were taken out by studios keen to be featured in the pages of these magazines with the hope of being spotted by a client with a pot of cash to spend on a new packaging range or a property brochure. (In reality, this rarely happened and designers ended up succeeding only in 'promoting' themselves to other designers.)

In the new publishing terrain, criticality was avoided and the status quo was carefully protected – 'design is good for business'; 'don't upset the clients'; 'don't criticise fellow professionals'. In the 1980s and 1990s design became embedded in the great service sector boom. Big design groups got bigger, charged higher fees and became indistinguishable from management consultants. But at the same time, a new radicalism entered design publishing with the arrival of small, agile publications, owned, edited, and designed by designers.

Designers as publishers

Octavo (1986) offered a single-minded exploration of the neo-modernist trends in European typography. Uncompromising, asymmetric and sometimes wilfully obscure, designers Hamish Muir, Mark Holt, Simon Johnston and Michael Burke produced a publication in the grand tradition of artists' statements: it was a catalogue of their own obsessions and an emphatic rebuttal of the dominant stylistic tropes of 1980s design.

Another counterpoint to the prevailing orthodoxy came in the shape of *Emigre* (1984), a publication founded by type designers Rudy VanderLans and Zuzana Licko. As design writer Michael Dooley has noted: '*Emigre* became a full-fledged graphic design journal in 1988 with issue ten, produced by students at Cranbrook Academy of Art in Michigan. VanderLans concentrated on work that was being neglected by other design publications, either because it didn't adhere to traditional canons or it was still in its formative stages.'[3] Widely regarded as the first design magazine of the computer age, *Emigre's* defiantly anti-commercial position, and its iconoclastic approach to graphic design formalism and good taste, caused widespread controversy amongst the design establishment. Massimo Vignelli was an especially virulent critic, accusing the magazine of being shallow, inelegant and lacking a sense of history.

PM
1934–42
USA

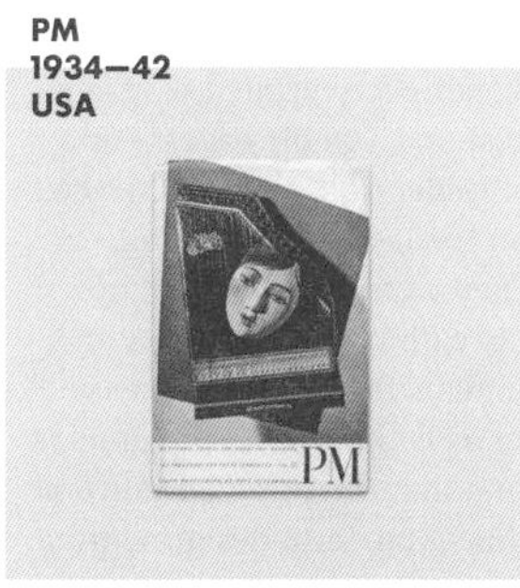

Idea
1953–present
Japan

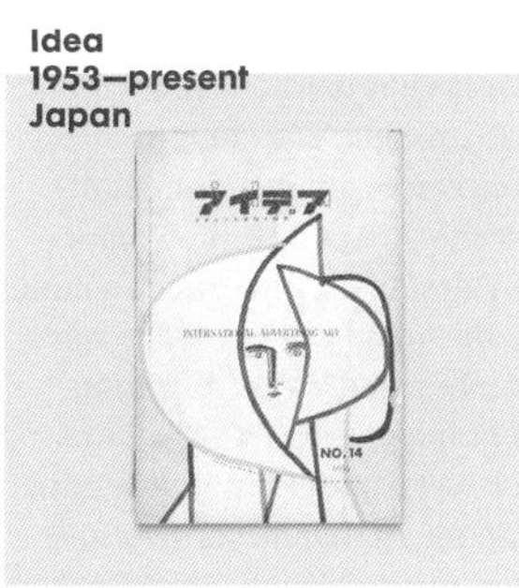

Emigre
1984–2005
USA

These publications, however, were only following a trend in independent designer-led journals that had been pioneered years before by *The Push Pin Graphic* (1957, USA), and *Neue Grafik* (1958, Switzerland). *The Push Pin Graphic* was the work of Milton Glaser and Seymour Chwast, two giants of the mid-20th century New York graphic arts scene. The publication was launched as an item to send to clients and friends, but ended up as a vehicle for alerting people to the Push Pin Studios (run by Glaser and Chwast), and later as a promotional aid when the studio began representing illustrators. The magazine showed the range of expression that could be achieved by graphic arts practitioners. As Chwast has said: 'The *Graphic* was an extension of our passions not entirely satisfied by our day jobs.'[4] It had a dedicated following, and lasted for 23 years and 86 issues.

Neue Grafik was the work of Paul Lohse, Josef Müller-Brockmann, Hans Neuberg and Carlo Vivarelli. They set out, in their words, 'to create an international platform for the discussion of modern graphic and applied art. Contrary to that of existing publications, the attitude of *Neue Grafik* is characterised by exclusiveness, consistency and lack of compromise'. In that statement – especially in the words 'exclusiveness' and 'lack of compromise' – we find the clarion call adopted by nearly every independent publication that followed in *Neue Grafik's* wake.

Eye magazine, under the astringent editorship of Rick Poynor, was launched in 1990. Its strapline announced its bold agenda: The International Review of Graphic Design. It was perfect-bound, had good paper, superb reproduction, trilingual texts and sophisticated layouts by designer Stephen Coates. This was combined with sharp, critical writing that was unafraid to prick the bubbles of complacency and self-aggrandisement within which many end-of-the-millennium designers comfortably resided. Poynor gave up the editorship in 1997, and although present-day *Eye* has abandoned its role as a design world agitator, it remains an important voice in design under the proprietorship of John L Walters (editor) and Simon Esterson (art director).

Academia was slow to accept that graphic design ('visual communication' was often the preferred designation) was now a mature discipline. Although most designers were content with their role as passive signatories to the design-is-a-business-service charter, there were others who were helping to make the discipline more self aware and self critical and, most importantly, to develop an awareness of its political and sociological role in a modern complex world driven by information and services, rather than manufacturing. Academia, when it finally came to recognise that design was more than anonymised window-dressing, helped to accelerate this process.

Design Issues (1982) emerged from the School of Art and Design, University of Illinois, under the partial editorship of Victor Margolin. It maintains an uncompromising commitment to the academic study of graphic design. *Visible Language*, which began in 1967, brings rigour to the study and analysis of graphic design. These and other journals have added to the contemporary status of graphic design as something more than the mute foot soldiers of consumerism.

Print in the age of the Internet

The designer today has an abundance of choice. For every printed magazine there are a thousand websites, blogs and Pinterest and Tumblr pages. For a while, energetic fast-paced blogs, most notably 'Under Consideration' (2002) and 'Design Observer' (2003), both USA, took on the task of explaining, analysing and critiquing the world of design. They were characterised by smart writing, instant responses to developments within the profession and, for the first time, thanks to well-populated comments threads, a real sense of an active discourse within the profession. But as is the way in the utopian world of the Internet, we woke up one day to find that the ship had sailed at dawn. Social media had usurped the role of online long-form design writing. Where once 1000 words were needed to make a rounded argument, a 140-character Twitter blast appeared, for many, to suffice.

Rather than destroying the print medium for design journalism, it can be argued that blogs and social media have made it stronger, although in a less centralised and a more splintered way. Dominant voices are less dominant, and no single printed publication governs the scene. Instead, we now have shoals of small design publications, often run by designers, and often looking at fragments of a fragmented discipline. Perhaps this trend can be said to have started with *Dot Dot Dot* (2001), a deceptively modest-looking publication that began by poking around in odd corners of graphic design's attic, but which over time expanded its field of vision to cover a wider cultural terrain. It was a publication for designers who needed an alternative to puffery and boosterism, and who knew that graphic design was a lens through which to view the world beyond the narrow confines of clients, deadlines and brandspeak.

No one has quite filled the gap left by *Dot Dot Dot* when it ceased to be a printed publication in 2010, but the spirit of independence and singularity of vision lives on in *Back Cover* (2008, France), *Slanted* (2004, Switzerland), and *Graphic* (2007, South Korea), all magazines with a clear purpose and a commitment to intelligent documenting of the current – and historical – importance of graphic design.

Young designers emerging into today's scene are well served by the vast amount of design material that can be found online. The blogs and Tumblr pages are an important first step on the journey to a deeper understanding of the craft. Dedicated people doing it for the love of the subject maintain the best blogs, and they do a first-rate job at presenting material in a clear and respectful manner. They add greatly to the fund of material that might otherwise go unseen.

But it would appear that, even for the most dedicated Internet trawler, after a period of endless 'online grazing', there develops a need for something less ephemeral. We can see this in the world of book publishing where, sales of ebooks have fallen, and sales of printed books have revived.[5] The instant buzz of most online design blogs is short- lived. Only printed magazines, with their small bands of hard-working, low paid editorial toilers, and smart designers making dynamic use of the real estate of the printed page, can offer the hope for a deeper understanding of the craft, and of the history and theory of design.

Whatever happens, we have good reason to think that the fate of design magazines is not the same as that which befell the British music press. In the 1960s, 1970s and 1980s there was a vibrant print culture surrounding music. At their best, weekly tabloid publications such as *NME* (*New Musical Express*), *Sounds* and *Melody Maker*, avoided pandering to the record industry (whose advertising bucks they needed), and allowed a cohort of smart music writers the freedom to write about the attributes that made pop music the great cultural force it was in the second half of the 20th century.

Today there is almost nothing left of that inky world. Many of the writers have gone on to become influential cultural critics (Julie Burchill, Jon Savage, Paul Morley). Others have excellent blogs (Simon Reynolds) and others are now respected critics (Ian Penman). But nothing has replaced the pungent weekly explosions of critical and iconoclastic music writing. We must fervently hope that the same fate does not apply to design journals.

Dot Dot Dot
2001–11
UK/Netherlands

My strong feeling is that oblivion is not the destiny of design publications. Many of the publications featured in this book refute that notion. But I'm biased. As a self-taught designer, I was partly educated by the design press. In my early career, I relied heavily on various design journals to navigate my way through a sometimes-bewildering world. At first I was content to use design publications as a way of gazing wonder-struck at how other designers seemed effortlessly to do the work I wanted to do. I was a fan, and I enjoyed reading about the people I admired. Later, when I'd worked out a few survival strategies of my own (largely through reading the design press), I demanded more from the periodicals I was reading. I even appeared in a few of them when editors and journalists featured my studio's work in their pages. Later still I contributed to one or two magazines as a writer and commentator, and thanks to the support of some kindly editors I finally ended up with a hybrid practice of designer and design writer.

Grafik
2003–present
UK

Like many designers, I owe these publications a debt of gratitude. I buy them by the armful. Some I keep; others I throw away. Some I read cover to cover; others I skim. Sometimes I even find myself buying – at inflated prices – copies of magazines I once owned. But without them I doubt I'd be the person I am today, and I doubt that design would be anything like it is today. The next few years are critical (aren't they always?). Will there be any printed design publications in ten years' time? In my view, yes there will. Paper, glue and ink are fundamentals of the design life. Like fibre, vegetables and fresh fruit, they are essential for a healthy diet and a long life.

Eye
1990–present
UK

1 Steven Heller and Jason Godfrey, *100 Classic Graphic Design Journals* (London: Laurence King, 2014).
2 Richard Hollis, *Graphic Design: A Concise History* (London: Thames & Hudson, 1997).
3 Michael Dooley, 'Critical Conditions: Zuzana Licko, Rudy VanderLans, and the Emigre Spirit', *emigre.com*, first published in *Graphic Design USA 18*, 1998. (www.emigre.com/Editorial.php?sect=3&id=8)
4 Seymour Chwast, *The Push Pin Graphic* San Francisco: (Chronicle Books, 2004).
5 Alison Flood, 'Ebook sales falling for the first time, finds new report.' The Guardian, 3 February 2016. (www.theguardian.com/books/2016/feb/03/ebook-sales-falling-for-the-first-time-finds-new-report)

Grafische Revue
Country: Netherlands

Design: unidentified

Grafische Revue
Country: Netherlands

Design: unidentified

04.1923

GRAFISCHE
REVUE

NUMMER 10
APRIL 1923
ZEVENDE JAARGANG

UITGAVE VAN DEN BOND
VAN TYPOGRAFISCHE STUDIEGEZELSCHAPPEN IN
SAMENWERKING MET DE LEERLINGEN-COMMISSIËN
EN DE ORGANISATIES IN DE GRAFISCHE BEDRIJVEN

014

Grafische Revue
Country: Netherlands

Design: unidentified

VERLAG ENGLERT UND SCHLOSSER IN FRANKFURT AM MAIN

2

DAS NEUE FRANKFURT

MONATSSCHRIFT FÜR DIE FRAGEN DER GROSSTADT-GESTALTUNG 1926-1927

Das Neue Frankfurt
Country: Germany

Cover Design:
Hans & Grete Leistikow

JAHRGANG 4
HEFT NR 1
GEBRAUCHSGRAPHIK
MONATSSCHRIFT ZUR FÖRDERUNG KÜNSTLERISCHER REKLAME
INTERNATIONAL ADVERTISING ART
MONTHLY MAGAZINE FOR PROMOTING ART IN ADVERTISING

1927
HERAUSGEBER: PROF. H·K FRENZEL EDITOR
PHÖNIX ILLUSTRATIONSDRUCK U. VERLAG G·M·B·H BERLIN SW 68 LINDENSTR.2

Gebrauchsgraphik
Country: Germany

Design: unidentified

VERLAG ENGLERT UND SCHLOSSER IN FRANKFURT AM MAIN

DAS NEUE FRANKFURT

MONATSSCHRIFT FÜR DIE FRAGEN DER GROSSTADT-GESTALTUNG 1926-1927

Das Neue Frankfurt
Country: Germany

Cover Design:
Hans & Grete Leistikow

Das Neue Frankfurt
Country: Germany

Cover Design:
Hans & Grete Leistikow

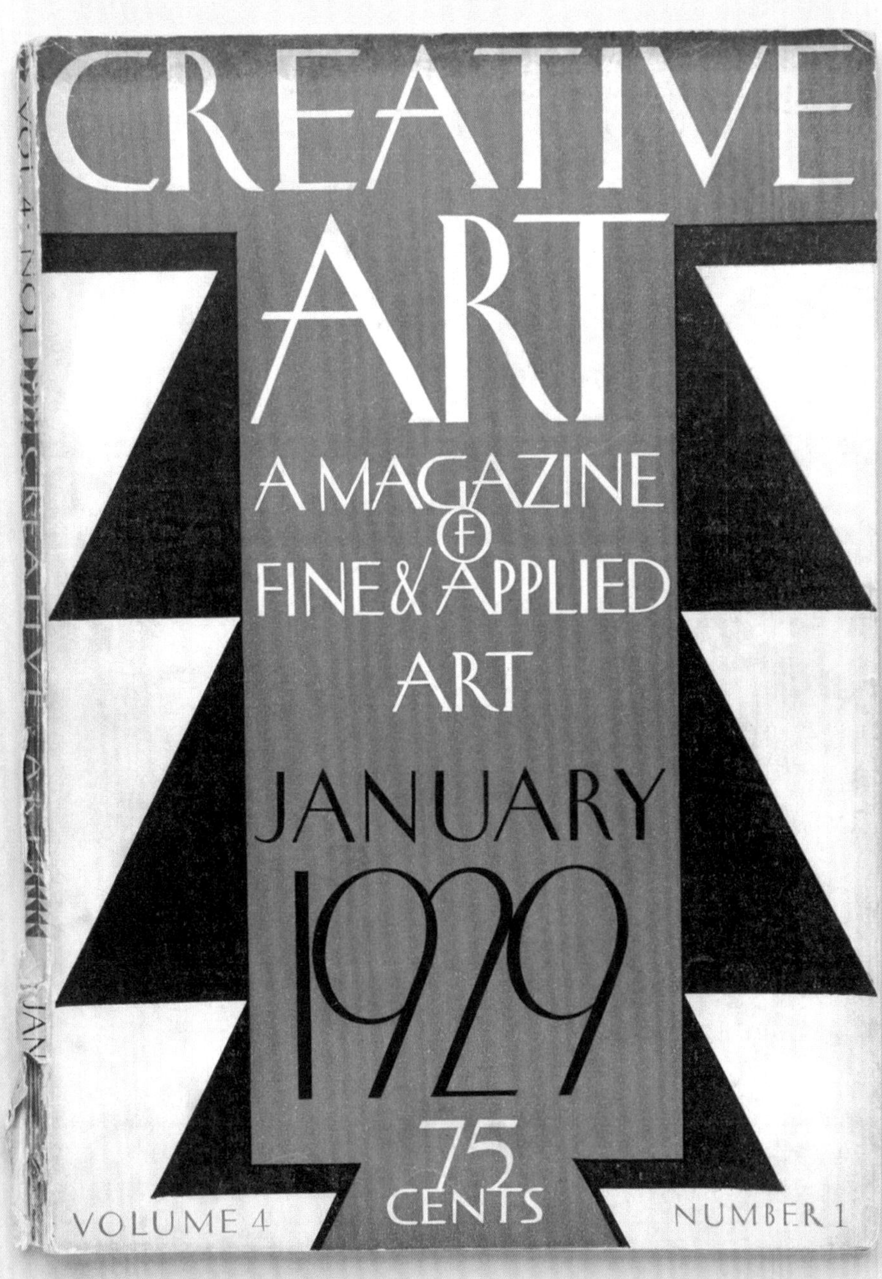

Creative Art
Country: USA

Design: unidentified

VERLAG ENGLERT UND SCHLOSSER IN FRANKFURT AM MAIN

6

DAS NEUE FRANKFURT

MONATSSCHRIFT FÜR DIE PROBLEME MODERNER GESTALTUNG / 3. JAHRG. 1929

III. JAHRGANG · JUNI 1929

schweiz

Das Neue Frankfurt
Country: Germany

Cover Design:
Hans & Grete Leistikow

VERLAG ENGLERT UND SCHLOSSER IN FRANKFURT AM MAIN

8

DAS NEUE FRANKFURT

INTERNATIONALE MONATSSCHRIFT FÜR DIE PROBLEME KULTURELLER NEUGESTALTUNG

Film

Film

IV. JAHRGANG · AUGUST 1930

Das Neue Frankfurt
Country: Germany

Cover Design:
Hans & Grete Leistikow

Domas
Country: Latvia

Cover Design: Niklāvs Strunke

Domas
Country: Latvia

Cover Design: Niklāvs Strunke

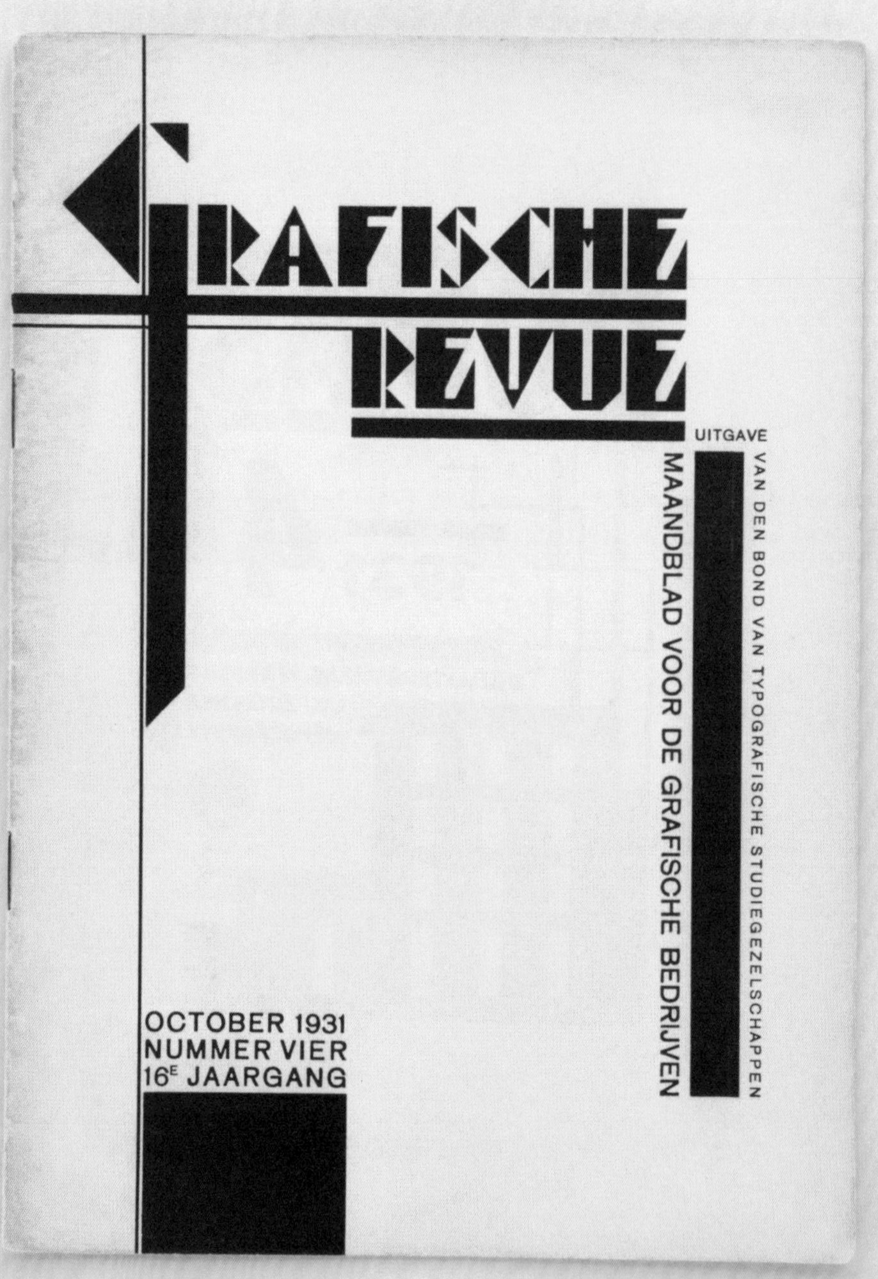

GRAFISCHE
REVUE
UITGAVE
VAN DEN BOND VAN TYPOGRAFISCHE STUDIEGEZELSCHAPPEN
MAANDBLAD VOOR DE GRAFISCHE BEDRIJVEN
OCTOBER 1931
NUMMER VIER
16E JAARGANG

Grafische Revue
Country: Netherlands

Design: unidentified

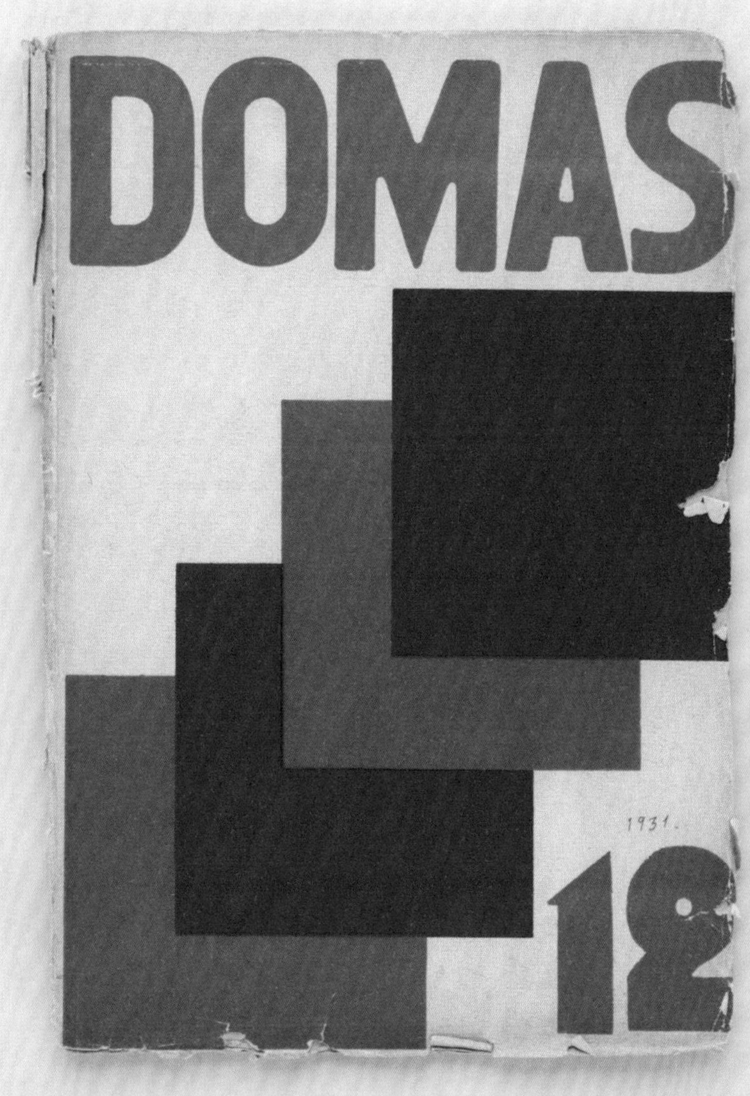

Domas
Country: Latvia

Cover Design: Niklāvs Strunke

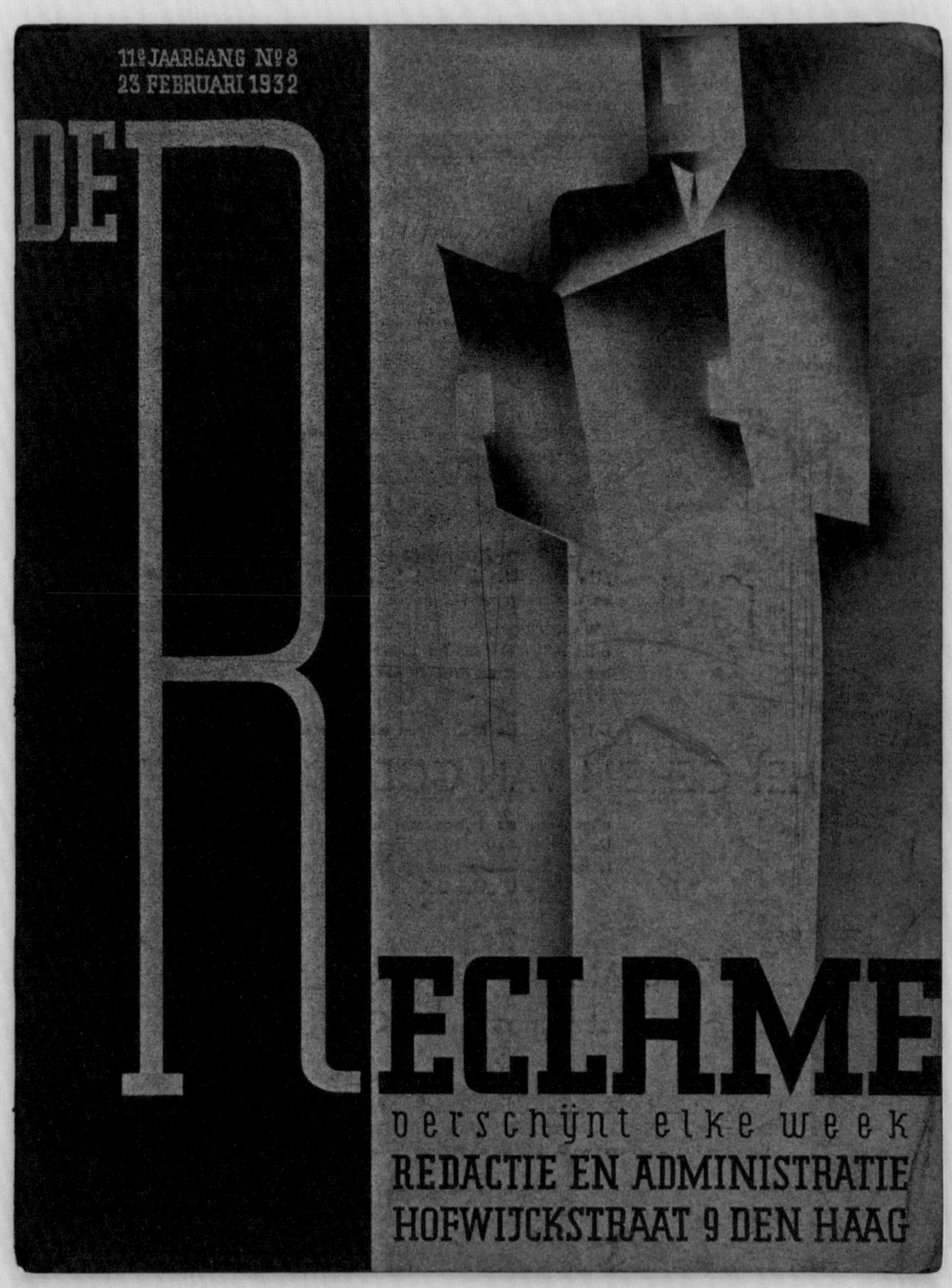

De Reclame
Country: Netherlands

Design: unidentified

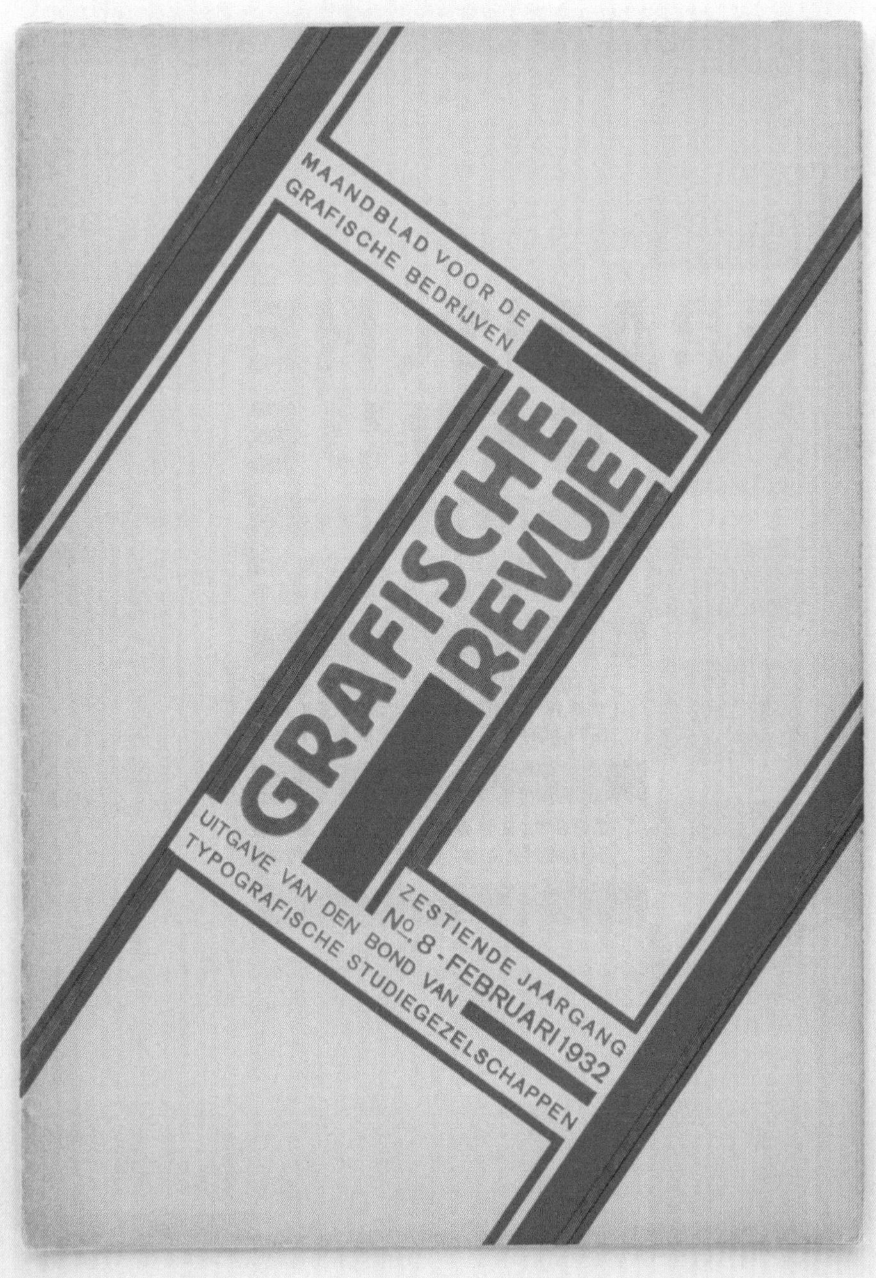

Grafische Revue
Country: Netherlands

Design: unidentified

03.1932

Grafische Revue
Country: Netherlands

Design: unidentified

Domas
Country: Latvia

Cover Design: Niklāvs Strunke

06.1932

Grafische Revue
Country: Netherlands

Design: unidentified

03.1933

jakžijeme

3

obsah

J. Hora: Pokrok a svoboda
B. Václavek: Literatura minulosti a budoucnosti
V. Volavka: Jubilejní výstava Umělecké besedy 1913-1933
E. F. Burian: Šlágr a dnešní periferie
B. Novák: Válečná trilogie B. Benešové
E. Hruška: Pražská náměstí
F. Tetauer: Divadlo jako představa a skutečnost
V. Volavka: Ivan Meštrović
L. Žák: Jak žijeme — jak bydlíme
Gramofonové desky
Poznámky

Jak žijeme • obrázkový kulturní magazin • ročník 1, čís. 3 • v Praze v červnu 1933

Jakzijeme (later Magazin DP)
Country: Czechoslovakia

Cover Design: Ladislav Sutnar

04.1933

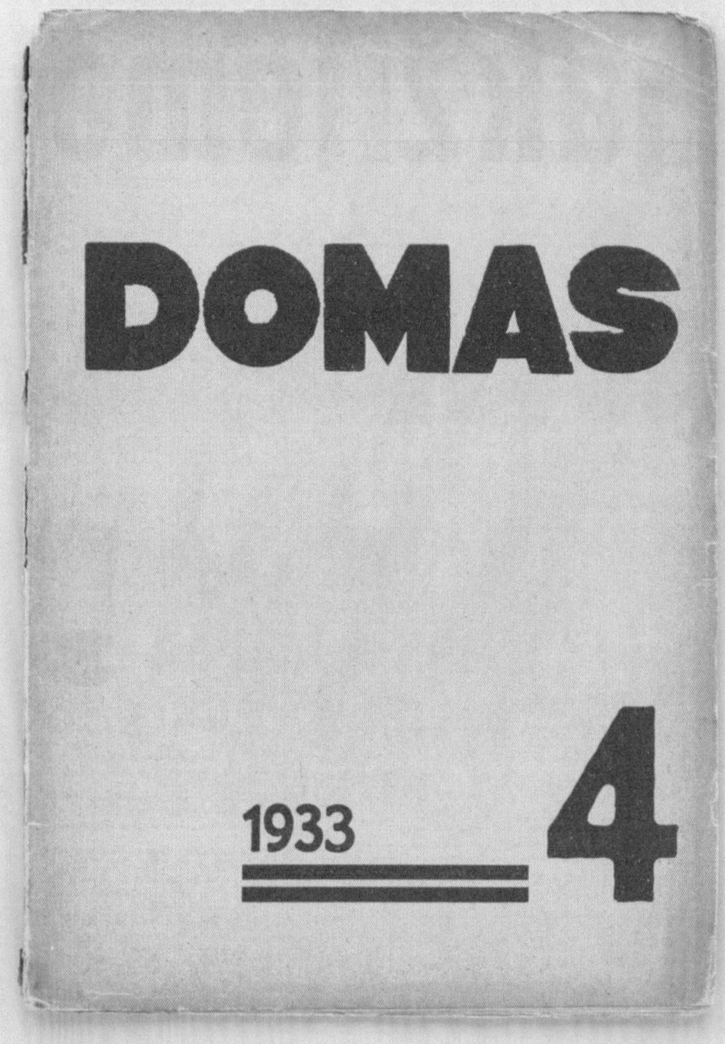

Domas
Country: Latvia

Cover Design: Niklāvs Strunke

Magazin DP
Country: Czechoslovakia

Cover Design: Ladislav Sutnar

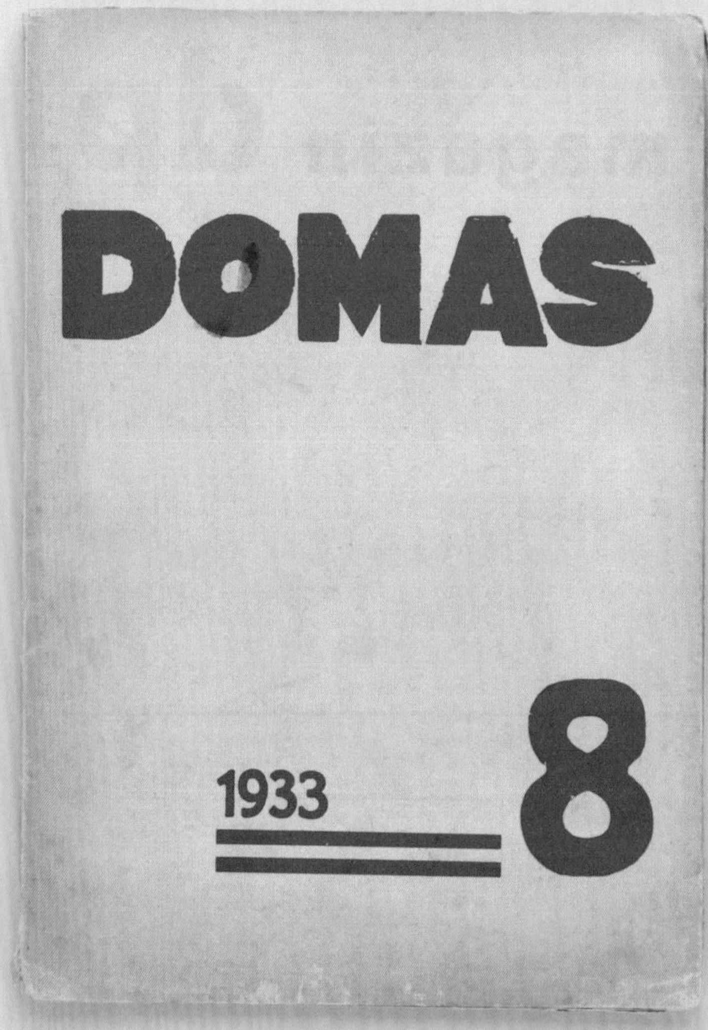

Domas
Country: Latvia

Cover Design: Niklāvs Strunke

19e jaargang
nummer 2
augustus 1934

grafische
revue

maandblad
voor de grafische
bedrijven

uitgave
van den bond
van
typografische
studie
gezelschappen

Grafische Revue
Country: Netherlands

Design: unidentified

11.1934

PM
Country: USA

Art Director: Martin J Weber

PM
Country: USA

Art Director: Martin J Weber

Grafische Revue
Country: Netherlands

Design: unidentified

Grafische Revue
Country: Netherlands

Design: unidentified

03.1935

PM
Country: USA

Art Director: Martin J Weber

PM
Country: USA

Art Director: Martin J Weber

03.1936

PM
Country: USA

Cover Design: Lucian Bernhard

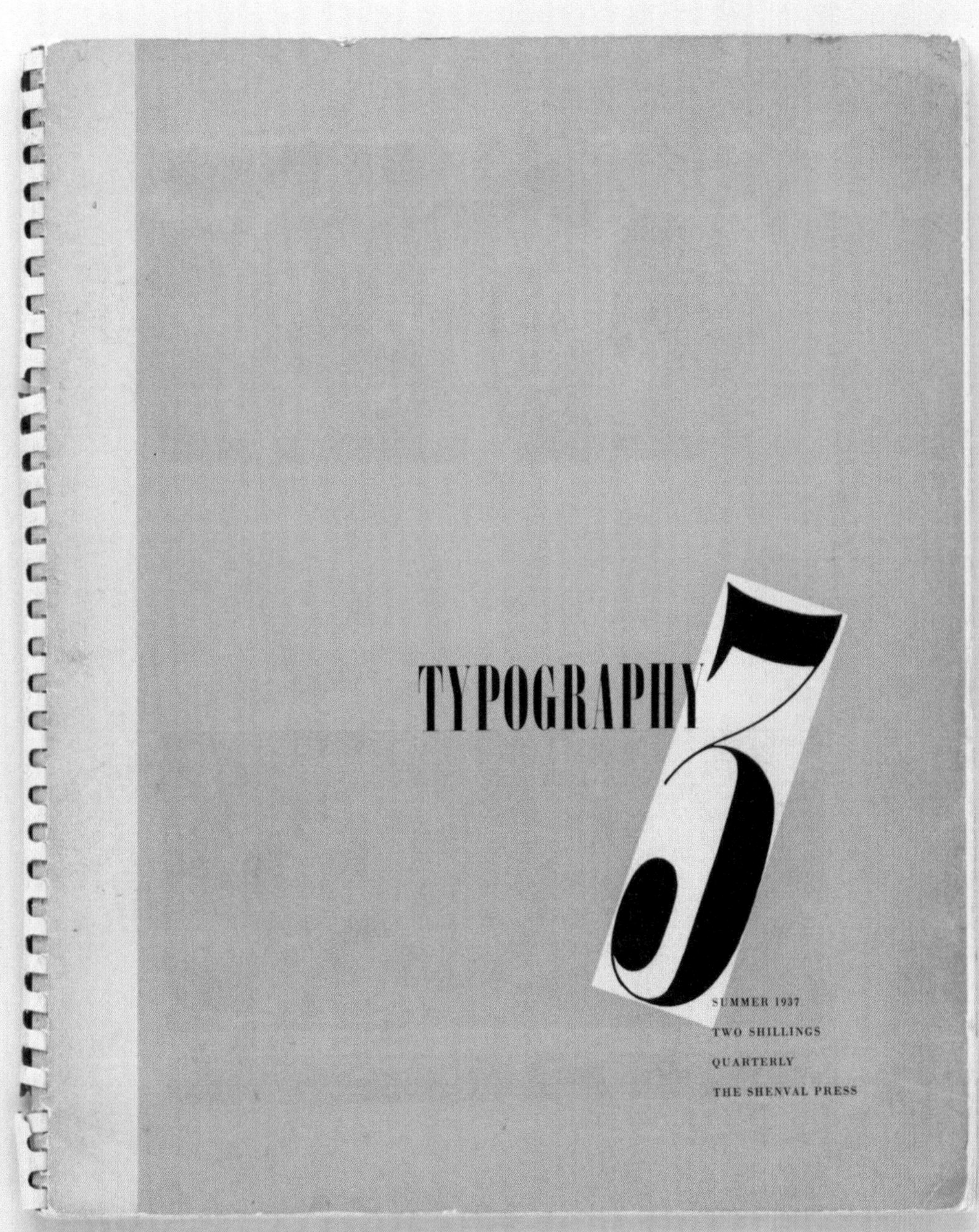

Typography
Country: UK

Design: unidentified

10.1937

PM
Country: USA

Cover Design:
Samuel Bernard Schaeffer

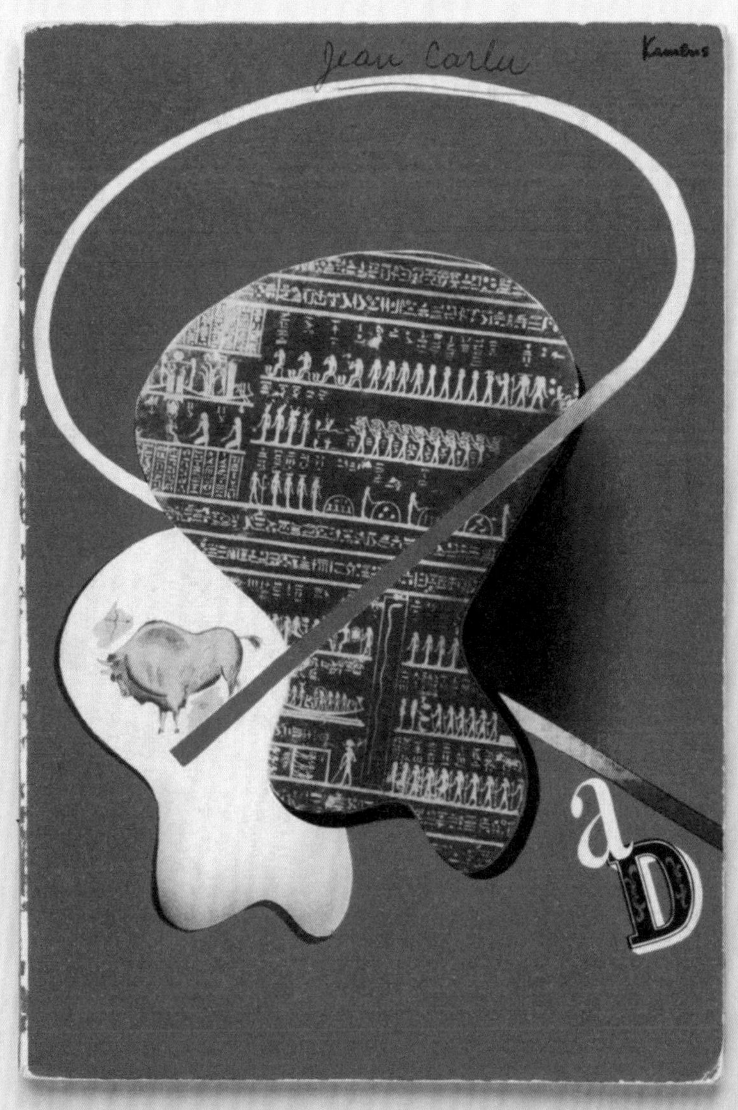

PM
Country: USA

Cover Design: Irvine Kamens

02.1941

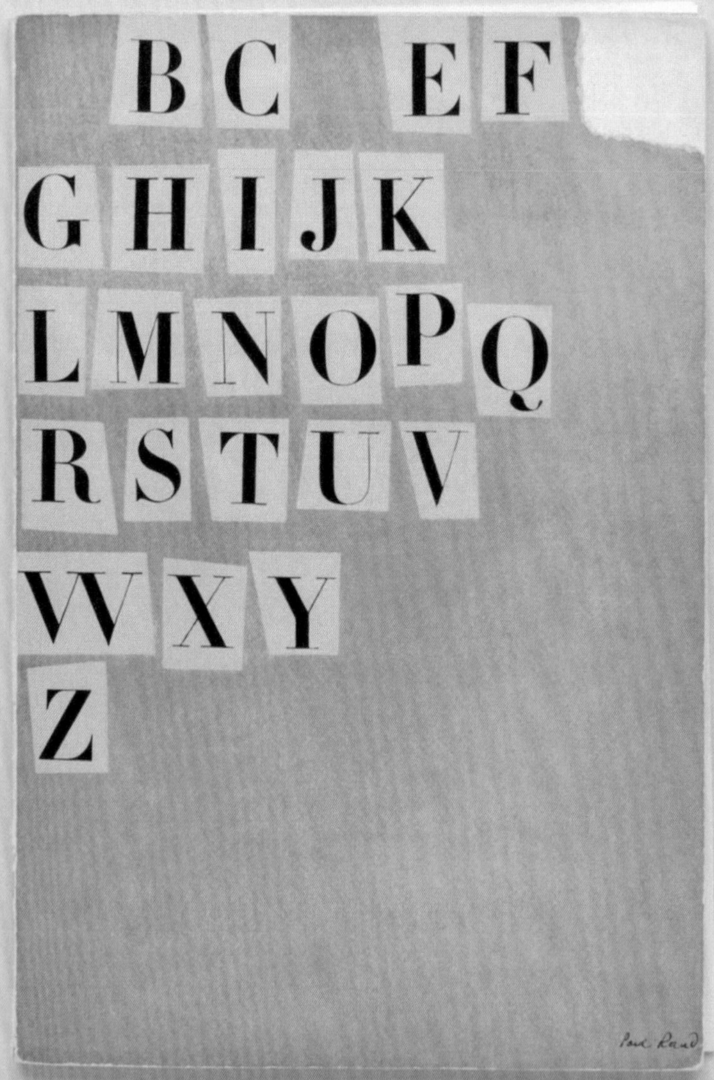

AD
Country: USA

Cover Design: Paul Rand

AD
Country: USA

Cover Design: Alex Steinweiss

12.1941

AD
Country: USA

Cover Design: E Mcknight Kauffer

Q As a historian and researcher of lettering, calligraphy and typography, what are the most important early journals that you would recommend students to study to gain an understanding of the origins of the graphic arts?

A The answer depends on the country you are studying. My expertise is the United States. *The Inland Printer* (1883–2011), *The Printing Art* (1903–25), *The American Printer* (1883–2011) are some of the journals you need to look at to understand graphic design in America from 1890 to about 1930. For Germany, you need to look at *Gebrauchsgraphik* (1923–50), *Typographische Mitteilungen* (1903–33) and others. In England it is *The Studio* (1893–1964), *Monotype Recorder* (1902–present), *The Penrose Annual* (1895–1982) and more. For France you need to look at *Arts et Métiers Graphiques* (1927–39) and others. For Italy, you need to look at *Campo Grafico* (1933–39), *Tipografia* and *Il Risorgimento Grafico* (1815–14). And so on. But those are general magazines, not ones that are necessarily specialised for lettering, etc. Some titles off the top of my head are *The Imprint* (1913, UK), *The Fleuron* (1923–30, UK), *Die Zeitgemäße Schrift* (1928–45, Germany) and newsletter of the *Society for Italic Handwriting* (1954–2000, UK). Anyone who wants to know more specifically about calligraphy and lettering should order a copy of my two *Alphabet* issues devoted to the field from 1850 to 2000 which have all sorts of information on individual articles.

Q What is the role of *Codex* – your journal of typography – at a time when nearly everything can be seen online?

A *Codex* (2011–13) is no longer a journal. It has not been one since the end of 2013 when we took the name over from John Boardley and turned what should have been *Codex* No.4 into *The Eternal Letter*. We are now trying to make *Codex* into a book series. We are slowly working on our second title and have a few others underway. But I still think there is a role for Prints today. I wish we could have saved *Codex*. The problem was not online competition but the cost of distribution. Print offers tactility, scale, materiality, sequencing and surprise that online periodicals cannot match. Print is also likely to last longer. We know the longevity of paper (even poor wood pulp paper) but we have no idea how long digital material will last due to changes in hardware, software and platforms. And, of course, print does not require power or an infrastructure to be read. My view is that long-form texts and those that we want to refer to in the future belong in print. Texts that are of the moment belong online. So I think printed journals that aim for short, quick articles are making a mistake. Do the teasers online and then give people the real meal in print.

Gebrauchsgraphik
1923–50
Germany

Q Which, if any, of the current design journals have impressed you the most in the field of scholarship in the graphic arts?

A None, if you really mean scholarship. I have enjoyed *Eye* (1990–present, UK) since the beginning, and it often has had useful and interesting design history articles but they have not been seriously scholarly, even if they are necessary fodder for such scholarship. The same is true of *Progetto Grafico* (2003–present, Italy). We don't really have much in the way of scholarship in the graphic arts, despite the explosion of design history books. Too many are just hagiographic monographs or portfolio pieces. Rare are books like those Robin Kinross wrote about Anthony Froshaug, Chris Burke on Paul Renner and Jan Tschichold, or the Unit Editions' book on Herb Lubalin. I think we are still in the infancy of graphic design history. We have very few properly trained scholars. We either have practitioners with a passion for the profession or academics who are full of jargon and usually clueless about what actually goes on in graphic design.

Eye
1990–present
UK

Q Regarding the great design journals of the 20th century – which ones stand out for you as having made a major contribution to the evolution of the graphic arts?

A *The Fleuron*, *Neue Grafik* (1958–65, Switzerland), *U&lc* (1970–99, USA), *Emigre* (1984–2005, USA). These are ones that have influenced the course of graphic design, as opposed to those which have merely been of interest to designers and thus may have influenced individuals rather than the practice as a whole, such as *Typographica* (1949–67, UK), *Motif* (1958–67, UK) or *Graphis* (1944–present, Switzerland).

Q Can you name a non-design magazine that exemplifies the best of contemporary design practice?

A I don't read non-design magazines, so I can't really answer the question. I don't have enough time to keep up with design publications, let alone non-design ones. About the only non-design publication that I read regularly is *The New York Times* (1851–present, USA).

Paul Shaw is a designer and a design historian. For three decades he has researched and written about the history of graphic design, with a focus on typography, lettering and calligraphy.

Typographica
1949–67
UK

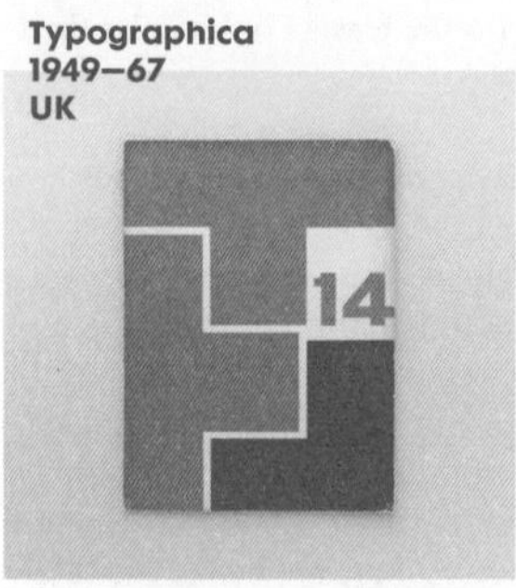

Motif
1958–67
UK

AD
Country: USA

Cover Design: Will Burtin

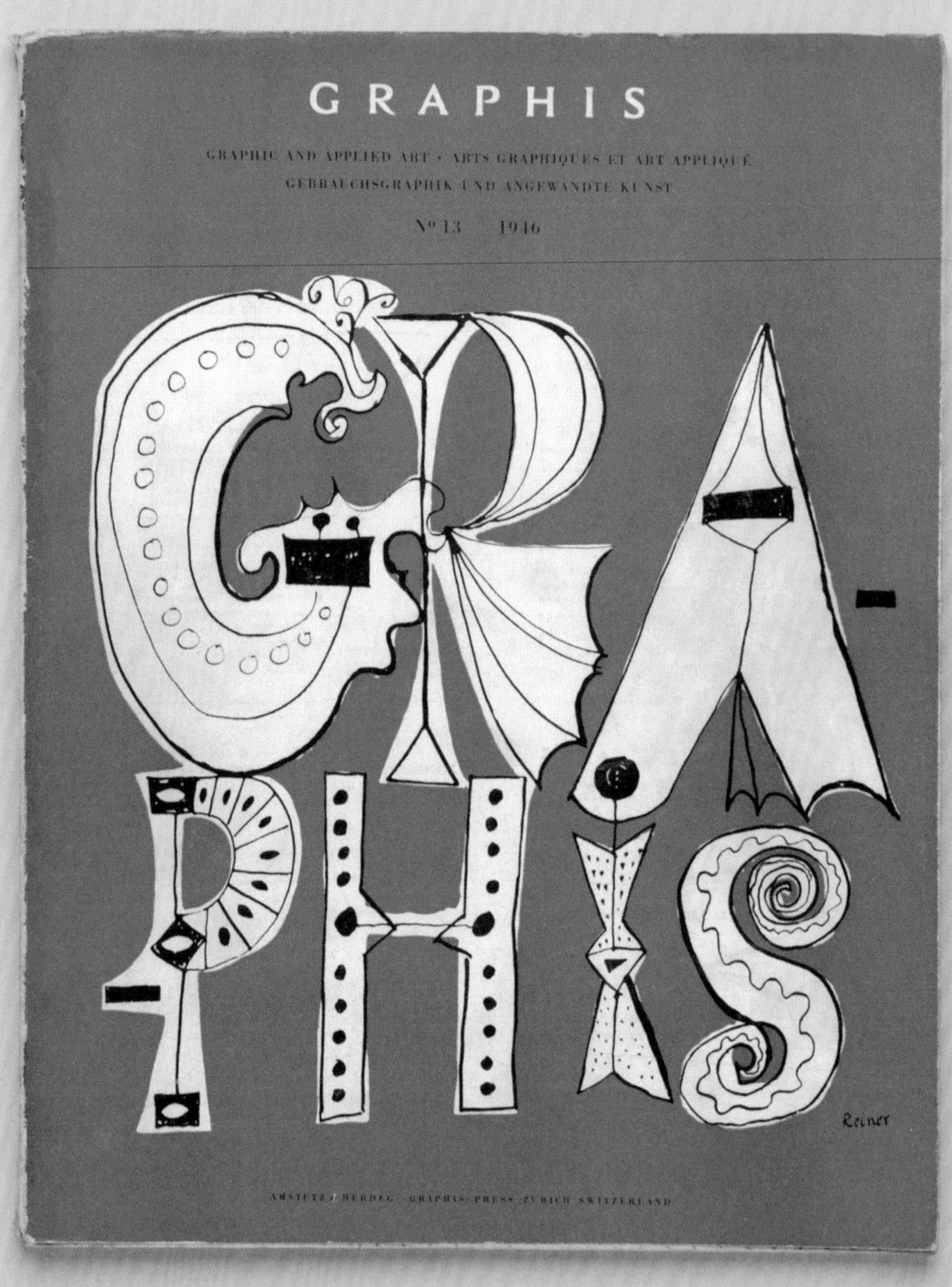

Graphis
Country: Switzerland

Cover Design: Imre Reiner

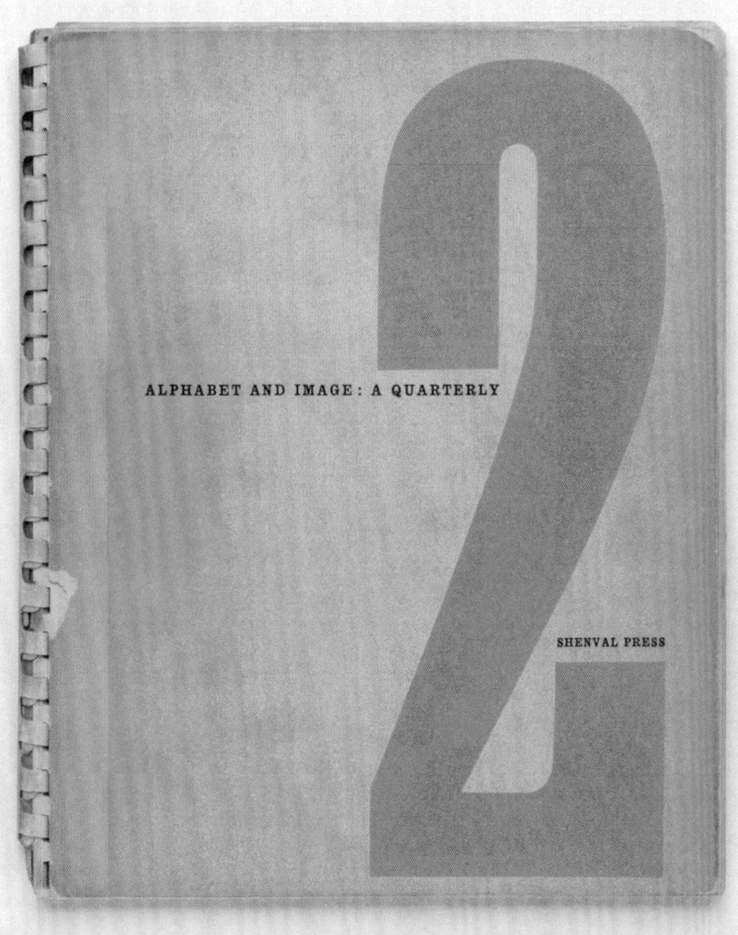

Alphabet and Image
Country: UK

Cover Design: Robert Harling

10.1946

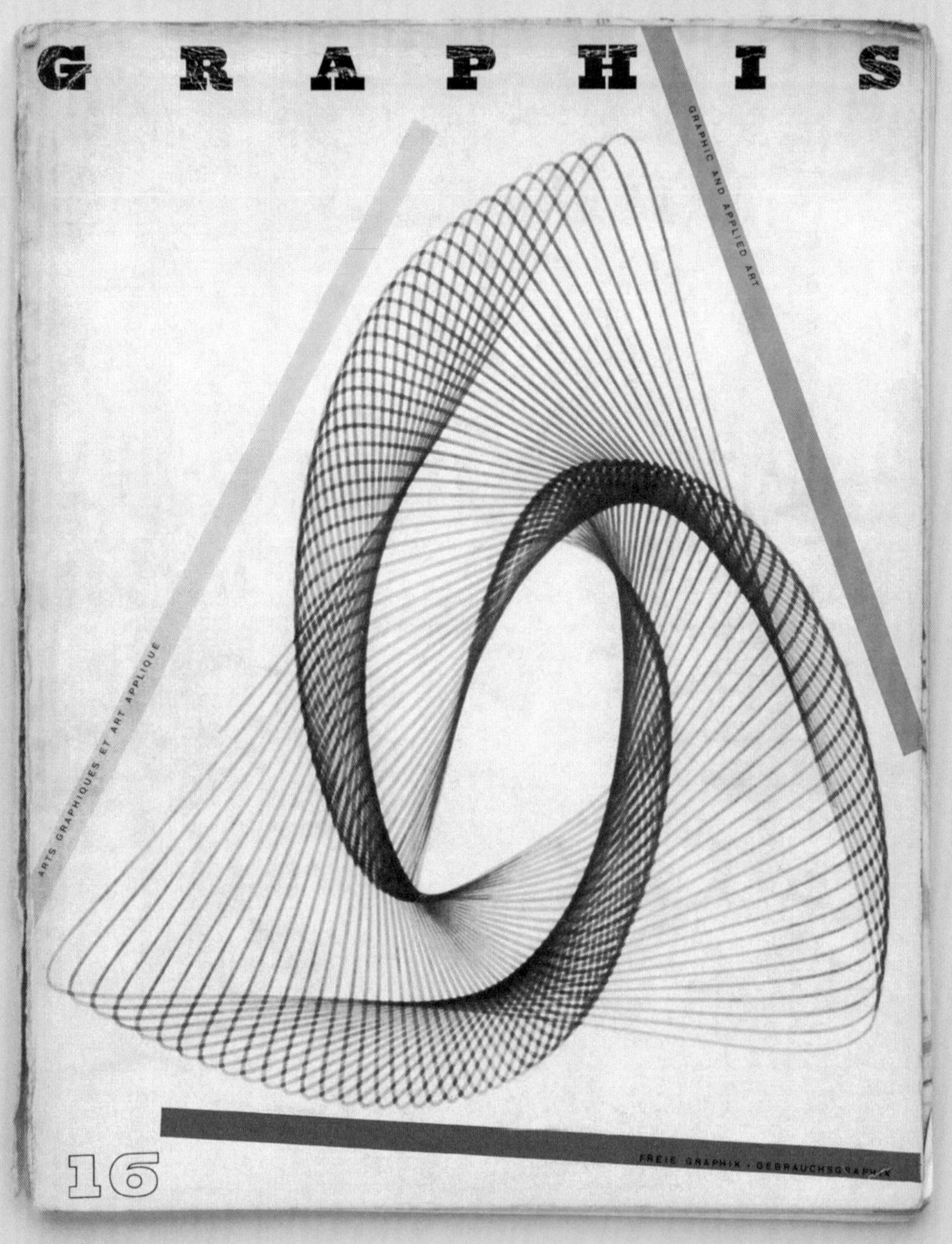

Graphis
Country: Switzerland

Cover Design: Walter Herdeg

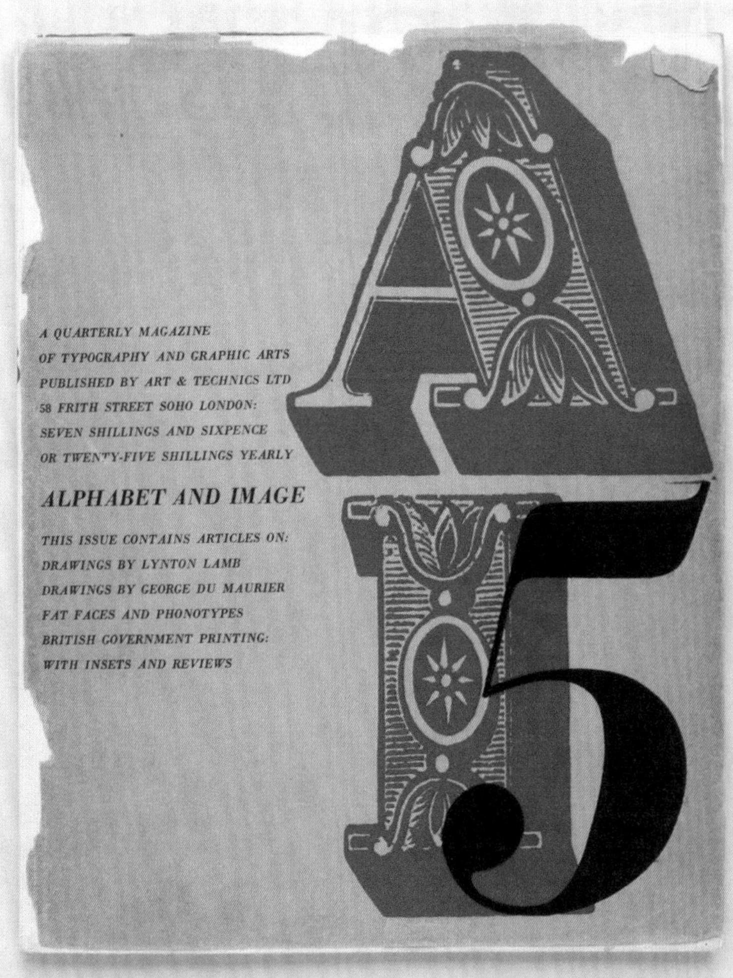

A QUARTERLY MAGAZINE
OF TYPOGRAPHY AND GRAPHIC ARTS
PUBLISHED BY ART & TECHNICS LTD
58 FRITH STREET SOHO LONDON:
SEVEN SHILLINGS AND SIXPENCE
OR TWENTY-FIVE SHILLINGS YEARLY
ALPHABET AND IMAGE
THIS ISSUE CONTAINS ARTICLES ON:
DRAWINGS BY LYNTON LAMB
DRAWINGS BY GEORGE DU MAURIER
FAT FACES AND PHONOTYPES
BRITISH GOVERNMENT PRINTING:
WITH INSETS AND REVIEWS
A
5

Alphabet and Image
Country: UK

Cover Design: Robert Harling

10.1947

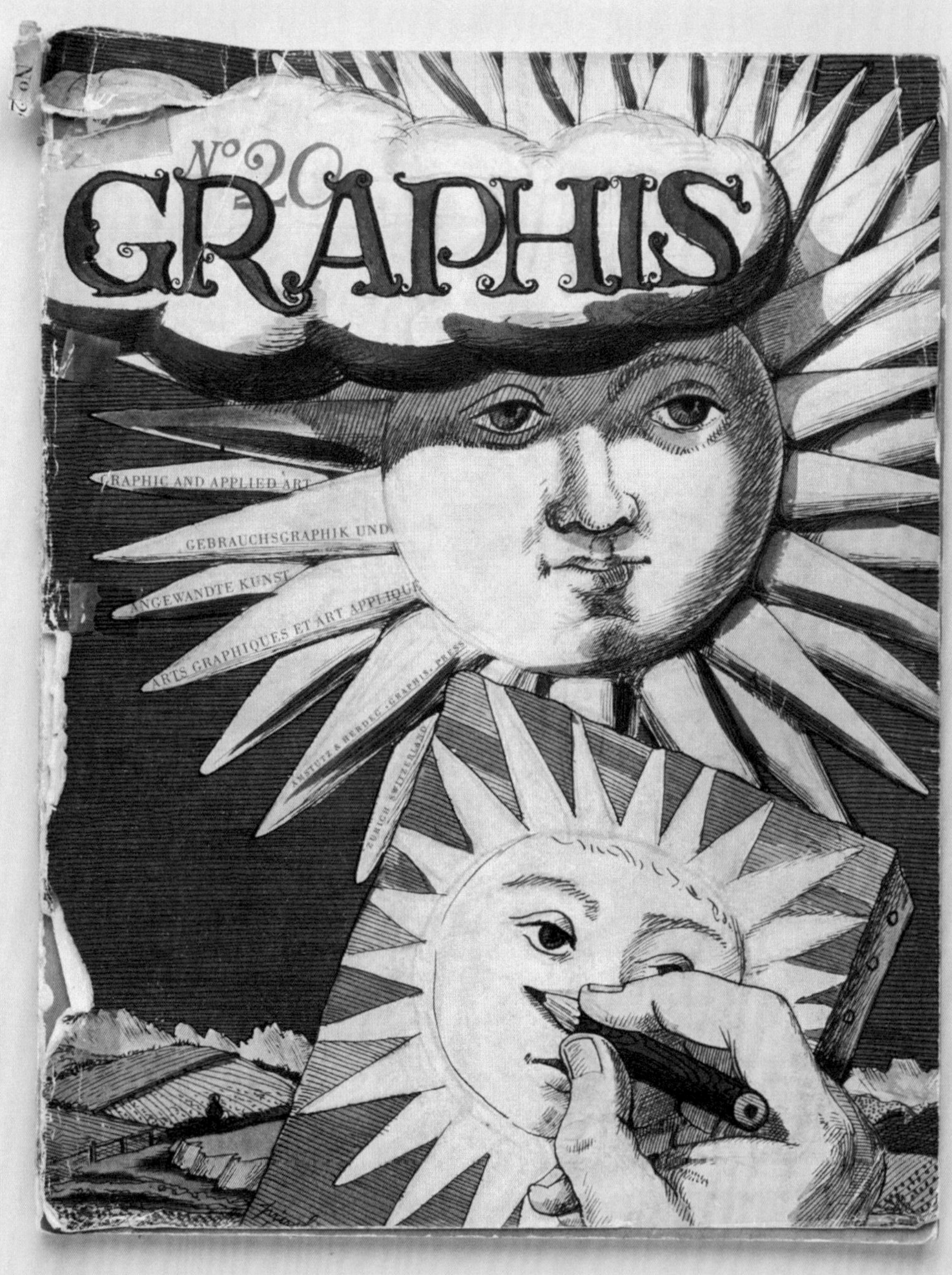

Graphis
Country: Switzerland

Cover Design: Piero Fornasetti

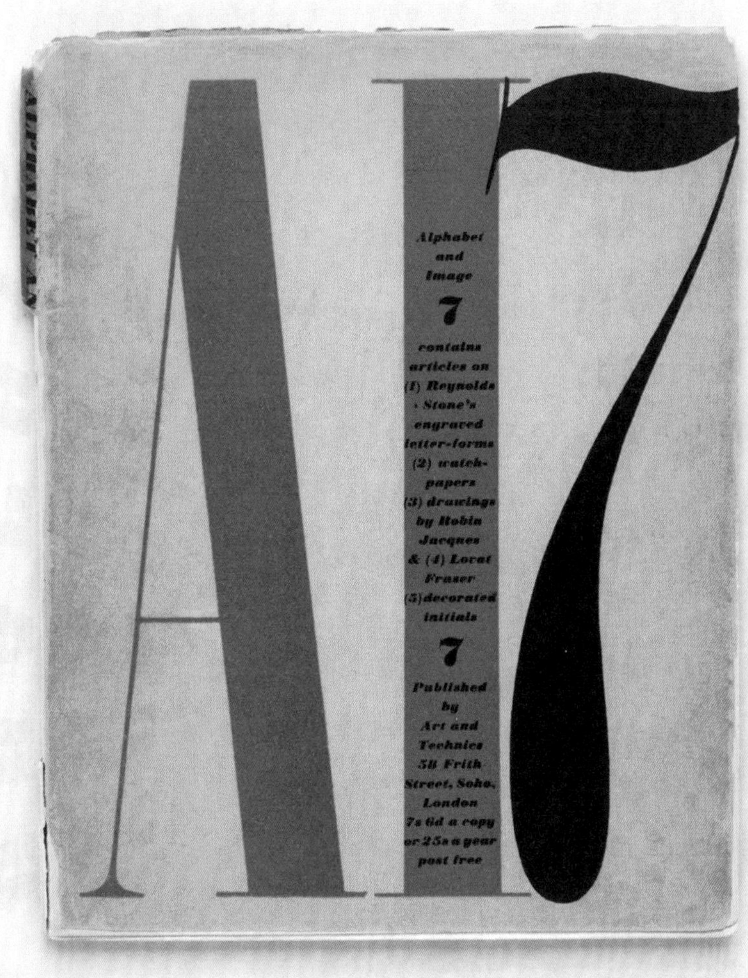

Alphabet and Image
Country: UK

Cover Design: Robert Harling

07.1948

Graphis
Country: Switzerland

Cover Design: Joseph Binder

67. JAHRGANG HEFT 10 OKTOBER 1948

10

SCHWEIZER GRAPHISCHE MITTEILUNGEN

REVUE SUISSE DE L'ART ET DES INDUSTRIES GRAPHIQUES

THE SWISS PRINTING REVIEW

ZOLLIKOFER & CO. ST. GALLEN

SGM (Schweitzer Graphische Mitteilungen)
Country: Switzerland

Cover Designer: Rudolf Hosteller

67. JAHRGANG HEFT 12 DEZEMBER 1948

12

SGM

SCHWEIZER GRAPHISCHE MITTEILUNGEN
REVUE SUISSE DE L'ART ET DES INDUSTRIES GRAPHIQUES
THE SWISS PRINTING REVIEW

Heinrich Jost †	Eine Gutenberg-Gedenkstätte in Eltville am Rhein
Adolfhanns Schirmann	Praktische Fachchemie
Walter Ballmer	Italienische Reklametypographie (Beilage)
Hermann Strehler	Graphisches Gewerbe — graphische Industrie
Paul Renner	Kleine Farbenlehre
Ernst Schmid	Die automatische Ausrückvorrichtung
Pierre Mornand	La Bibliophilie en France

ZOLLIKOFER & CO. ST. GALLEN

SGM (Schweitzer Graphische Mitteilungen)
Country: Switzerland

Cover Designer: Rudolf Hosteller

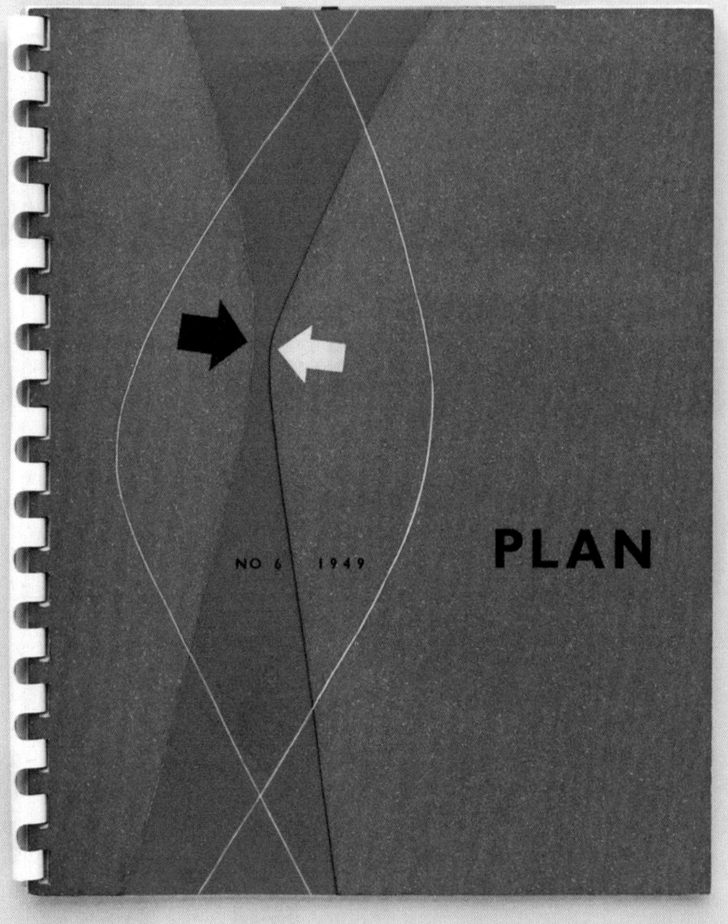

Plan
Country: UK

Cover Design: Plan Group

01.1950

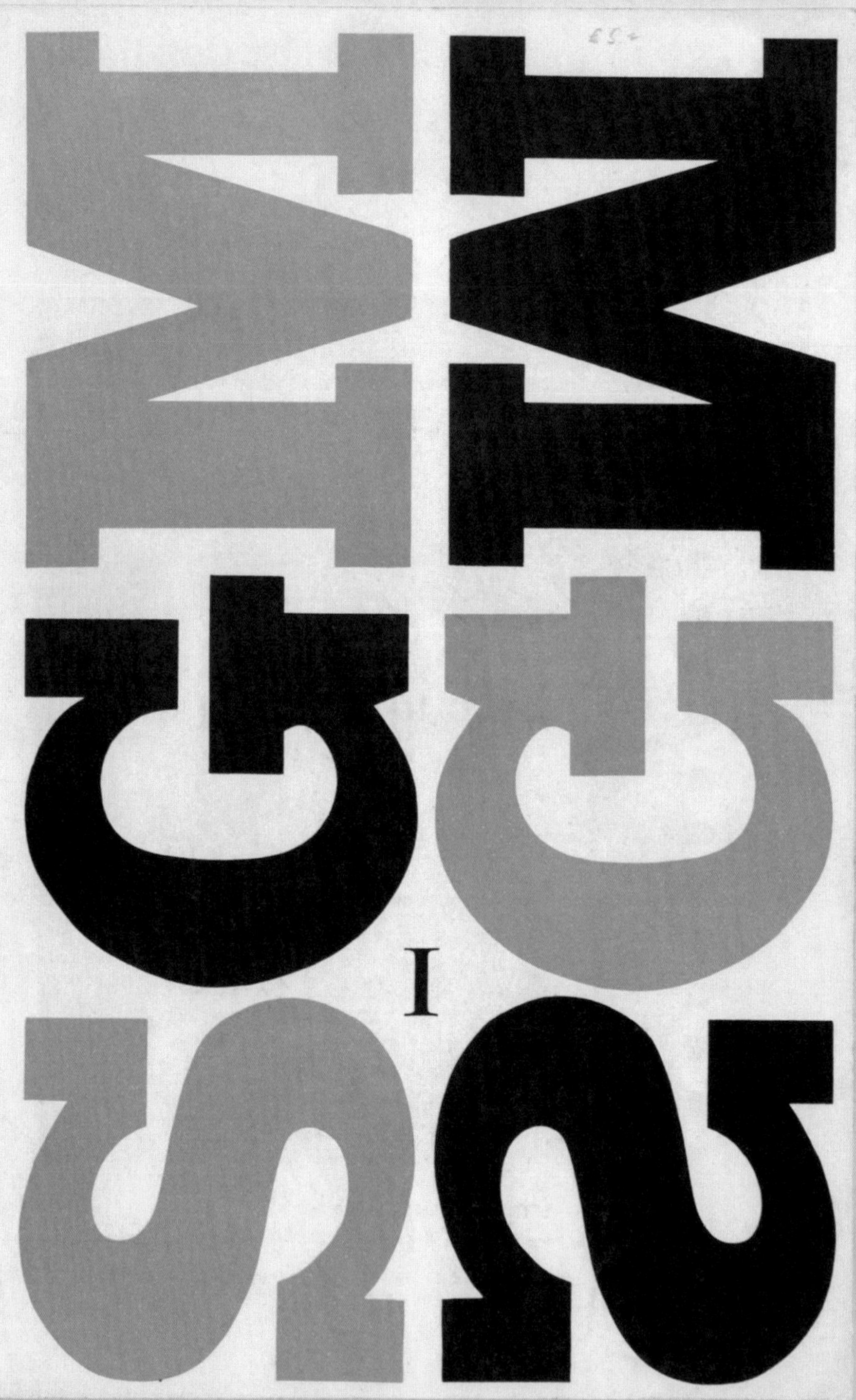

Schweizer Graphische Mitteilungen · Revue suisse de l'Art et des Industries graphiques · The Swiss Printing Review
SGM
I

SGM (Schweitzer Graphische Mitteilungen)
Country: Switzerland

Cover Designer: Rudolf Hosteller

02.1950

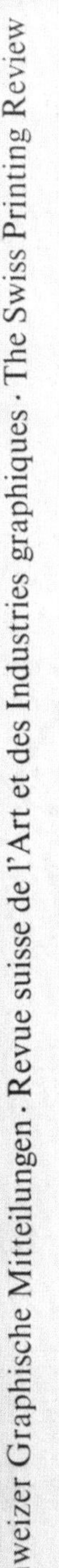

SGM (Schweitzer Graphische Mitteilungen)
Country: Switzerland

Cover Design: René Ponot

03.1950

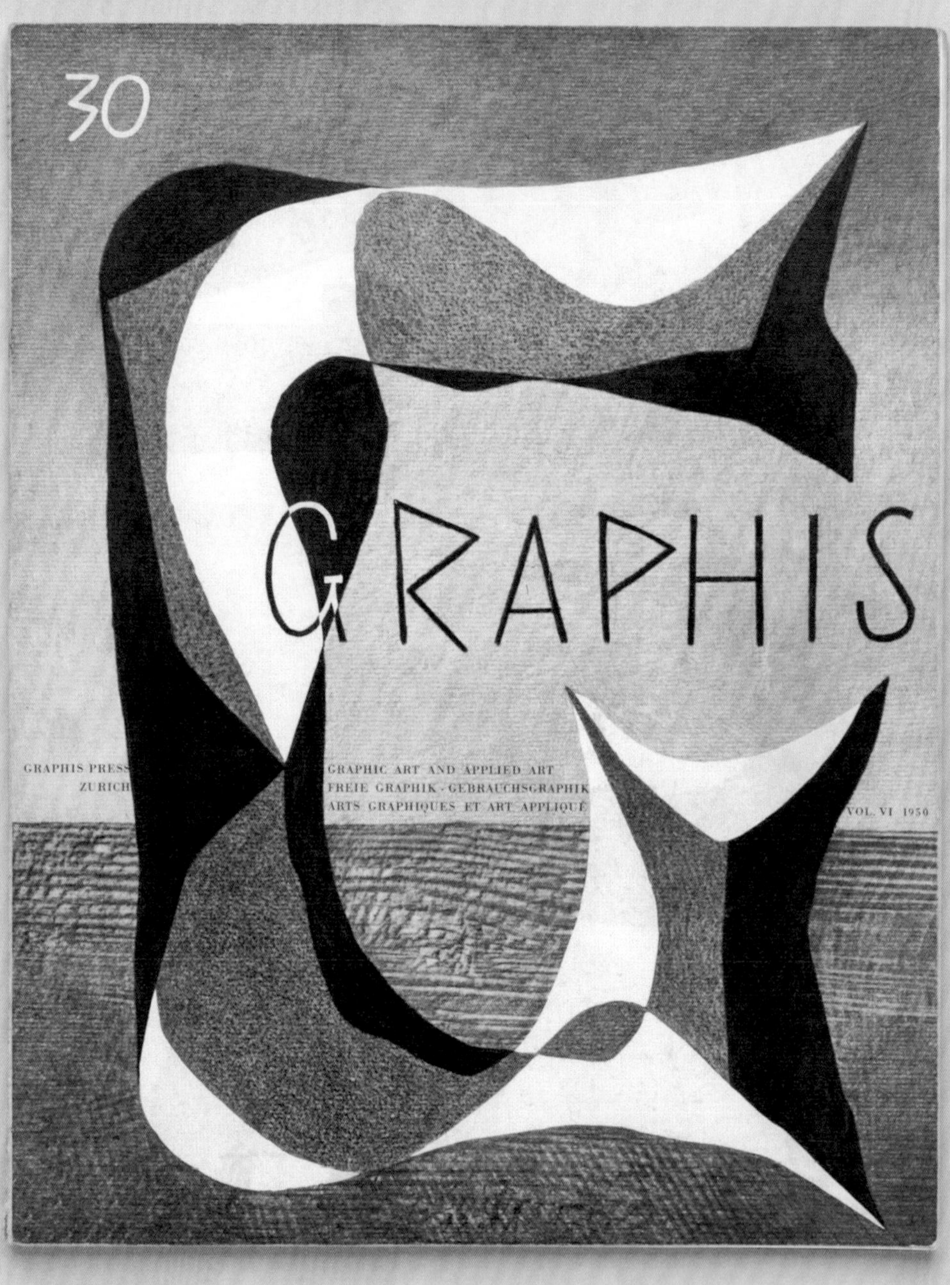

Graphis
Country: Switzerland

Cover Design: Jan Bons

Portfolio
Country: USA

Art Director: Alexey Brodovitch

Sondernummer

1951

Der
Fortschritt
im graphischen
Gewerbe

Schweizer Graphische Mitteilungen Revue suisse des industries graphiques The Swiss Printing Review

sgm

1

1 Erich Reber
2 Dr. Hans Bachmann
3 Josef Specker
4 Hans Lips
5 H. Hösli
6 Dr. G. O. Baerlocher
7 Siegfried Stoeckli
8 Ernst Leuenberger

SGM (Schweitzer Graphische Mitteilungen)
Country: Switzerland

Design: unidentified

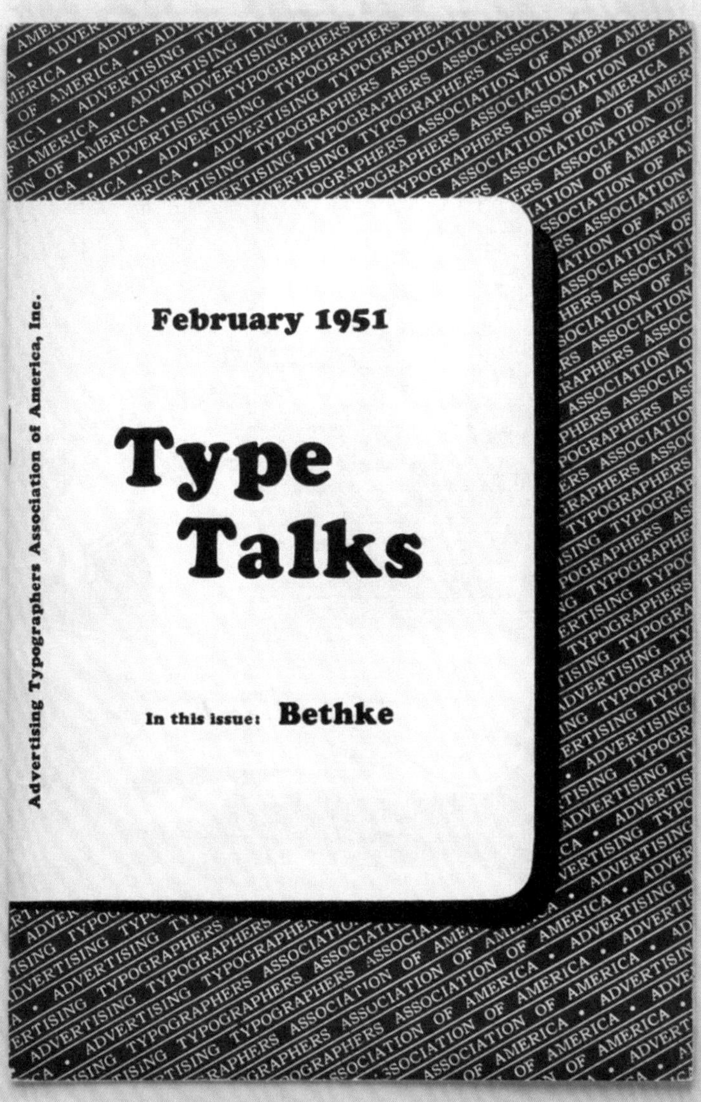

Type Talks
Country: USA

Design: unidentified

09.1951

Graphis
Country: Switzerland

Cover Design: FHK Henrion

TM (Typographische Monatsblätter)
Country: Switzerland

Design: unidentified
Courtesy of syndicom

1951

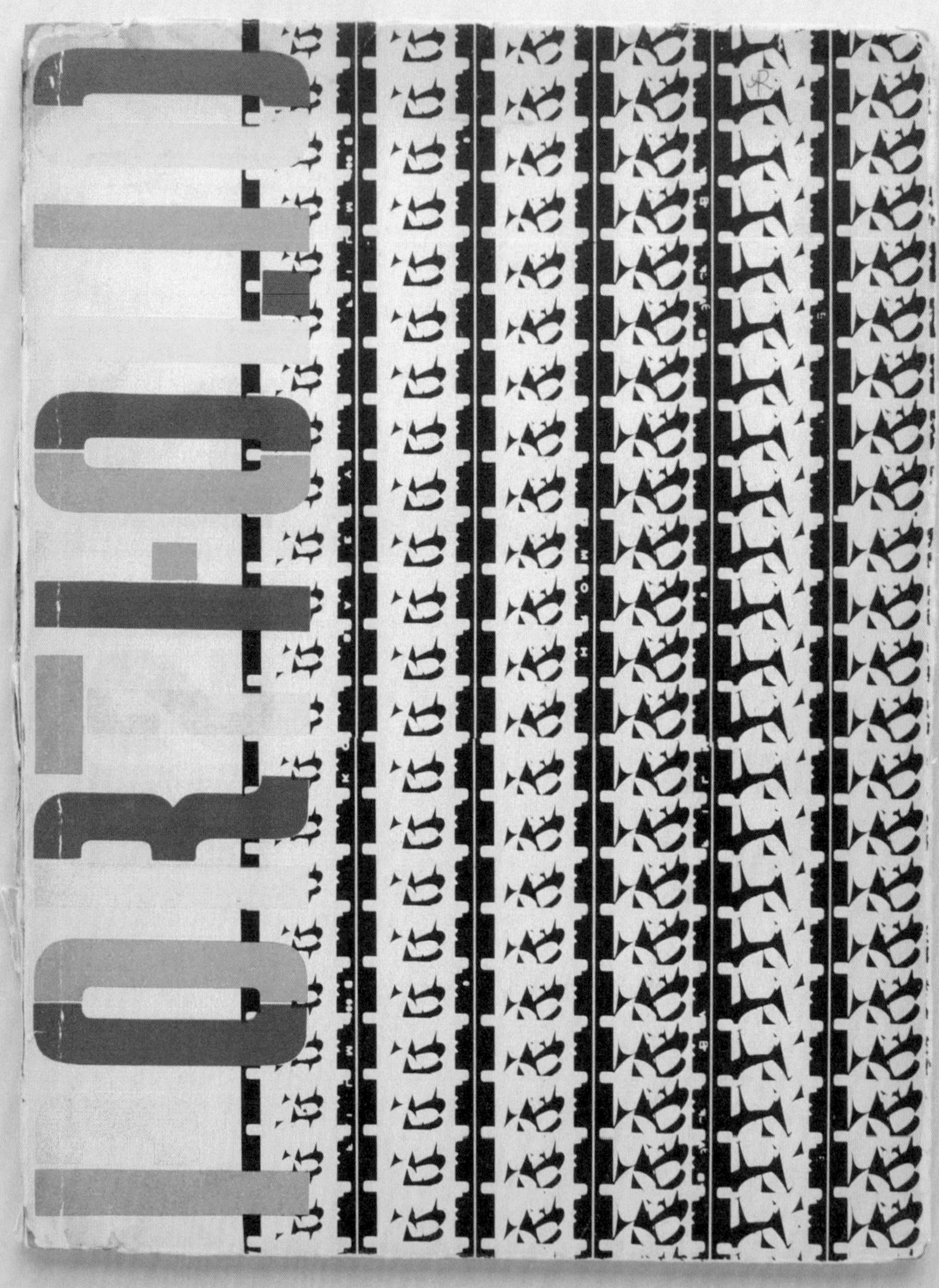

070

Portfolio
Country: USA

Art Director: Alexey Brodovitch

Graphis
Country: Switzerland

Cover Design: Olle Eskell

09.1952

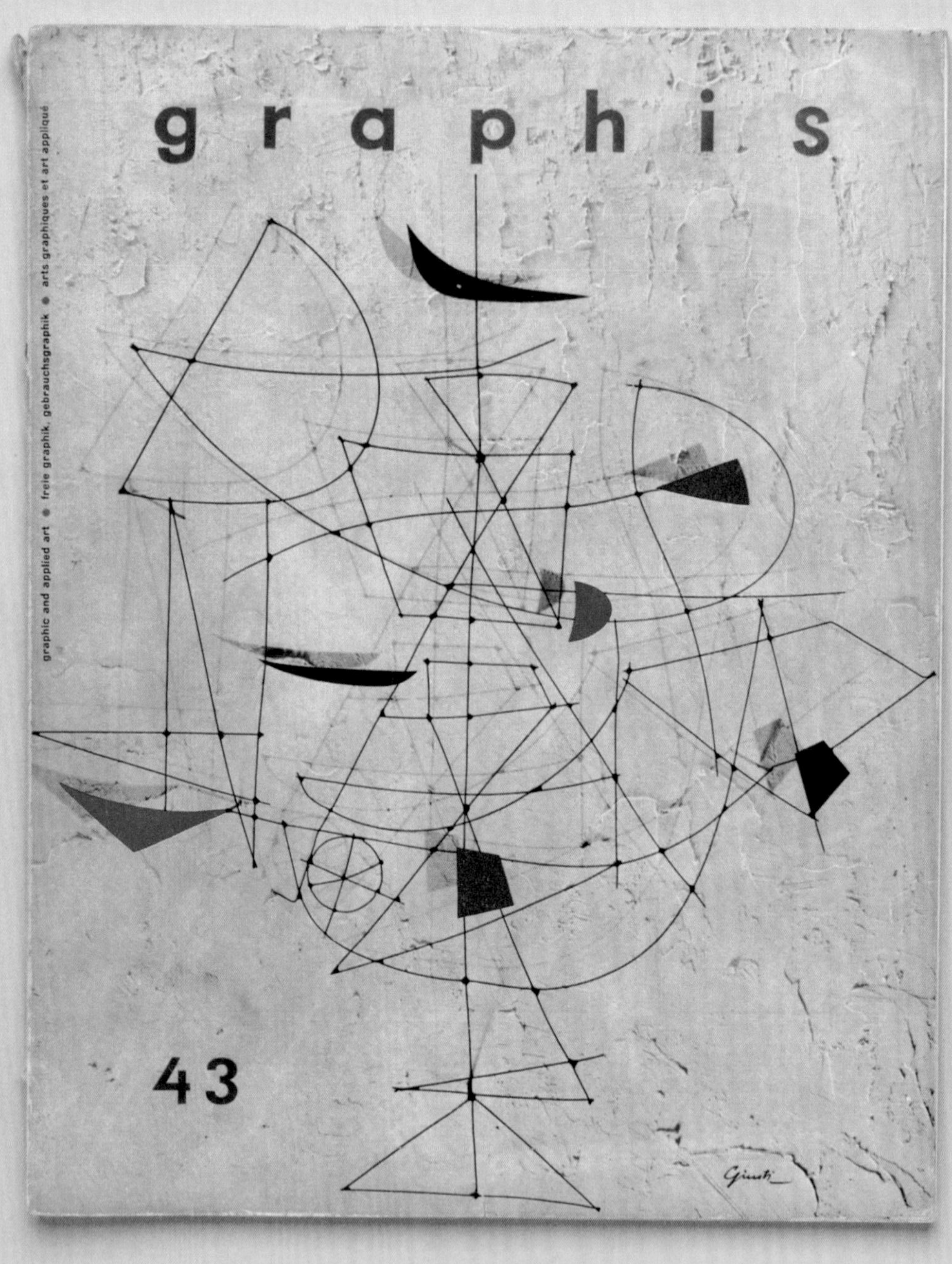

072

Graphis
Country: Switzerland

Cover Design: George Giusti

Interview: Richard Hollis

Q What are the ingredients needed for a good design journal?

A Well, as you might know, I don't approve of design journals [laughs]. But perhaps that's just me. I did a review for *Eye* (1990–present, UK) recently, and they sent me a copy. The issue was really good. It told me what people are doing and thinking – and it does it internationally. So I think there is a place for magazines, but speaking personally, because I'm not a designer any more, I don't tend to read them now.

They are useful however, for design historians because you can see what was interesting to people at the time. On the other hand, one of the reasons I've always felt that design magazines were pernicious was because students would go to them to find a style that they could imitate. Of course, people learn by imitation, but if you don't understand the context then it's just mindless copying. Today, so much graphic design is intended for online use anyway – which is wonderful because it means that you can see 'the real thing'. And that's another problem with printed magazines – you get a small reproduction and the scale can be misleading.

Q In your book *Concise History of Graphic Design* (1994) you talk about some of the first design publications: *The Poster* (1898–1900, UK), *Inland Printer* (1883–1900, USA), and the *Monotype Recorder* (1902–relaunched 2014, UK). What do you think was the earliest example of a graphic design journal?

A The earliest ones were part of the Arts and Crafts movement, and so graphic design was incorporated alongside other things. In *The Studio* (1893–1964, UK) magazine there were articles on Will Bradley and Aubrey Beardsley – but not what you'd call graphic design. *Das Plakat* (1910–21, Germany), and *Les Maîtres de l'Affiche* (1895–1900, France) – published in sections as I remember – were early examples. Unfortunately, today most archives insist on binding magazines and journals into folders, which makes photography difficult. But of course so many magazines – mostly architecture and interiors publications – are now online. It's changed research – everything's much easier. But I don't like reading online so I'm always printing everything out.

Q You have strong views on captions, don't you?

A I do. I used to complain about the captions in *Eye*, and one day a woman bumped into a friend of mine – the designer Robin Fior – who lived in Portugal and had come over to London because his daughter had designed an architectural exhibition at the Royal Academy. He was going up the steps at the RA and a woman recognised him. She introduced herself as a copy editor on *Eye*. And he said, 'Oh, you and your bloody captions.' And the woman said, 'Ah, you must be a friend of Richard Hollis?' [laughs]

With *Neue Grafik* (1958–65, Switzerland), because it was in several languages, in the original layout – I think it was by Carlo Vivarelli – all pictures had numbers that corresponded to captions, so you had to search for the caption. On the second or third issue, Max Bill said, 'I'm putting the caption next to the picture'. And it's really that simple. To do otherwise is a failure on the part of the designer to think about the reader. You see something mentioned and you want to find out about it. To my generation it's just idiotic not to put the caption as close to the picture as possible.

Q Can we talk about the sort of writing you look for in a journal? You make a clear distinction between what we could call texts that deal with theoretical or cultural reflection, as opposed to practical texts on use of materials, choice of printer, etc.

A Can these two avenues ever be reconciled? How do you bring the two together? Well, if you're writing about a piece of work, you put it into context, which involves nearly every aspect of a project. So, if space allows, everything should really be a case study. Today, this is perhaps less interesting, because everyone uses the same technology, and more or less works in the same way. And of course clients are completely different now; they think they know everything they need to know – and that's why I'm very pleased I stopped designing.

Neue Grafik
1958–65
Switzerland

Neue Grafik
New Graphic Design
Graphisme actuel
1

Q Despite your low opinion of design magazines, which ones were successful in bringing about change? For instance, I would say that *Emigre* (1984–2005, US) was a real game-changer.

A I'm talking about sixty years ago – but *Kwadraat-Bladen* (1955–74, Netherlands) by Pieter Brattinga was very influential. So too was *Stile Industria* (1954–63, Italy), although it was a general design publication and not a graphic one. Also from Italy, *Linea Grafica* (1945–2011). In Britain, Herbert Spencer's *Typographica* (1949–67) was also important. It introduced us to people we knew almost nothing about. For example, he did an issue with Franco Grignani. And from a slightly later period – *Octavo* (1986–92, UK). It was an example of a manifesto.

Neue Grafik, of course. It was made and written by designers. The practitioner is speaking. It was from the horse's mouth, so to speak, and that lends authenticity to what's being said. And, of course, Switzerland was relatively near and you could go and meet Swiss designers, and that makes all the difference.

When I was first teaching at London School of Printing and Graphic Arts, the interesting magazines were mainly American. *Communication Arts* (1959–present) and *Print* (1940–present), because we were as much interested in the USA as in Europe. There was an American 'do-it-yourself' magazine in the 1980s. I had an issue. It was one of the leading American designers telling you how to do it. People like Lester Beall.

The school also subscribed to something called the Graphic Samples Service. Exposing students to the real things was important, because everyone has to be reminded that a reproduction is not the real thing. In those days, designers would send their work to *Graphis* magazine (1944–present, Switzerland) to be reproduced. Well, either having used it or not, the actual objects were sent to subscribers. Push Pin posters and covers, that sort of thing. And so every month, on the wall, were put the original things, and you could handle them. And that's why, for my generation, going to see designers and talking to them was what we did.

Richard Hollis is a graphic designer, book designer, writer and lecturer on design history. He is the author of the best-selling Graphic Design: A Concise History (1994) *and* Swiss Graphic Design: The Origins and Growth of an International Style, 1920–65 (2006).

Linea Grafica
1945–2011
Italy

Print
1940–present
USA

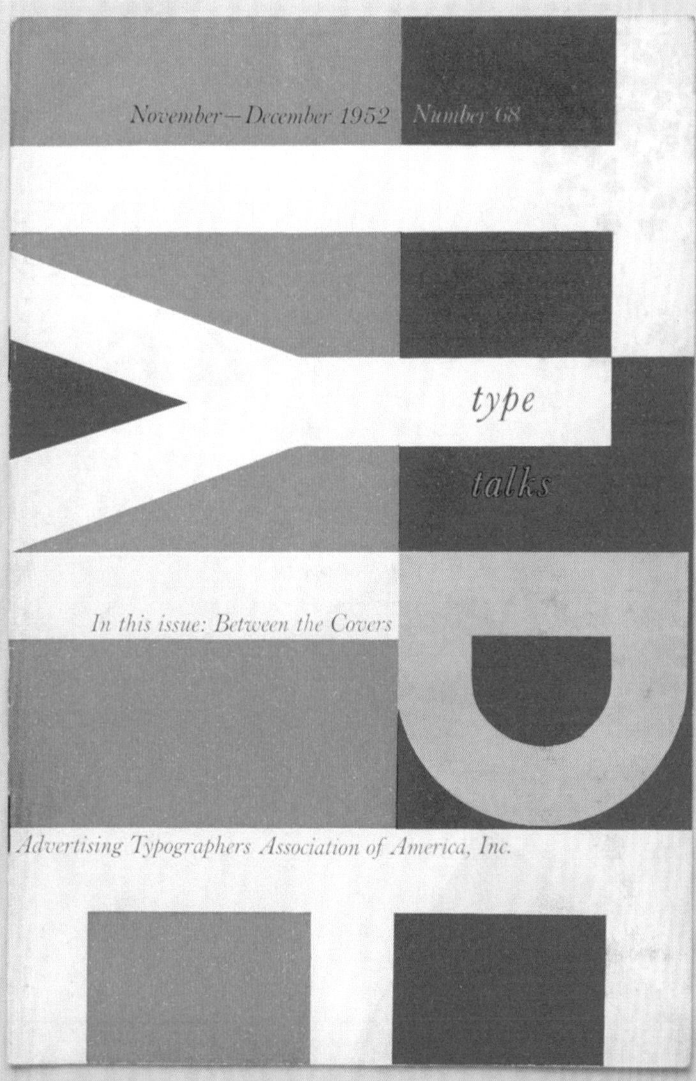

November—December 1952
Number 68
type
talks
In this issue: Between the Covers
Advertising Typographers Association of America, Inc.

Type Talks
Country: USA

Design: unidentified

03.1953

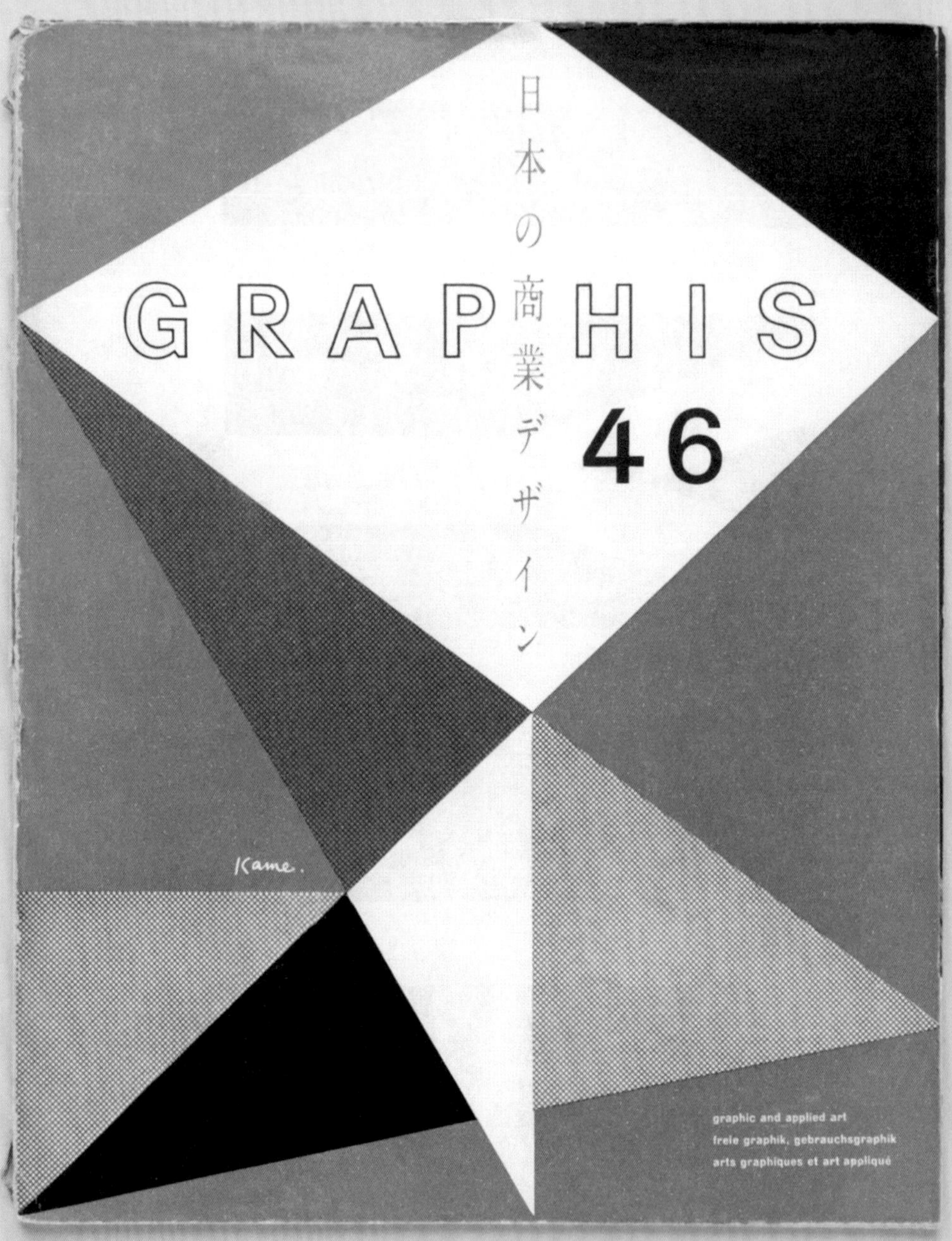

Graphis
Country: Switzerland

Cover Design: Yusaku Kamekura

11.1953

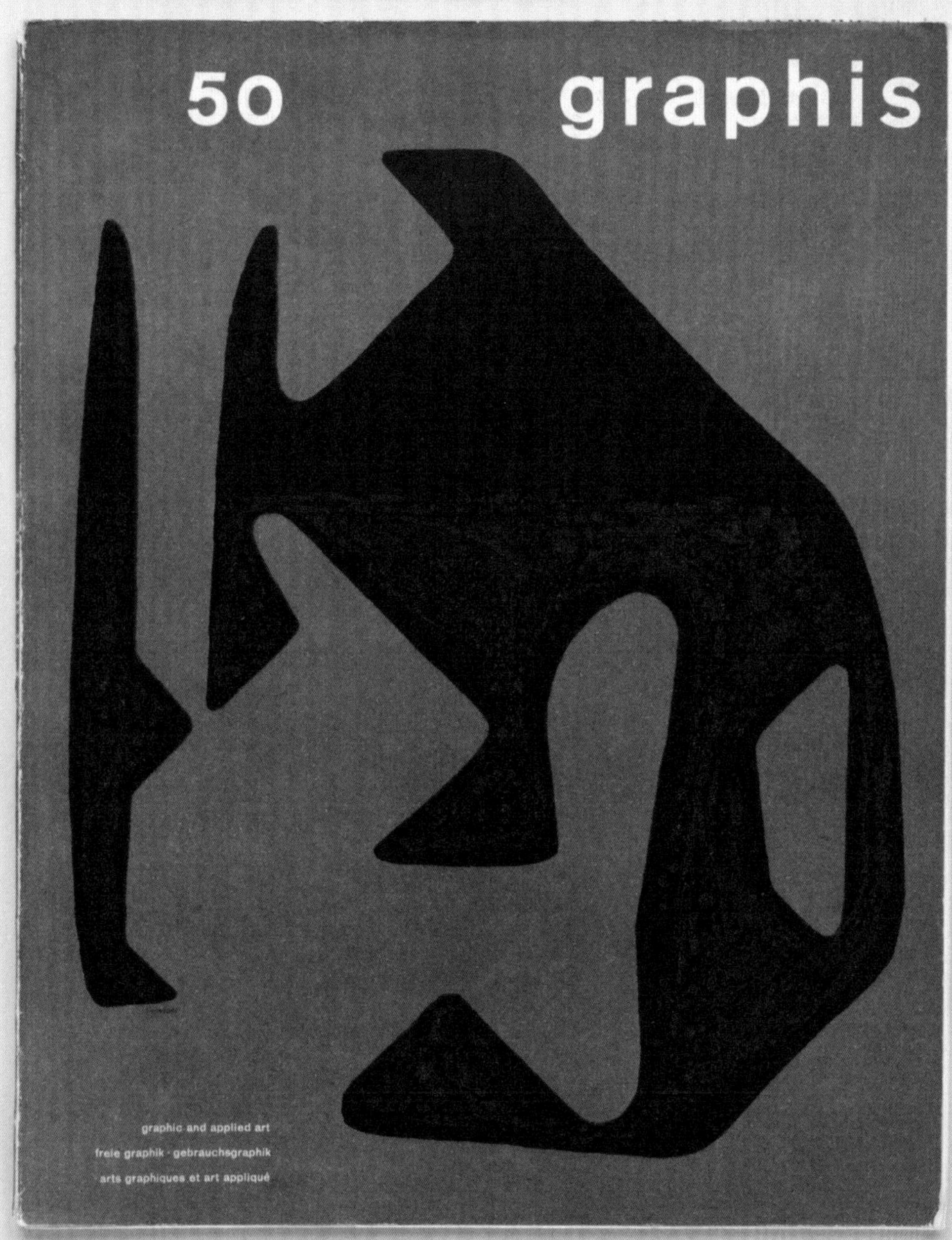

Graphis
Country: Switzerland

Cover Design:
Gottfried Honegger

Building + Home

2 Bauen+Wohnen

Construction + Habitation 1954

Bauen+Wohnen
Country: Germany

Design: unidentified

Building | Home

Büro- u. Verwaltungsbauten
Bâtiments commerciaux et administratifs
Office and administrative buildings

Ausstellungshalle
Hall d'exposition
Exhibition hall

3 Bauen+Wohnen

Kirche
Eglise
Church

Formgestaltung
Dessign industriel
Industrial design

Wettbewerb Hansaviertel Berlin
Concours: Hansaviertel Berlin
Contest: Hansaviertel Berlin

Construction | Habitation

1954

Art Director & Studio News
Country: USA

Cover Design: Robert Flynn

Building | Home

Ausstellungspavillon
Pavillon d'exposition
Exhibition pavilion

Verwaltungsbau
Bâtiment administratif
Administrative offices

4 Bauen+Wohnen

Tankstellen
Postes d'essence
Petrol stations

Wohnbauten
Bâtiments d'habitation
Dwelling houses

Construction | Habitation

1954

05.1954

Building + Home

Einkaufszentren
Shopping Centers
Shopping Centers

Victor Gruen, Architekt, New York
Dr. Carlo Pagani, Architekt, Mailand

Einzelläden
Magasins isolés
Single Shops

E. Zietzschmann, Architekt SIA, Zürich
Bräuning, Leu, Dürig, Architekten, Basel
Rolf Rhyner, Innenarchitekt, Zürich
Dipl.-Ing. E. Frh. von der Lippe, Architekt BDA, München

Sitzmöbel
Sièges
Chairs

Hans Eckstein, München

Schreibtische
Bureaux
Writing-tables

Friedrich Pütz, Architekt, München
Dr. Karl Hammann, Düsseldorf

5 Bauen+Wohnen

Construction + Habitation 1954

082

Bauen+Wohnen
Country: Germany

Design: unidentified

Building | Home

Einfamilienhäuser

Habitations Privées
Private Houses

Wochenendhäuser

Maisons de Week-end
Week-end Houses

6 Bauen+Wohnen

Prämiierte Bauten in Hannover

Bâtiments Couronnés à Hanovre
Prize-winning Buildings at Hanover

Construction | Habitation

1954

Design: unidentified

06.1954

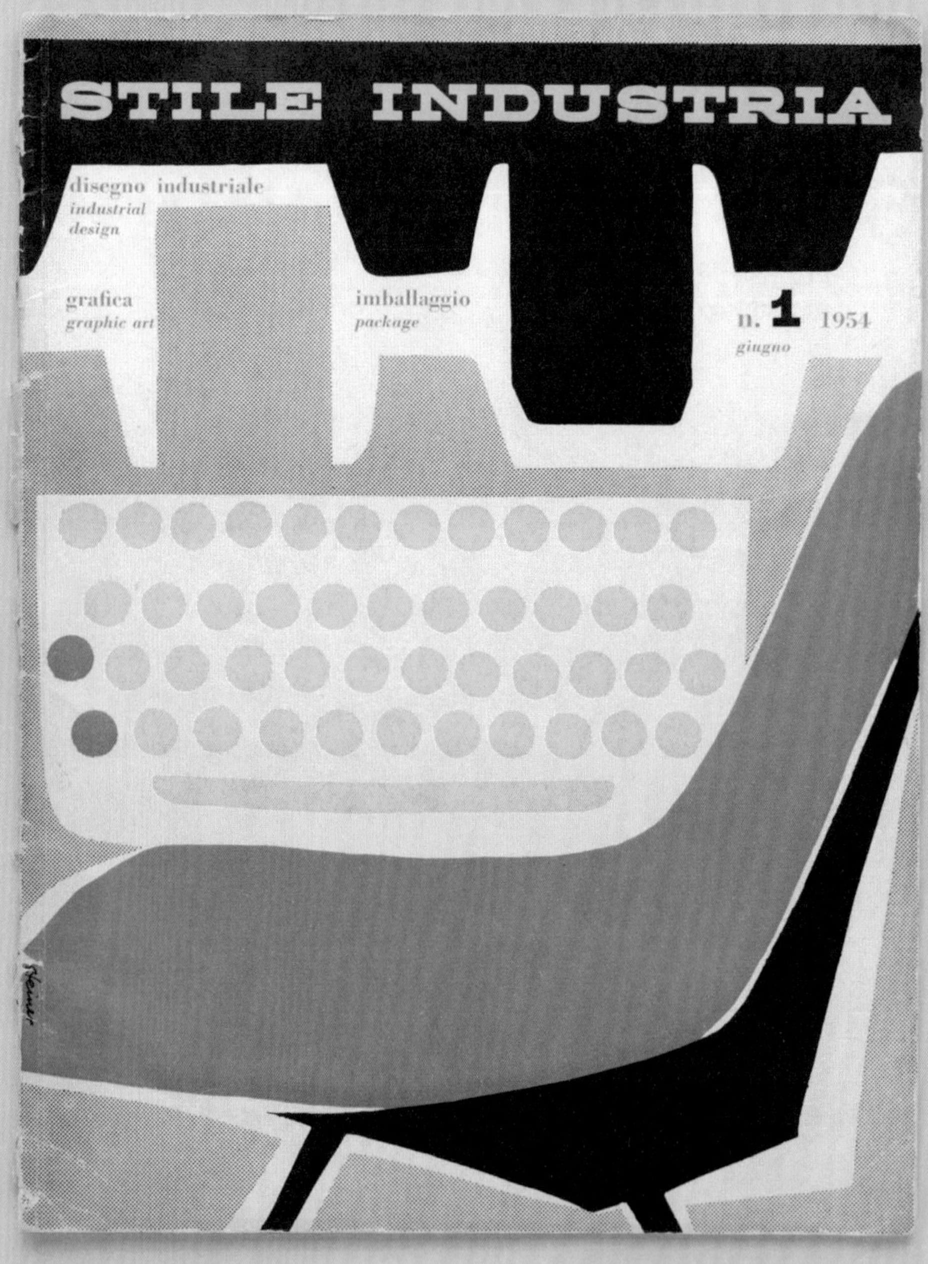

Stile Industria
Country: Italy

Cover Design: Albe Steiner

Building | Home

Schulen
Ecoles
Schools

Studenten-Clubhaus
Cercle des Etudiants
Students' Club-house

7 Bauen Wohnen

Mädchenheim
Home de jeunes Filles
Girls' Home

Kindergarten
Ecole maternelle
Kindergarten

Construction | Habitation

1954

Building | Home

Wohnbauten
Habitations
Dwellings

Bauten des Verkaufs
Bâtiments de Vente
Buildings for the Sale of Goods

8 Bauen+Wohnen

Fabrikbauten
Bâtiments Industriels
Industrial Buildings

Möbel
Meubles
Furniture

Werner Stücheli, Architekt BSA/SIA, Zürich

G. Addor, Architekt EPF/SIA, Genf
Prof. Eduard Ludwig, Architekt, Berlin

Hans Coray, SWB, Zürich
Prof. Eduard Ludwig, Architekt, Berlin
Nisse Stringing, Architekt, Stockholm

Ernst Zietzschmann, Architekt SIA, Zürich
C. Rathgeb & Sohn, Architekten SIA, Zürich

Richner und Anliker, Architekten SIA, Aarau

Prof. Dr.-Ing. Friedrich Wilhelm Kraemer, Braunschweig
Deutsche Mannesmannröhren-Werke AG, Düsseldorf
Friedrich Pütz, Architekt, München
Hans Eckstein, München

Dr. K. Hammann und Obering. E. Müller, Düsseldorf

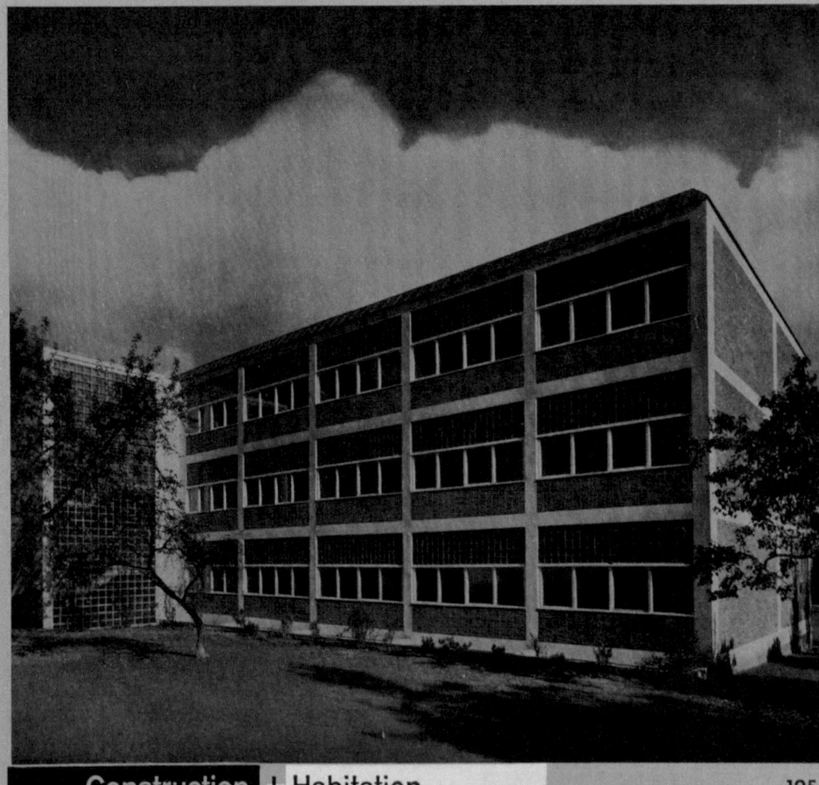

Construction | Habitation

1954

Bauen+Wohnen
Country: Germany

Design: unidentified

Building | Home

Verwaltungsbauten
Bâtiments administratifs
Office buildings

Kleine Markthalle
Marché couvert
Covered market

9 Bauen+Wohnen

Bauten am Wasser
Bâtiments sur l'eau
Buildings on the water

Innenräume
Intérieurs
Interiors

Sitzmöbel
Sièges
Sitting furniture

Stadtbaurat Dipl.-Ing. Walther Schmidt, Augsburg
Hans Eckstein, München
Prof. Hermann Mattern, Architekt BDA, Kassel
Prof. Martin Elsässer, Architekt BDA, Stuttgart
Dipl.-Ing. W. Schlegtendal, Arch. BDA, Nürnberg
Dipl.-Ing. Friedrich Lindau, Arch. BDA, Hannover
Dipl.-Ing. Günther Gottwald, Architekt,
Gerhard Weber, Architekt BDA, Frankfurt
E. und F. Burckhardt, Architekten BSA/SIA, Zürich
Hermann Blomeier, Dipl.-Architekt, Konstanz

Prof. Willy Kreuer, Architekt, Berlin

Dipl.-Ing. Ferdinand Kramer, Arch., Frankfurt
Prof. Georg Leowald, Architekt, Düsseldorf
Reg.-Baum. a. D. Dr.-Ing. M. E. Feuchtinger, Ulm
H. G. Nolde, Bonn

Friedrich Ruser, Weil am Rhein

Helmuth de Haas, München
Richard P. Lohse, SWB, Zürich
Dr.-jur. Cordes, Fechta
Dr.-Ing. Gerhard Dressel, Stuttgart

Dr. A. Foulon, Darmstadt

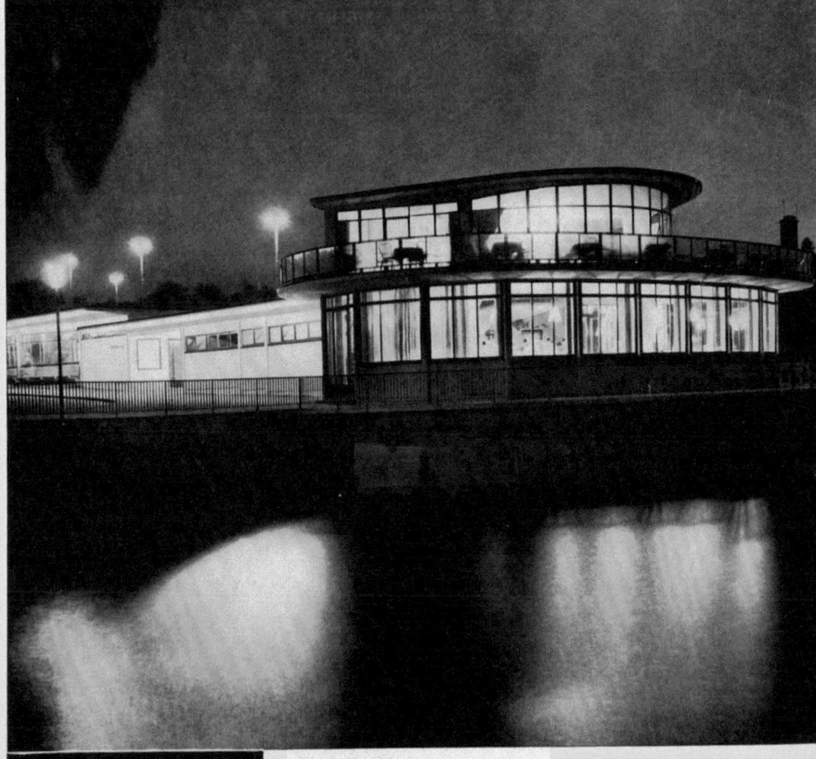

Construction | Habitation 1954

Bauen+Wohnen
Country: Germany

Design: unidentified

Industrial Design (later I.D.)
Country: USA

Art Director: Martin Rosenzweig

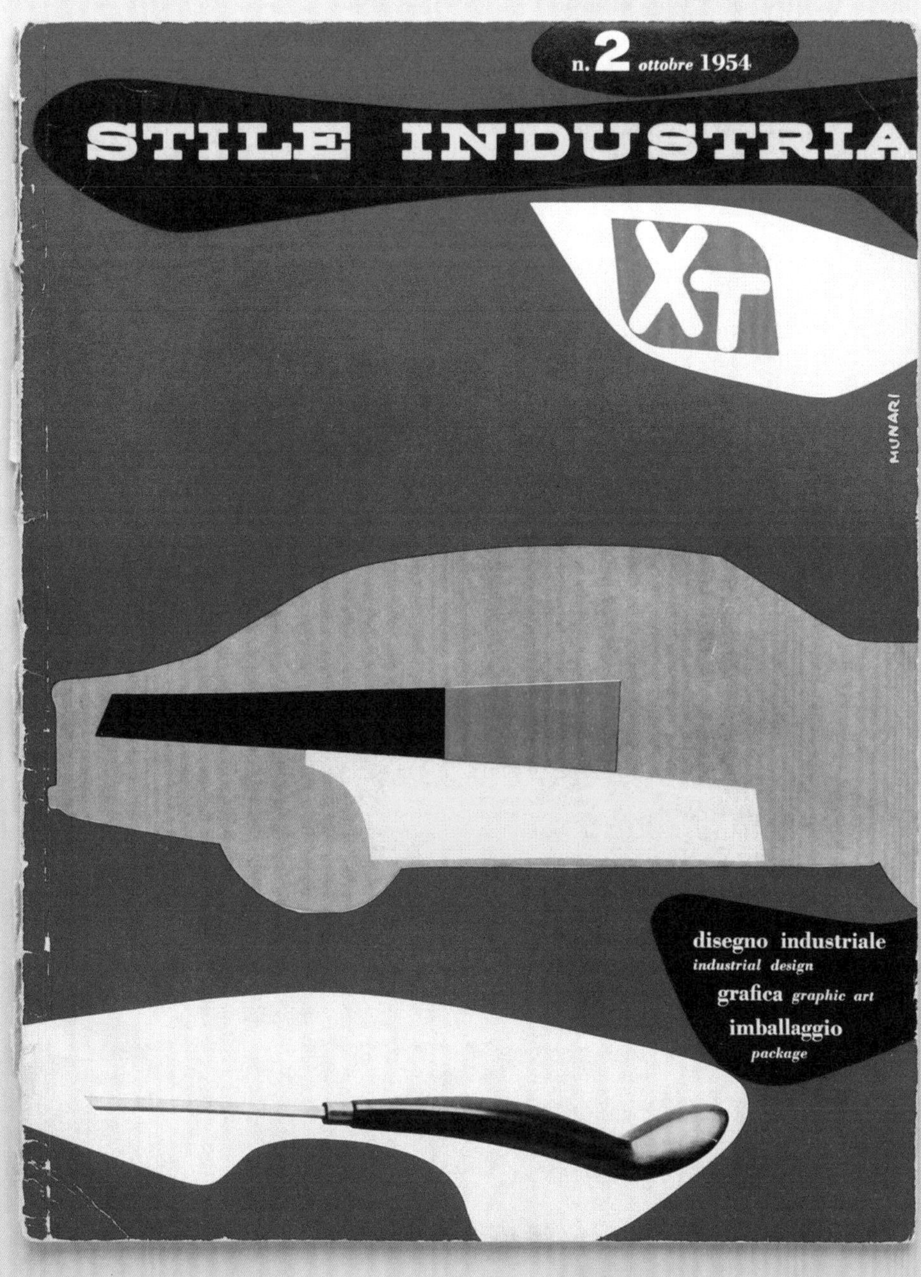

Stile Industria
Country: Italy

Cover Design: Bruno Munari

Building + Home

Geschäftshaus
Bâtiment commercial
Office block

Wohnbauten
Habitations
Blocks of flats

12 Bauen+Wohnen

Einfamilienhäuser
Habitations familiales
Single houses

Hans Eckstein, München
Dr.-Ing. Jürgen Joedicke, Stuttgart

W. Belart, Architekt SIA,
H. Frey, Architekt BSA/SIA, Olten
Ralph Rapson, J. van der Meulen, Architekten

Otto Apel, Architekt BDA, Frankfurt a. M.

Otto Glaus, Architekt BSA/SIA, Zürich
Richard J. Neutra, Architekt, Los Angeles

Willy Boesiger, Architekt, Zürich

Dipl.-Ing. Paul Schneider-Esleben,
Architekt BDA, Düsseldorf
Dipl.-Ing. Werner und Grete Wirsing,
Architekten, München

Peter Thomas, Oberingenieur VDI, Kiel

Erwin O. Genzsch, Hamburg

Construction + Habitation 1954

Bauen+Wohnen
Country: Germany

Design: unidentified

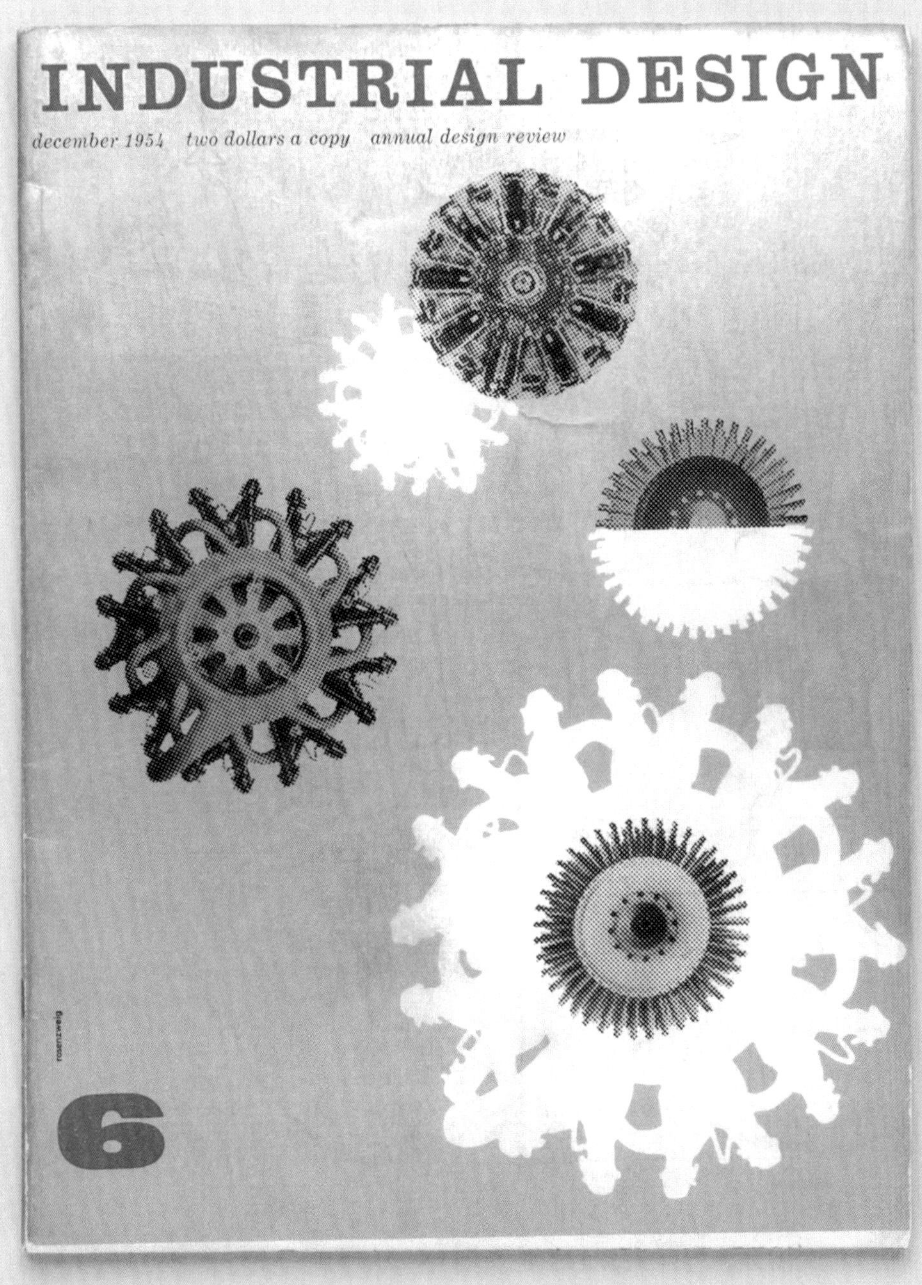

Industrial Design (later I.D.)
Country: USA

Art Director: Martin Rosenzweig

Stile Industria
Country: Italy

Cover Design: Giovanni Pintori

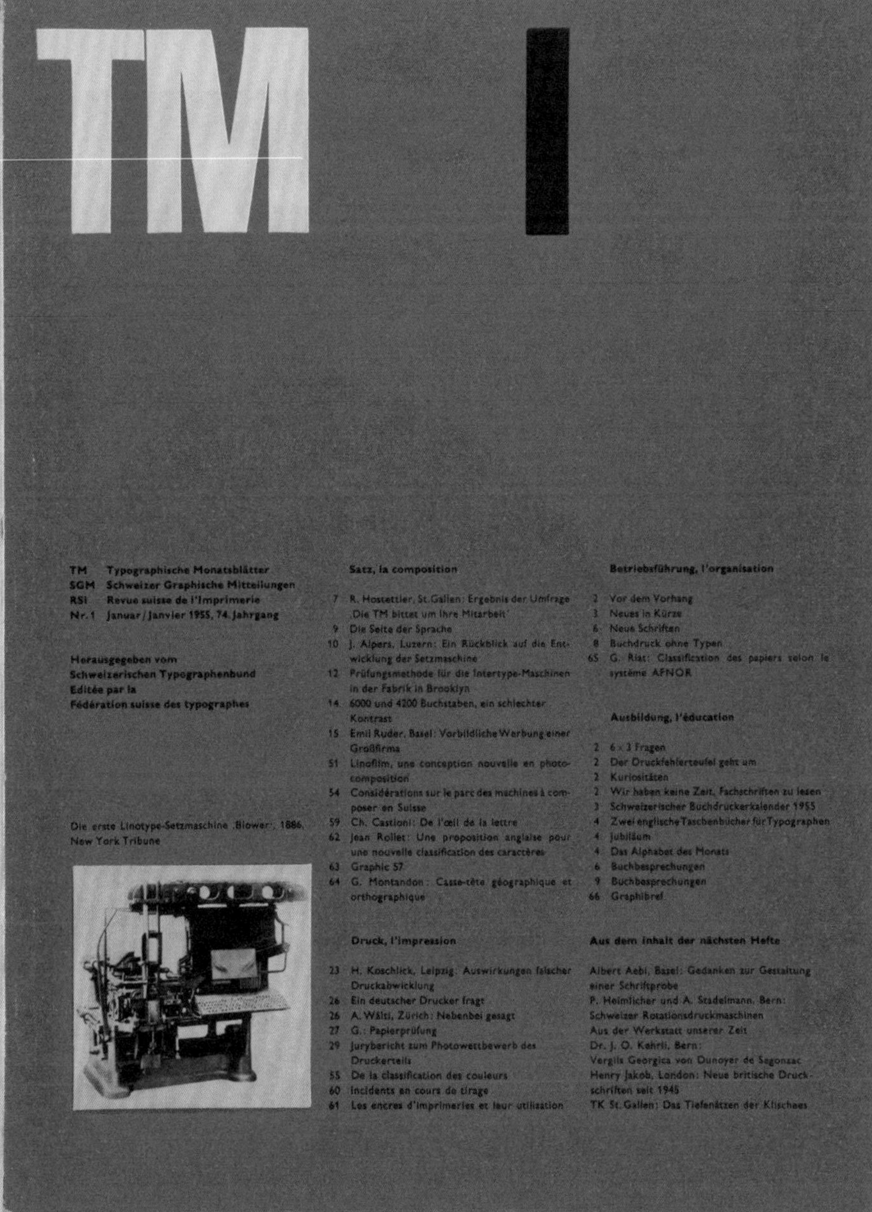
TM

1

TM Typographische Monatsblätter
SGM Schweizer Graphische Mitteilungen
RSI Revue suisse de l'Imprimerie
Nr. 1 Januar/Janvier 1955, 74. Jahrgang

Herausgegeben vom
Schweizerischen Typographenbund
Editée par la
Fédération suisse des typographes

Die erste Linotype-Setzmaschine ‚Blower', 1886, New York Tribune

Satz, la composition

Druck, l'impression

Betriebsführung, l'organisation

Ausbildung, l'éducation

Aus dem Inhalt der nächsten Hefte

Albert Aebi, Basel: Gedanken zur Gestaltung einer Schriftprobe
P. Heimlicher und A. Stadelmann, Bern: Schweizer Rotationsdruckmaschinen
Aus der Werkstatt unserer Zeit
Dr. J. O. Kehrli, Bern: Vergils Georgica von Dunoyer de Segonzac
Henry Jakob, London: Neue britische Druckschriften seit 1945
TK St. Gallen: Das Tiefenätzen der Klischees

TM (Typographische Monatsblätter)
Country: Switzerland

Design: unidentified
Courtesy of syndicom

02.1955

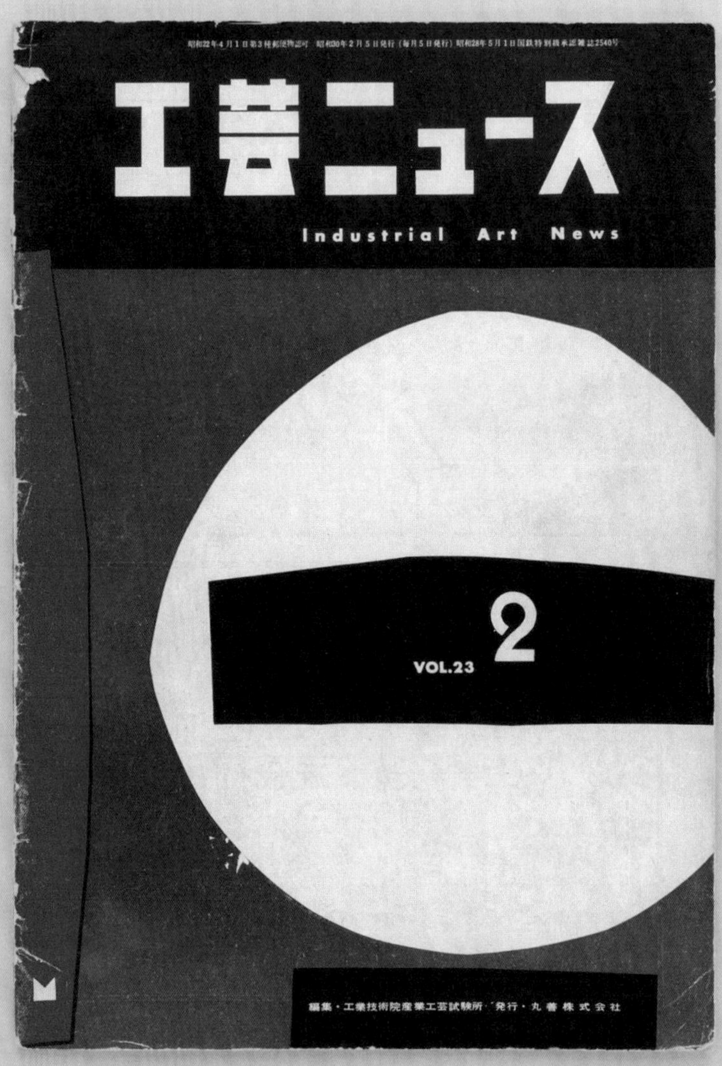

Industrial Art News
Country: Japan

Cover Design:
Murai Masanari

TM 

TM Typographische Monatsblätter
SGM Schweizer Graphische Mitteilungen
RSI Revue suisse de l'Imprimerie
Nr. 2 Februar / Février 1955, 74. Jahrgang

Herausgegeben vom
Schweizerischen Typographenbund
Editée par la
Fédération suisse des typographes

Papierrollenstern mit Klebevorrichtung
und automatischer Papierrollenbremse, Wifag

Satz, la composition

Druck, l'impression

Betriebsführung, l'organisation

Ausbildung, l'éducation

Aus dem Inhalt der nächsten Hefte

Henry Jacob, London:
Neue britische Druckschriften seit 1945
Albert Steiner, Winterthur:
Nordische Buchkunst
Meier, Zürich: Etwas über den Begriff Faktor
Sondernummer Setzmaschinen
Die Matrizensammlung mit Hindernissen
Day-Glo für Millionenauflagen im Buchdruck

TM (Typographische Monatsblätter)
Country: Switzerland

Design: unidentified
Courtesy of syndicom

03.1955

Idea
Country: Japan

Cover Design: Herbert Bayer

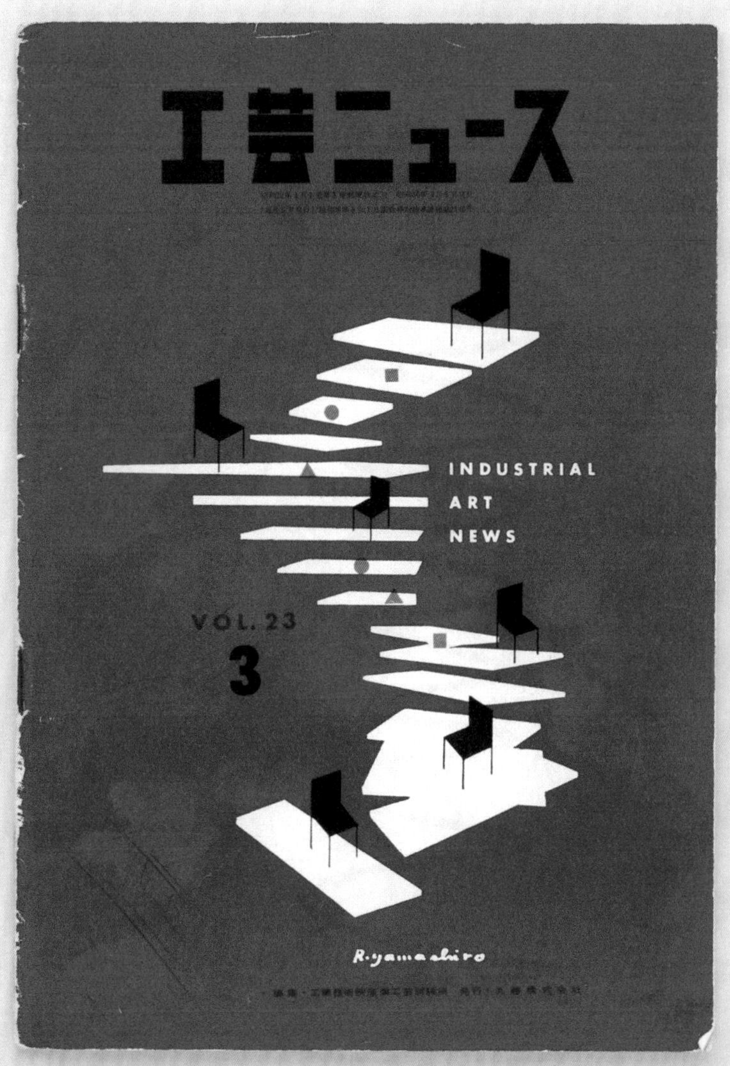

Industrial Art News
Country: Japan

Cover Design:
Yamashiro Ryuichi

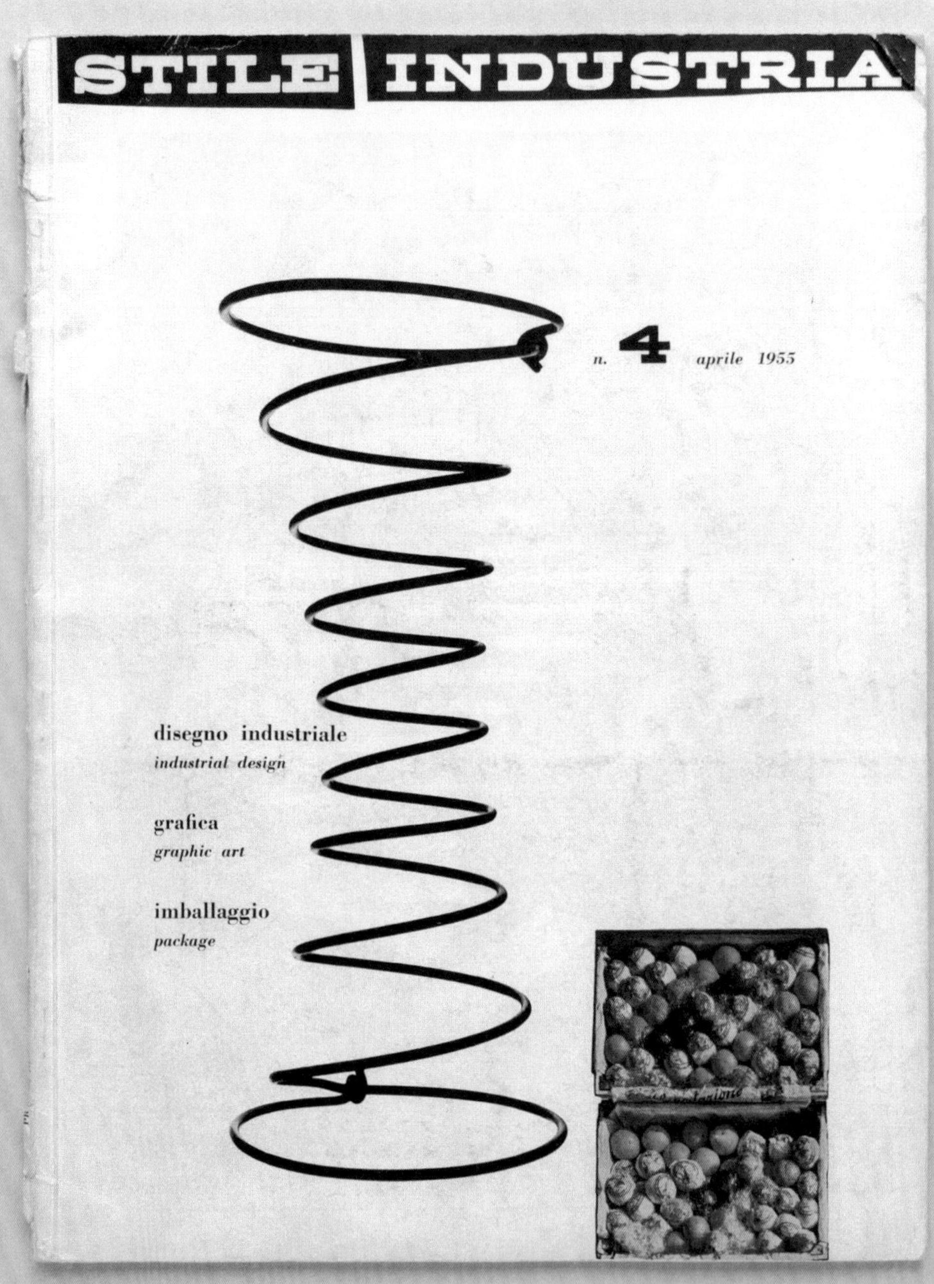

Stile Industria
Country: Italy

Cover Design:
G Casali, K Helmer-Petersen

TM (Typographische Monatsblätter)
Country: Switzerland

Design: unidentified
Courtesy of syndicom

05.1955

Graphis
Country: Switzerland

Cover Design: George Giusti

05.1955

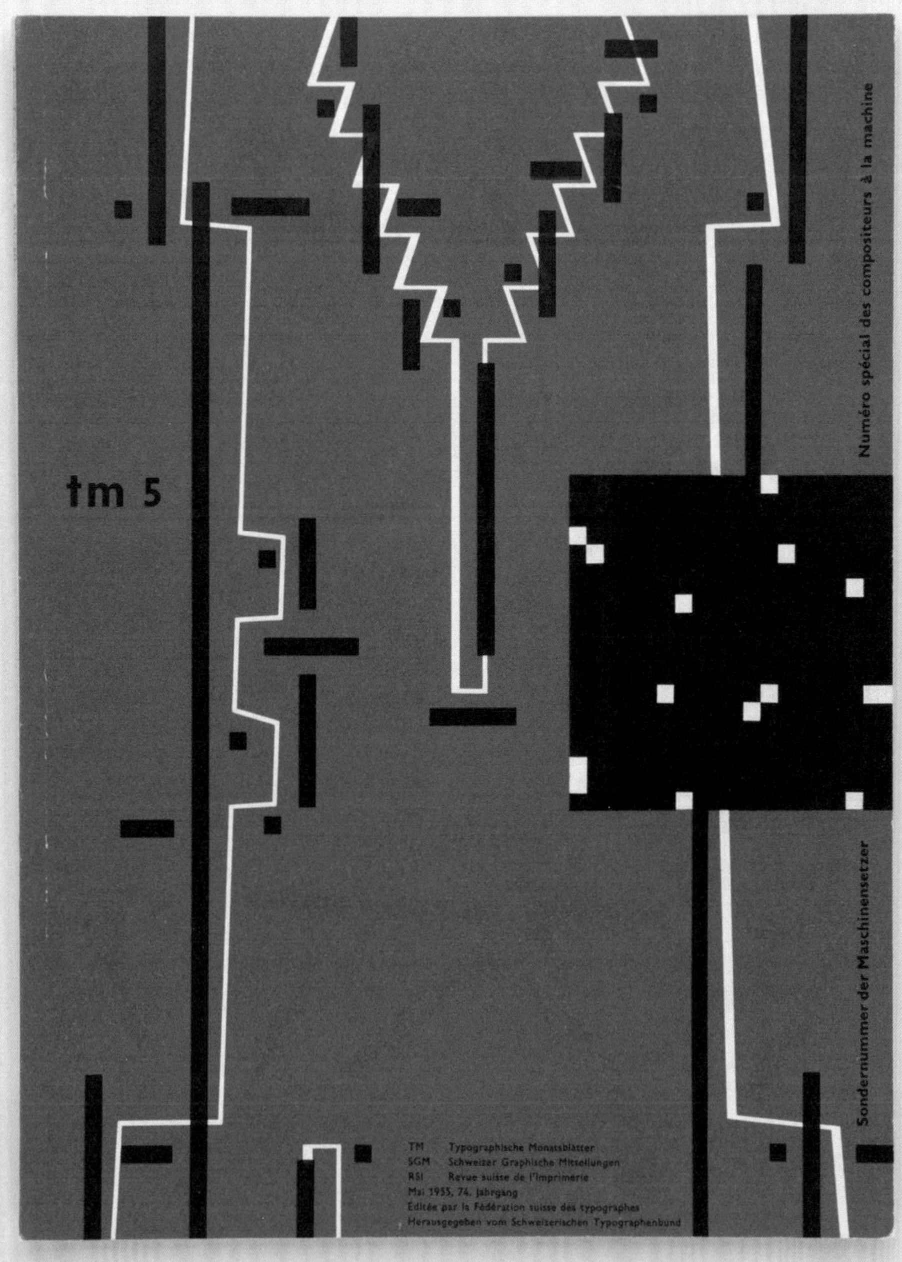

Numéro spécial des compositeurs à la machine
tm 5
Sondernummer der Maschinensetzer
TM Typographische Monatsblätter
SGM Schweizer Graphische Mitteilungen
RSI Revue suisse de l'Imprimerie
Mai 1955, 74. Jahrgang
Editée par la Fédération suisse des typographes
Herausgegeben vom Schweizerischen Typographenbund

TM (Typographische Monatsblätter)
Country: Switzerland

Design: unidentified
Courtesy of syndicom

06.1955

Industrial Design (later I.D.)
Country: USA

Art Director: Martin Rosenzweig

TM (Typographische Monatsblätter)
Country: Switzerland

Design: unidentified
Courtesy of syndicom

10.1955

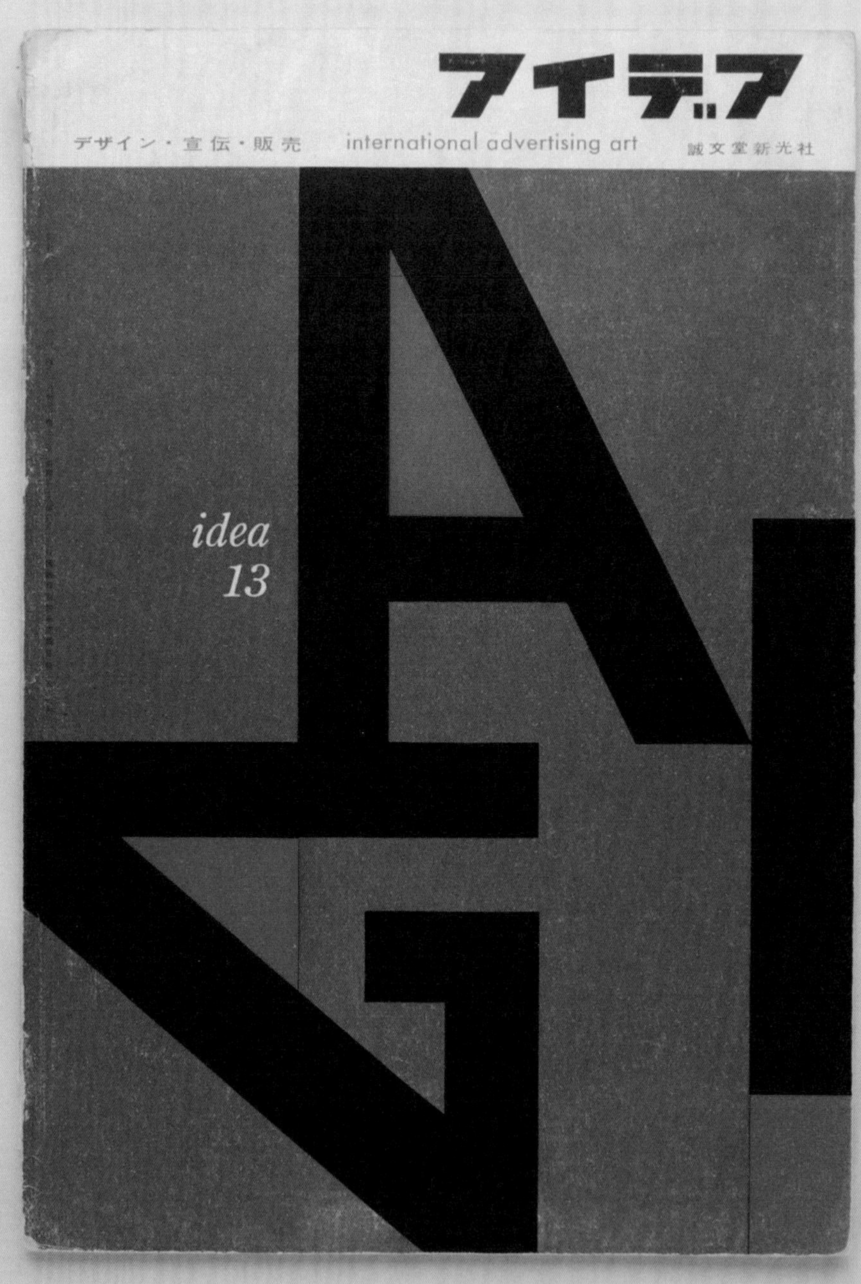

104

Idea
Country: Japan

Cover Design: Hiromu Hara

10.1955

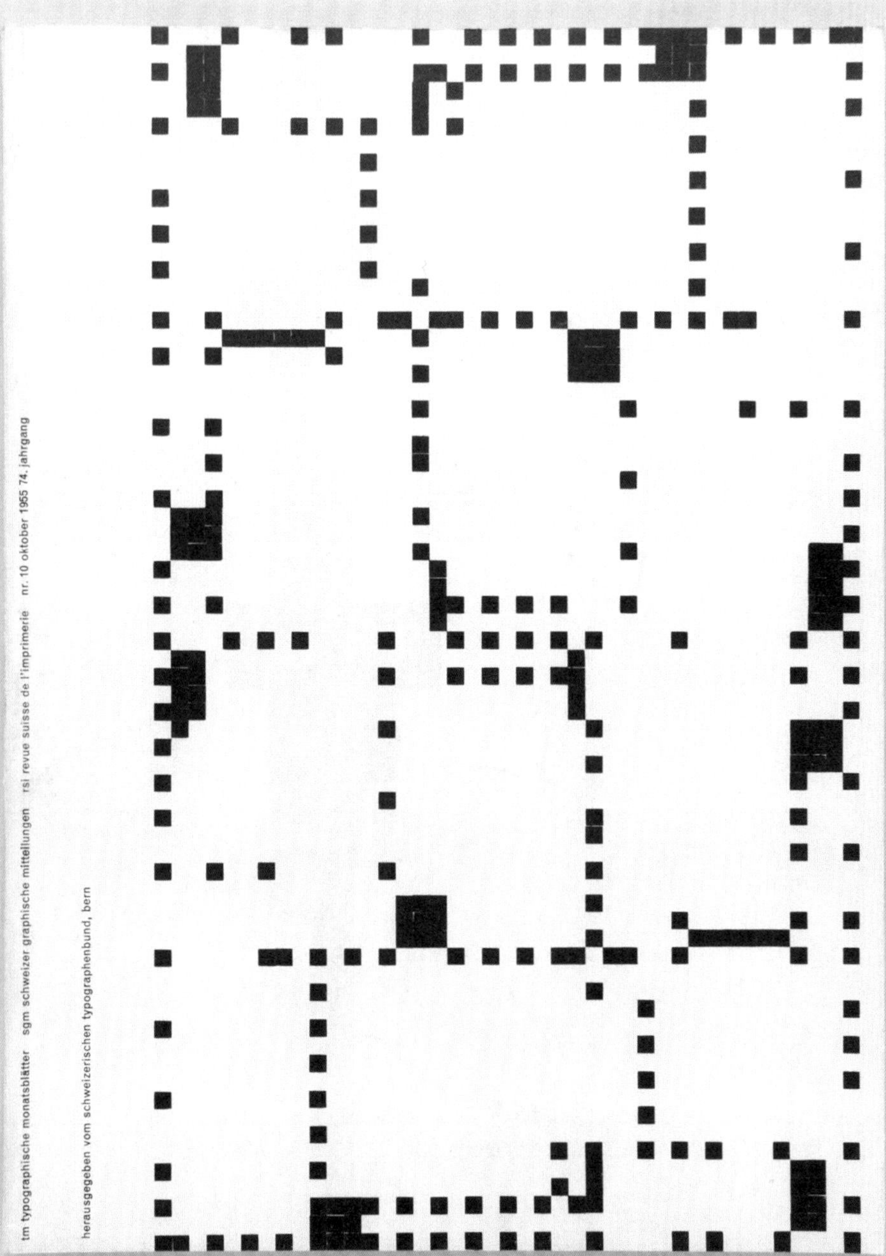

TM (Typographische Monatsblätter)
Country: Switzerland

Design: unidentified
Courtesy of syndicom

11.1955

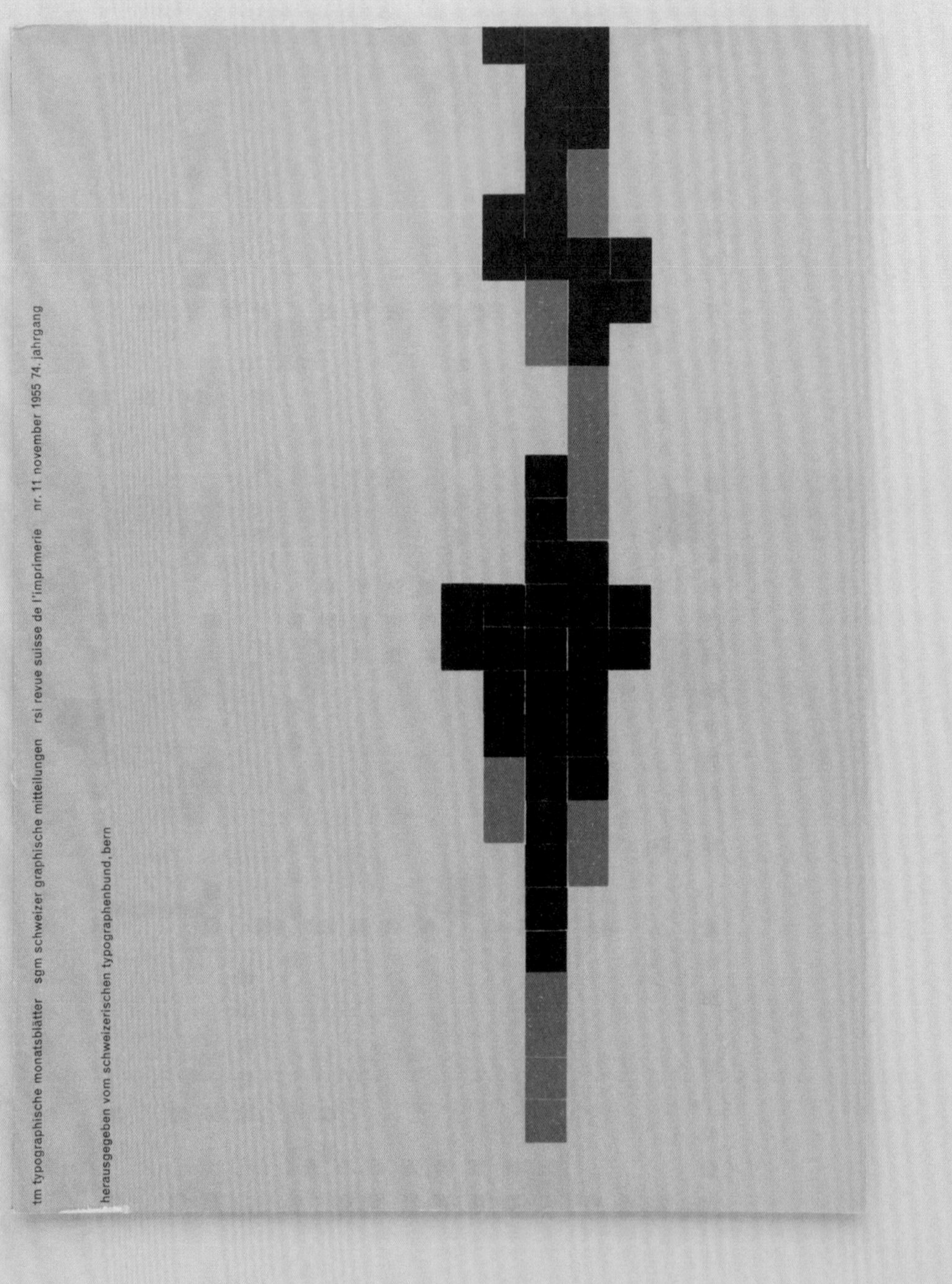

TM (Typographische Monatsblätter)
Country: Switzerland

Design: unidentified
Courtesy of syndicom

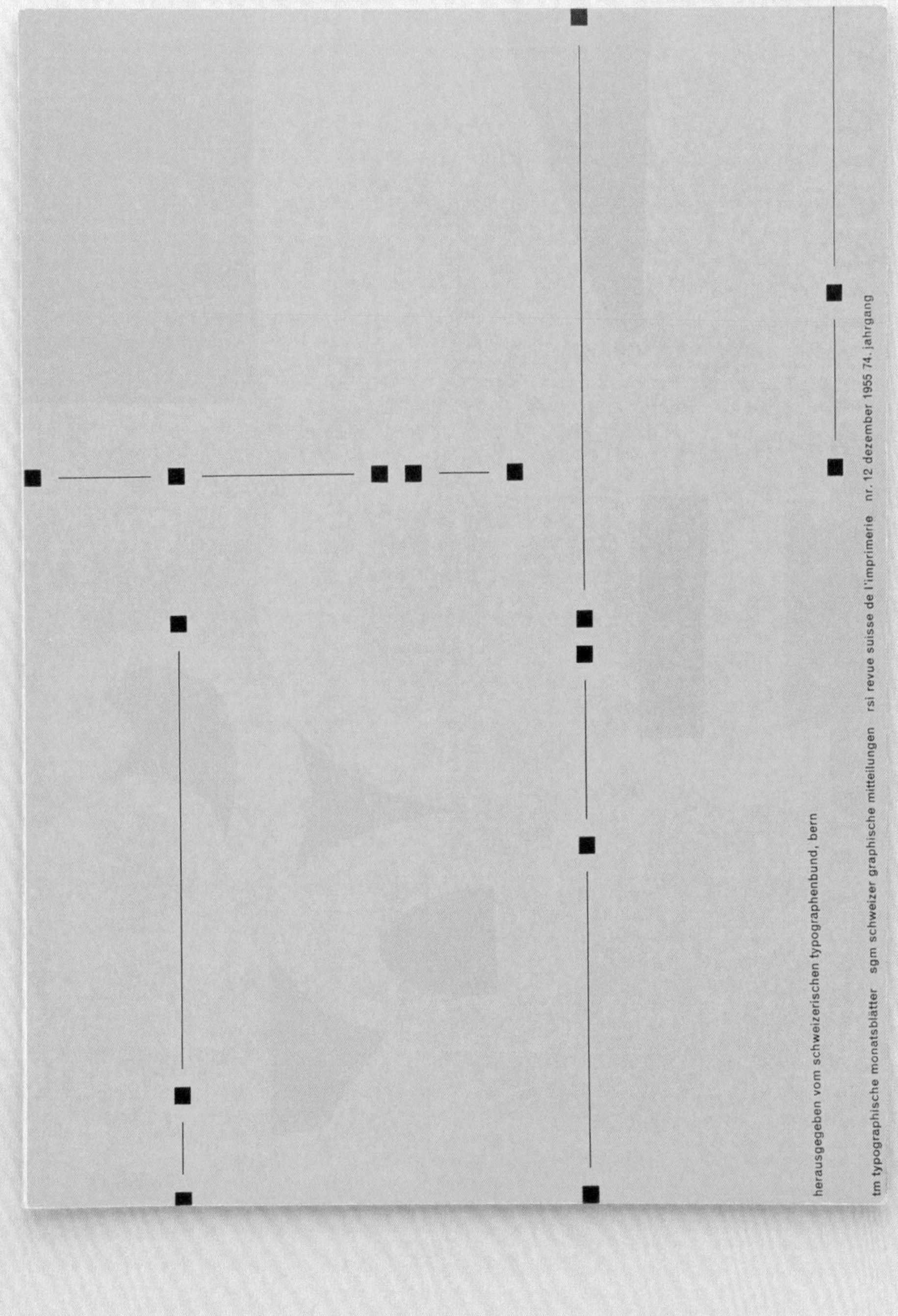

TM (Typographische Monatsblätter)
Country: Switzerland

Design: unidentified
Courtesy of syndicom

12.1955

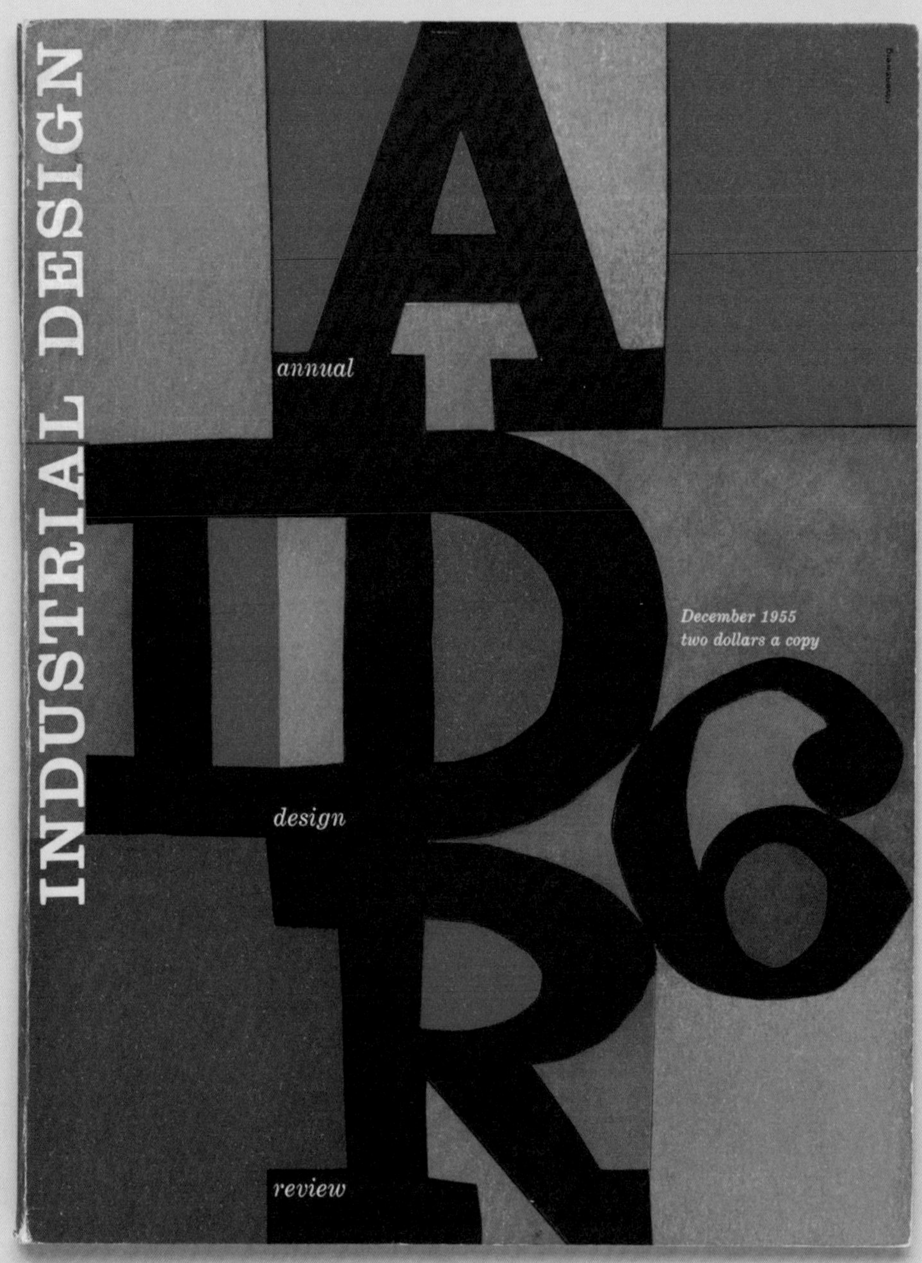

Industrial Design (later I.D.)
Country: USA

Art Director: Martin Rosenzweig

01.1956

Industrial Art News
Country: Japan

Design:
Toyoguchi Katsuhei,
Akashi Kazuo, Yoshitake Mosuke

01.1956

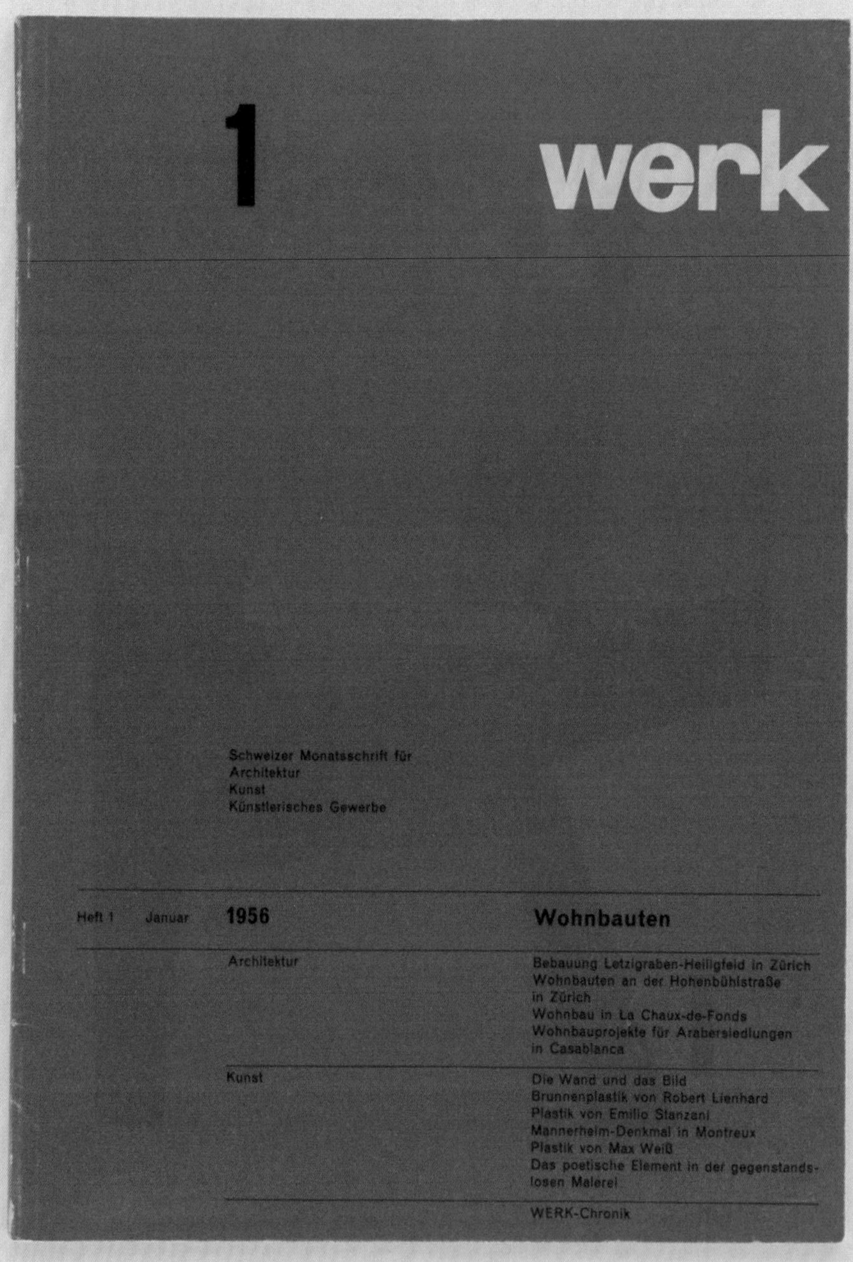

(Das) Werk
Country: Switzerland

Cover Design: Karl Gerstner

Design
Country: UK

Cover Design: Ken Garland

Q Your first important job after graduation was as art editor of *Design* (1949–99, UK). Richard Hollis has described the design of the publication prior to you taking over as having a 'bloodless centred layout'. How did you approach the task of changing this?
A Slowly, somewhat to the impatience of my contemporaries who were anticipating a dramatic transformation: in fact, the appearance of the magazine was not to my satisfaction until I had been in the post about five years, and even then I left some things still to be done. Regarding the covers, I commissioned every third one. The choice of designer was left to me.

Q Which publications were your inspirations at that time?
A *Industrial Design* (1954–2009, USA), *Stile Industria* (1954–63, Italy), *Domus* (1928–present, Italy).

Q Is there a sense in which designers of design magazines have an easy ride?
A Yes, because their colleagues are in sympathy with them; and no, because too much is expected of them.

Q Which, if any, of today's design publications catch your attention?
A *Creative Review* (1981–present, UK), *Typography Papers* (1996–present, UK).

Q What is the role of the design publication today?
A If you are referring to printed publications: to be a permanent record of achievement when all the online sources have slid into oblivion.

Ken Garland is a graphic designer, photographer, writer and educator. In 1962 he formed Ken Garland & Associates (until 2009) in Camden, London, where he continues to live and work.

Industrial Design/I.D
1954–2009
USA

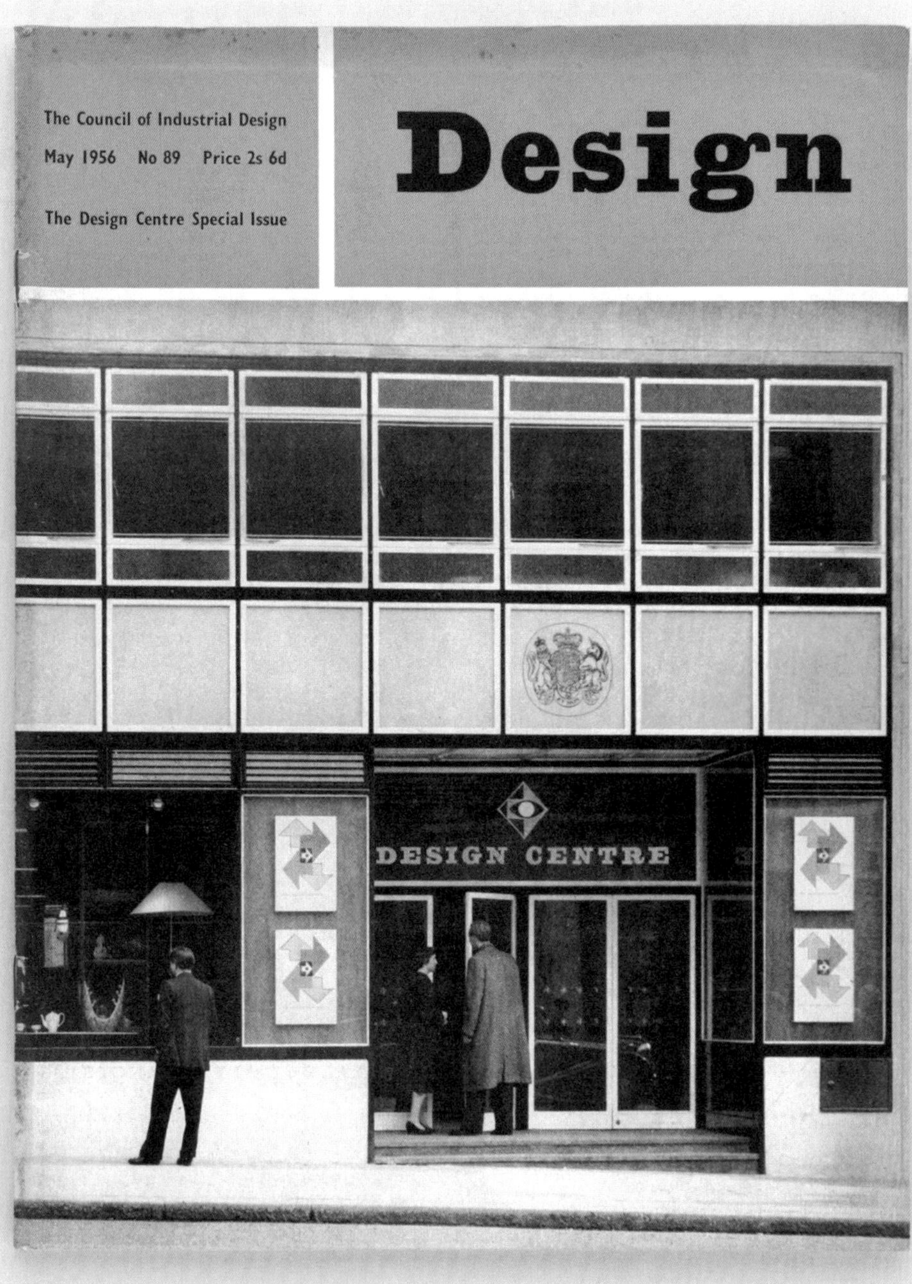

Design
Country: UK

Cover Design: Ken Garland

05.1956

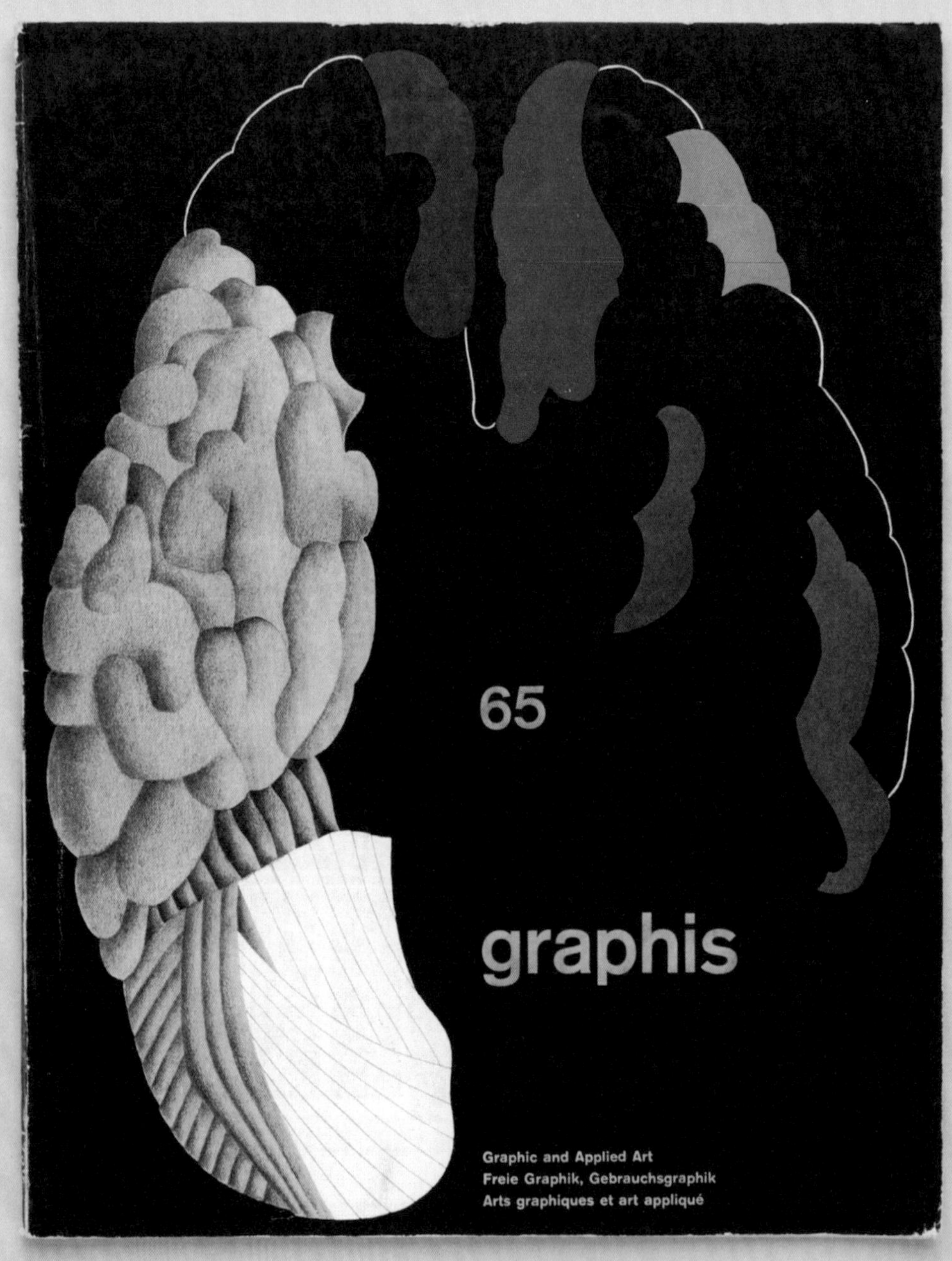

65
graphis
Graphic and Applied Art
Freie Graphik, Gebrauchsgraphik
Arts graphiques et art appliqué

Graphis
Country: Switzerland

Cover Design: Gottfried Honegger

Industrial Art News
Country: Japan

Cover Design:
Yamashiro Ryuichi

08.1956

Industrial Art News
Country: Japan

Cover Design: Kitadai Shozo

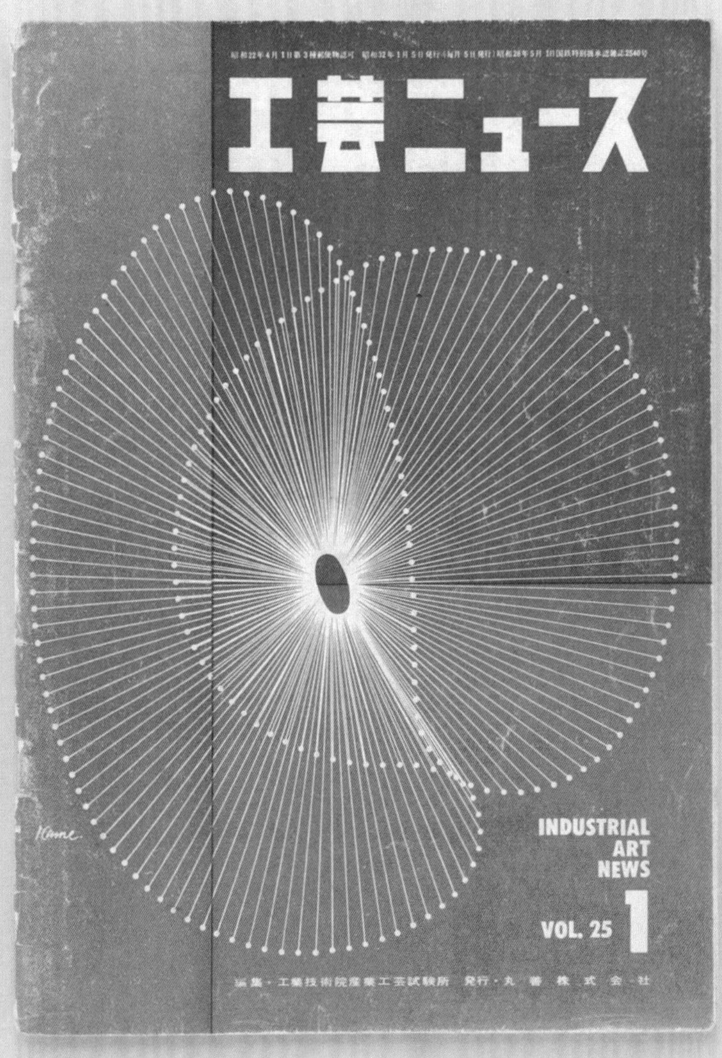

Industrial Art News
Country: Japan

Cover Design:
Toyoguchi Katsuhei,
Akashi Kazuo, Yoshitake Mosuke

03.1957

The Council of Industrial Design

March 1957 No 99 Price 3s

Design

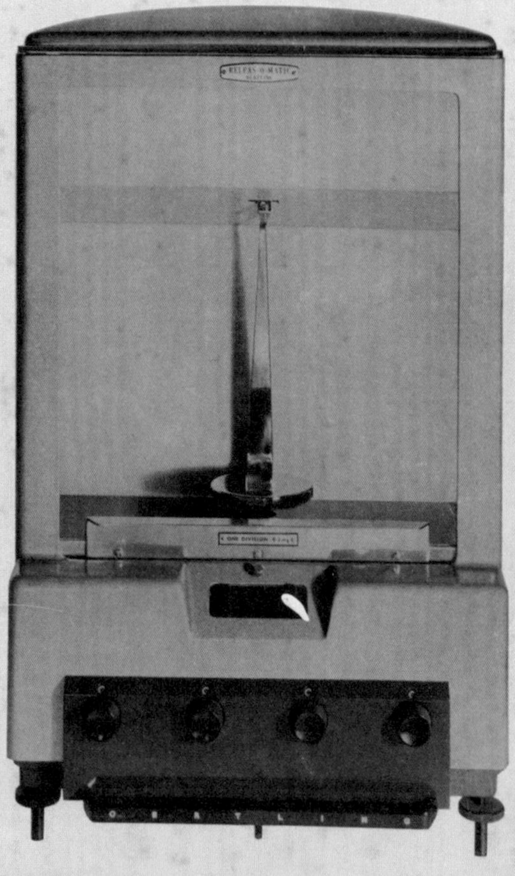

Design
Country: UK

Cover Design: Ken Garland

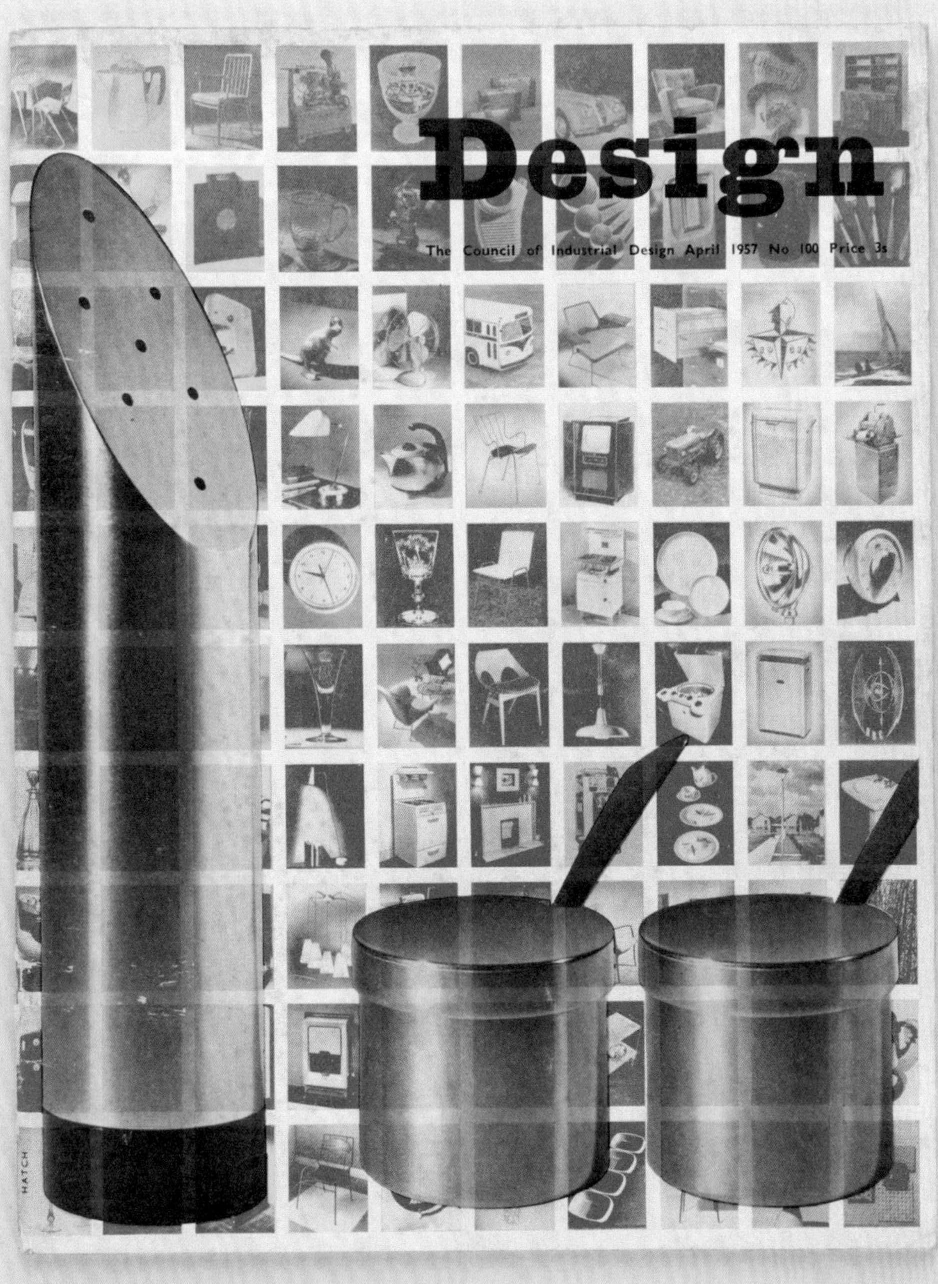

Design
Country: UK

Cover design: "Hatch"

06.1957

Design
Country: UK

Cover Design: Ken Garland

Idea
Country: Japan

Cover Design:
Matthew Leibowitz

10.1957

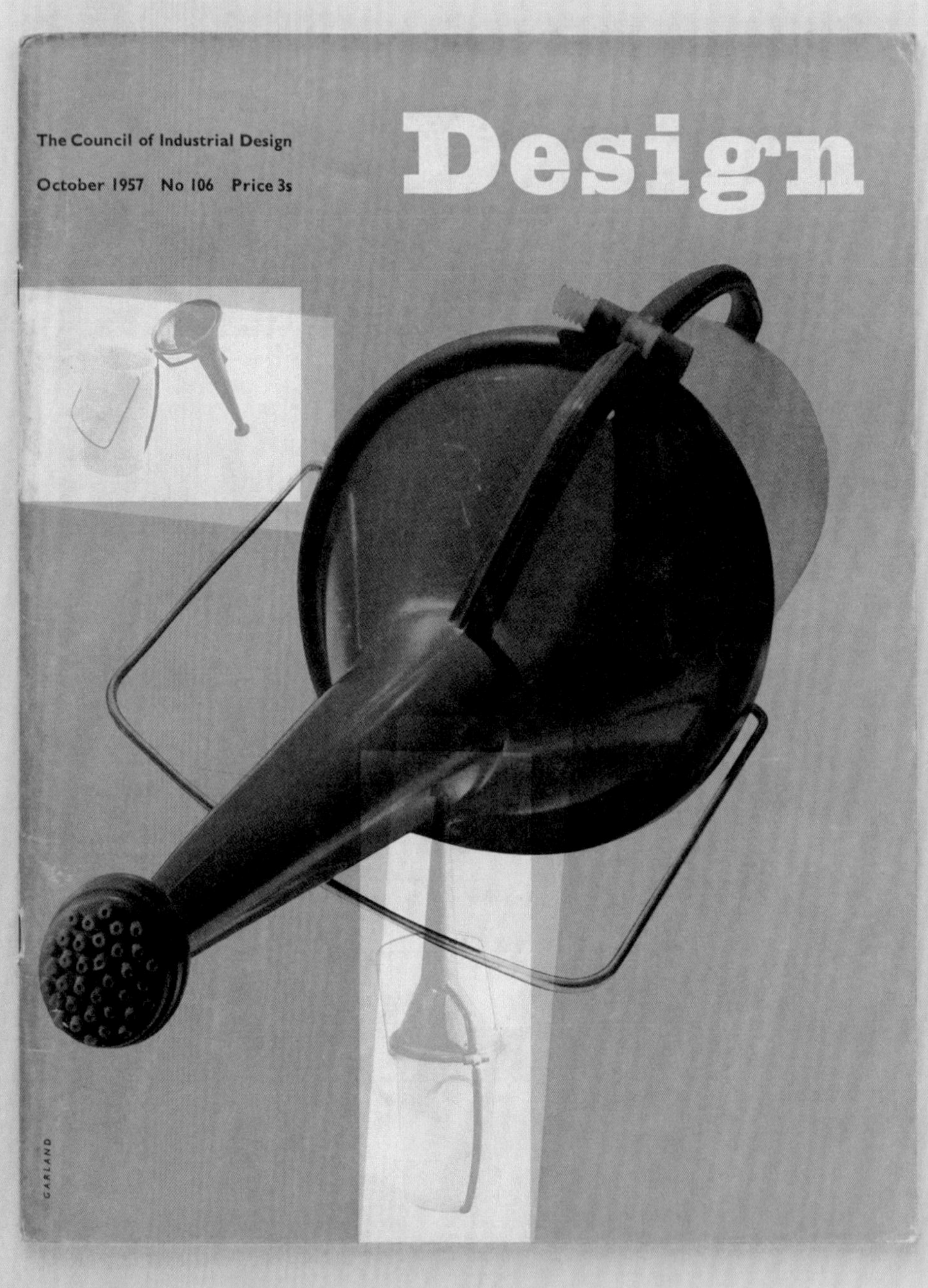

Design
Country: UK

Cover Design: Ken Garland

10.1957

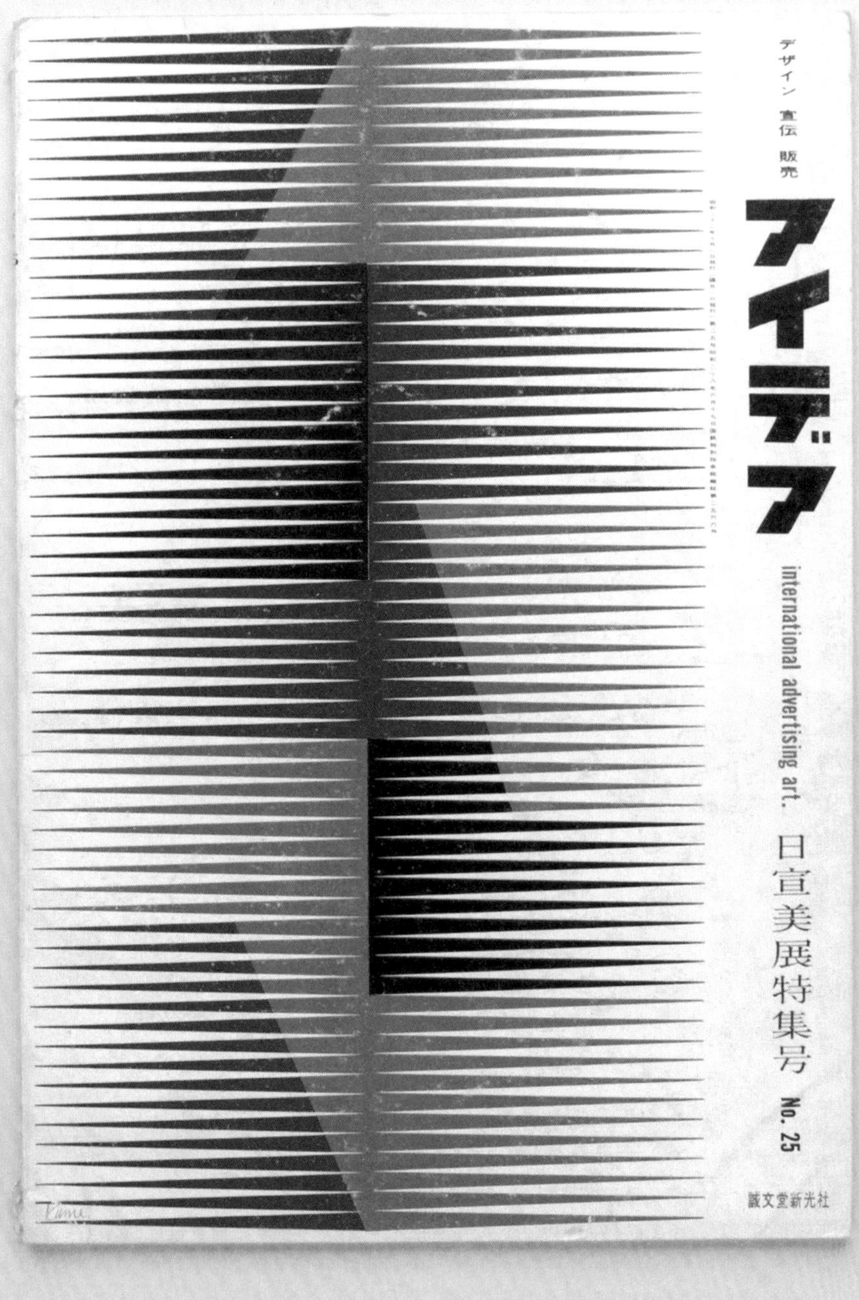

Idea
Country: Japan

Cover Design:
Yusaku Kamekura

11.1957

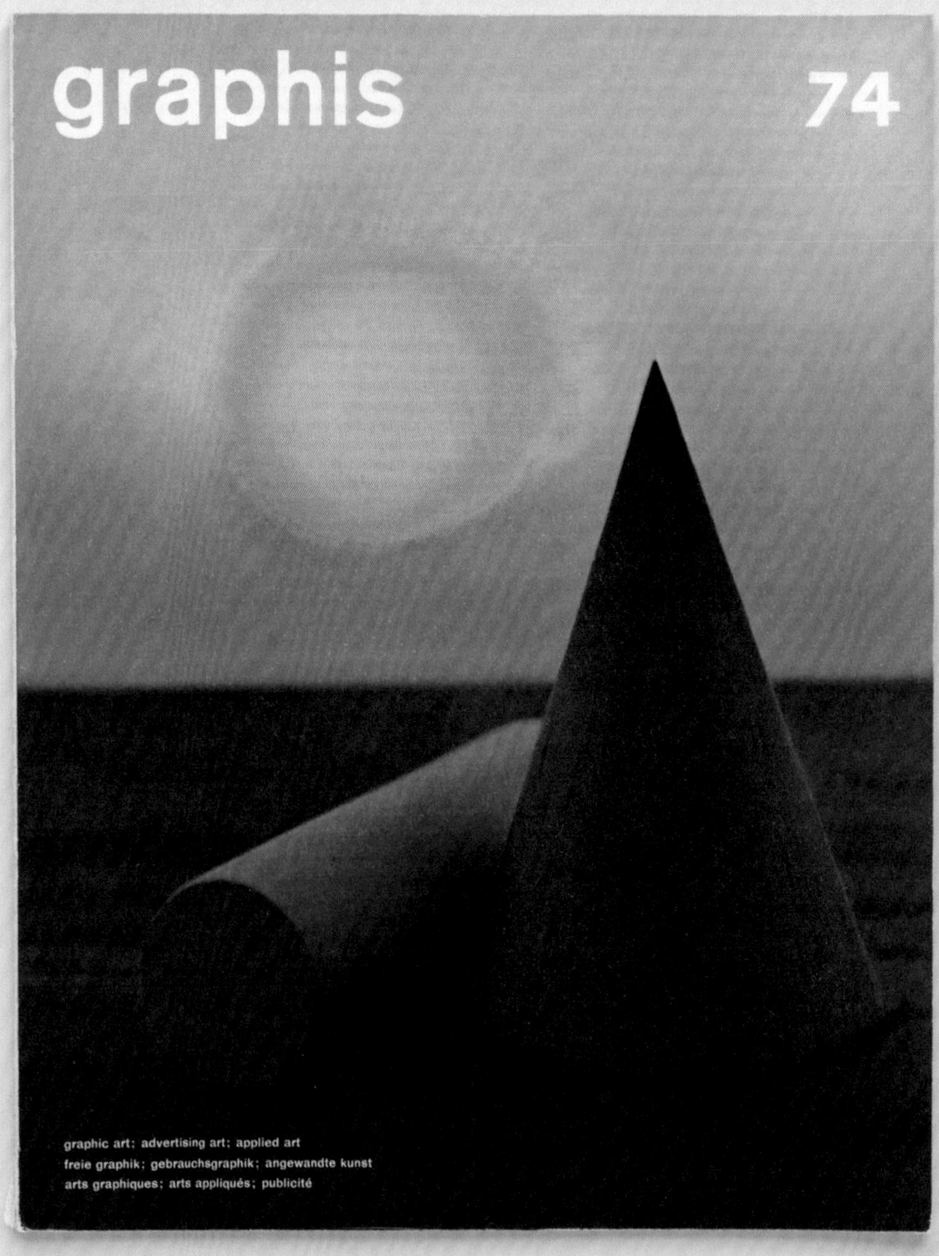

graphis
74
graphic art; advertising art; applied art
freie graphik; gebrauchsgraphik; angewandte kunst
arts graphiques; arts appliqués; publicité

Graphis
Country: Switzerland

Design: unidentified

01.1958

Type Talks
Country: USA

Design: unidentified

04.1958

Idea
Country: Japan

Cover Design: Tadao Ujihara

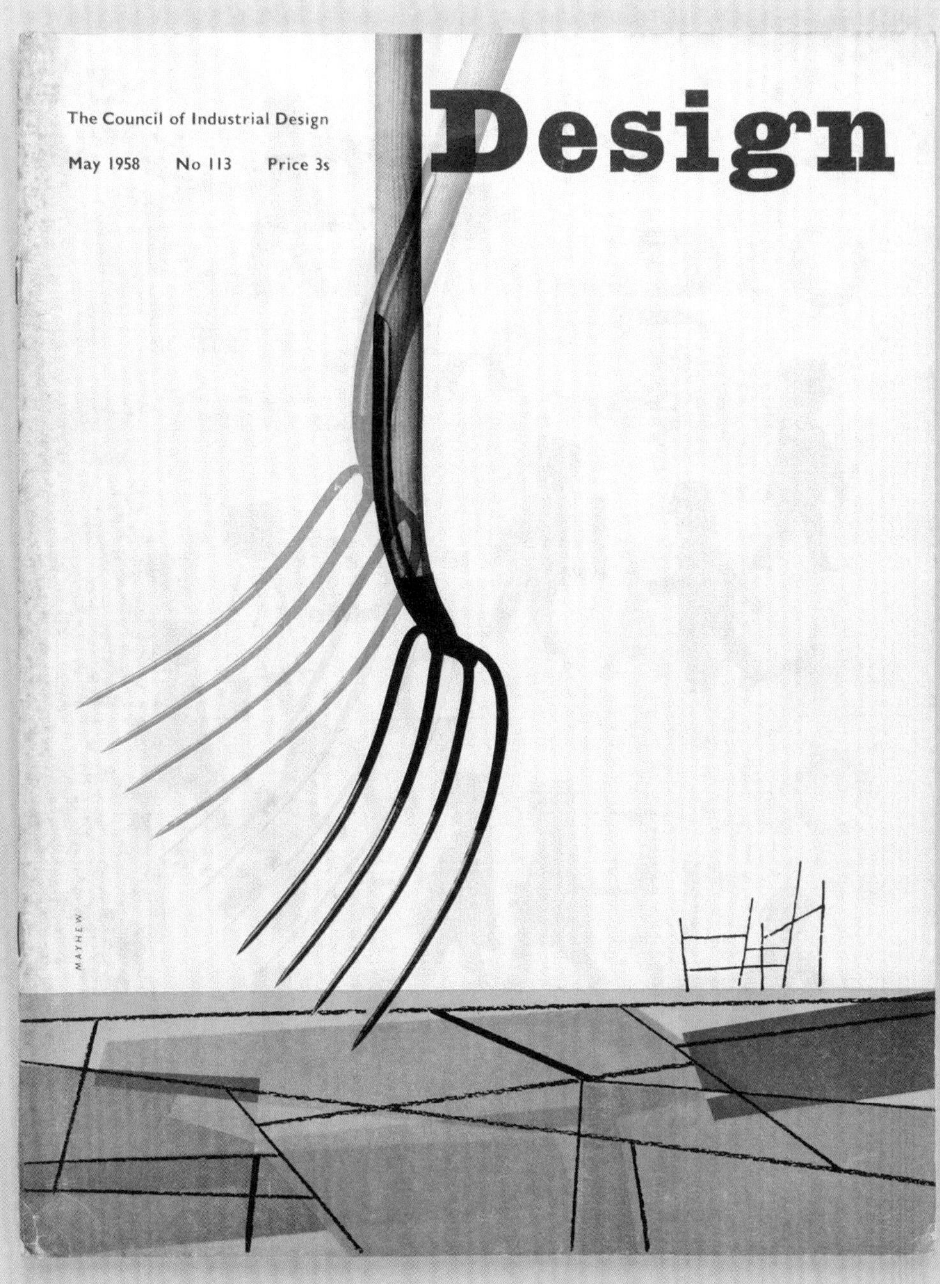

Design
Country: UK

Cover Design: George Mayhew

05.1958

Gebrauchsgraphik
Country: Germany

Art Director: Hans Kuh

Design
Country: UK

Cover Design:
Dick Negus, Philip Sharland

08.1958

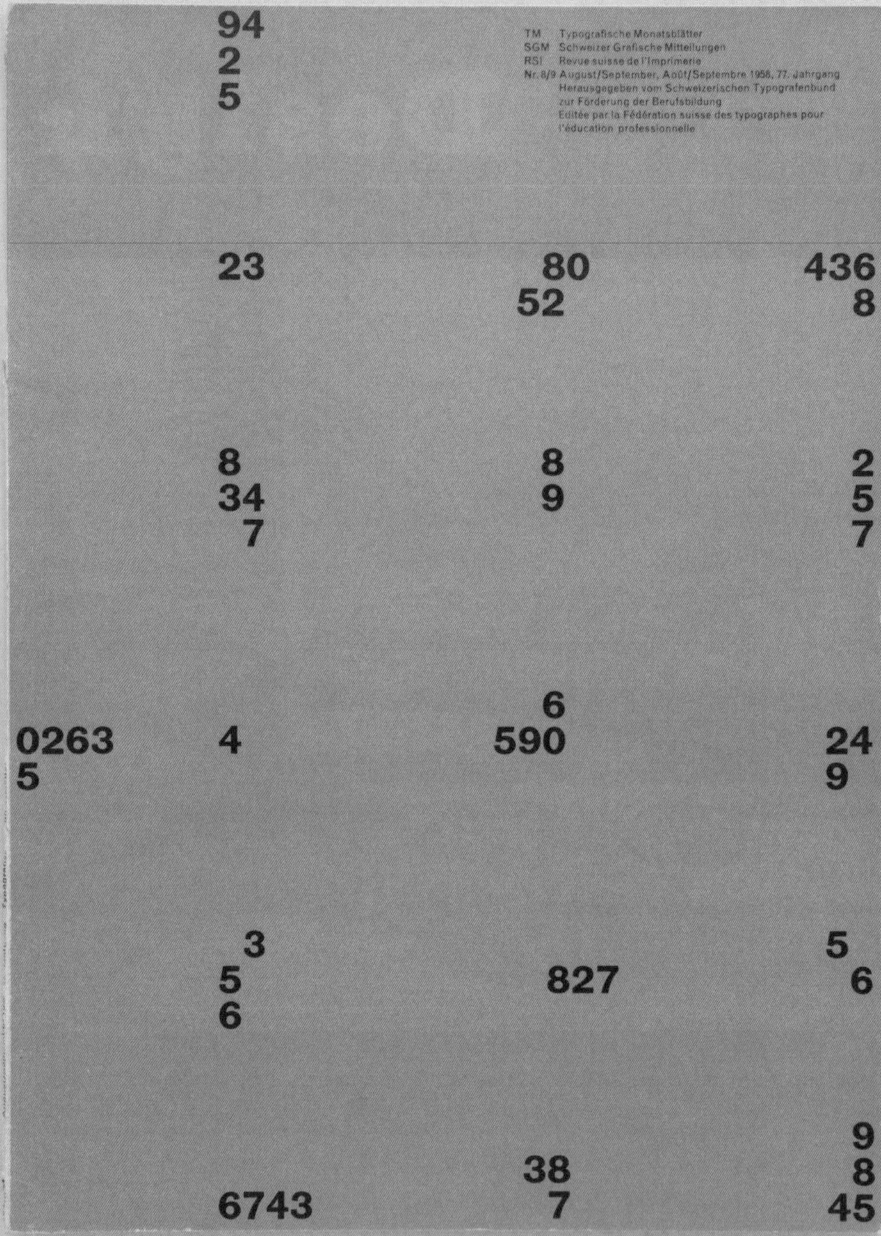

94
2
5

TM Typografische Monatsblätter
SGM Schweizer Grafische Mitteilungen
RSI Revue suisse de l'Imprimerie
Nr. 8/9 August/September, Août/Septembre 1958, 77. Jahrgang
Herausgegeben vom Schweizerischen Typografenbund
zur Förderung der Berufsbildung
Editée par la Fédération suisse des typographes pour
l'éducation professionnelle

23 80 436
52 8

8 8 2
34 9 5
7 7

6
0263 4 590 24
5 9

3 5
5 827 6
6

9
38 8
6743 7 45

TM (Typographische Monatsblätter)
Country: Switzerland

Cover Design: Yves Zimmermann
Courtesy of syndicom

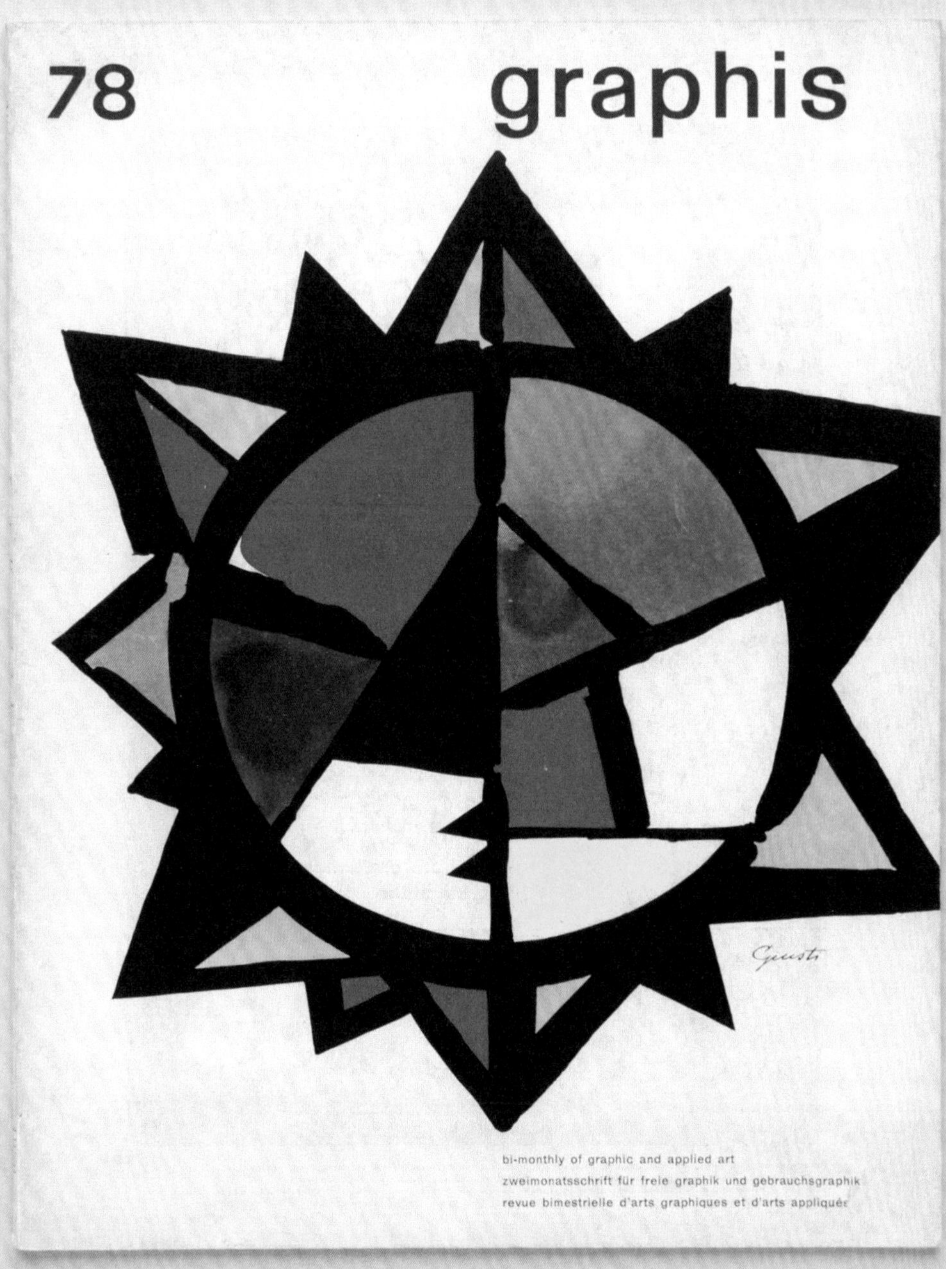

78
graphis
Giusti
bi-monthly of graphic and applied art
zweimonatsschrift für freie graphik und gebrauchsgraphik
revue bimestrielle d'arts graphiques et d'arts appliqués

Graphis
Country: Switzerland

Cover Design: George Giusti

08.1958

Industrial Art News
Country: Japan

Cover Design:
Toyoguchi Katsuhei,
Hattori Shigeo, Yoshitake Mosuke

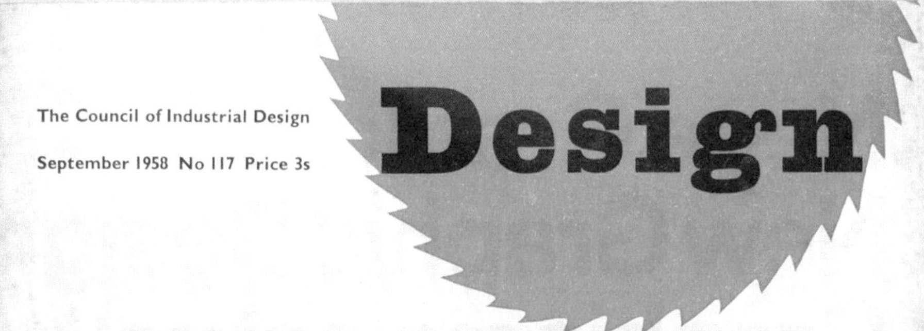

The Council of Industrial Design
September 1958 No 117 Price 3s
Design

Design
Country: UK

Cover Design: John Sewell

09.1958

Neue Grafik
New Graphic Design
Graphisme actuel

Internationale Zeitschrift für Grafik und verwandte Gebiete
Erscheint in deutscher, englischer und französischer Sprache

International Review of graphic design and related subjects
Issued in German, English and French language

Revue internationale pour le graphisme et domaines annexes
Parution en langue allemande, anglaise et française

1

Ausgabe September 1958

Inhalt

LMNV	Einführung
Richard P. Lohse SWB/VSG, Zürich	Der Einfluß der modernen Kunst auf die zeitgenössische Grafik
Hans Neuburg SWB/VSG, Zürich	Industrie-Grafik
LMNV	Foto-Experimente für die Grafik
Hans Neuburg SWB/VSG, Zürich	Die besten neuzeitlich gestalteten Schweizer Plakate 1931-1957
Ernst Scheidegger SWB, Zürich	Experiment Ulm und die Ausbildung des Grafikers
Max Bill SWB, Zürich	«Die unbekannte Gegenwart.» Eine thematische Schau des Warenhauses Globus, Zürich
	Chronik
	Buchbesprechungen
	Hinweise
	Pro domo

Einzelnummer Fr. 15.–

Issue for September 1958

Contents

Introduction
The Influence of Modern Art on Contemporary Graphic Design
Industrial Design
Experimental Photography in Graphic Design
The best recently designed Swiss Posters 1931-1957
The Ulm Experiment and the Training of the Graphic Designer
"The Unknown Present." An Exhibition with a special theme for the Globus store, Zurich
Miscellaneous
Book Reviews
Memoranda
Pro domo

Single number Fr. 15.–

Fascicule septembre 1958

Table des matières

Introduction
L'influence de l'art moderne sur la graphique contemporaine
Graphique industrielle
Photo expérimentale pour la graphique
Les meilleures affiches suisses actuelles 1931-1957
L'expérience d'Ulm et la formation du graphiste
«L'actualité inconnue.» Exposition thématique des Grands Magasins Globus, Zurich
Chronique
Bibliographie
Indications
Pro domo

Le numéro Fr. 15.–

Herausgeber und Redaktion
Editors and Managing Editors
Editeurs et rédaction

Richard P. Lohse SWB/VSG, Zürich
J. Müller-Brockmann SWB/VSG, Zürich
Hans Neuburg SWB/VSG, Zürich
Carlo L. Vivarelli SWB/VSG, Zürich

Druck/Verlag
Printing/Publishing
Imprimerie/Edition

Verlag Otto Walter AG, Olten
Schweiz/Switzerland/Suisse

Neue Grafik
Country: Switzerland

Cover Design: Carlo Vivarelli

Schweizer Monatsschrift für
Architektur
Kunst
Künstlerisches Gewerbe

50 Jahre

Bund
Schweizer Architekten

9

werk

Fr. 3.75 September 1958

Der BSA – sein Wesen und seine Tätigkeit
Die Entwicklung des Wohnungsbaus von 1908 bis 1930
Siedlungsbau 1930 bis 1958
25 Jahre Landesplanung in der Schweiz
Kurze Entwicklungsgeschichte des schweizerischen Schulbaus
Abriß über den Spitalbau der Schweiz in den letzten 50 Jahren
Die Entwicklung des Industriebaus in den letzten 50 Jahren
Reformierter Kirchenbau der letzten 50 Jahre
Der katholische Kirchenbau in den letzten 50 Jahren
La Fédération des Architectes suisses FAS et les relations internationales
Exposition Nationale 1964
Malerei und Plastik am Bau
Die Kollegialität im BSA

WERK-Chronik

(Das) Werk
Country: Switzerland

Cover Design: Karl Gerstner

ulm 1

Vierteljahresbericht
der Hochschule für Gestaltung, Ulm
Oktober 1958

Preis pro Nummer DM 1.–/SFr 1.–/ÖS 7.50
Jahresabonnement DM 4.–/SFr 4.–/ÖS 30
portofrei

Quarterly bulletin
of the Hochschule für Gestaltung, Ulm
October 1958

Price per issue 2s6d/$0.50
Yearly subscription 10s/$2.00 post paid

Bulletin trimestriel
de la Hochschule für Gestaltung, Ulm
Octobre 1958

Prix du numéro 125 frs/L 175
Abonnement annuel 500 frs/L 700 port payé

Hochschule für Gestaltung

Die Hochschule für Gestaltung bildet Fachkräfte aus für zwei entscheidende Aufgaben der technischen Zivilisation:
die Gestaltung industrieller Produkte
(Abteilung Produktform und Abteilung Bauen);
die Gestaltung bildhafter und sprachlicher Mitteilungen
(Abteilung visuelle Kommunikation und Abteilung Information).

Die Hochschule für Gestaltung bildet damit Gestalter heran für die Gebrauchs- und Produktionsgüterindustrie sowie für die modernen Kommunikationsmittel Presse, Film, Funk und Werbung. Diese Gestalter müssen über die technologischen und wissenschaftlichen Fachkenntnisse verfügen, die für eine Mitwirkung in der heutigen Industrie erforderlich sind. Gleichzeitig müssen sie die kulturellen und gesellschaftlichen Konsequenzen ihrer Arbeit erfassen und berücksichtigen.

Die Hochschule für Gestaltung ist als eine Schule für höchstens 150 Studierende konzipiert, um ein günstiges Zahlenverhältnis zwischen Studierenden und Dozenten zu gewährleisten.

Dozenten und Studierende kommen aus verschiedenen Ländern und geben der Hochschule einen internationalen Charakter.

The Hochschule für Gestaltung educates specialists for two different tasks of our technical civilization:
The design of industrial products
(industrial design department and building department);
The design of visual and verbal means of communication
(visual communication department and information department).

The school thus educates designers for the production and consumer goods industries as well as for present-day means of communication: press, films, broadcasting, television, and advertising. These designers must have at their disposal the technological and scientific knowledge necessary for collaboration in industry today. At the same time they must grasp and bear in mind the cultural and sociological consequences of their work.

The Hochschule für Gestaltung is conceived as a school for a maximum number of 150 students, in order to ensure a favourable proportion between the number of students and faculty. Faculty and students come from many different countries, thus giving the school an international character.

La Hochschule für Gestaltung s'attache à former des spécialistes appelés à remplir deux tâches d'importance décisive dans notre civilisation technique:
la création dans le domaine des produits industriels
(section «Industrial Design» et section «Industrialisation du Bâtiment»),
la création dans le domaine de la communication visuelle et verbale
(section «Communication Visuelle» et section «Information»).

La Hochschule für Gestaltung forme des créateurs qui s'appliquent tant à l'étude d'objets industriels de consommation et de production, qu'à celle des moyens modernes de communication (presse, film, radiodiffusion, télévision, publicité). Ces créateurs devront posséder les connaissances techniques et théoriques aujourd'hui nécessaires à une collaboration fructueuse avec l'industrie. Ils devront aussi considérer et mesurer la portée des conséquences sociales et culturelles de leur travail.

La Hochschule für Gestaltung est conçue de manière à recevoir un maximum de 150 étudiants, afin d'assurer une proportion numérique favorable aux rapports entre étudiants et professeurs, qui viennent de tous les horizons et donnent à l'Ecole son caractère international.

Ulm
Country: Germany

Cover Design: Anthony Froshaug

Interview: Mason Wells

Q You are a connoisseur and collector of design and typography journals of mid-century Modernism – *Neue Grafik* (1958–65, Switzerland), *Ulm Bulletin* (1958–1968, Germany), *Form* (1966–69, UK). All three journals had austere covers that spoke to a certain kind of design sensibility. But what makes a good cover for a design magazine today?

A I find the conventional cover structures found on many magazines too noisy. Graphics on graphics is not usually a good combination – and that's probably why I love the simplicity of the magazines mentioned in your question. Understandably there is a need to sell the product, but I think good design is usually indicative of good content and this has become apparent with many recent (usually independent) magazines – *The Gentlewoman* (2010–present, UK) is one that springs to mind.

Q If you were asked to design a cover for a contemporary design magazine, how would you approach it?

A I like the idea of a visual narrative – to enhance the identity of the publication. Thinking holistically about how the cover becomes an evolving design as opposed to designing each cover in isolation.

Q Beyond the three examples mentioned above, can you name a favourite 20th-century magazine cover?

A My favourite is the classic *Esquire* (1933–present, USA), Muhammad Ali by George Lois – masthead, image, small line of copy. Perfect.

Q Can you do the same for a current design publication?

A I have always liked the Japanese style and design magazines. I have no understanding of the language, and this enhances their exotic appeal. One that I particularly like is called *Brutus* (1980–present, Japan) – which has a great masthead.

Q Do we still need design magazines in the age of the Internet – hasn't the role been taken over by blogs, Pinterest, Instagram, and other social media platforms?

A Magazines are analogue – the tactile pleasure of flicking (or poring) through a magazine, smelling the ink, feeling the paper, experiencing the photography cannot be rivalled by a web browser.

Mason Wells is a co-founder of Bibliothèque, where he works with clients such as Tate Modern and Adidas on corporate identity programmes, exhibitions and publications.

Neue Grafik
1958–65
Switzerland

10.1958

ulm 2

Vierteljahresbericht
der Hochschule für Gestaltung, Ulm
Oktober 1958

Preis pro Nummer DM 1.–/SFr 1.–/ÖS 7.50
Jahresabonnement DM 4.–/SFr 4.–/ÖS 30
portofrei

Quarterly bulletin
of the Hochschule für Gestaltung, Ulm
October 1958

Price per issue 2s6d/$0.50
Yearly subscription 10s/$2.00 post paid

Bulletin trimestriel
de la Hochschule für Gestaltung, Ulm
Octobre 1958

Prix du numéro 125 frs/L 175
Abonnement annuel 500 frs/L 700 port payé

Tomás Maldonado

Neue Entwicklungen in der Industrie und die Ausbildung des Produktgestalters

Die Anschauungen, die die Ideologie des Bauhauses bestimmt haben, lassen sich ein Vierteljahrhundert nach Schließung dieses Instituts schwer in die Sprache unserer heutigen Problematik übertragen. Mehr noch: wir müssen einige dieser Anschauungen, wie wir sehen werden, mit größter Entschiedenheit, aber auch mit größter Objektivität, zurückweisen.

New Developments in Industry and the Training of the Designer

The ideas which supply the basis for what might be called the Bauhaus ideology are today, a quarter of a century after that institution closed, difficult to translate into the language of our present-day preoccupations. Furthermore, as we shall see, some of these ideas must now be refuted with the greatest vehemence as well as with the greatest objectivity.

Les nouvelles perspectives industrielles et la formation du «designer»

Les conceptions qui servirent de fondement à ce que l'on pourrait appeler l'idéologie du Bauhaus, sont aujourd'hui, un quart de siècle après la fermeture de cet institut, difficiles à traduire dans le langage de nos préoccupations actuelles. Plus encore, quelques-unes de ces conceptions doivent être maintenant réfutées avec la plus grande véhémence ainsi qu'avec la plus grande objectivité.

Ulm
Country: Germany

Cover Design: Anthony Froshaug

The Council of Industrial Design

November 1958 No 119 Price 3s

Design

WILDBUR

Design
Country: UK

Cover Design: Peter Wildbur

TM (Typographische Monatsblätter)
Country: Switzerland

Cover Design: Yves Zimmermann
Courtesy of syndicom

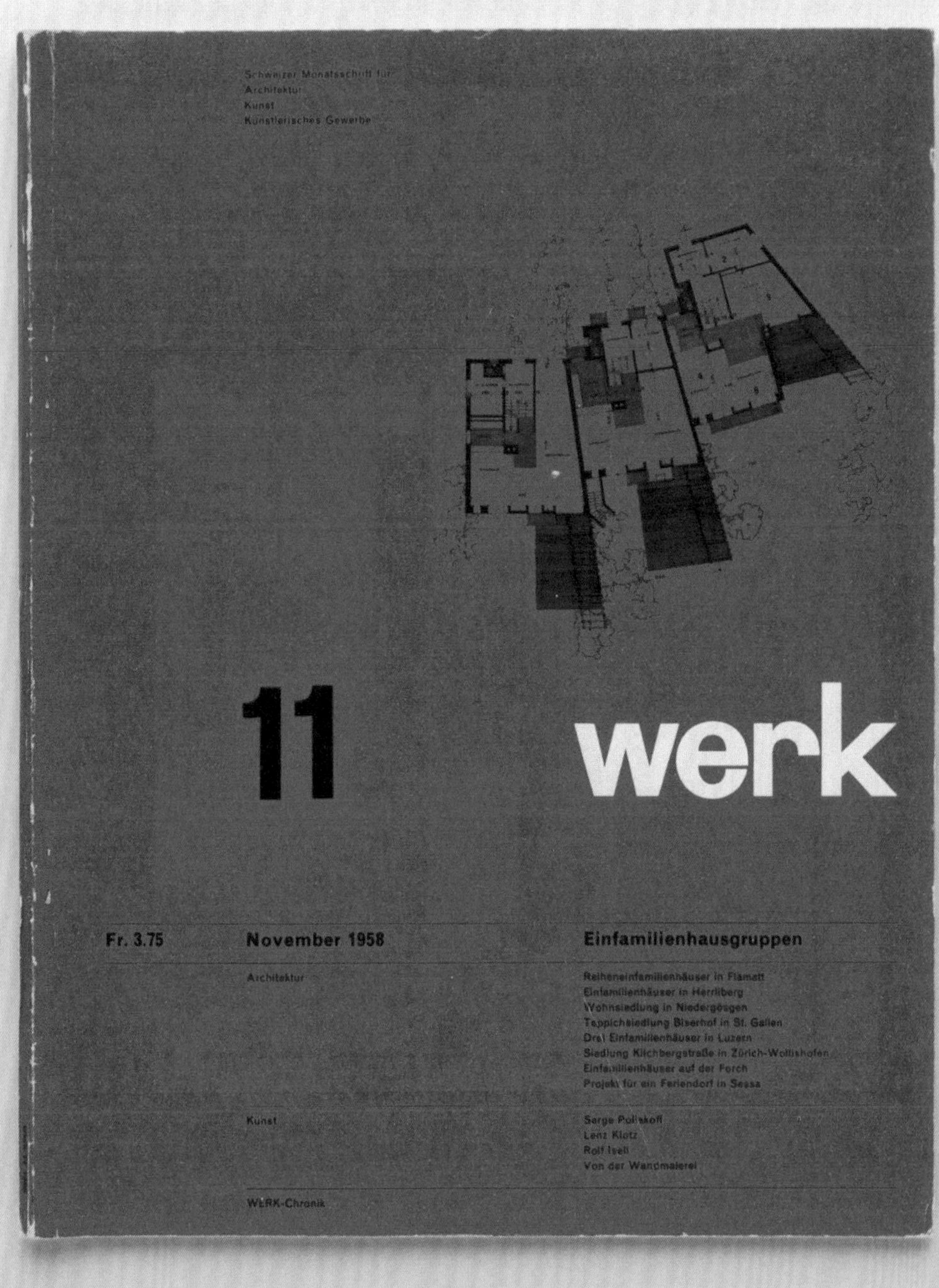

Schweizer Monatsschrift für
Architektur
Kunst
Künstlerisches Gewerbe
11
werk
Fr. 3.75
November 1958
Einfamilienhausgruppen
Architektur
Reiheneinfamilienhäuser in Flamatt
Einfamilienhäuser in Herrliberg
Wohnsiedlung in Niedergösgen
Teppichsiedlung Biserhof in St. Gallen
Drei Einfamilienhäuser in Luzern
Siedlung Kilchbergstraße in Zürich-Wollishofen
Einfamilienhäuser auf der Forch
Projekt für ein Feriendorf in Sessa
Kunst
Serge Poliakoff
Lenz Klotz
Rolf Iseli
Von der Wandmalerei
WERK-Chronik

(Das) Werk
Country: Switzerland

Cover Design: Karl Gerstner

12.1958

The Council of Industrial Design

December 1958 No 120 Price 3s

Design

Design
Country: UK

Cover Design: Ken Garland

Typographica
Country: UK

Cover Design: Herbert Spencer

01.1959

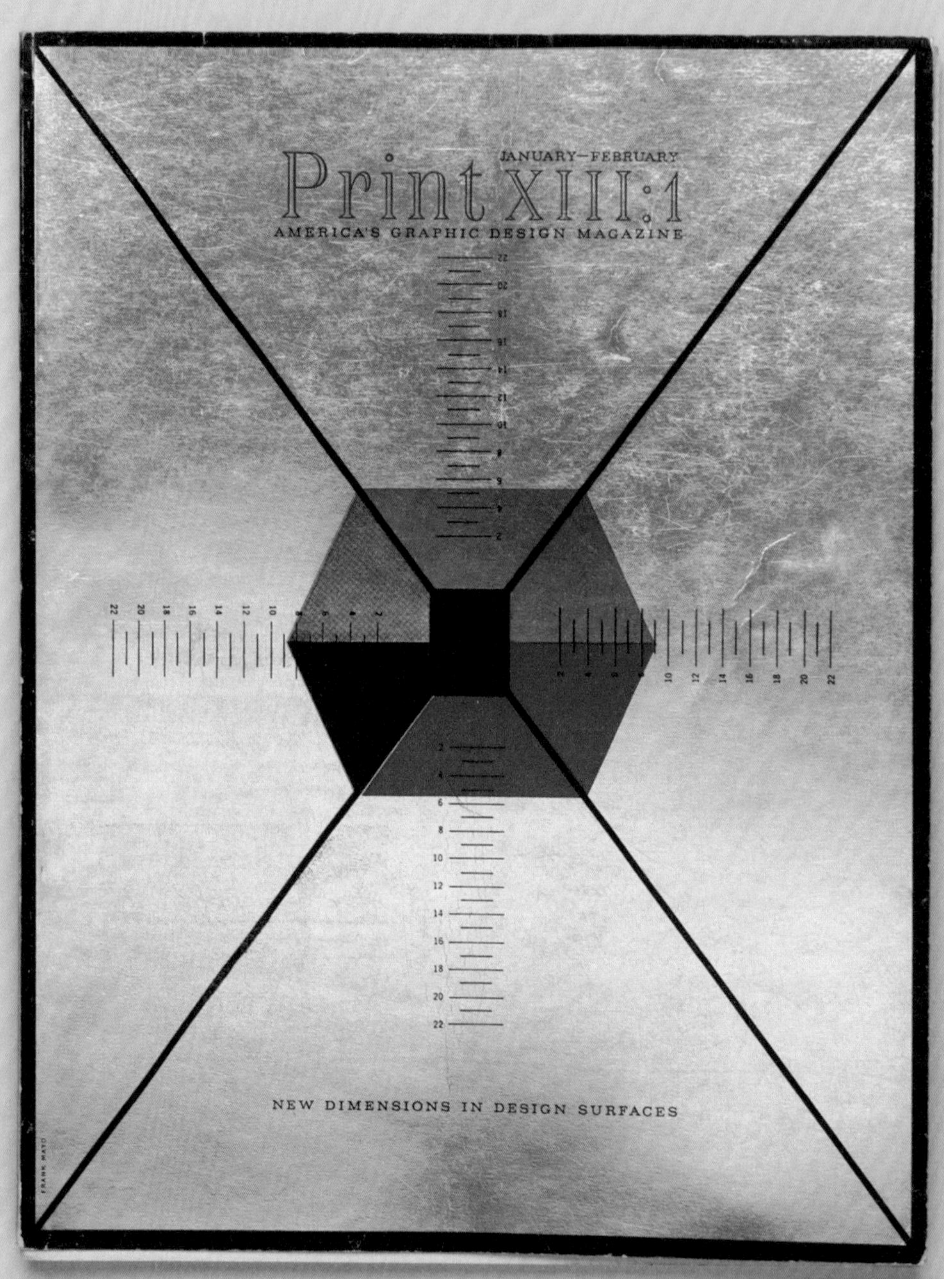

Print
Country: USA

Cover Design: Frank Mayo

01.1959

ulm 3

Vierteljahresbericht
der Hochschule für Gestaltung, Ulm
Januar 1959

Preis pro Nummer DM 1.–/SFr 1.–/ÖS 7.50
Jahresabonnement DM 4.–/SFr 4.–/ÖS 30
portofrei

Quarterly bulletin
of the Hochschule für Gestaltung, Ulm
January 1959

Price per issue 2s6d/$0.50
Yearly subscription 10s/$2.00 post paid

Bulletin trimestriel
de la Hochschule für Gestaltung, Ulm
Janvier 1959

Prix du numéro 125 frs/L 175
Abonnement annuel 500 frs/L 700 port payé

Ulm
Country: Germany

Cover Design: Anthony Froshaug

03.1959

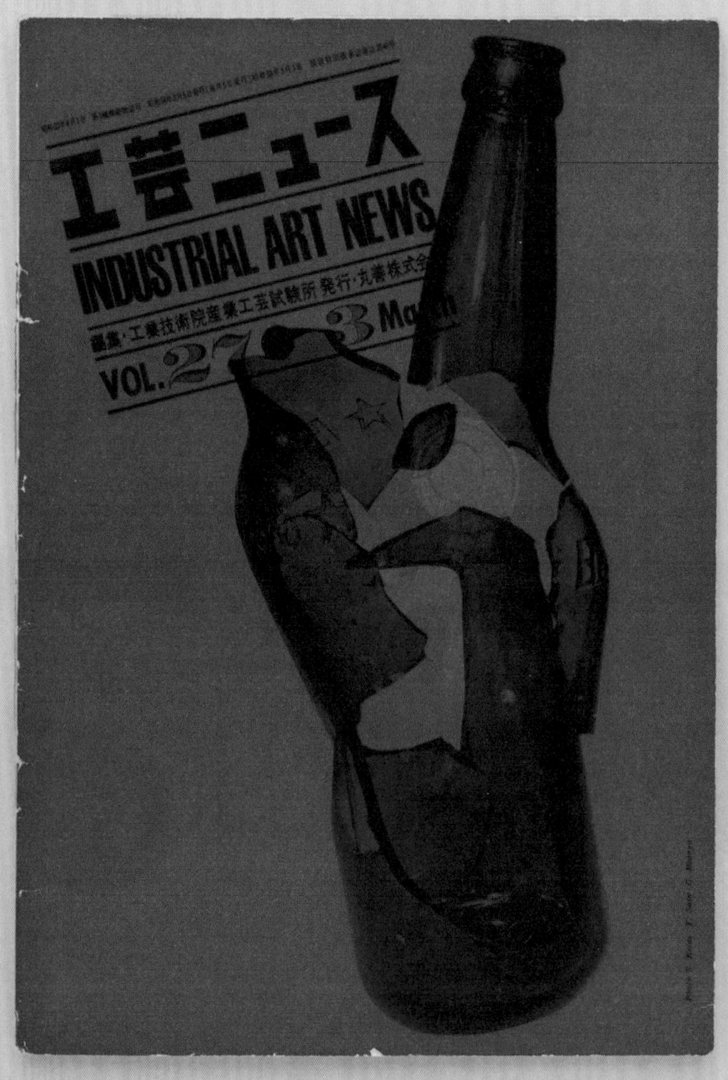

Industrial Art News
Country: Japan

Cover Photography:
G Hosaya, S Kitai, T Sato

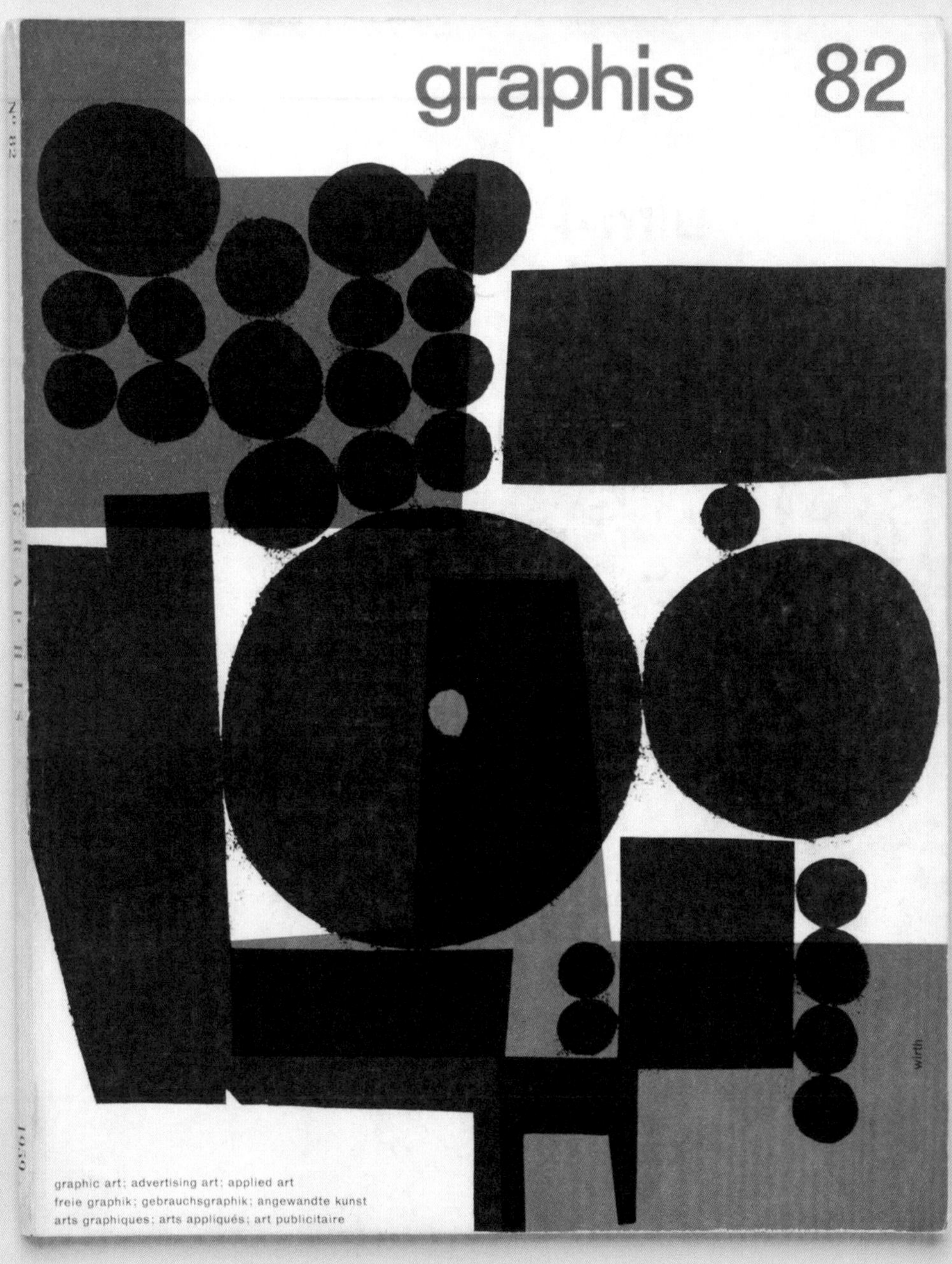

graphis 82
Nº 82
GRAPHIS
1959
wirth
graphic art; advertising art; applied art
freie graphik; gebrauchsgraphik; angewandte kunst
arts graphiques; arts appliqués; art publicitaire

Graphis
Country: Switzerland

Cover Design: Kurt Wirth

ulm 4

Vierteljahresbericht
der Hochschule für Gestaltung, Ulm
April 1959

Preis pro Nummer DM 1.–/SFr 1.–/ÖS 7.50
Jahresabonnement DM 4.–/SFr 4.–/ÖS 30
portofrei

Anthony Fröshaug

Visuelle Methodik

1. Aufgabenstellung

Die ersten Aufgaben, die in der Grundlehre der HfG innerhalb des Faches Visuelle Methodik gestellt werden, haben zu berücksichtigen, daß die Studierenden eine unterschiedliche Vorbildung besitzen und daß kaum methodologische Vorkenntnisse vorausgesetzt werden können. Auch beherrschen sie die Darstellungstechniken nicht in gleicher Weise.

Daher werden am Anfang Aufgaben gestellt, die nicht nur die Darstellungsfertigkeiten entwickeln, sondern auch ohne besondere methodologische Voraussetzungen zu lösen sind. Die Studierenden sollen dazu angeleitet werden, diese Aufgaben nicht nur intuitiv zu bearbeiten, sondern, soweit wie möglich, systematisch an sie heranzugehen und sich auf diese Weise einige methodologische Kenntnisse anzueignen. Schließlich sollen die Aufgaben in einem thematischen Zusammenhang mit der späteren Arbeit in den Abteilungen stehen.

Es empfiehlt sich, Aufgaben zu wählen, die eine übersehbare Anzahl von Lösungen besitzen. Eine solche Aufgabe ist zum Beispiel die Darstellung von Kommunikationsverhältnissen durch zwei- oder dreidimensionale Graphe. Unter einem Graph versteht man ein System von Punkten und Verbindungslinien zwischen diesen Punkten (1.1).

Gleichzeitig läßt sich auf diese Weise experimentell untersuchen, ob sich für die Gestaltung von Informationsträgern Prinzipien entwickeln lassen, deren Anwendung die Informationsvermittlung optimalisiert: ein Problem, das für alle Abteilungen der HfG in gleicher Weise von Bedeutung ist.

Quarterly bulletin
of the Hochschule für Gestaltung, Ulm
April 1959

Price per issue 2s6d/$0.50
Yearly subscription 10s/$2.00 postpaid

Visual Methodology

1. Problems set

In the foundation course at the HfG, the first problems set in the subject of visual methodology have to take into consideration the facts that the previous education of the students varies; that hardly any basic methodological knowledge can be presupposed; and also that their command of representation by means of technical drawing is uneven.

For these reasons, at the beginning of the school year problems were set, which not only develop skill in technical drawing but which are also soluble without previous specialised knowledge of methodology. In this way an attempt is made to guide students to have, as far as possible, a systematic approach – rather than merely to work intuitively; thus to acquire some knowledge of method. Finally, the problems must be related in theme to the work which the students will carry out later on in the various departments of the Hochschule.

It is advisable to choose problems which have a clearly visible number of solutions. An example of this sort of problem is the representation of communication relationships by means of two- and three-dimensional graphs. A graph is understood as a system composed of points and connections between such points (1.1).

Simultaneously, one can in this way make an experimental investigation into the design of sign vehicles, to discover whether certain principles can be developed whose application will lead to an optimal transmission of information: a problem which is of equal significance for all departments of the HfG.

Bulletin trimestriel
de la Hochschule für Gestaltung, Ulm
Avril 1959

Prix du numéro 125 frs/L 175
Abonnement annuel 500 frs/L 700 port payé

Méthodologie visuelle

1. Enoncé des problèmes

Les premiers problèmes posés en méthodologie visuelle, une des branches du cours fondamental de la HfG, doivent s'adapter à la formation antérieure très inégale des étudiants; on ne peut exiger d'eux des notions méthodologiques préalables. Par ailleurs, ils ne maitrisent pas de manière uniforme les techniques de représentation.

On commence donc par poser des problèmes qui développent l'habileté à représenter, sans exiger pour autant des bases méthodologiques. Il faut amener les étudiants à ne pas se contenter d'aborder les problèmes par l'intuition seule, mais, dans la mesure du possible, à les étudier systématiquement afin d'acquérir ainsi quelques connaissances méthodologiques. En outre, les thèmes des problèmes doivent se rattacher aux travaux ultérieurs des différentes sections.

Il vaut mieux choisir des problèmes ayant un nombre limité de solutions. Représenter des réseaux de communication par des graphes à deux ou trois dimensions constitue un exemple de ce genre de problèmes. Par graphe, on entend un système de points et de lignes reliant ces points les uns aux autres (1.1).

En même temps, on peut, par ce moyen, vérifier expérimentalement s'il est possible de déduire des principes pour la représentation de porteurs d'information dont l'application permettrait un transfert optimal d'information. Ce problème intéresse également toutes les sections de la HfG.

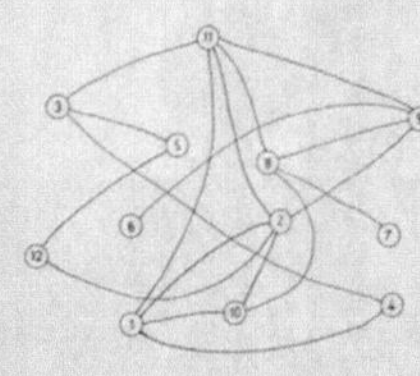

(1.1)

Ulm
Country: Germany

Cover Design: Anthony Froshaug

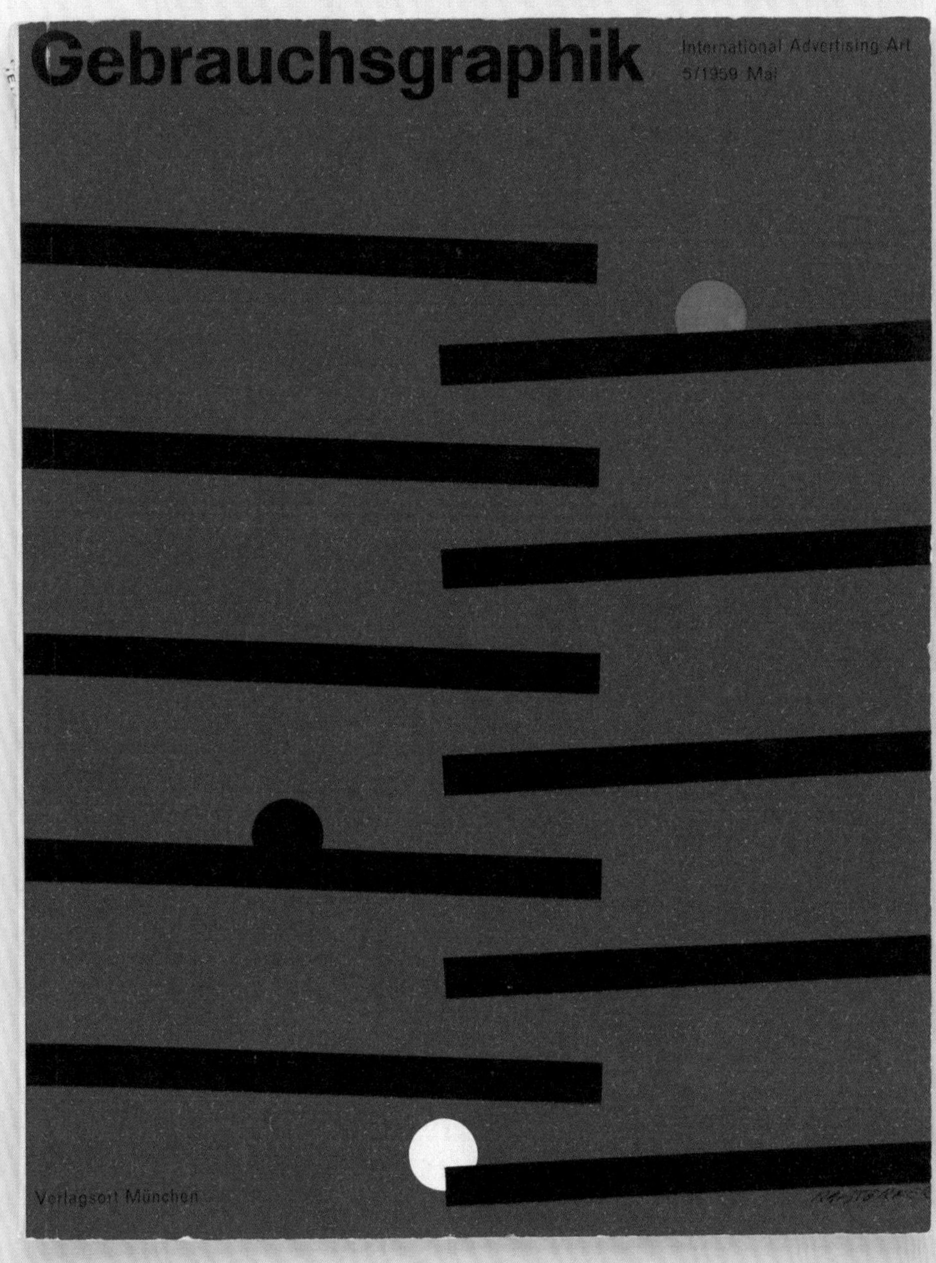

Gebrauchsgraphik
Country: Germany

Cover Design:
Hermann Rastorfer

05.1959

TM (Typographische Monatsblätter)
Country: Switzerland

Design: unidentified
Courtesy of syndicom

Design For Industry
Country: UK

Art Editor: Margaret Webb

ulm 5

Vierteljahresbericht
der Hochschule für Gestaltung, Ulm
Juli 1959

Preis DM 1.–/SFr 1.–/ÖS 7.50

Quarterly bulletin
of the Hochschule für Gestaltung, Ulm
July 1959

Price 2s6d/$ 0.50

Bulletin trimestriel
de la Hochschule für Gestaltung, Ulm
Juli 1959

Prix 125 frs/L 175

Tomás Maldonado

Kommunikation und Semiotik

(Der Verfasser beansprucht nicht, das folgende Thema systematisch und erschöpfend zu behandeln. Der Text ist eine Zusammenstellung von Notizen zu Vorlesungen über Semiotik an der HfG.)

Die Kommunikation zwischen Menschen vollzieht sich durch das Medium von Zeichen, was sie von anderen Arten der Kommunikation unterscheidet. Die Kommunikation ohne Zeichen, nur mittels Signalen, ist keine spezifisch zwischenmenschliche Kommunikation. Tiere wie Maschinen kommunizieren miteinander durch Signale. Aber während das Signal in der Tierwelt als »angeborenes Schema« auftritt (K. Lorenz, 1942), als höchst rituelle Zweckbewegung (N. Tinbergen, 1953; J. B. S. Haldane, 1953), muß in der Welt der Maschinen das Signal in einem rein physikalischen Sinn verstanden werden, d.h. als Materialisation einer Botschaft (H. Nyquist, 1924; R. W. Hartley, 1928; C. Shannon, 1948). Zeichen und tierische Signale, insofern sie materialisierte Botschaften sind, können reduziert werden auf Signale in rein physikalischem Sinn. Daher können auch einige Maschinen als Modelle für die Darstellung und Erklärung psychophysiologischer Vorgänge des menschlichen und tierischen Verhaltens dienen (A. Rosenblueth, N. Wiener und J. Bigelow, 1943; W. R. Ashby, 1951).

Die Behauptung, daß eine nur durch Signale erfolgende Kommunikation keine spezifisch menschliche sei, muß jedoch eingeschränkt werden: Menschen kommunizieren sehr oft auch mit einer Art von Signalen, die alle Mitglieder des zoologischen Bereichs gemeinsam haben. Der Großteil der mimischen, interjektiven und expressiven Repertoires gehört zu dieser Kategorie. Ausdruck, Appell und Darstellung sind die drei Dimensionen der kommunikativen Welt des Menschen (K. Bühler, 1943). In den ersten beiden Dimensionen spielt das Signal eine größere Rolle, in der dritten dagegen das Zeichen.

Communication and Semiotics

(The author does not pretend that the following theme is dealt with systematically and exhaustively. The text is assembled from notes for lectures on semiotics in the HfG.)

Human communication takes place through the medium of signs, thereby distinguishing itself from other types of communication. Communication without signs, merely by means of signals, is not specifically human communication. Animals, as well as machines, communicate with each other through signals. But whereas the animal signal appears as an 'innate scheme' (K. Lorenz, 1942), as a highly ritualized movement with a purpose (N. Tinbergen, 1953; J. B. S. Haldane, 1953), the signal in the sphere of machinery must be understood in a purely physical sense, i.e. as the materialization of a message (H. Nyquist, 1924; R. W. Hartley, 1928; C. Shannon, 1948). Signs and animal signals – insofar as they are materialized messages, can be reduced to signals in a purely physical sense. Therefore it is possible for some machines to serve as models for the presentation and explanation of psycho-physiological processes in human and animal behaviour (A. Rosenblueth, N. Wiener and J. Bigelow, 1943; W. R. Ashby, 1951).

The assertion that communication only through signals is not specifically human must, however, be qualified: humans, too, often communicate through a kind of signal which all members of the zoological kingdom have in common. The majority of mimical, interjective, and expressive repertoires belongs to this category. Expression, appeal, representation are the three dimensions of the human being's communicative world (K. Bühler, 1943). In the first two, the signal plays a greater role; in the third, on the other hand, the sign.

Communication et sémiotique

(L'auteur ne prétend pas que le thème suivant soit traité systématiquement et complètement. Ce texte est pris des notes pour conférences faites à la HfG sur le sujet de la sémiotique.)

La communication entre les hommes s'effectue par l'intermédiaire de signes, ce qui la distingue d'autres types de communication. La communication sans signes, uniquement au moyen de signaux, n'est pas une communication spécifiquement humaine. Les animaux entre eux et les machines entre elles, communiquent à l'aide de signaux. Mais alors que, dans le monde animal, le signal se présente comme un «schéma inné» (K. Lorenz, 1942) ou comme un mouvement fonctionnel à caractère très rituel (N. Tinbergen, 1953; J. B. S. Haldane, 1953); dans le monde des machines, il doit être envisagé dans un sens purement physique, c'est-à-dire comme matérialisation d'un message (H. Nyquist, 1924; R. W. Hartley, 1928; C. Shannon, 1948). Les signes et signaux des animaux, dans la mesure où ils sont des messages matérialisés, peuvent être traduits en des signaux purement physiques. C'est pourquoi certaines machines peuvent servir de modèles pour décrire et expliquer des processus psychophysiologiques du comportement humain et animal (A. Rosenblueth, N. Wiener et J. Bigelow, 1943; W. R. Ashby, 1951).

Il est inexact d'affirmer de façon absolue qu'une communication limitée aux signaux ne puisse pas être spécifiquement humaine: les hommes communiquent aussi très souvent au moyen de certains signaux communs à tous les membres du règne animal. La plus grande partie du répertoire mimique, interjectionnnel et expressif appartient à cette catégorie. L'expression, l'appel et la figuration forment les trois dimensions de l'univers de la communication humaine (K. B. Bühler, 1943) Le grand rôle est tenu dans les deux premières dimensions par le signal; dans la troisième, en revanche, par le signe.

Ulm
Country: Germany

Cover Design: Anthony Froshaug

TM (Typographische Monatsblätter)
Country: Switzerland

Design: unidentified
Courtesy of syndicom

11.1959

Print
Country: USA

Design: unidentified

Idea
Country: Japan
Cover Design: Hiroshi Ohchi

12.1959

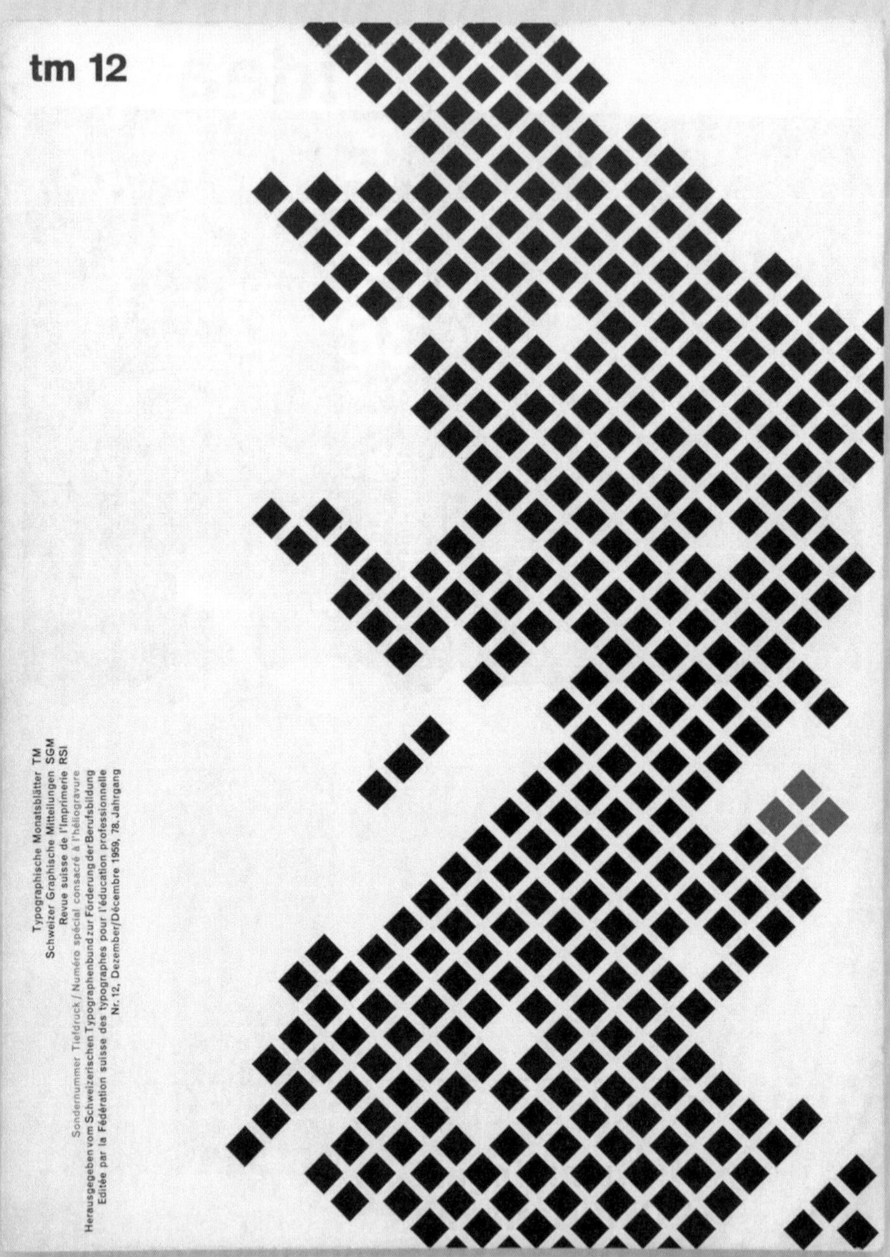

TM (Typographische Monatsblätter)
Country: Switzerland

Design: unidentified
Courtesy of syndicom

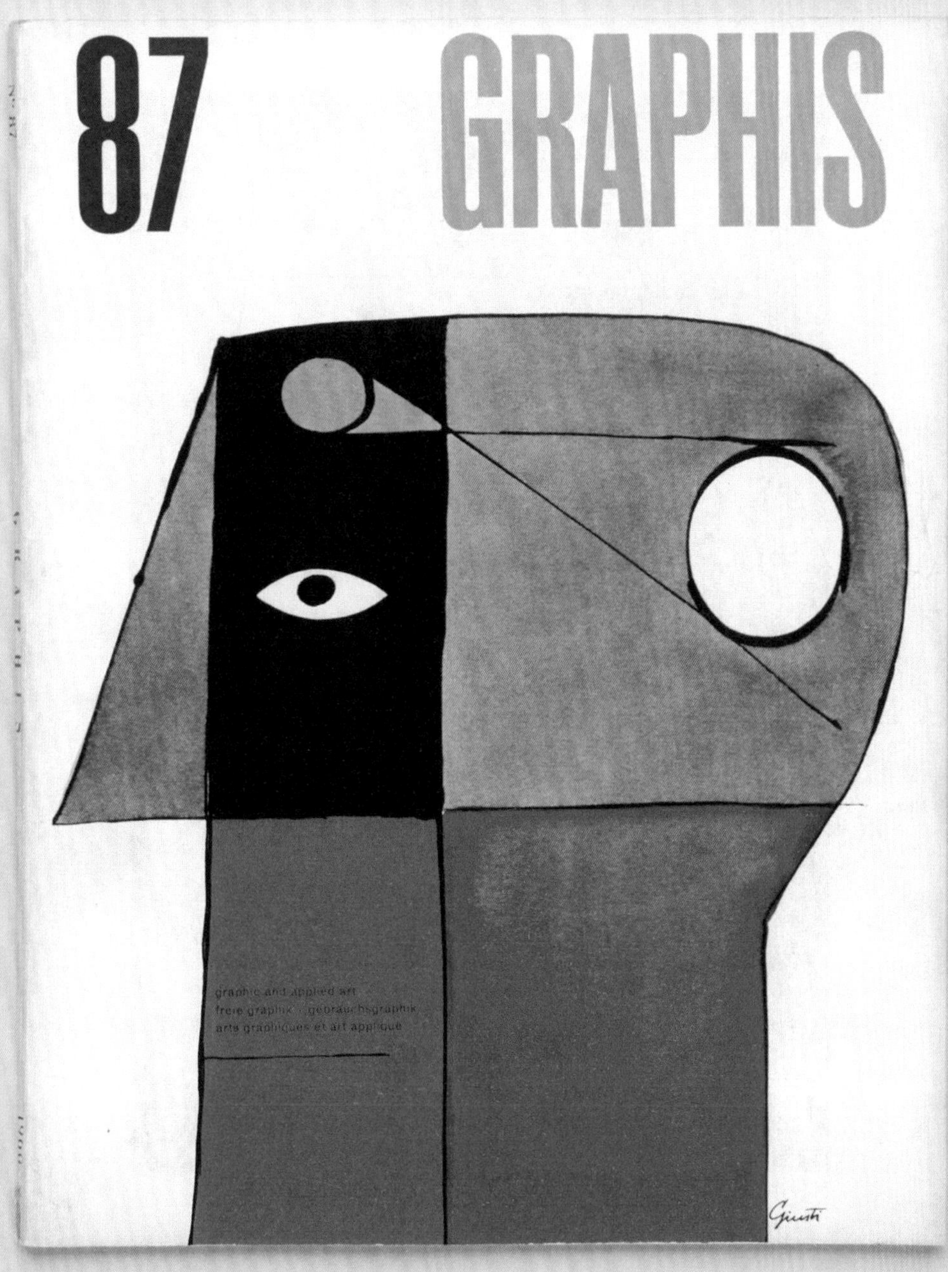

Graphis
Country: Switzerland

Cover Design: George Giusti

01.1960

Type Talks
Country: USA

Design: unidentified

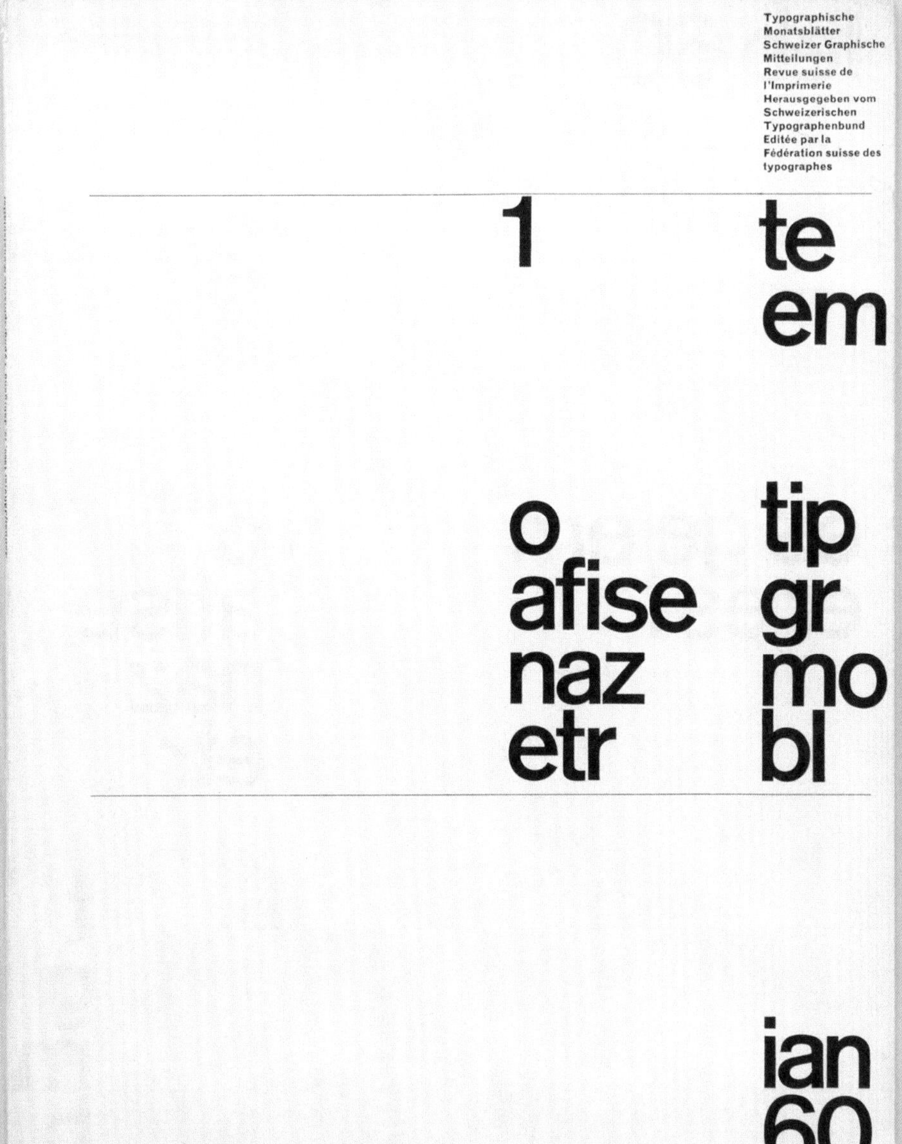

Typographische
Monatsblätter
Schweizer Graphische
Mitteilungen
Revue suisse de
l'Imprimerie
Herausgegeben vom
Schweizerischen
Typographenbund
Editée par la
Fédération suisse des
typographes

1 te
em

o tip
afise gr
naz mo
etr bl

ian
60

TM (Typographische Monatsblätter)
Country: Switzerland

Cover Design: Yves Zimmerman
Courtesy of syndicom

02.1960

feb 60

Typographische Monatsblätter
Schweizer Graphische Mitteilungen
Revue suisse de l'Imprimerie
Herausgegeben vom
Schweizerischen Typographenbund
zur Förderung der Berufsbildung
Editée par la
Fédération suisse des typographes
pour l'éducation professionnelle

Februar/Février 1960, 79. Jahrgang Typographische Monatsblätter Nr. 2

2

es ge em
er es i

o
afise
naz
etr

t
g
m
b

TM (Typographische Monatsblätter)
Country: Switzerland

Cover Design: Yves Zimmerman
Courtesy of syndicom

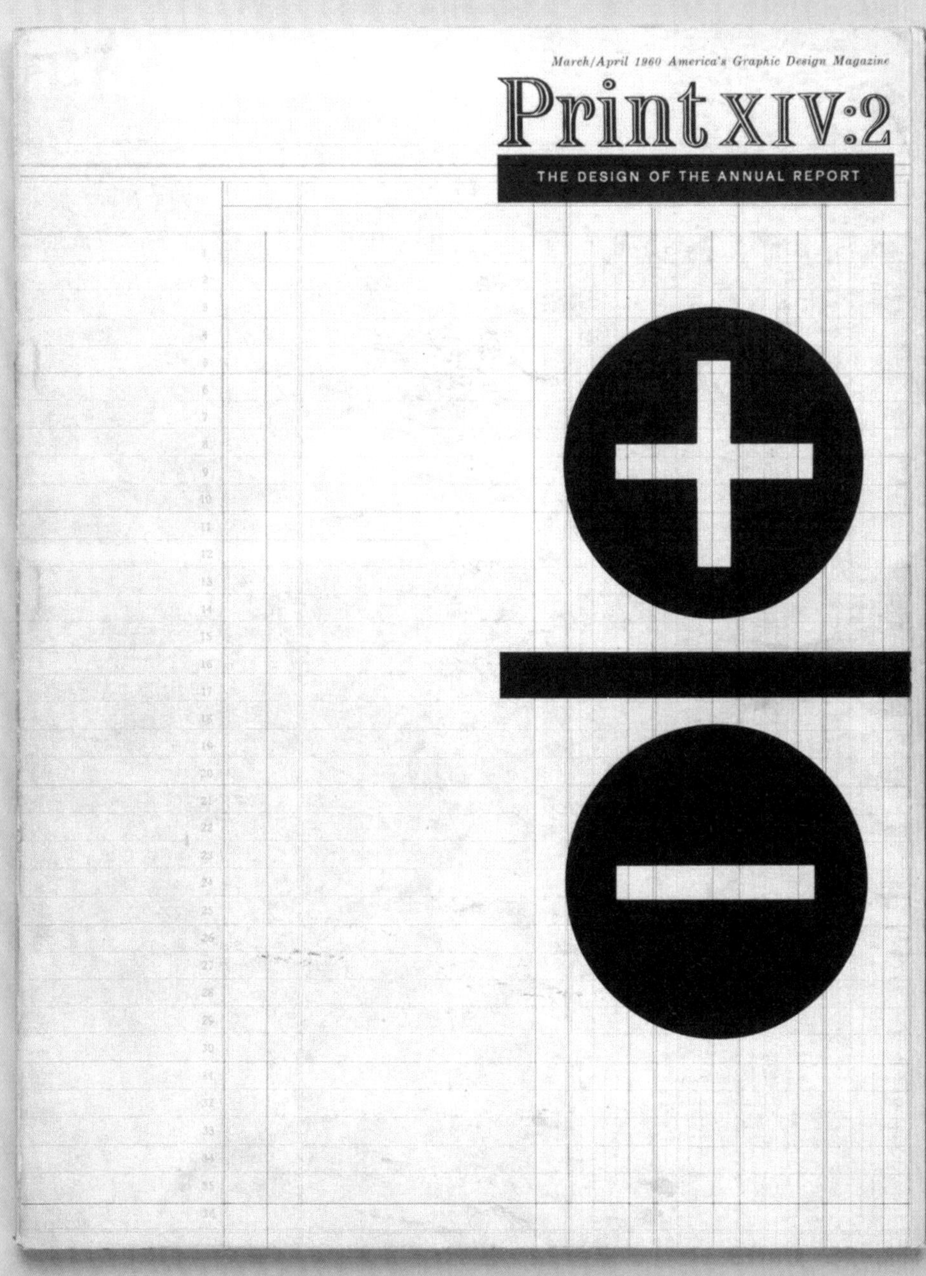

March/April 1960 America's Graphic Design Magazine
Print XIV:2
THE DESIGN OF THE ANNUAL REPORT

Print
Country: USA

Cover Design: Jack Golden

03.1960

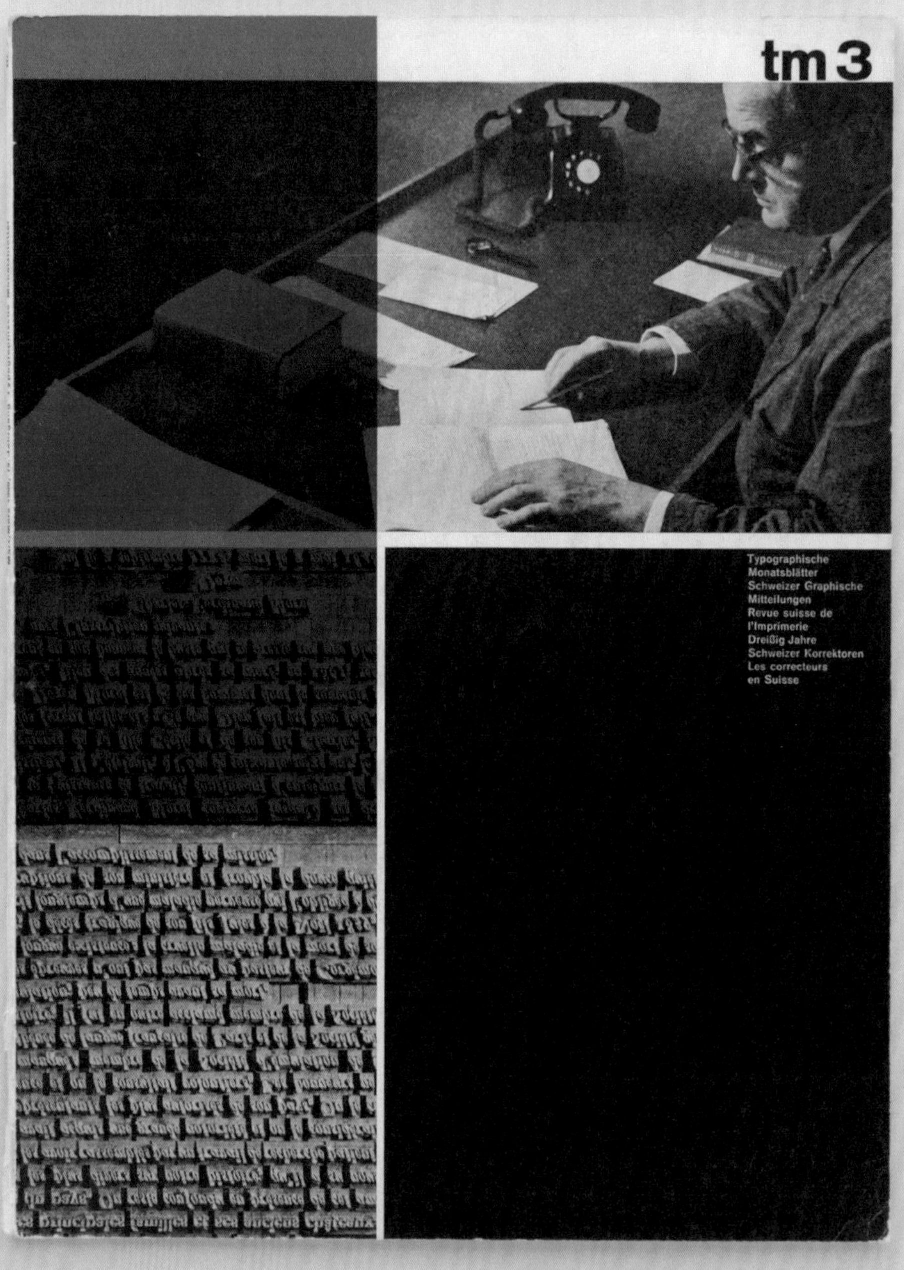

TM (Typographische Monatsblätter)
Country: Switzerland

Design: unidentified
Courtesy of syndicom

Type Talks
Country: USA

Design: unidentified

04.1960

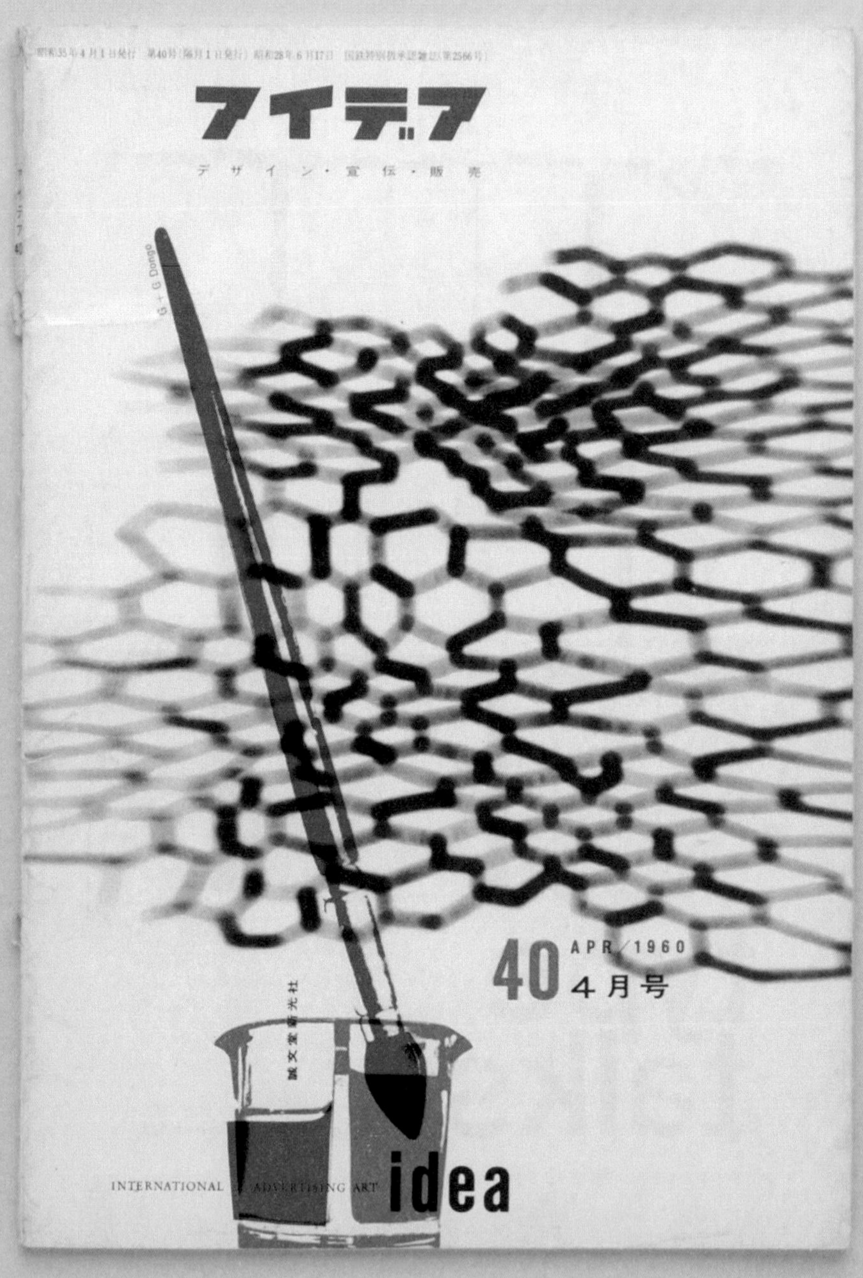

Idea
Country: Japan

Cover Design:
Günter & Gisela Dongowski

04.1960

TM (Typographische Monatsblätter)
Country: Switzerland

Cover Design: Siegfried Odermatt
Courtesy of syndicom

06.1960

TM (Typographische Monatsblätter)
Country: Switzerland

Cover Design: Siegfried Odermatt
Courtesy of syndicom

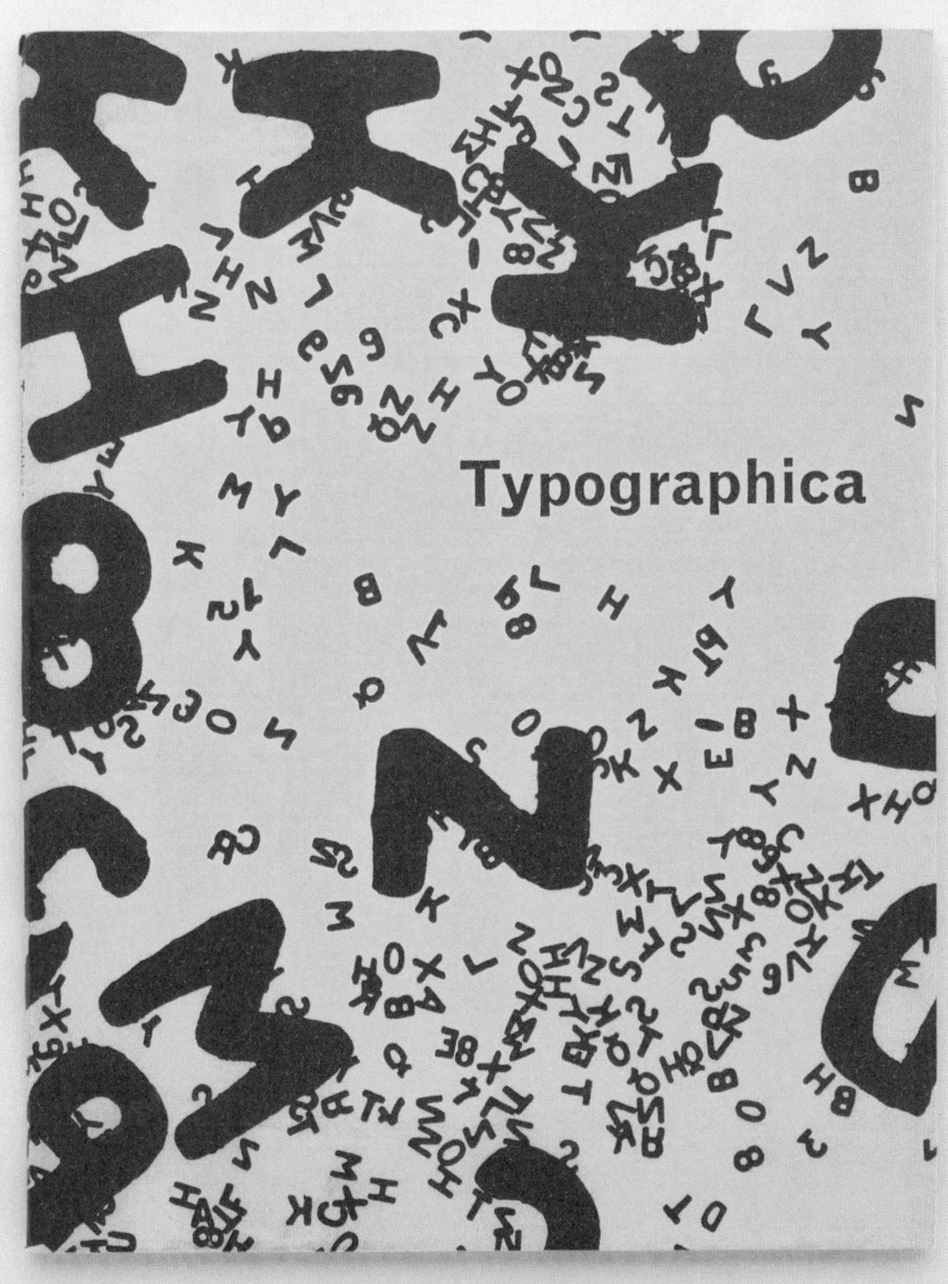

Typographica
Country: UK

Cover Design: Herbert Spencer

Idea
Country: Japan

Cover Design: Theo Dimson

TM (Typographische Monatsblätter)
Country: Switzerland

Cover Design: Siegfried Odermatt
Courtesy of syndicom

08.1960

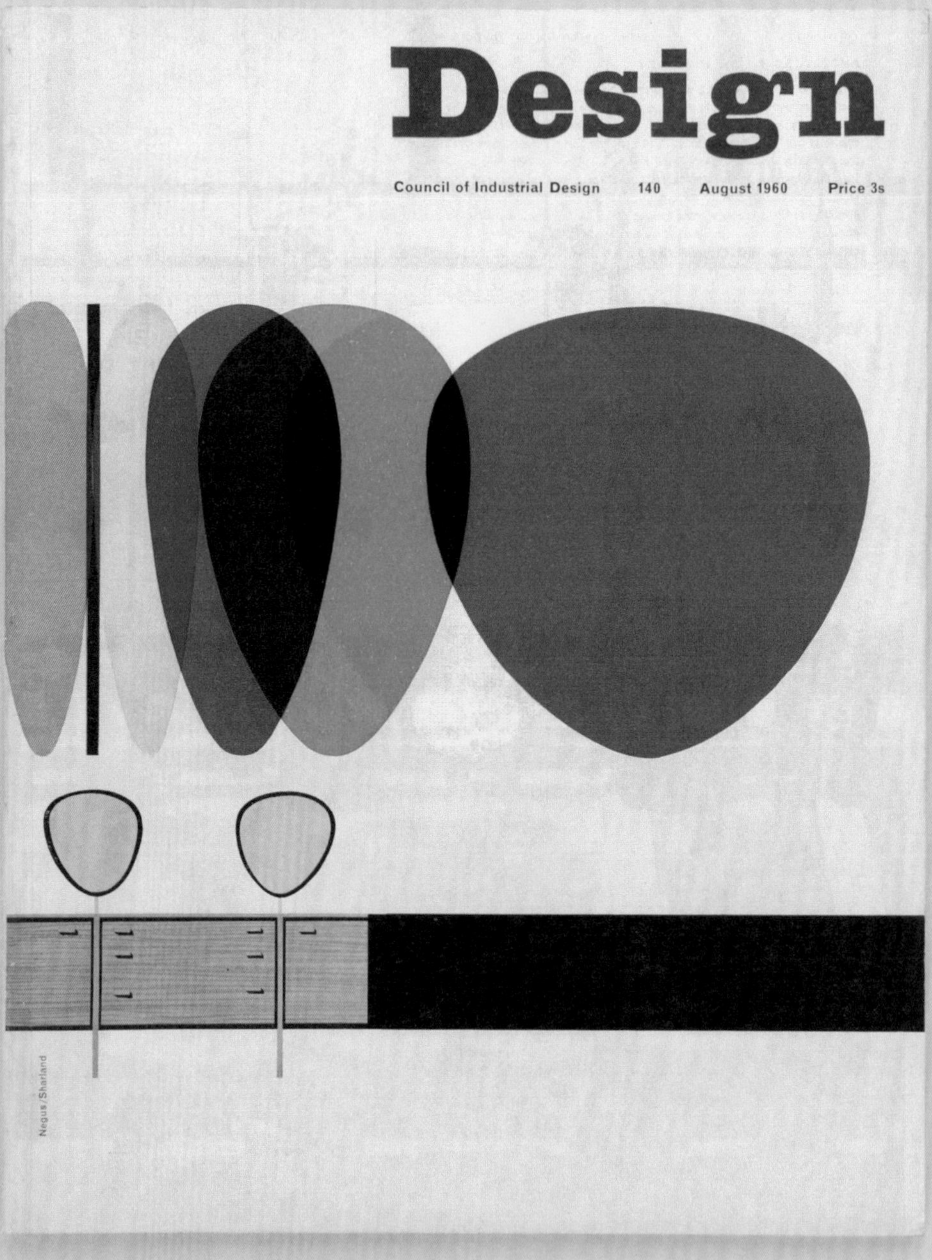

Design
Country: UK

Cover Design:
Dick Negus, Philip Sharland

Idea
Country: Japan

Cover Design:
Fritz Fischer, Dorothea Nosbisch

10.1960

Idea
Country: Japan

Cover Design: Jacques Richez

10.1960

TM (Typographische Monatsblätter)
Country: Switzerland

Cover Design: Siegfried Odermatt
Courtesy of syndicom

11.1960

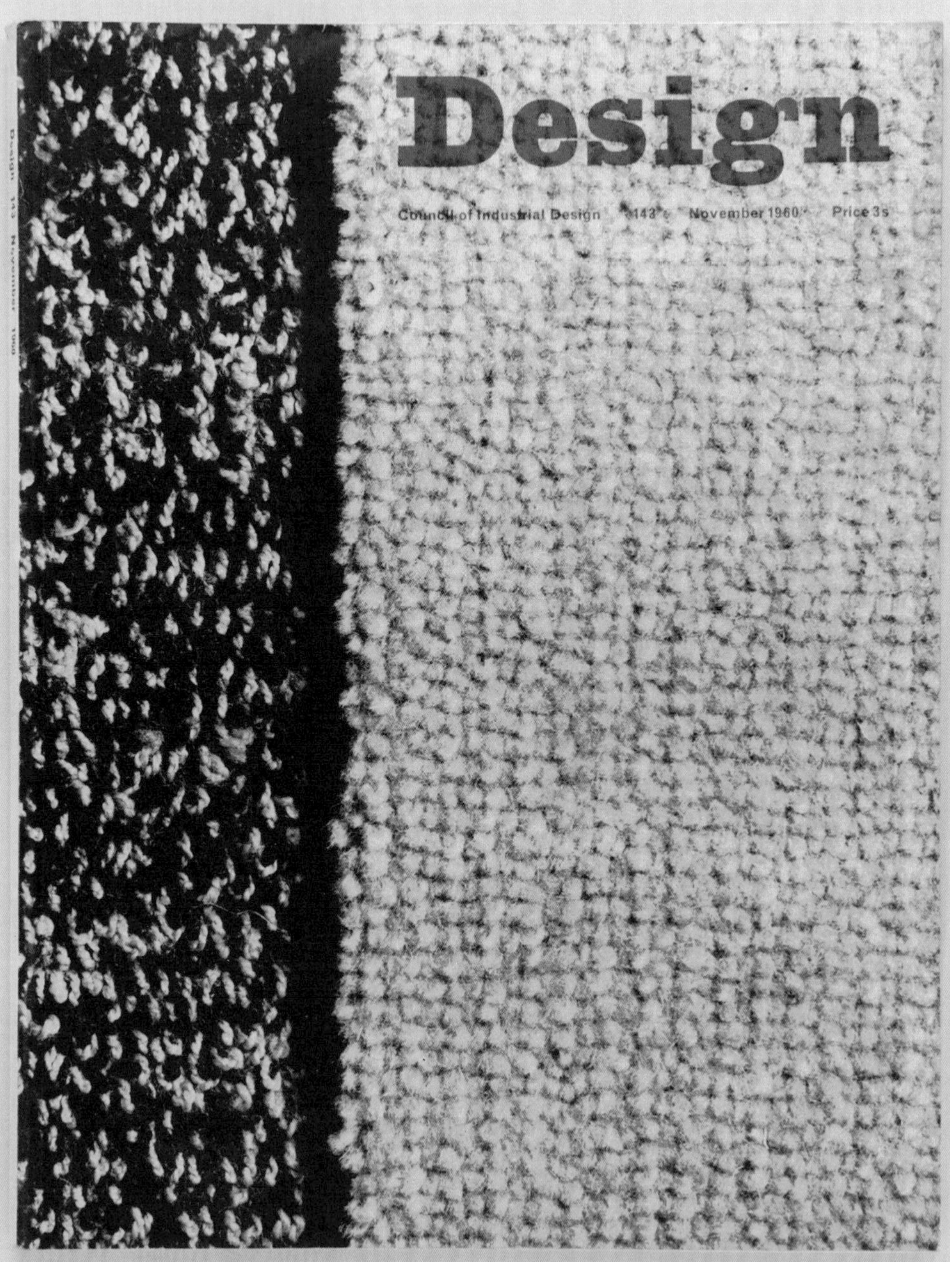

Design
Country: UK

Art Editor: Ken Garland

Graphis
Country: Switzerland

Cover Design: Alan Fletcher

12.1960

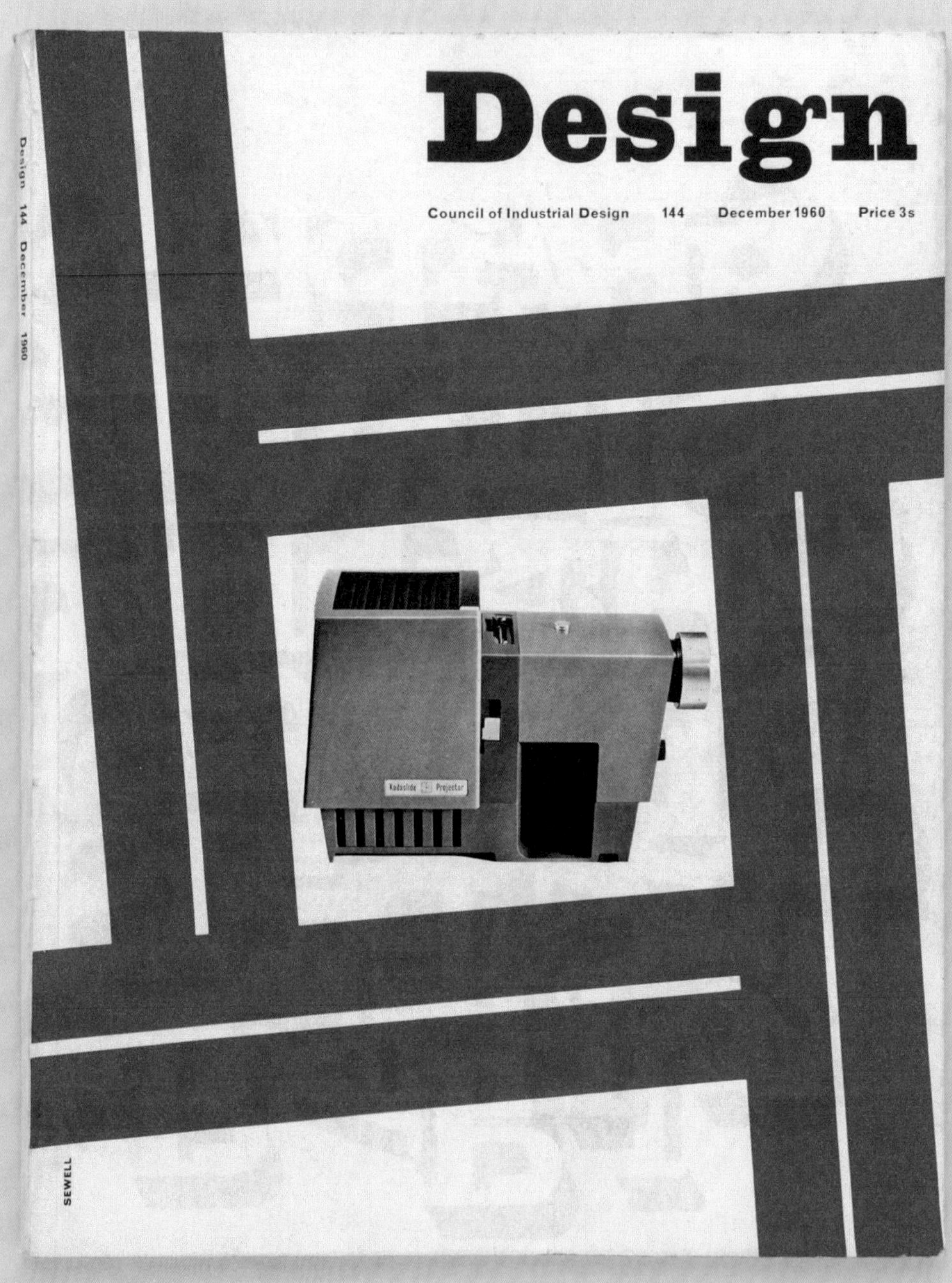

Design
Country: UK

Cover Design: John Sewell

Q Paul Rand said that he didn't like designing photography books because the work is already done for him, meaning that the photographs do all the work and the design merely supports them. Is this also true of design magazines? Or does the designer have to work extra hard to please a knowing audience?

A Designing a magazine about design presents a unique challenge to the designer, since the readership will be a very design-aware one. This is the case whichever of the two directions you (correctly) propose is chosen; the designer has to work extra hard either way. The difference between design and photography, though, is that design is often an object or a thing that needs to be photographed especially for the magazine, whereas a photography book is usually only presenting finished, flat images. The work is indeed done. My opinion is that the subject itself should be the star of the piece. If the design of the pages is too complex it will detract from the work being presented on those pages. But the styling and art direction of the photography of the objects to be featured comes into play too, whether it's a car, a vase, or any other piece of design. For instance, it might be tempting to design a magazine about the Memphis group in a very colourful, geometric manner to reflect the styles and devices of the furniture. But would it help the non-follower understand the work? The decision on which direction to take also depends on the nature of the magazine project. If it covers a general area of design it will more likely be minimal in on-page intervention. If it is more specific and manifesto-like in its dedication to a style or movement it will more likely want to reflect that movement's ethos, whatever it might be.

Q For non-publication designers, the role of the editor in magazine design is often regarded as mysterious. Can you say something about their input here – especially in relation to design magazines?

A Essentially the editor takes the lead on commissioning the texts and the designer works with photographers and/or illustrators and brings all these elements together on the page. But a good editor should have a strong eye for design, just as a designer needs to understand the text being designed. This has become more relevant now that both parties are working with the same technology and can work together to forge pages. At that stage they share the role of visual journalist. Both have a curatorial role, all the more so on a design magazine, and should be able to offer direction across each other's disciplines. To achieve the best results they should have equal status, and be open to suggestions from each other. Most great magazines have benefited from strong partnerships between the disciplines in this way.

Design
1949–99
UK

Q In your opinion can you name the best-designed design publications from the past – and from the present?

A Ken Garland's *Design* (1949–99, UK) and 8vo's *Octavo* (1986–92, UK) come to mind in terms of graphic design; *Nest* (1997–2004, USA) was a wonderful OTT interiors mag that completely flies in the face of my advice above. Today, there are many great new examples of small magazines covering aspects of design, such as the architecture title *Real Review* (launched 2016), *MacGuffin* (2015–present), about everyday objects, and the more journal-like *Disegno* (2011-present).

Octavo
1986–92
UK

Q How are design publications learning to survive with the competition that comes from online design activity – blogs, Pinterest, and so on?

A The big one! Many struggle, but to succeed they need a point of view and clear opinion. Online there's too much 'this is nice' and 'look at this!' (see It's Nice That, for example). Which is fine, but a print magazine can engage more deeply by having a strong standpoint.

Drawing from twenty-five years' experience, Jeremy Leslie founded magCulture in 2006 as a resource for connoisseurs of editorial design. This was followed by a design studio in 2010 and a shop in 2015.

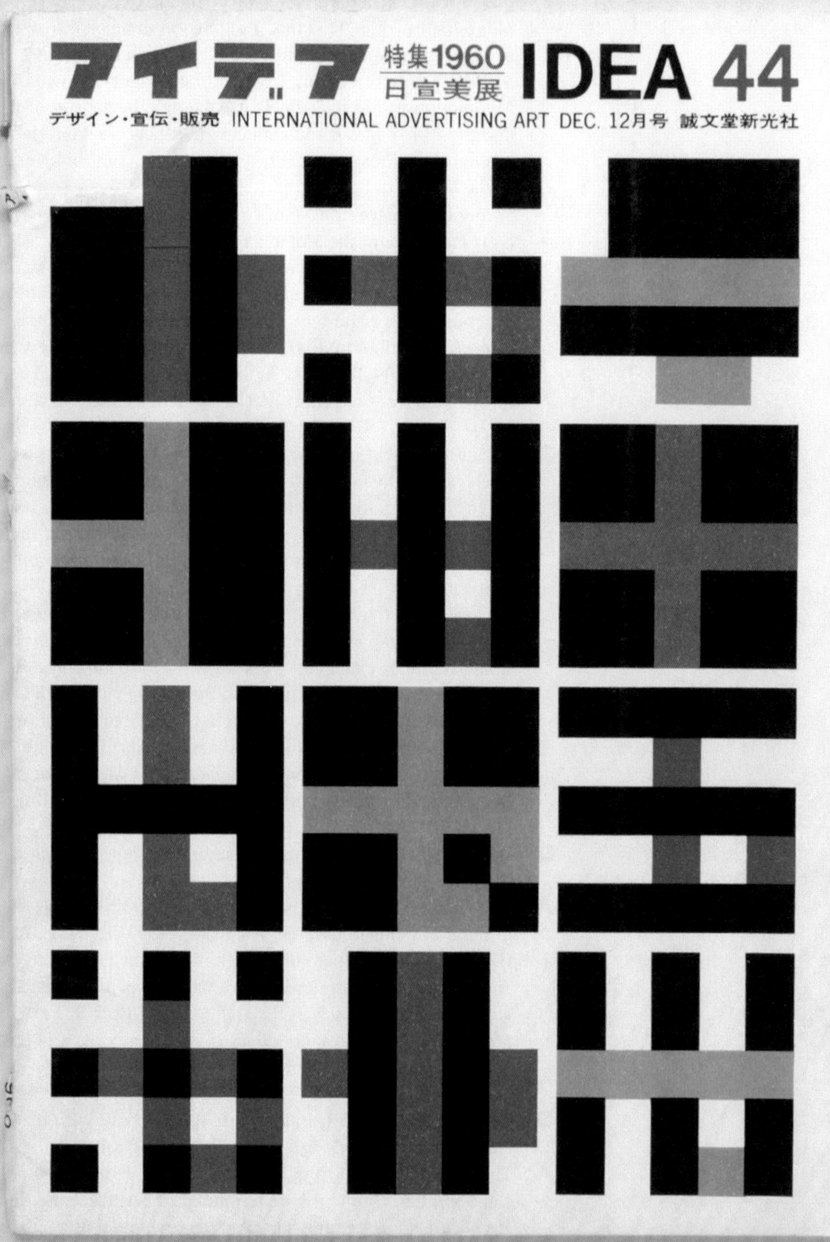

Idea
Country: Japan

Cover Design: Ikko Tanaka

12.1960

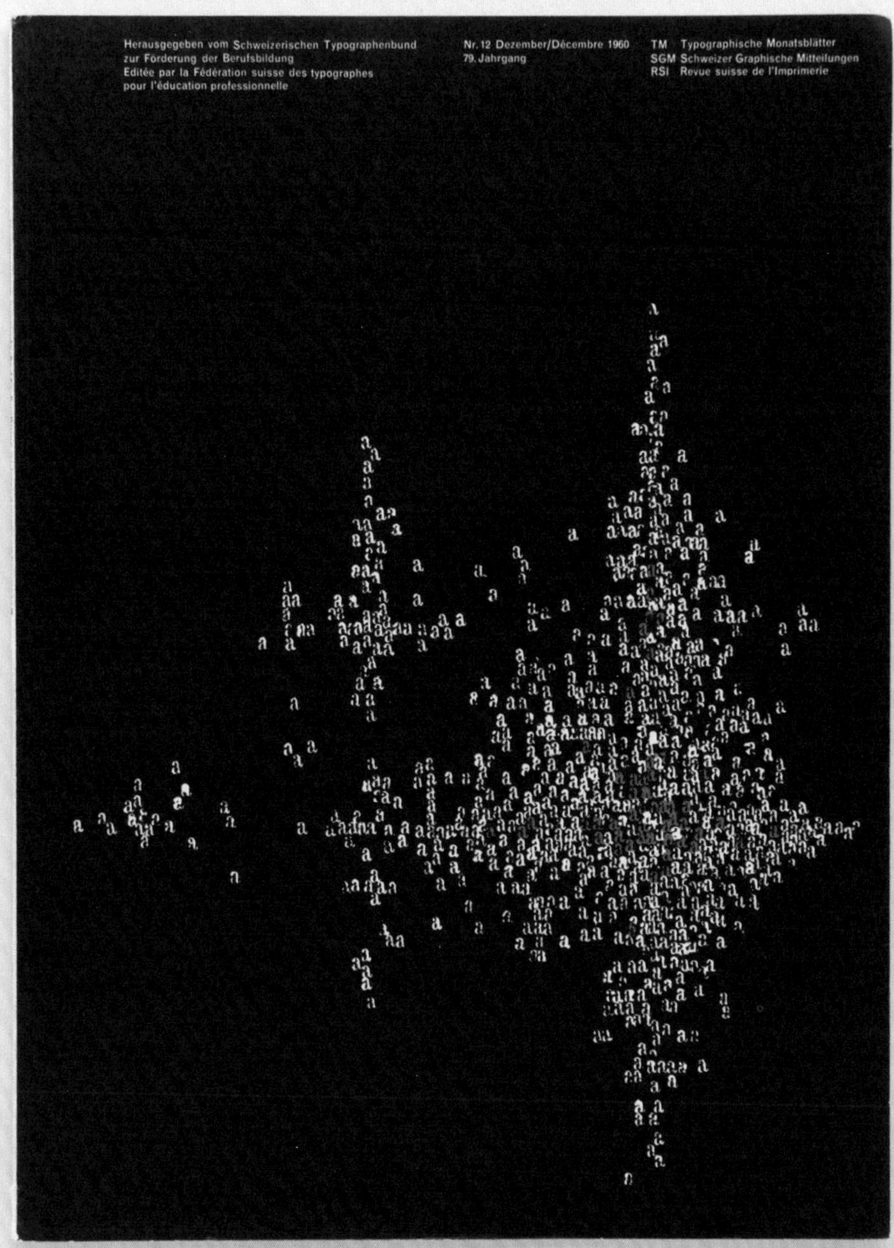

TM (Typographische Monatsblätter)
Country: Switzerland

Design: unidentified
Courtesy of syndicom

01.1961

Gebrauchsgraphik
Country: Germany

Art Director: Hans Kuh

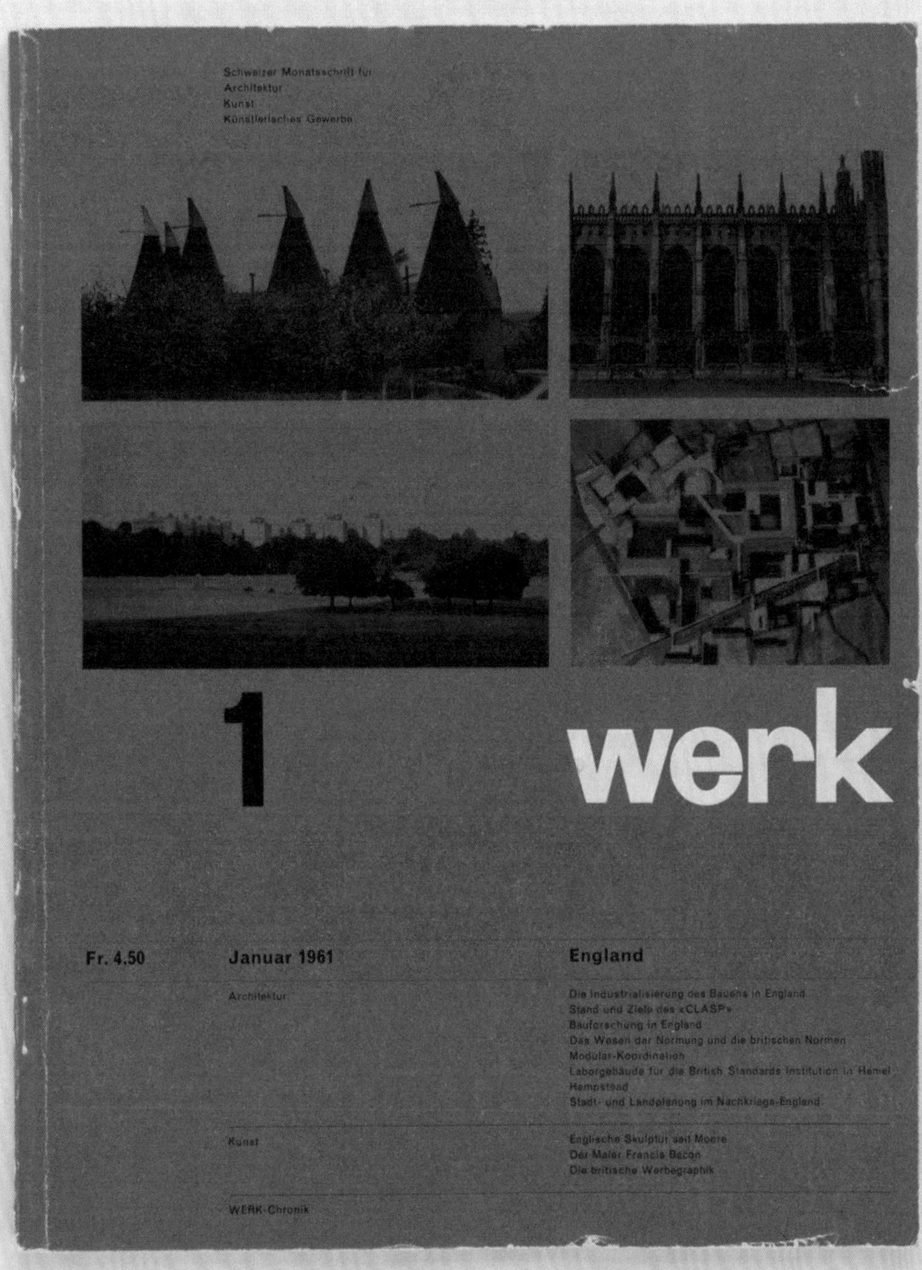

Schweizer Monatsschrift für
Architektur
Kunst
Künstlerisches Gewerbe
1
werk
Fr. 4.50
Januar 1961
England
Architektur
Die Industrialisierung des Bauens in England
Stand und Ziele des «CLASP»
Bauforschung in England
Das Wesen der Normung und die britischen Normen
Modular-Koordination
Laborgebäude für die British Standards Institution in Hemel Hempstead
Stadt- und Landplanung im Nachkriegs-England
Kunst
Englische Skulptur seit Moore
Der Maler Francis Bacon
Die britische Werbegraphik
WERK-Chronik

(Das) Werk
Country: Switzerland

Cover Design: Karl Gerstner

02.1961

Design
Country: UK

Art Editor: Ken Garland

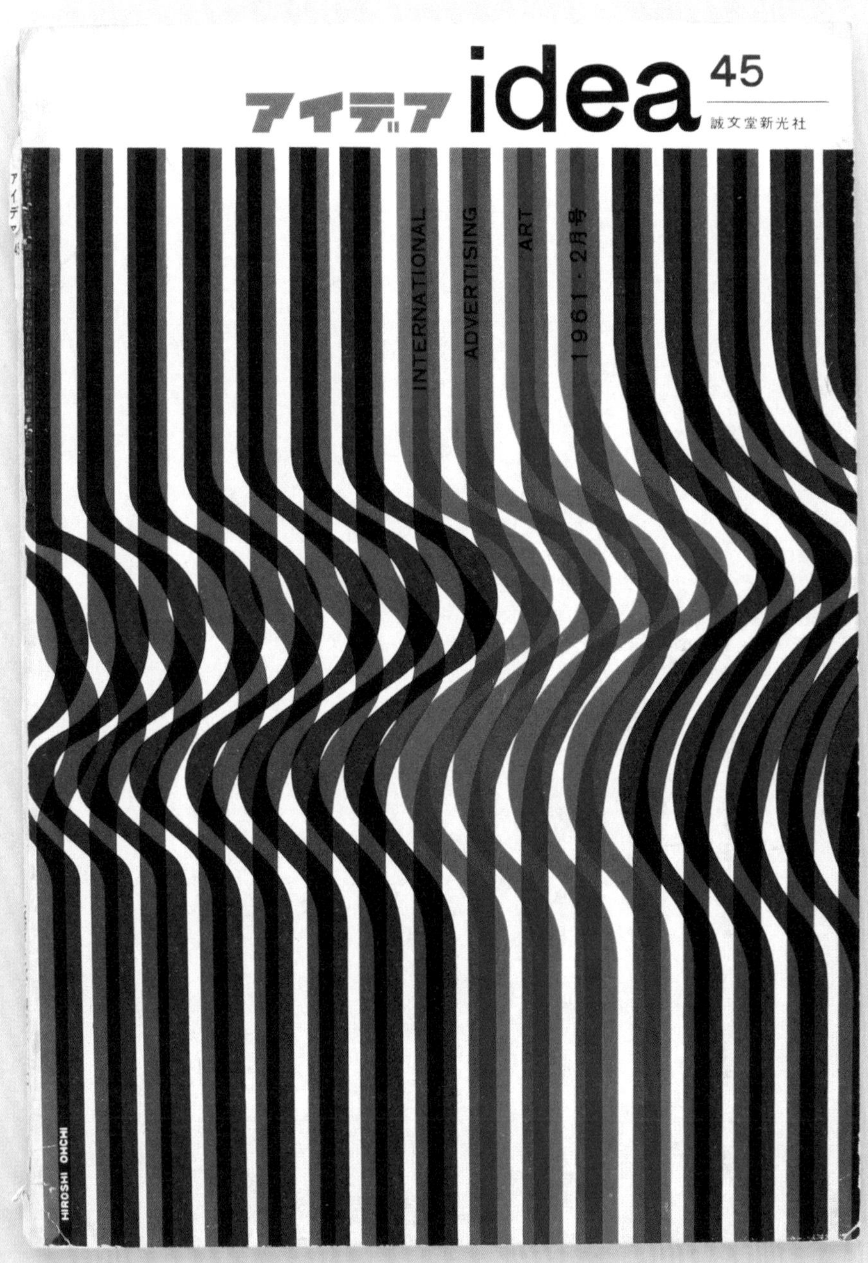

Idea
Country: Japan

Cover Design: Hiroshi Ohchi

03.1961

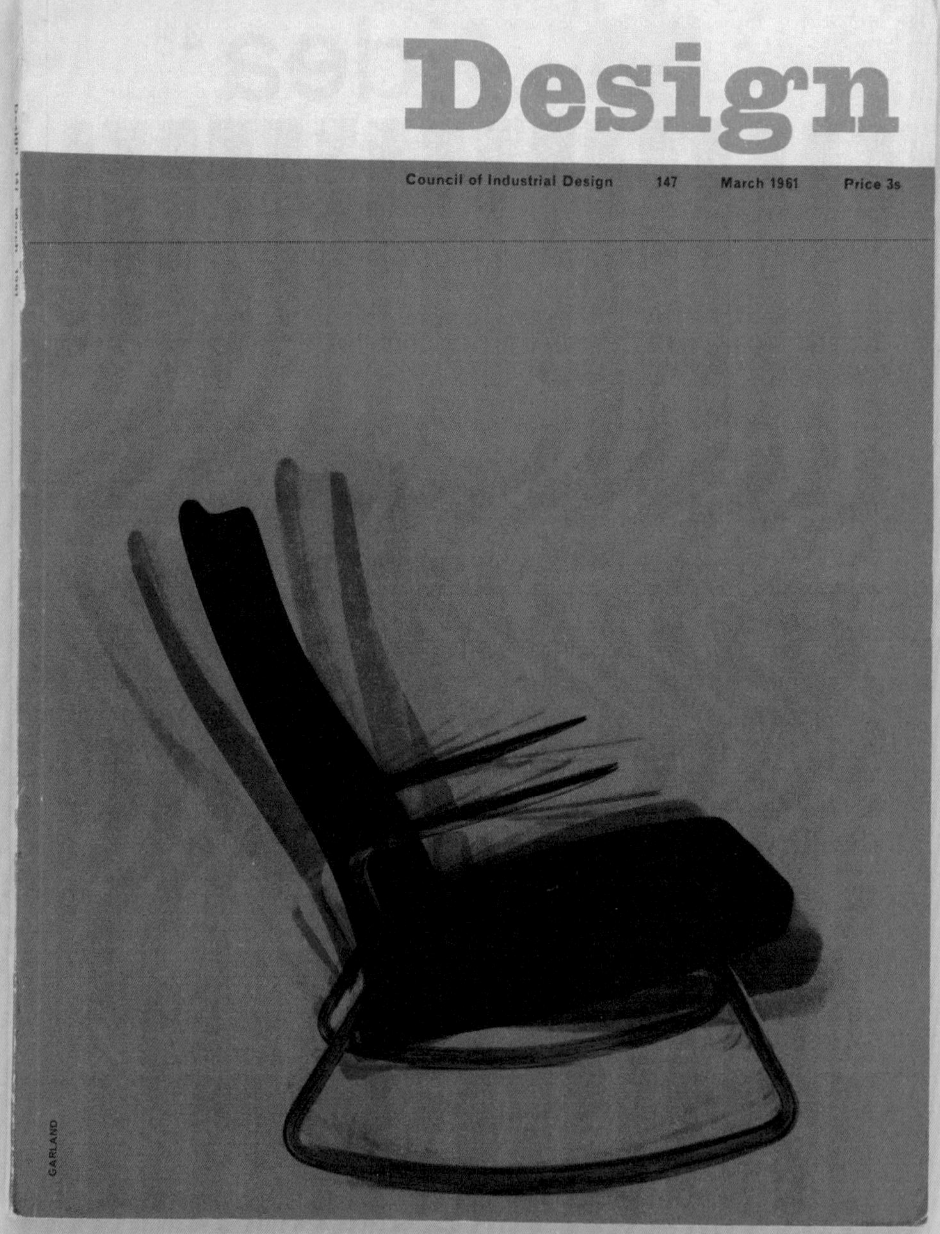

Design
Country: UK

Cover Design: Ken Garland

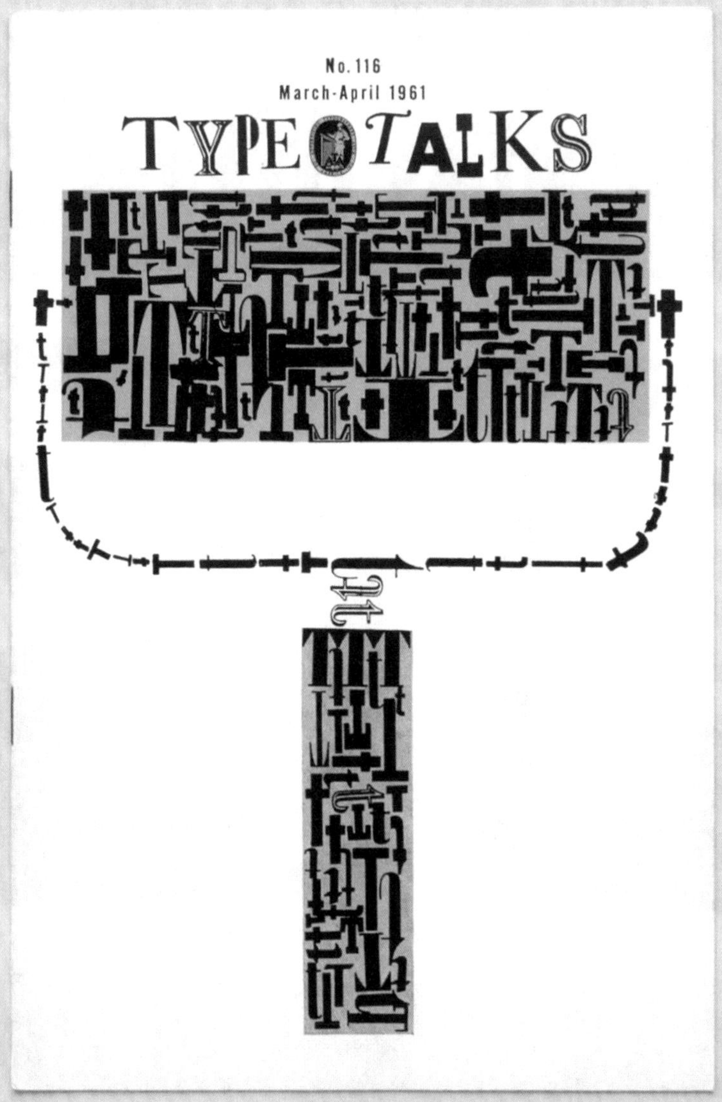

Type Talks
Country: USA

Design: unidentified

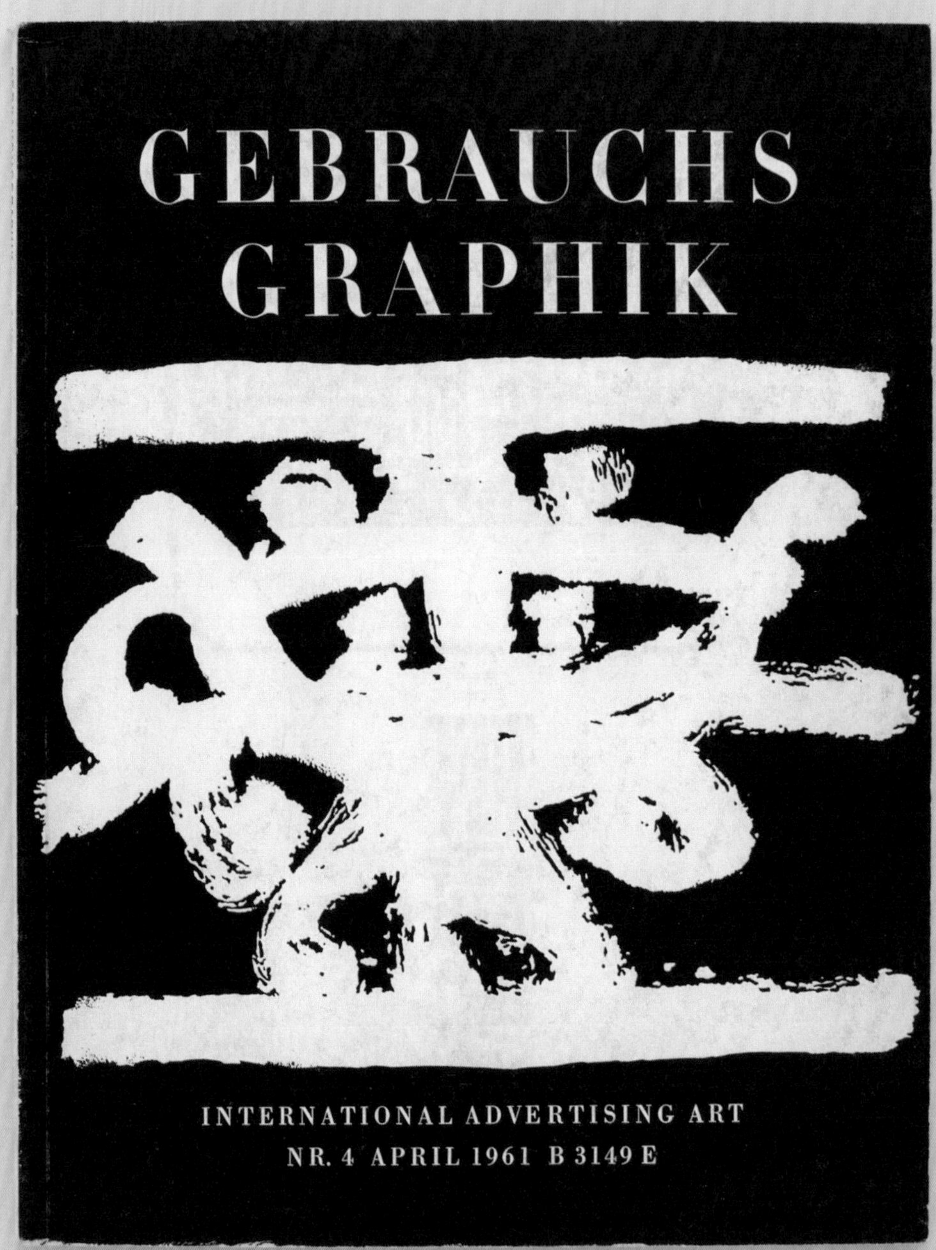

GEBRAUCHS
GRAPHIK
INTERNATIONAL ADVERTISING ART
NR. 4 APRIL 1961 B 3149 E

Gebrauchsgraphik
Country: Germany

Design: unidentified

Idea
Country: Japan

Cover Design: Hiroshi Ohchi

06.1961

Gebrauchsgraphik
Country: Germany

Cover Design: Erik Nitsche

06.1961

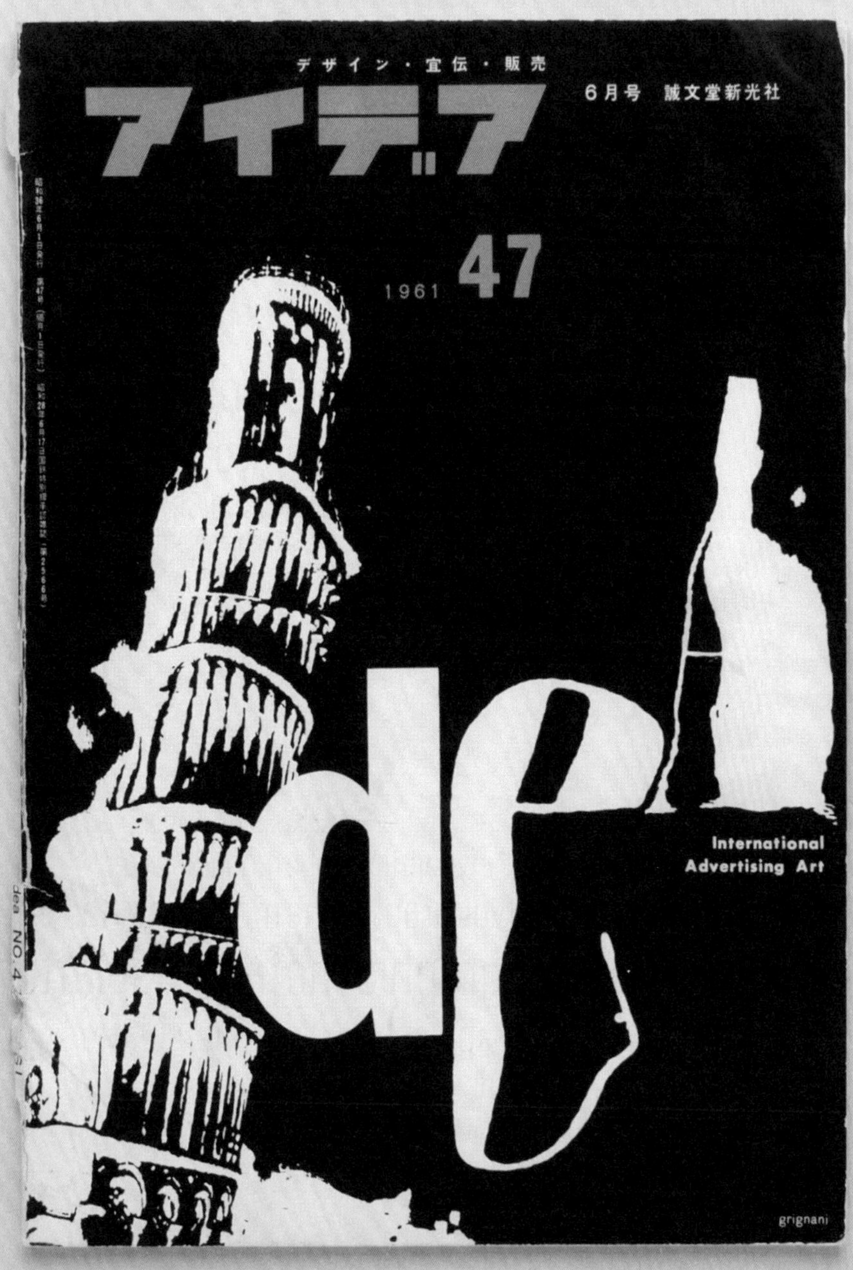

Idea
Country: Japan

Cover Design: Franco Grignani

06.1961

TM Typographische Monatsblätter
SGM Schweizer Graphische Mitteilungen
RSI Revue suisse de l'Imprimerie
Nr. 5 Juni/Juin 1961, 80. Jahrgang
Herausgegeben vom Schweizerischen Typographenbund zur Förderung der Berufsbildung
Editée par la Fédération suisse des typographes pour l'éducation professionnelle

typographische monatsblätter

TM (Typographische Monatsblätter)
Country: Switzerland

Cover Design: Emil Ruder
Courtesy of syndicom

Gebrauchsgraphik
Country: Germany

Cover Design: Günther Stiller

08.1961

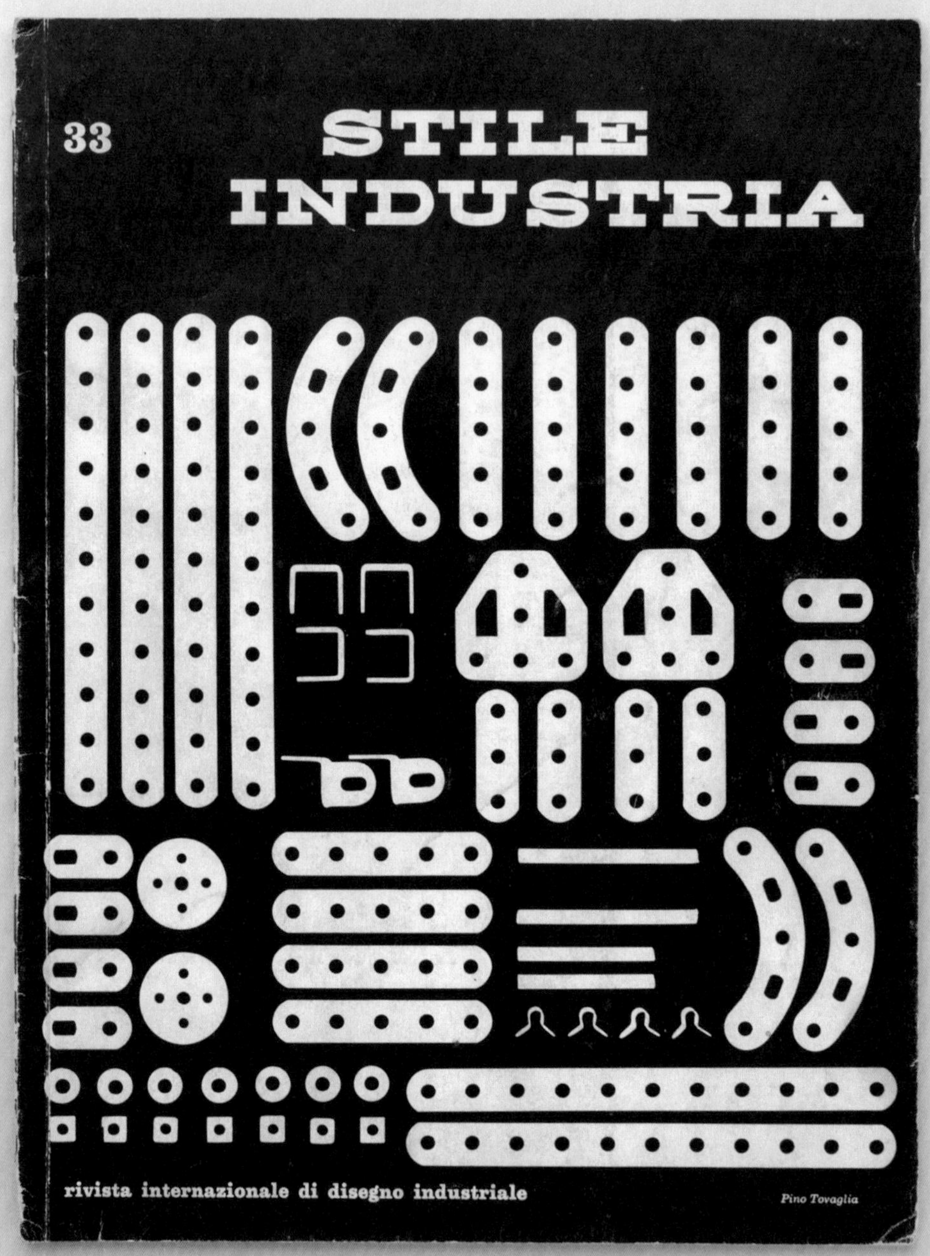

Stile Industria
Country: Italy

Cover Design: Pino Tovaglia

Gebrauchsgraphik
Country: Germany

Art Director: Hans Kuh

09.1961

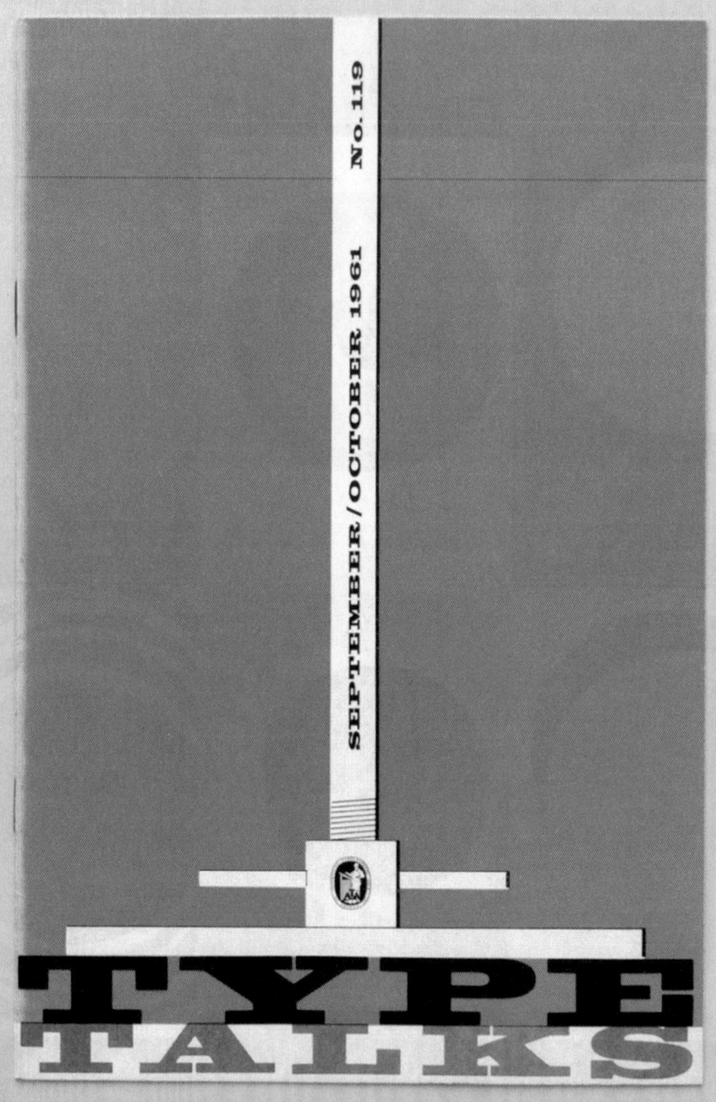

Type Talks
Country: USA

Design: unidentified

Design
Country: UK

Cover Design: Barry Trengove

Uppercase
Country: Germany

Editor: Theo Crosby

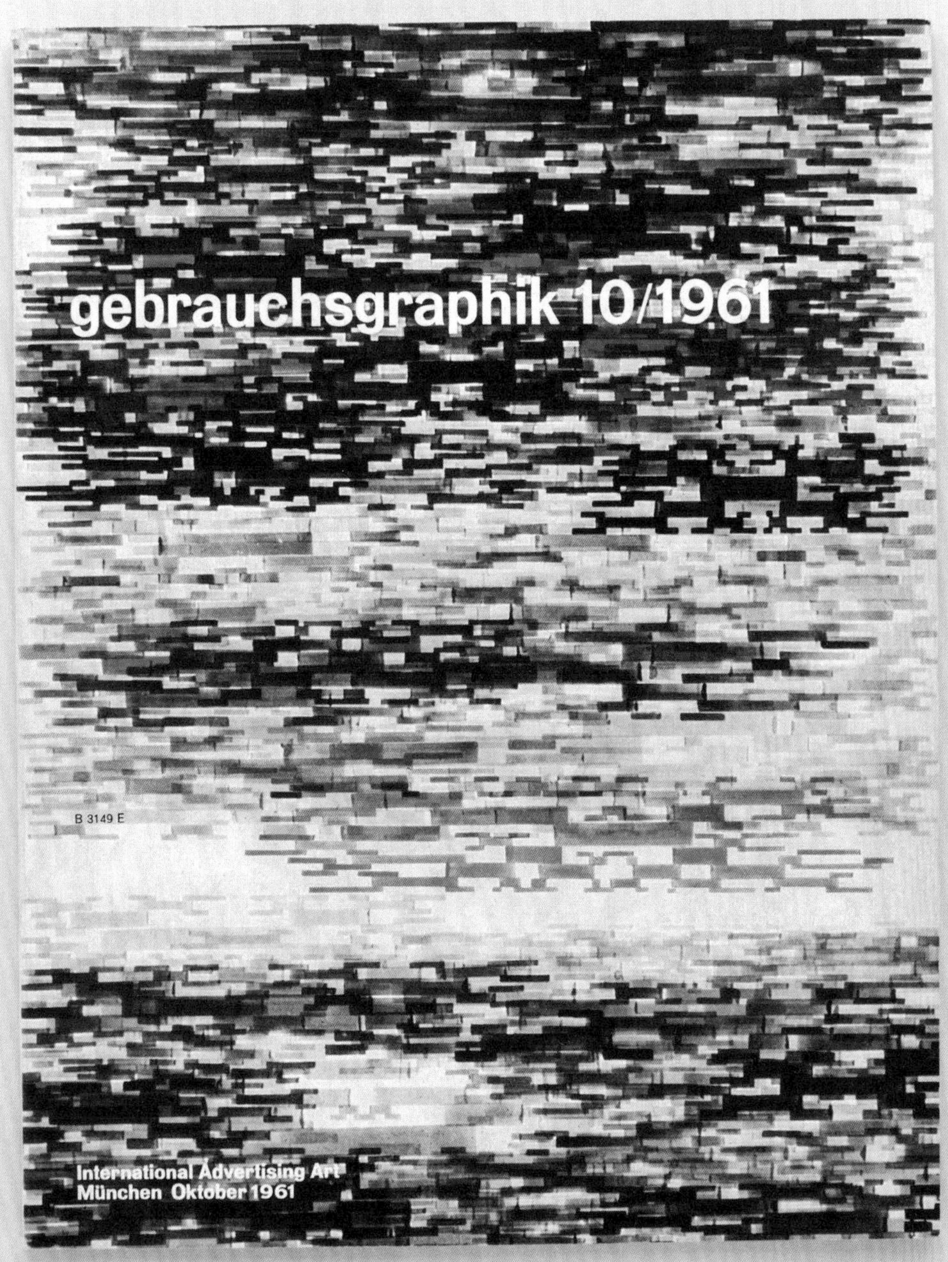

Gebrauchsgraphik
Country: Germany

Art Director: Hans Kuh

Idea
Country: Japan

Cover Design: Hiroshi Ohchi

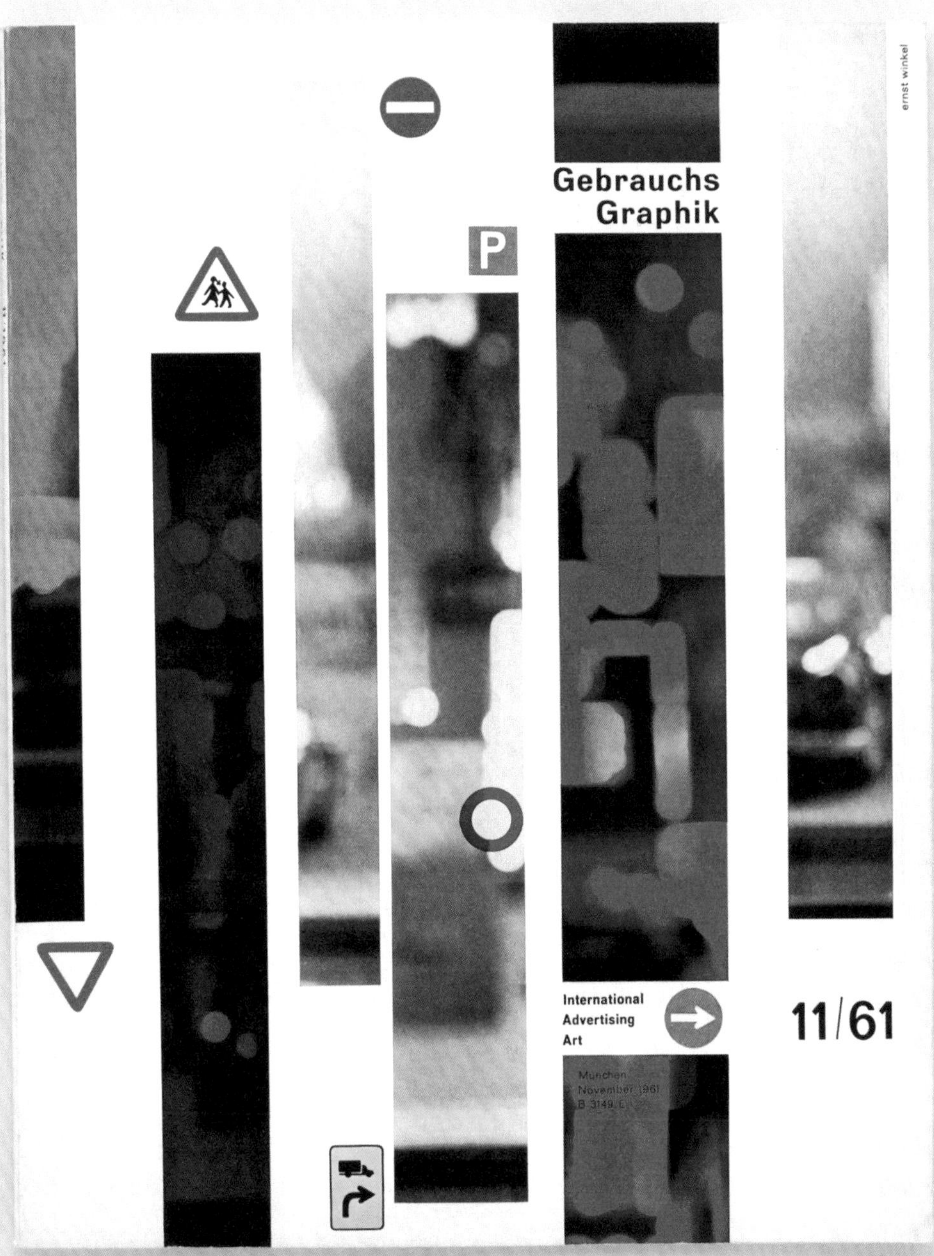

Gebrauchsgraphik
Country: Germany

Cover Design: Ernst Winkel

Typographische Monatsblätter TM
Schweizer Graphische Mitteilungen SGM
Revue suisse de l'Imprimerie RSI
November/Novembre 1961, 80. Jahrgang Nr. 11
Herausgegeben vom Schweizerischen Typographenbund
zur Förderung der Berufsbildung
Editée par la Fédération suisse des typographes
pour l'éducation professionnelle

typographische monatsblätter

TM (Typographische Monatsblätter)
Country: Switzerland

Cover Design: Emil Ruder
Courtesy of syndicom

Typographica
Country: UK

Cover Design:
Robert Brownjohn

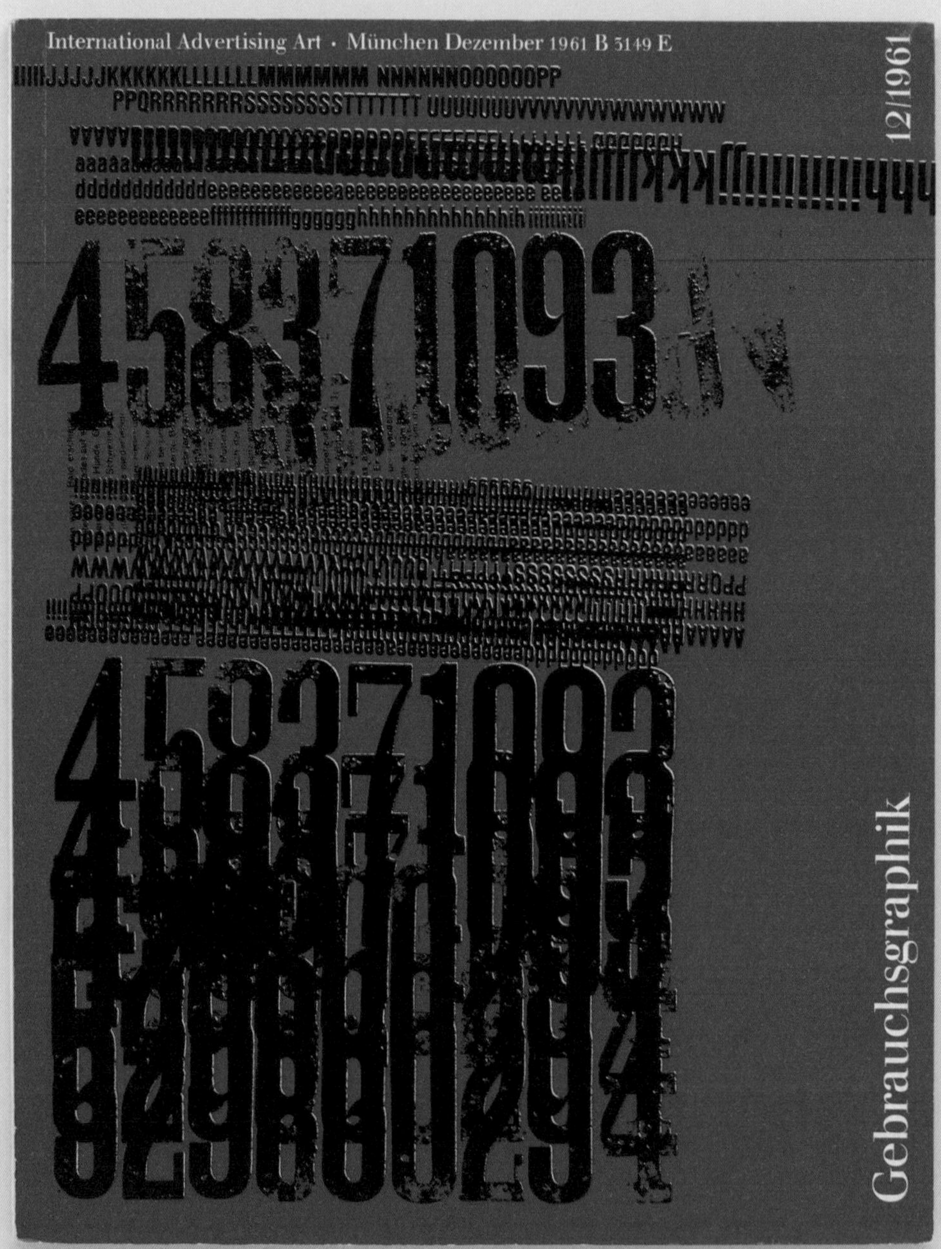

Gebrauchsgraphik
Country: Germany

Design: unidentified

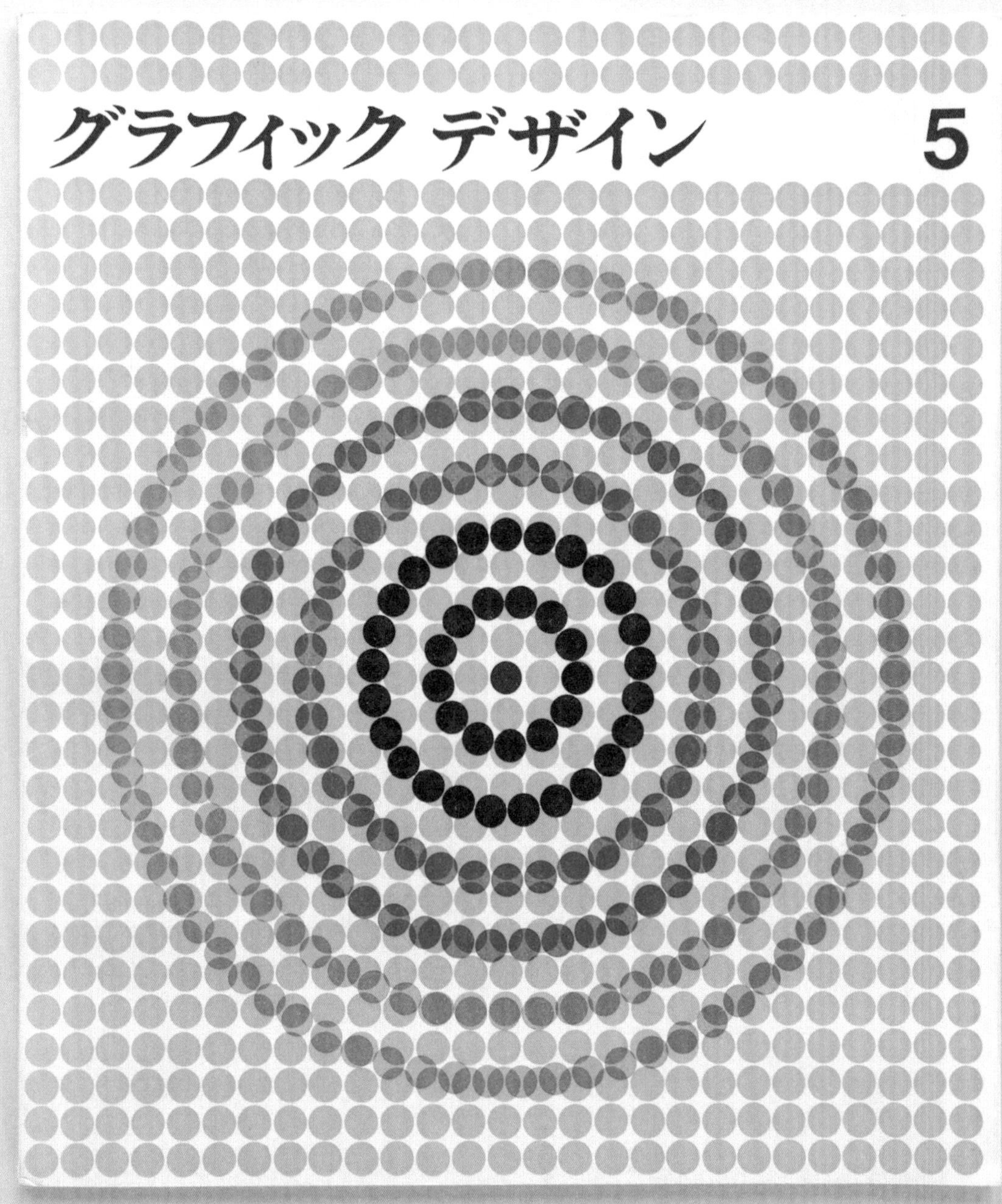

Graphic Design
Country: Japan

Cover Design:
Yusaku Kamekura

01.1962

Design
Country: UK

Cover Design: Ken Garland

Q Can you name the outstanding design magazines amongst the collection you have at the Graphic Design Department at UCA, Epsom?

A In late 2015, we were extremely lucky to acquire a 3,500-strong collection of design books, type specimens, magazines and exhibition catalogues from the seminal Nijhof & Lee Booksellers in Amsterdam (1988–2011). Whilst the shop lives on as part of the *Bijzondere Collecties* (Special Collections) at the University of Amsterdam, many of the books and publications that were retained by owner and bookseller Warren Lee when the shop closed are now housed in Epsom. The collection is a seemingly eclectic one, with the majority of the material dating from the early 20th century onwards and originating from all over the world. Historical magazines of note include *Kwadraat-Bladen* (1955–74, Netherlands), *Upper & Lower Case* (1970–99, USA), and the Japanese magazine dating from the 1960s and 1970s that is appropriately titled *Graphic Design* (1959–86, Japan).

Given that some of it is old shop stock, we are in the somewhat bizarre – and incredibly privileged – position of having multiple copies of influential design magazines that ceased production relatively recently, including *Emigre* (1984–2005, USA) and *Dot Dot Dot* (2001–11, UK/Netherlands). Alongside these familiar names are numerous small-run and often self-published magazines, many of which are student publications from the Rietveld, the Werkplaats Typografie, or further afield. When packing up the collection in Amsterdam, Warren had anecdotes that related to many of the items, which began to reveal how intrinsically linked many of them are and document the story behind their heritage. For example, the full set of *Graphic Design* magazine was gifted to the shop by Pieter Brattinga, the Dutch graphic designer and editor of *Kwadraat-Bladen*. There are sheets of his letterhead still interspersed between many of the issues.

Q How do you use design magazines as a teaching aid – especially the older ones – when design students (we are told) are only interested in looking at design online?

A It is a difficult time to be a design student, whereby the Mac that you use to create much of your work also serves as a means of communication, your TV, and your library (with multiple windows open at any given time). The majority of my teaching process focuses on working with students to engage with the subject in a different and often slower manner, and design magazines play a role within that. With students so accustomed to viewing work online, images of design have become permanently at a remove that renders the traditional PowerPoint more or less redundant in terms of teaching. The most successful design courses and schools have a history of valuing workshops, process and materials, and it is only logical to extend this approach to the history of the discipline through engaging with original artefacts wherever possible.

The formal teaching of design history is arguably out of vogue at undergraduate level, with many graphic design programmes having applied a cultural studies model to the theory of the discipline, which is in danger of leaving students with a piecemeal knowledge of those who have gone before. Without this prior knowledge it is easy to be at sea when researching online; I have encountered students referencing design work that has been done by a student at another college. Design magazines help to break some of this down and are an accessible way of tracing ideas back to the original object, designer, or era. Both historical and contemporary magazines are valuable, as they enable us to position work within a broader, social context – often a magazine will cover something ephemeral that has not been published elsewhere. Our students each receive a subscription to *Eye* (1990–present, UK) – long-form reading is increasingly important, and we will often use articles as the basis for discussion.

U&lc
1970–99
USA

Graphic Design
1959–86
Japan

Q Beyond teaching, what is the role of the printed design magazine in current culture? Similarly, what is the role of the material archive at a time when you can see everything online?

A Largely the same as it has always been – to document, to discuss, to challenge and to share. Accessing archives can open up the discipline in a different way. One of the advantages of archives is that they will often hold the material associated with something as well as (or indeed instead of) the object itself.

In addition to the Nijhof & Lee collection, we also hold the thirty-year archive of designer Vaughan Oliver's work at Epsom. Having held onto pretty much everything throughout his prolific career, it is now possible to view his initial sketches and paste-ups for album artwork alongside the completed record, billboard posters, and adverts for the albums within magazines. These position the object in context, and allow you to view it in a different manner from a stream of images that are based upon algorithms of past searches. Archives can be empowering, different methods of cataloguing can enable the discovery of something unexpected and the understanding of a subject or designer in an engaged, more tangible manner. I don't believe that you can replace materiality.

Rose Gridneff is the course leader for Graphic Design, University for the Creative Arts. She is also a designer working in letterpress, and has lectured and exhibited worldwide.

Emigre
1984—2005
USA

Dot Dot Dot
2001–11
UK/Netherlands

Gebrauchsgraphik
Country: Germany

Art Director: Hans Kuh

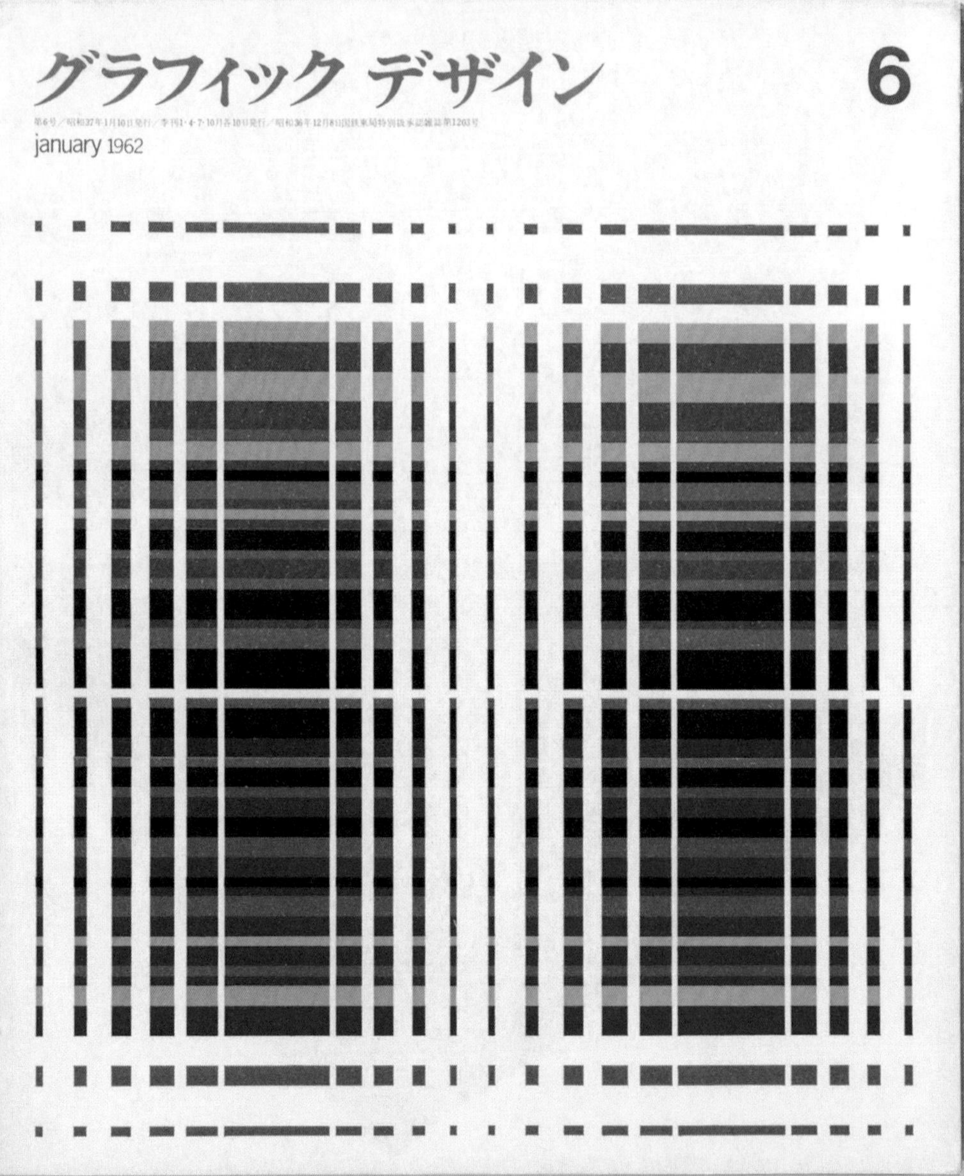

グラフィック デザイン
6
第6号／昭和37年1月10日発行／季刊1・4・7・10月各10日発行／昭和36年12月8日国鉄東局特別扱承認雑誌第1203号
january 1962

Graphic Design
Country: Japan

Cover Design: Sugiura Kohei

Graphis
Country: German

Cover Design: Reid Miles

02.1962

Design
Country: UK

Cover Design: Roy Laughton

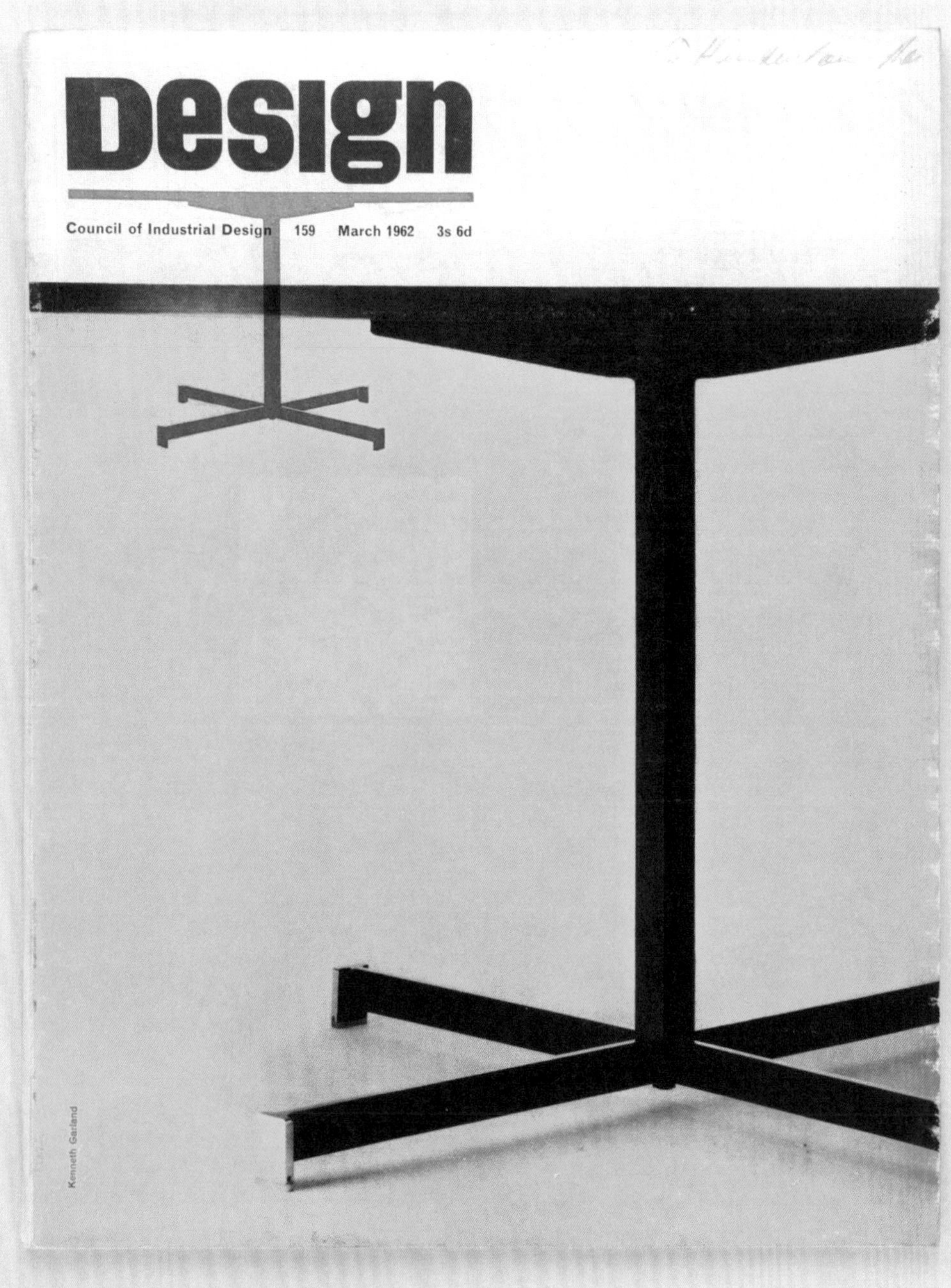

Design
Country: UK

Cover Design: Ken Garland

04.1962

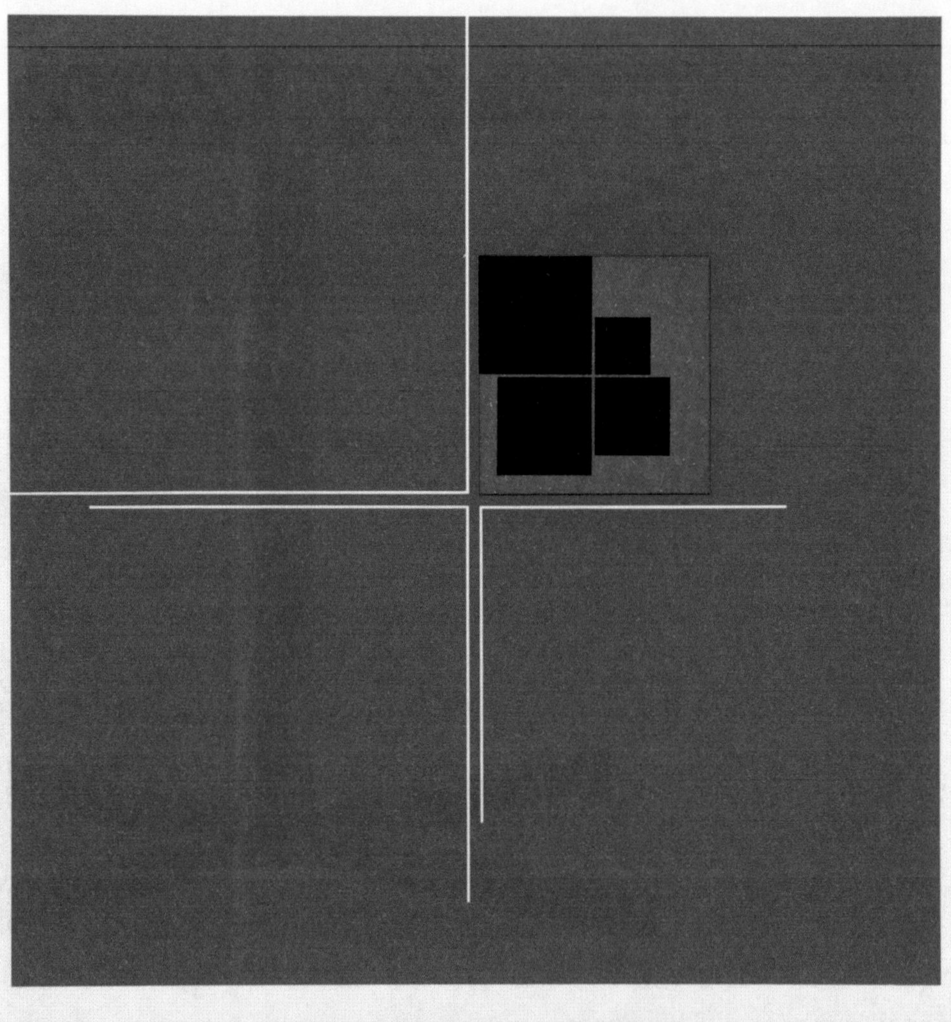

Graphic Design
Country: Japan

Cover Design: Nagai Kazumasa

04.1962

Typographische Monatsblätter
Schweizer Graphische Mitteilungen
Revue suisse de l'Imprimerie
Nr. 4, April/Avril 1962
81. Jahrgang
Herausgegeben vom
Schweizerischen Typographenbund
zur Förderung der Berufsbildung
Editée par la Fédération suisse
des typographes
pour l'éducation professionnelle
Sondernummer: Der Kleinoffsetdruck
Numéro spécial: La petite offset

TM (Typographische Monatsblätter)
Country: Switzerland

Cover Design:
André Gürtler, Bruno Pfäffli
Courtesy of syndicom

05.1962

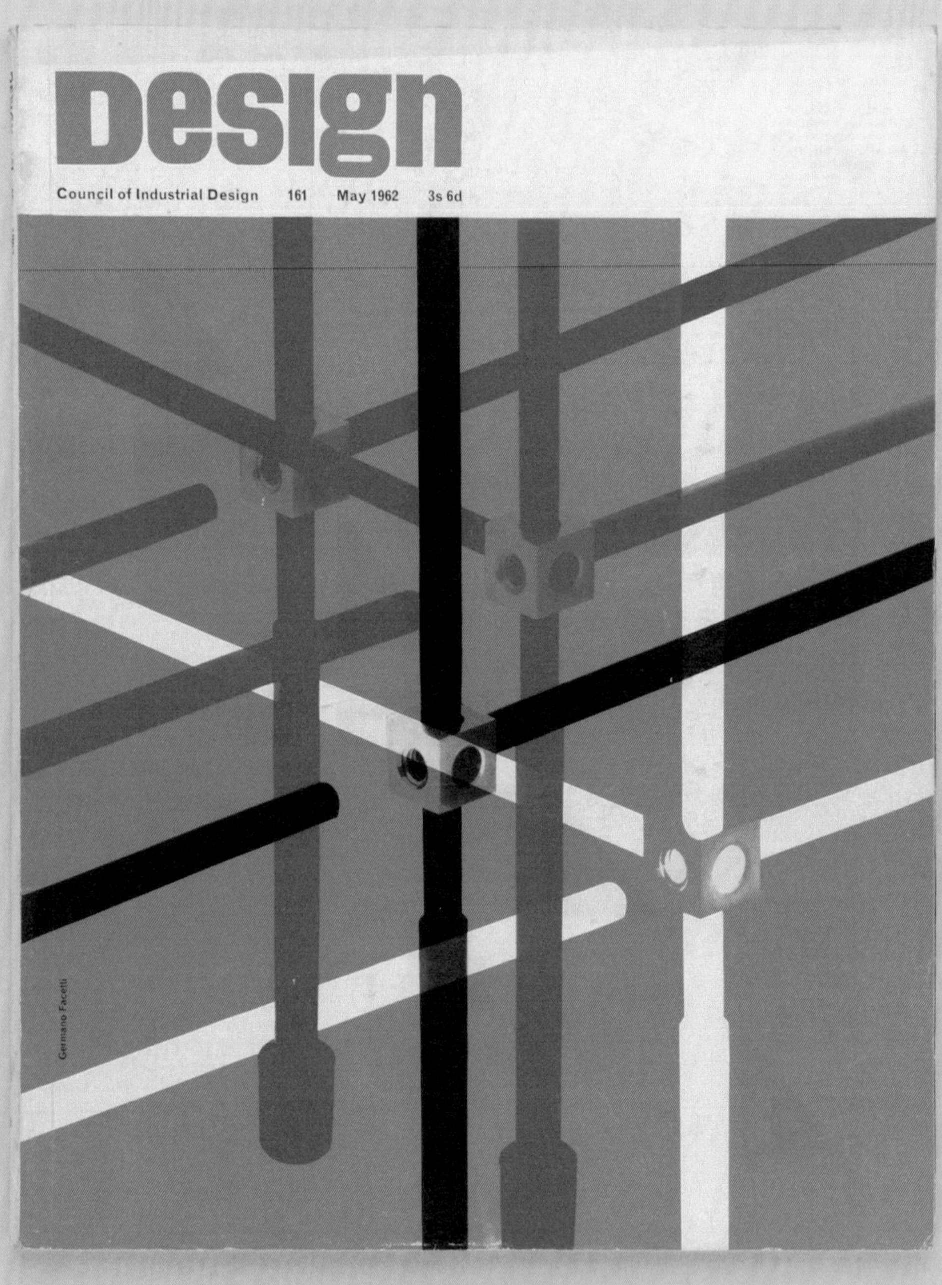

Design
Country: UK

Cover Design: Germano Facetti

Gebrauchsgraphik
Country: Germany

Art Director: Hans Kuh

06.1962

Design
Country: UK

Cover Design: Hans Schleger

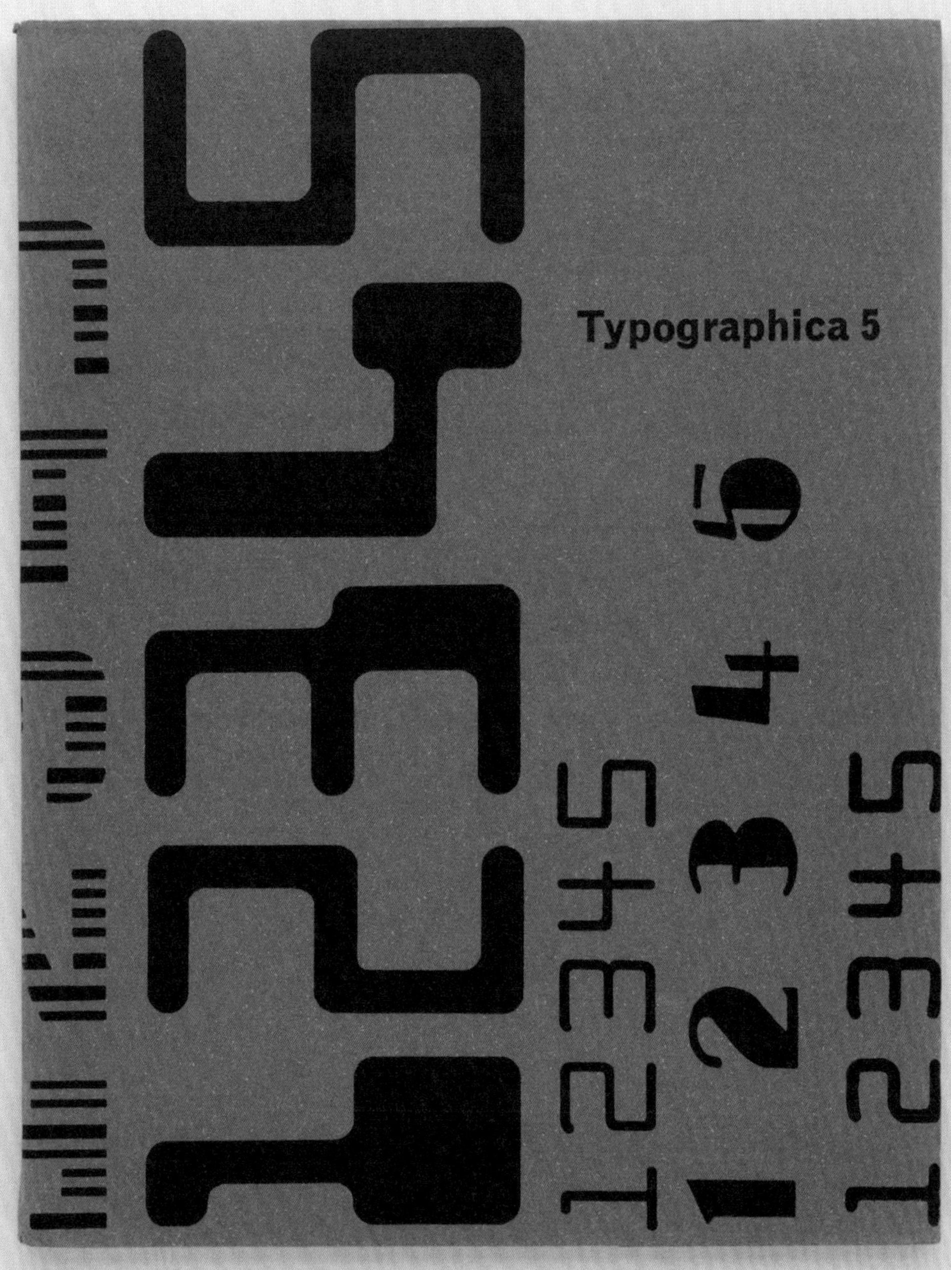

Typographica
Country: UK

Cover Design: Herbert Spencer

Idea
Country: Japan

Cover Design: Ivan Chermayeff

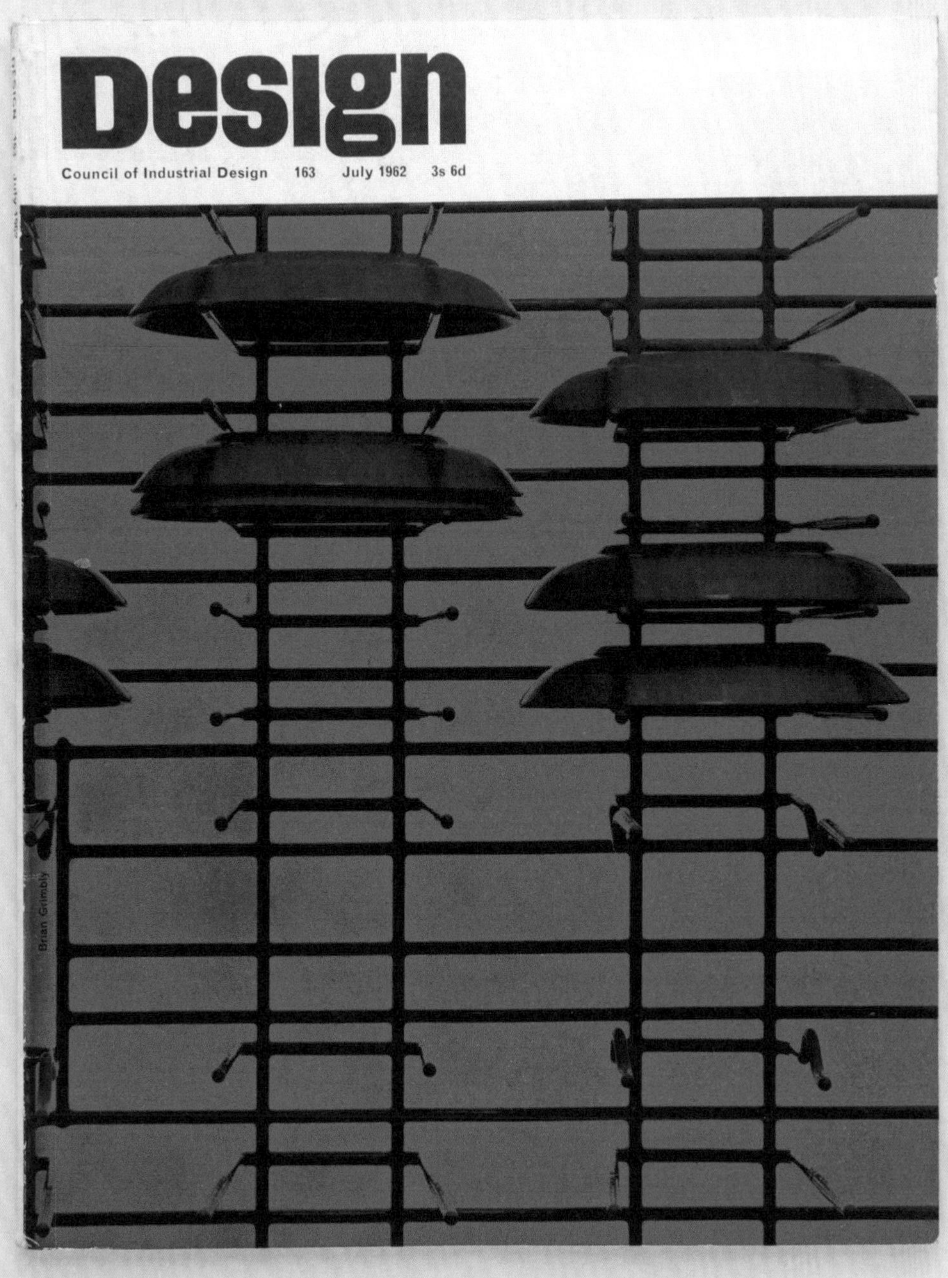

Design
Country: UK

Cover Design: Brian Grimbly

07.1962

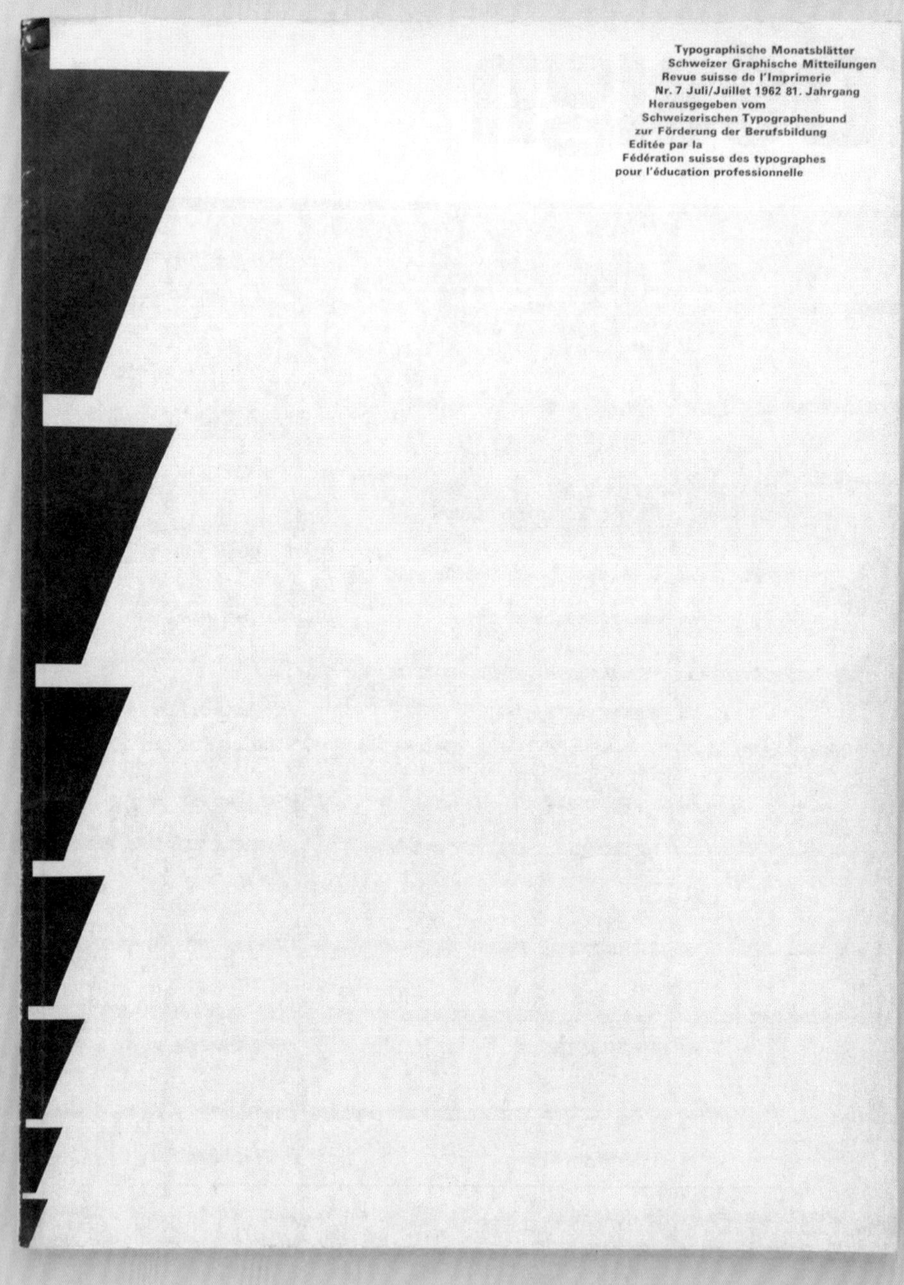

TM (Typographische Monatsblätter)
Country: Switzerland

Cover Design:
André Gürtler, Bruno Pfäffli
Courtesy of syndicom

Design

Council of Industrial Design 164 August 1962 3s 6d

Carter

Design
Country: UK

Cover Design: Larry Carter

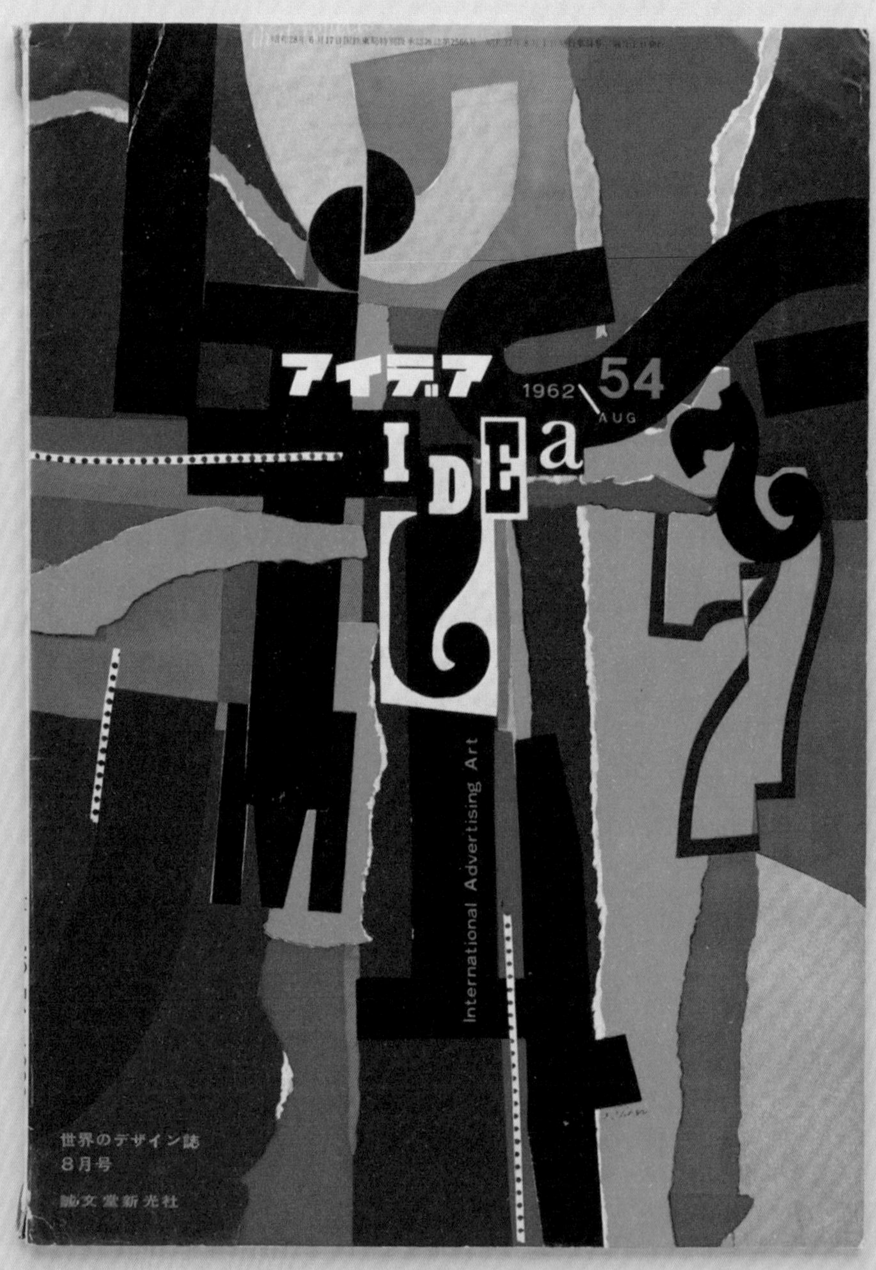

Idea
Country: Japan

Cover Design:
Fletcher Roger Sliker

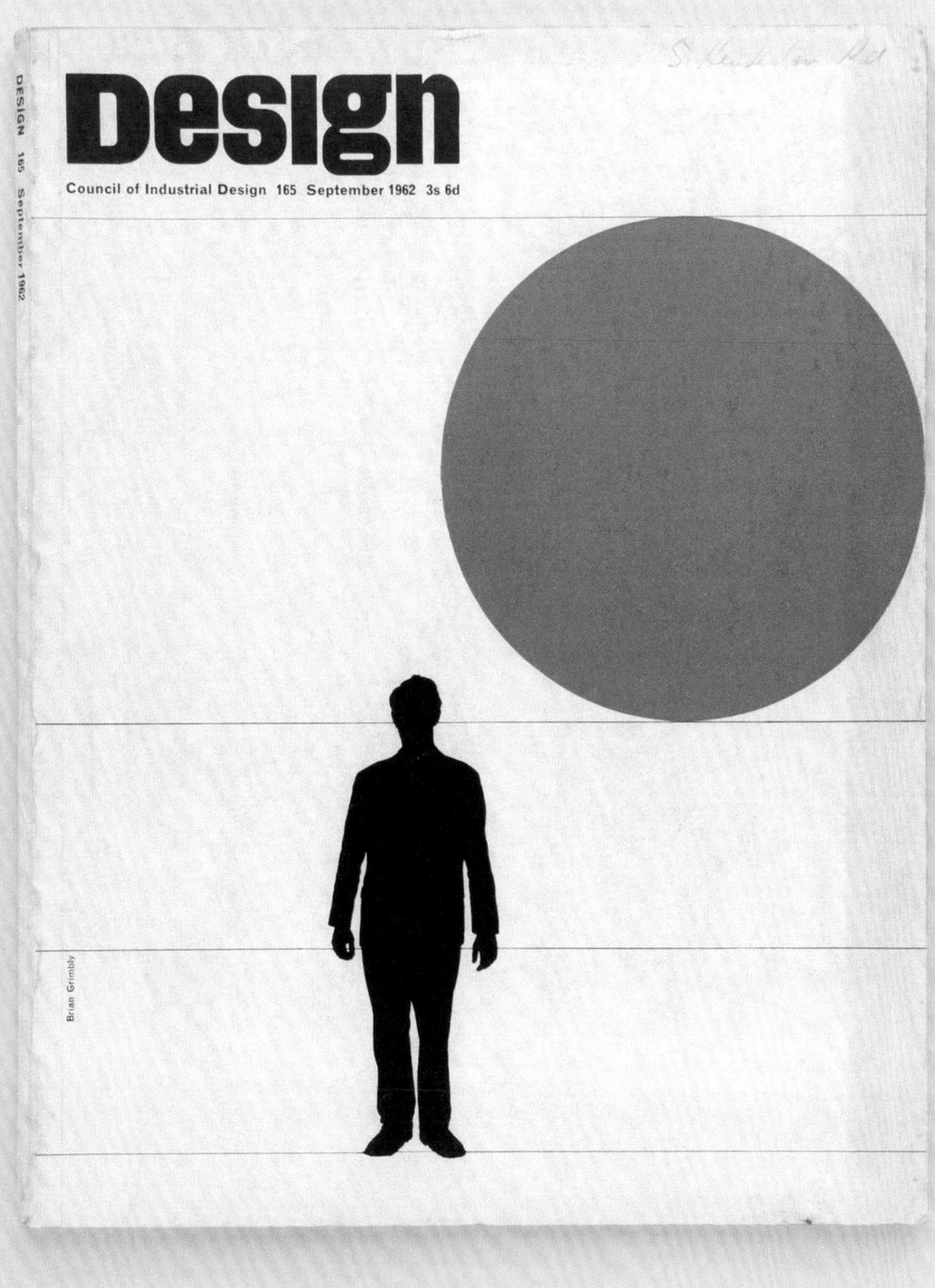

Design
Country: UK

Cover Design: Brian Grimbly

09.1962

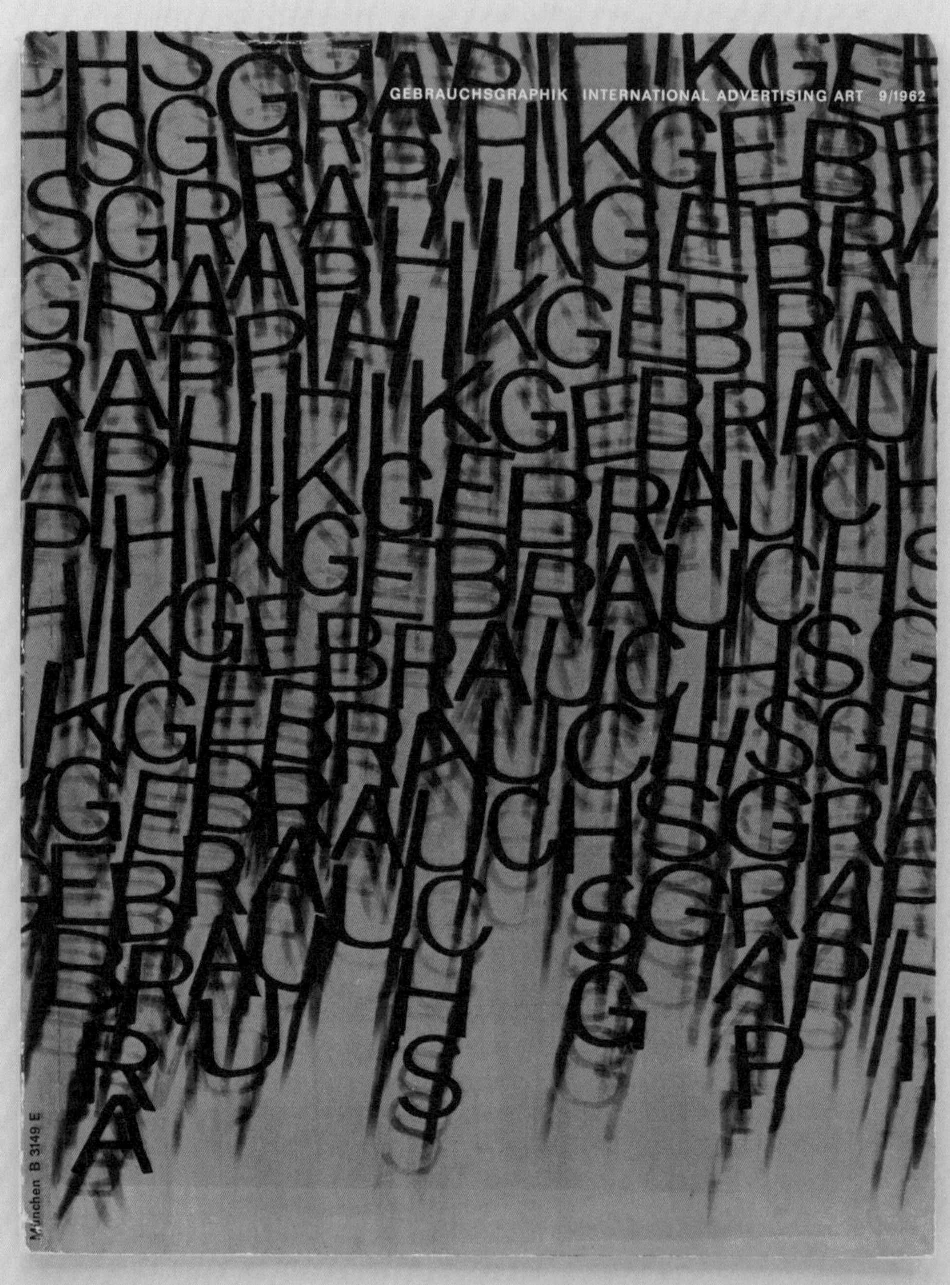

GEBRAUCHSGRAPHIK INTERNATIONAL ADVERTISING ART 9/1962
München B 3149 E

Gebrauchsgraphik
Country: Germany

Art Director: Hans Kuh

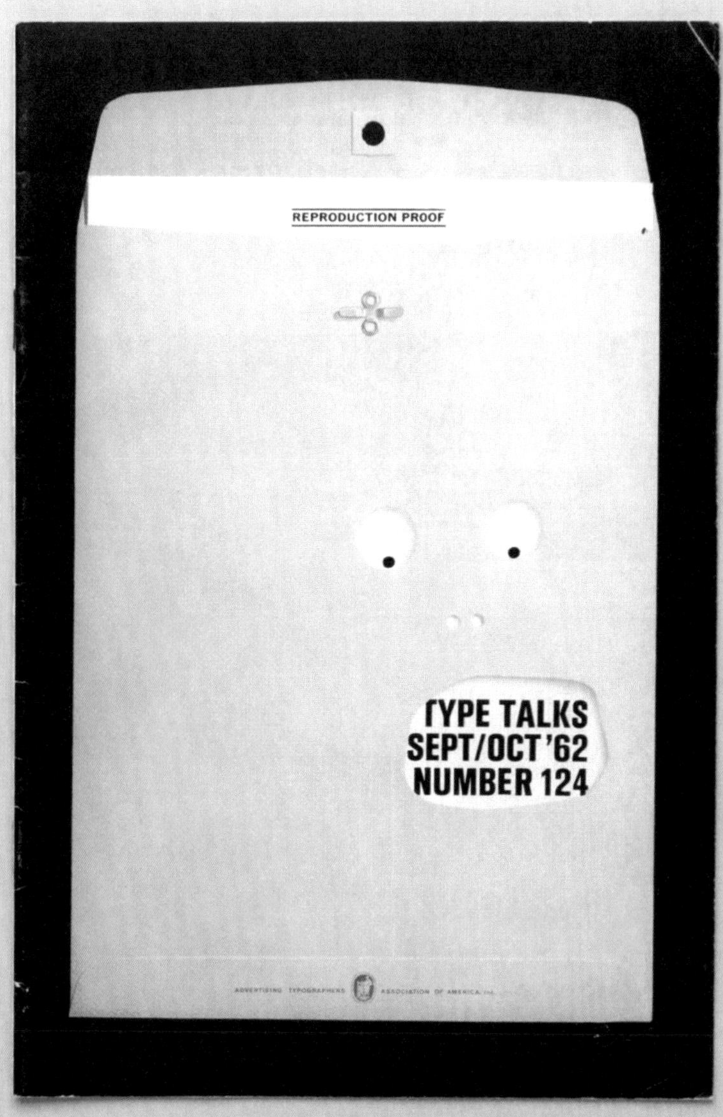

Type Talks
Country: USA

Design: unidentified

09–11.1962

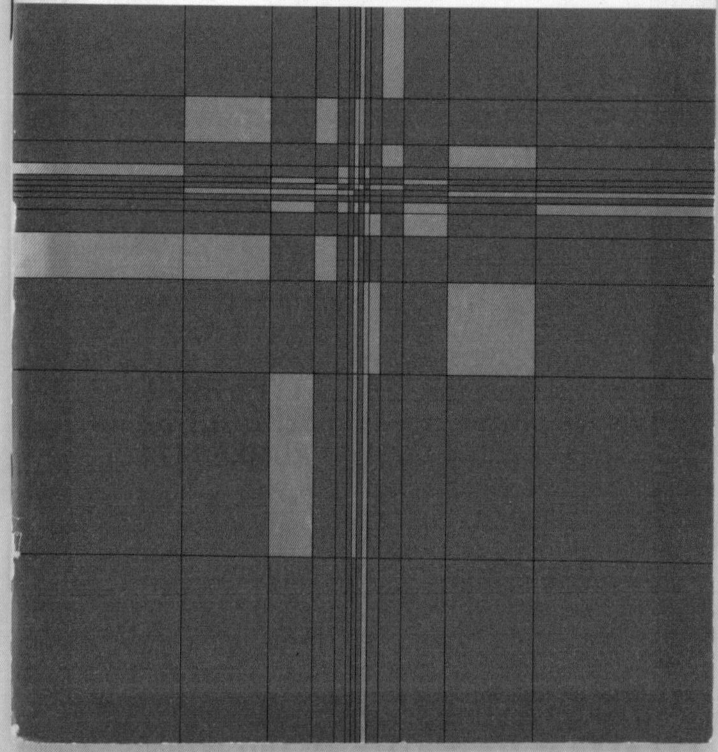

Industrial Art News
Country: Japan

Cover Design:
Miyabayashi Michio

Idea
Country: Japan

Cover Design: Tadashi Masuda

10.1962

ulm 6

Zeitschrift der Hochschule für Gestaltung

Journal of the Hochschule für Gestaltung

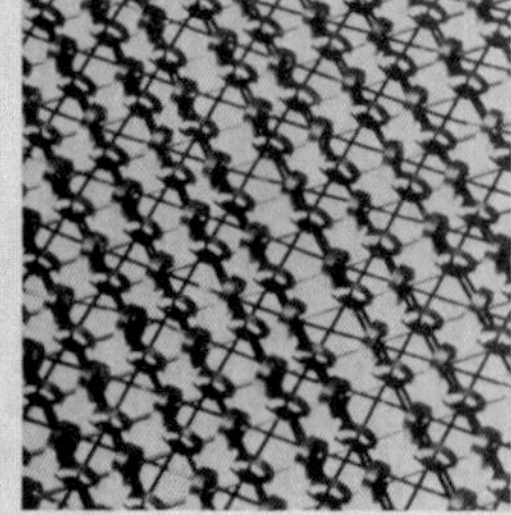

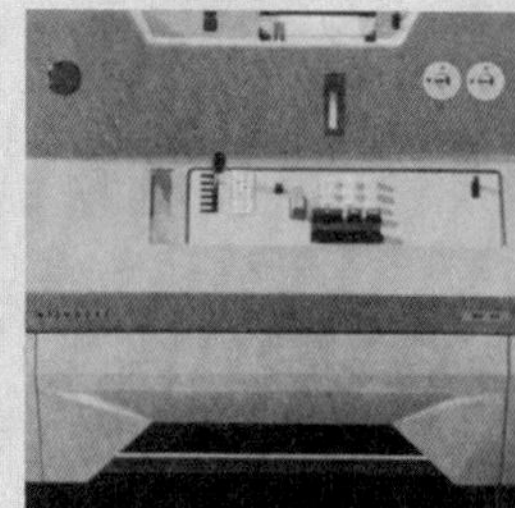

'ulm' – die Zeitschrift der Hochschule für Gestaltung (HfG) – erscheint wieder nach langer Unterbrechung. In der neuen Phase, die mit dieser Nummer beginnt, wird 'ulm' zwei Ziele anstreben: einerseits die Resultate der HfG in den Bereichen der Pädagogik, Forschung und Entwicklung dokumentieren sowie auch die theoretischen Grundlagen aufzeigen, mit Hilfe derer eben diese Resultate entstanden sind; andererseits zu einer Diskussion beitragen über noch offene Fragen der Designphilosophie, Designmethodik und Designpädagogik. Das eine Ziel ist so wichtig wie das andere; denn ein Vorweisen von Resultaten ohne Reflexion wird zu einer bloßen Selbstdarstellung, und eine Reflexion ohne Beleg zu einer bloßen Spekulation.

'ulm' – the journal of the Hochschule für Gestaltung (HfG) – now appears again after a long interruption. In the new series, starting with this edition, 'ulm' will strive to fulfill two aims: on the one hand it will document the achievements of the HfG in the fields of education, research and development and indicate the theoretical basis with the help of which these same achievements have been attained; on the other hand it will discuss unanswered questions of design philosophy, method and teaching. Both these aims are of equal importance; for a presentation of results without reflection is a mere self-representation, and a reflection without practical achievements is a mere speculation.

Ulm
Country: Germany

Cover Design: Tomás Gonda

11.1962

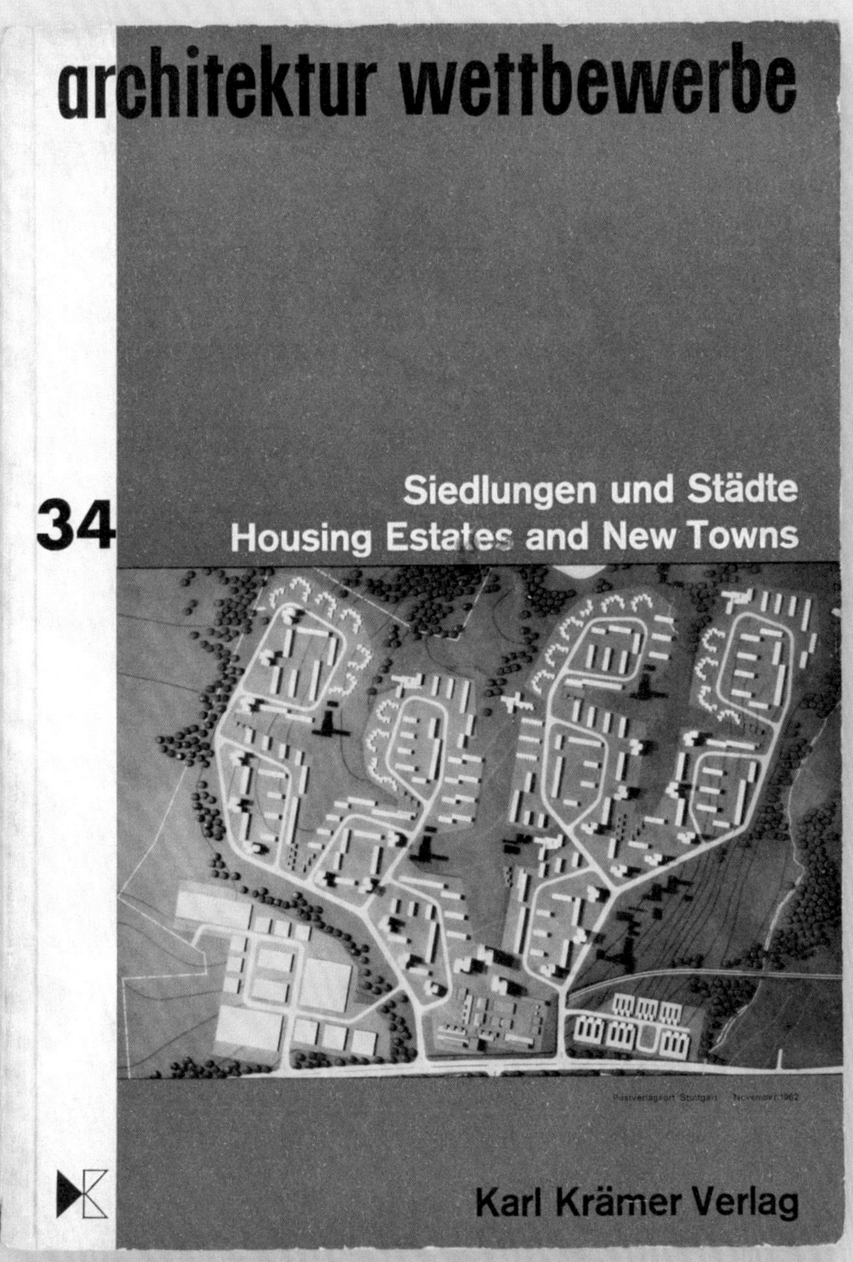

Architektur Wettbewerbe
Country: Germany

Design: unidentified

11.1962

Gebrauchsgraphik
Country: Germany

Cover Design: Pierre Mendell

12.1962

TM (Typographische Monatsblätter)
Country: Switzerland

Cover Design:
André Gürtler, Bruno Pfäffli
Courtesy of syndicom

12.1962

Typographica
Country: UK

Cover Design: Herbert Spencer

12—02.1962

Motif
Country: UK

Cover Design: Peter Blake

Design
Country: UK

Cover Design: Brian Grimbly

ulm 7

Zeitschrift der Hochschule für Gestaltung

Journal of the Hochschule für Gestaltung

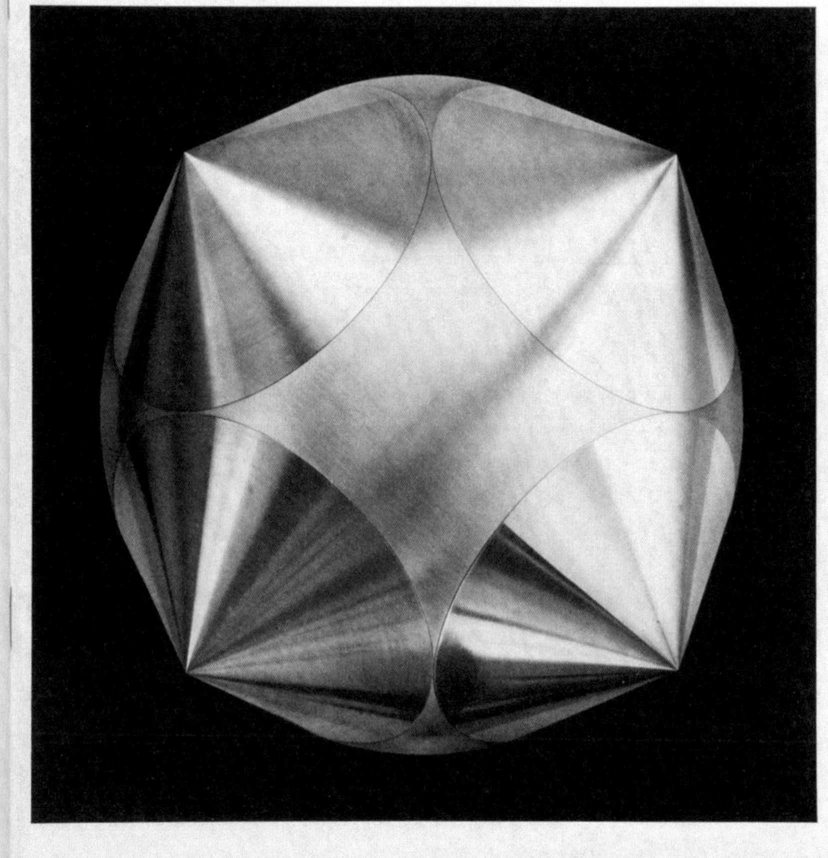

Ulm
Country: Germany

Cover Design: Tomás Gonda

02.1963

Design
Country: UK

Cover Design: Peter Wildbur

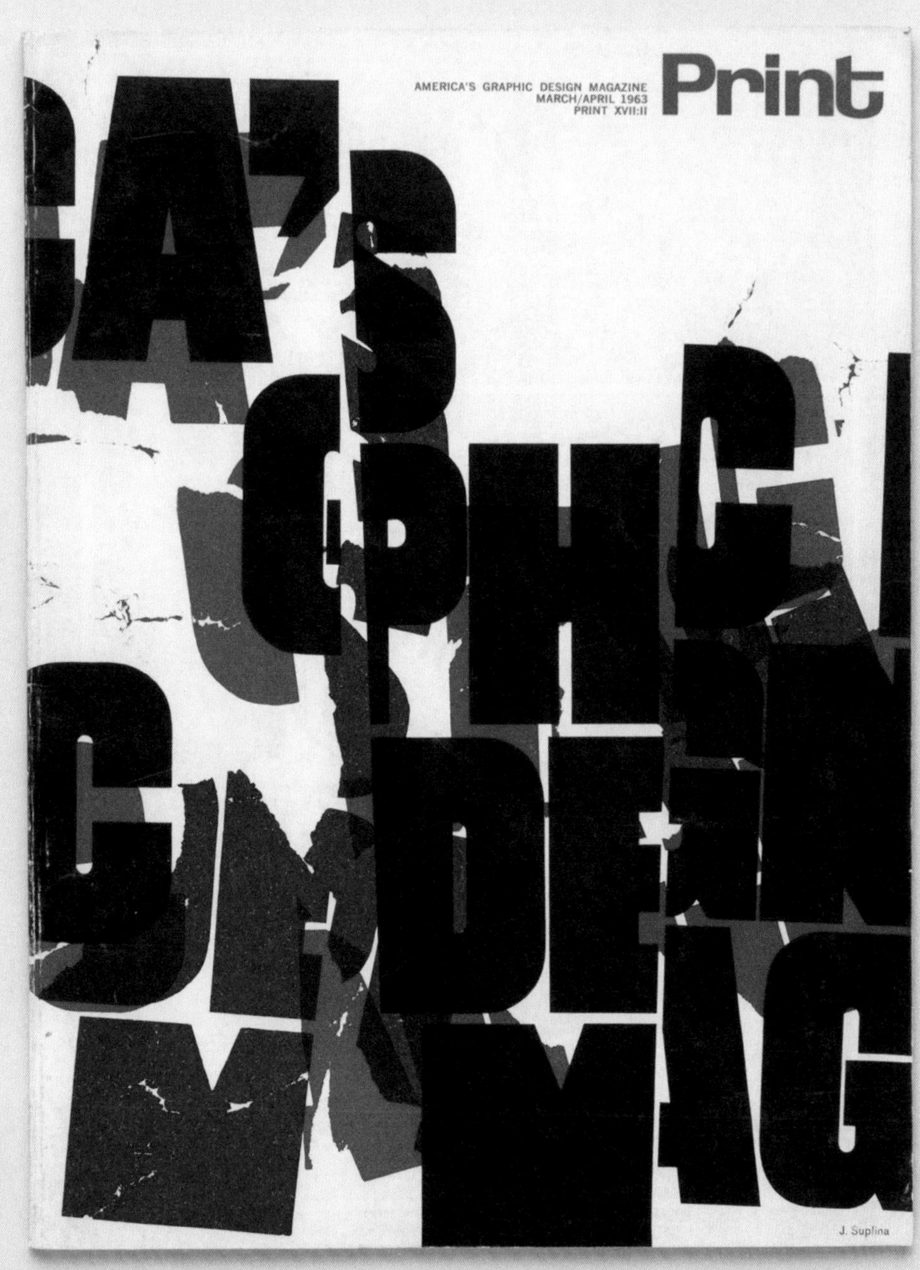

Print
Country: USA

Cover Design: Joseph Suplina

04.1963

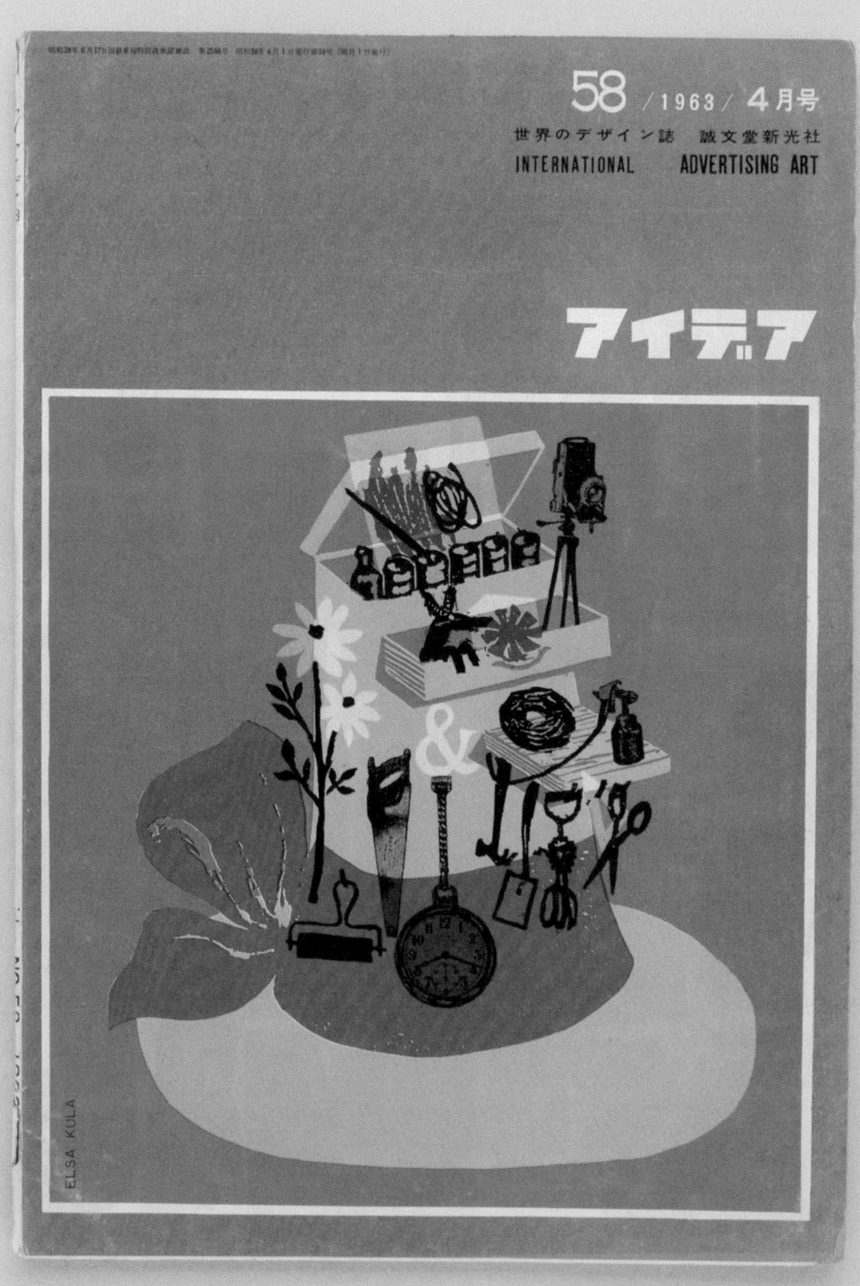

Idea
Country: Japan

Cover Design: Elsa Kula

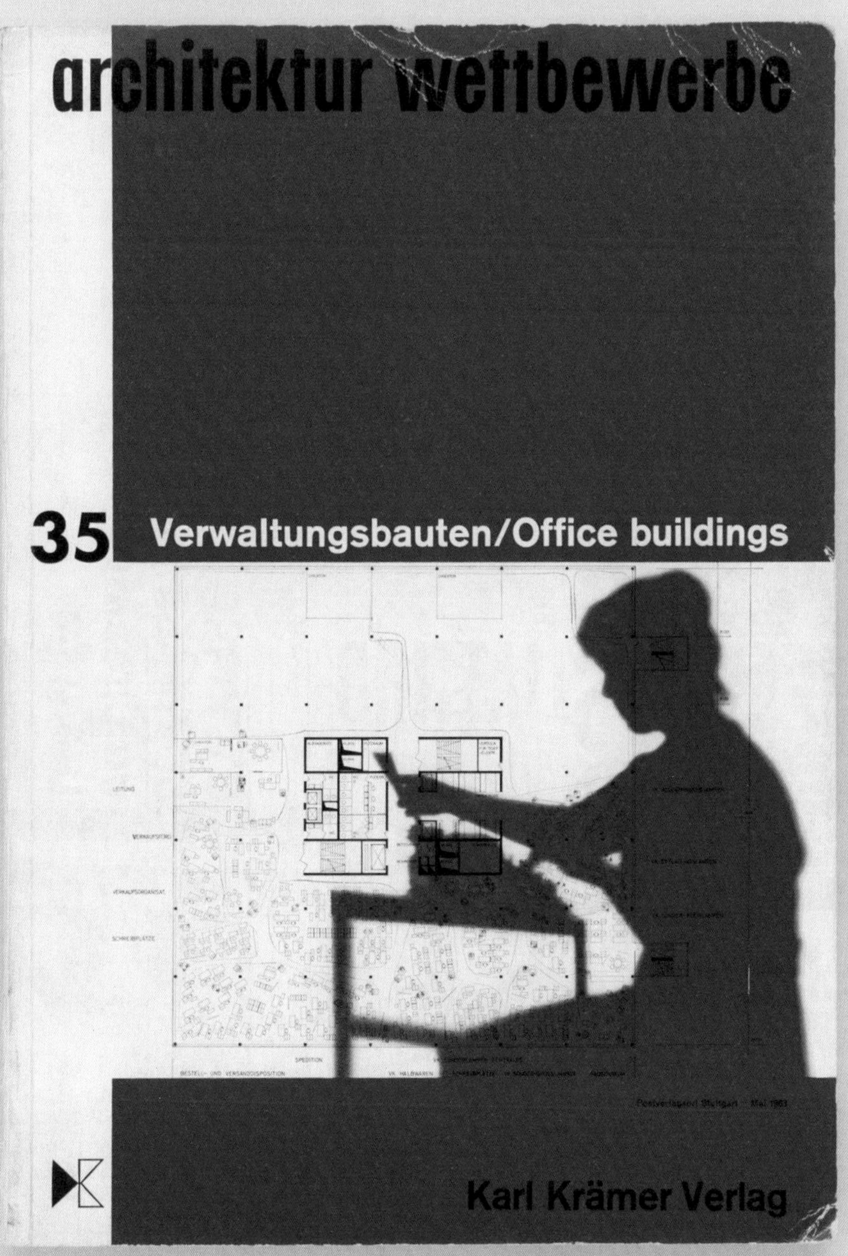

Architektur Wettbewerbe
Country: Germany
Design: unidentified

05.1963

Typographica
Country: UK

Cover Design: Herbert Spencer

Idea
Country: Japan

Cover Design: Fletcher/Forbes/Gill

07.1963

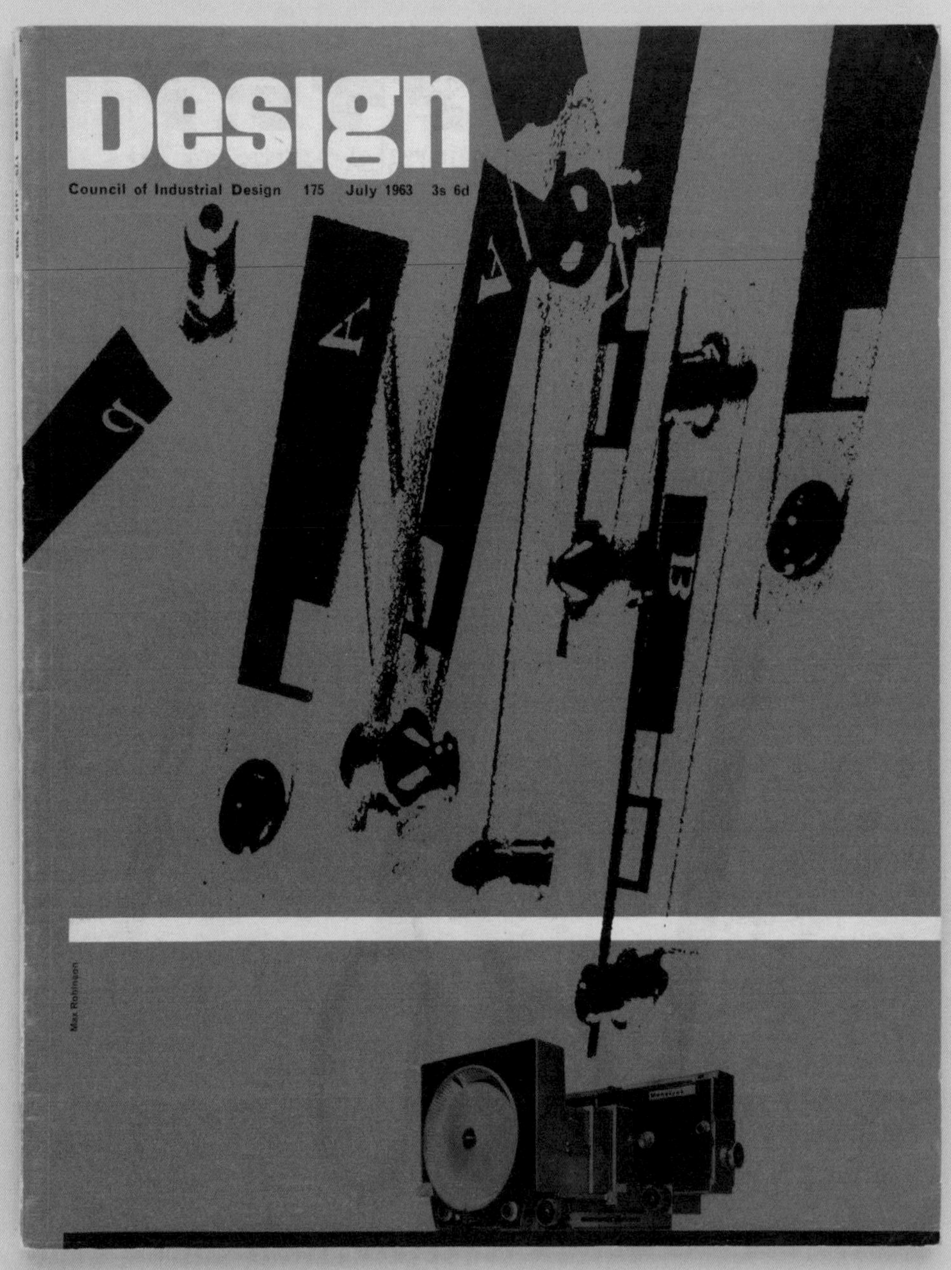

Design
Country: UK

Cover Design: Max Robinson

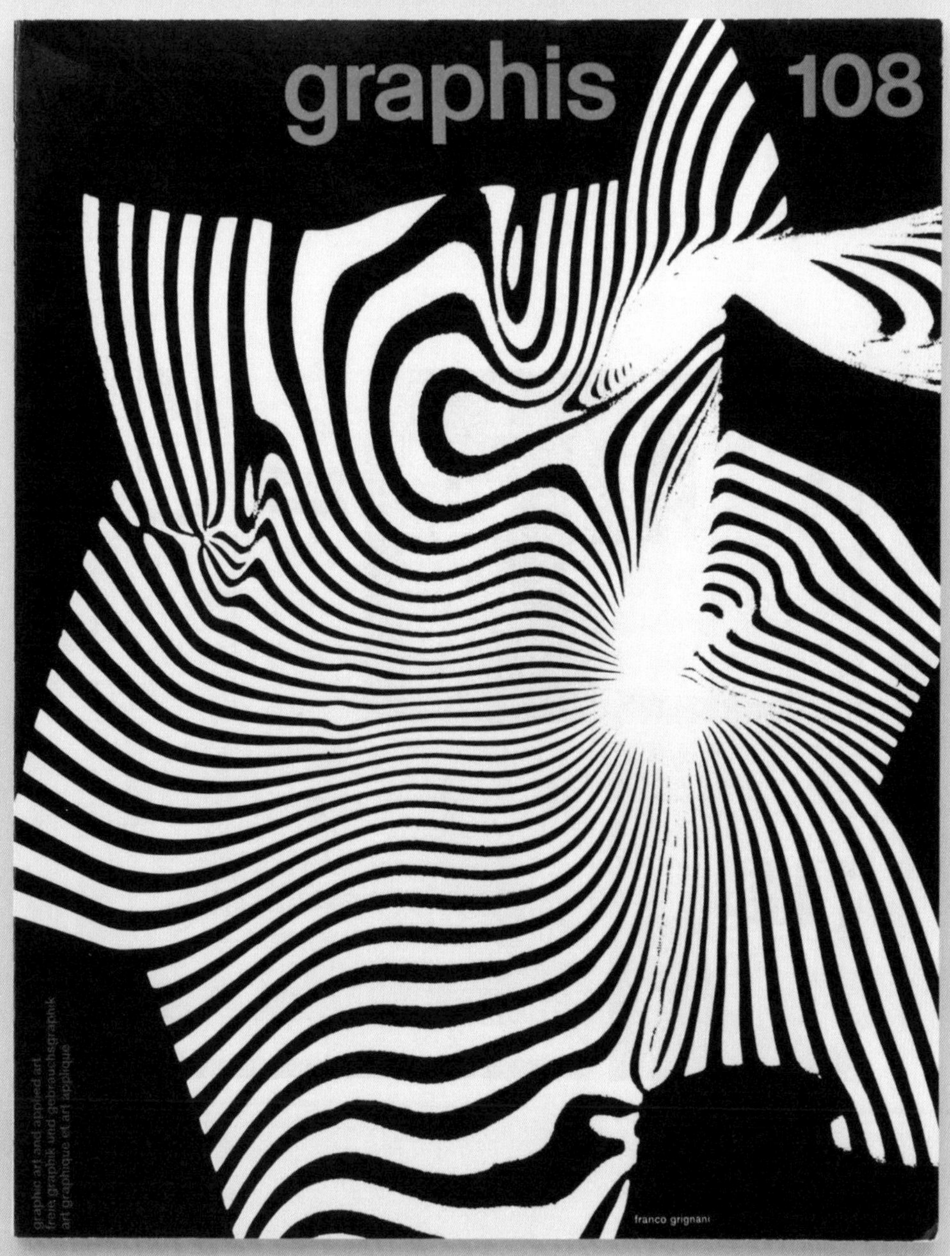

Graphis
Country: Switzerland

Cover Design: Franco Grignani

09.1963

ulm 8/9

Zeitschrift der Hochschule für Gestaltung   Journal of the Hochschule für Gestaltung

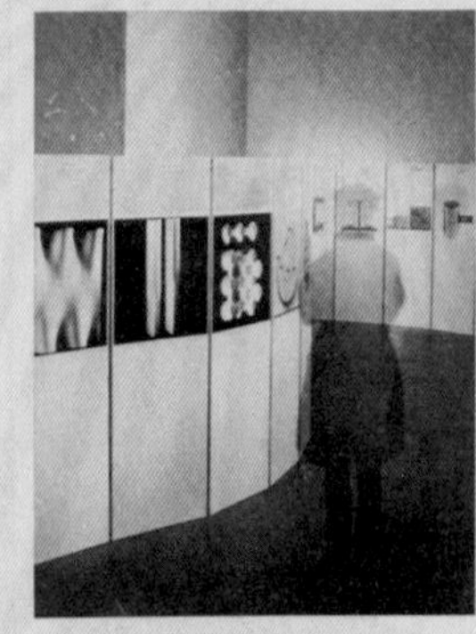

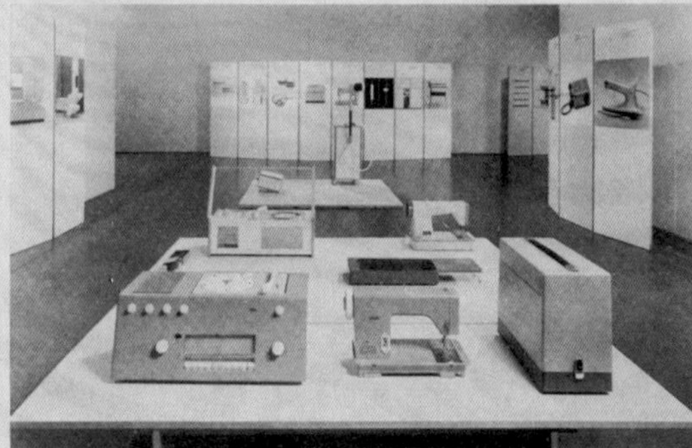

244

Ulm
Country: Germany

Cover Design: Tomás Gonda

Council of Industrial Design 178 October 1963 3s 6d

Cover Design: Anthony Froshaug

Q Some of the early Futurist publication covers look similar to covers of the early Italian design magazines – would you say that this melding of art and design was a defining feature of early and mid-20th-century Italian graphic design?

A It is a common opinion that boundaries between art and design in Italy have always been blurred. I'm not totally convinced that this is a defining feature of the Italian graphic design scene, but for sure, early Italian graphic designers usually had a background in fine arts and came from artistic movements. Many, indeed, were members of Futurism. In particular, exponents of the 'Second Futurism' were ideologically convinced that artists should engage with designing everyday objects and graphics. The influence of Futurism in the work of Italian graphic designers during the interwar years is undeniable. Yet, it was not the only one. *Campo Grafico* (1933–39, Italy), for example, was actually much more inspired by European Modernism and new typography, although its last issue was a kind of retrospective tribute to Marinetti's *Parole in libertà* (1914–15).

Q How did *Campo Grafico* and the other major Italian design publications contribute to the evolution of graphic design in Italy?

A I would say that *Campo Grafico* helped to spread avant-garde ideas to a wider audience of typographers and printing trade workers. Its modernist battles also stressed the need for designers to switch their attention from classic book typography to everyday printed matter. *Linea Grafica* (1945–2011) paved the way for the advancement of a modern, service-oriented graphic design profession in Italy. *Pagina* (1962–65) was an extraordinary platform for the free experimentations of graphic designers. Overall, these – and other – design publications contributed to the advancement of Italian graphic design not only through the quality of their layout and visual features but also by promoting critical debate among designers.

Q Which of the 20th-century Italian graphic design magazines would you recommend to students wishing to study Italian graphic design history?

A Magazines are an extraordinary source for anyone interested in doing research and in understanding graphic design history in Italy. I would recommend all graphic design magazines, as well as specialist periodicals in the fields of advertising, architecture, product design. Among design magazines, *Pagina* probably offers the most immediate window into the 'golden age' of Italian graphic design.

Q For British designers, the short-lived *Pagina* (only seven issues) holds a special fascination. It is said to be the first 'international contemporary graphics magazine'. In your view, does it deserve its special status?

A Definitely. *Pagina* is unique, not only for its international scope but also for its editorial formula. What has always intrigued me about *Pagina* is the inclusion of visual poetry, as well as designers' self-initiated 'verbo-visual experiments', in a publication aimed at addressing professional graphic designers. I think that Bruno Alfieri, founder and editor of the magazine, is a non-designer figure who deserves more attention in the history of Italian design.

Q As the design world migrates to an online existence, what does the future hold for printed design journals?

A I believe that there is still a need for printed design journals. Since 2003, *Progetto Grafico* has played an important role in developing the theoretical and historical discourse about graphic design in Italy. In 2011, when I joined the editorial board, the magazine changed its formula and it is now published as monographic issues. Further changes will appear in the near future.

Carlo Vinti (PhD, currently at the University of Camerino, Italy) is a writer and historical researcher and author/editor of several publications and articles on graphic design in Italy.

Linea Grafica
1945–2011
Italy

Linea grafica

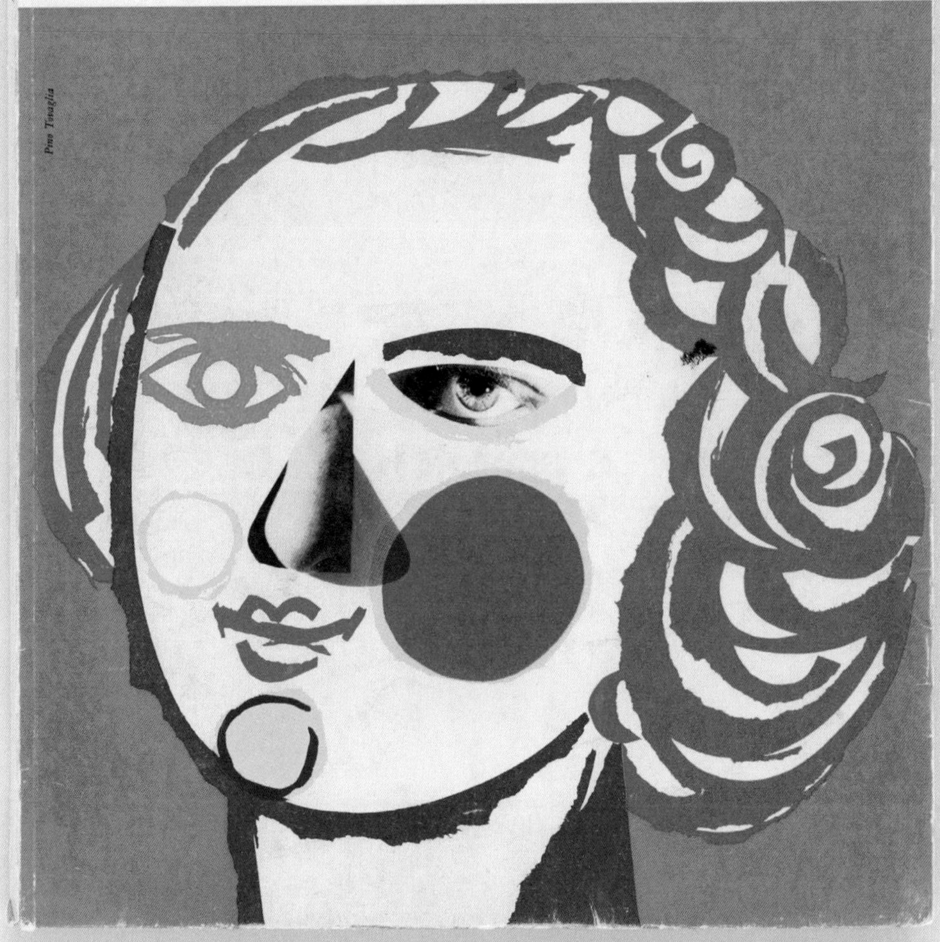

Pagina
Country: Italy

Cover Design: Pino Tovaglia

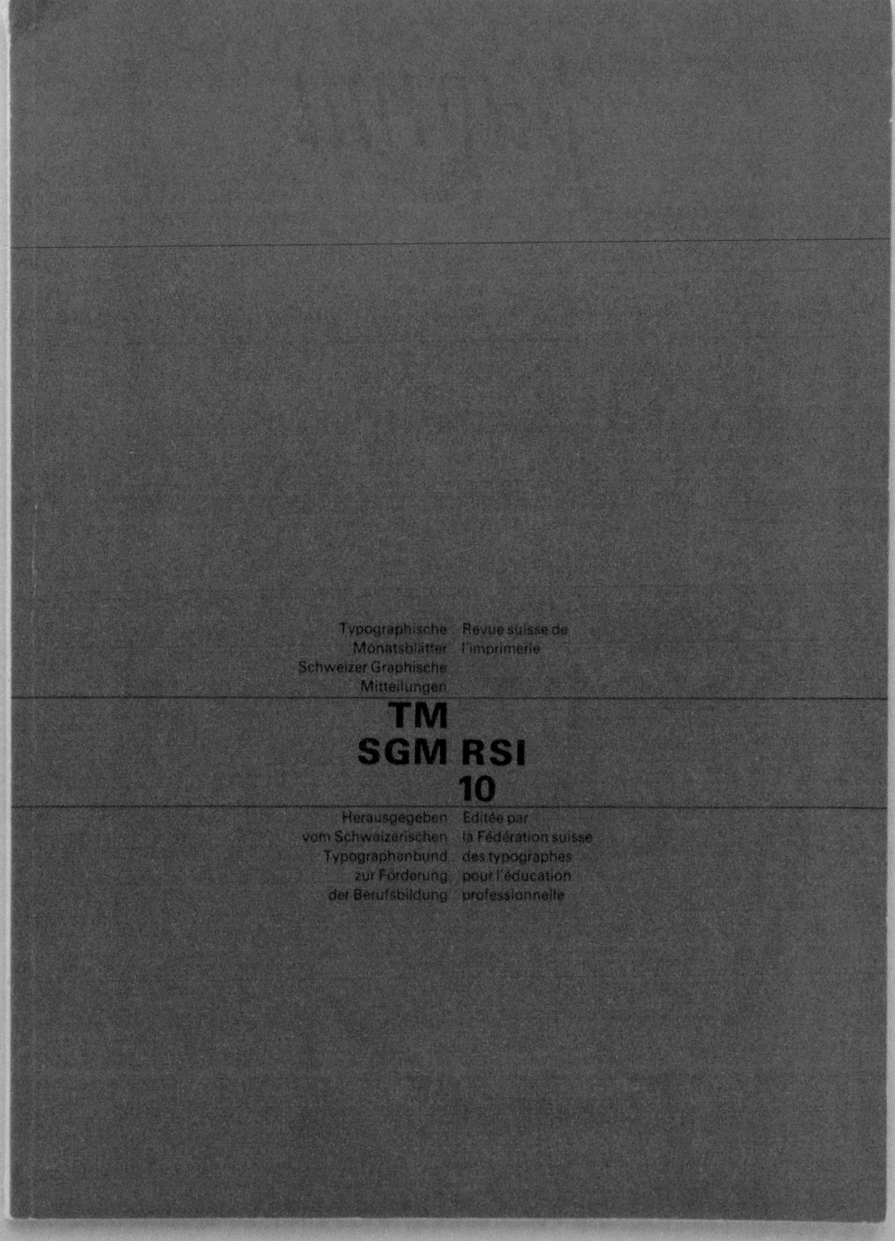

TM (Typographische Monatsblätter)
Country: Switzerland

Cover Design: Felix Berman
Courtesy of syndicom

Design
Country: UK

Cover Photography:
Alfred Lammer

12.1963

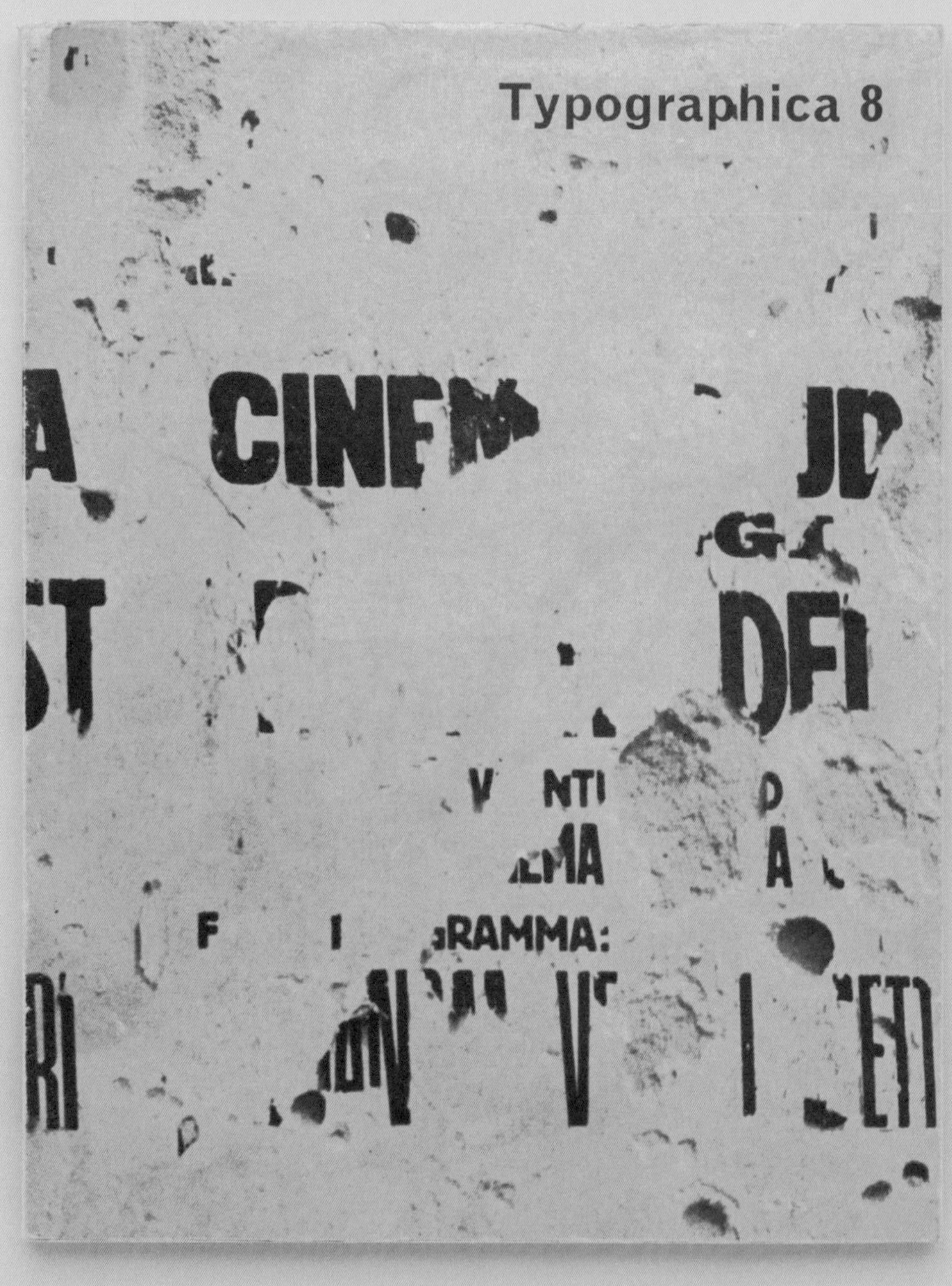

Typographica
Country: UK

Cover Design: Herbert Spencer

Motif
Country: UK

Cover Design: Eduardo Paolozzi

1963

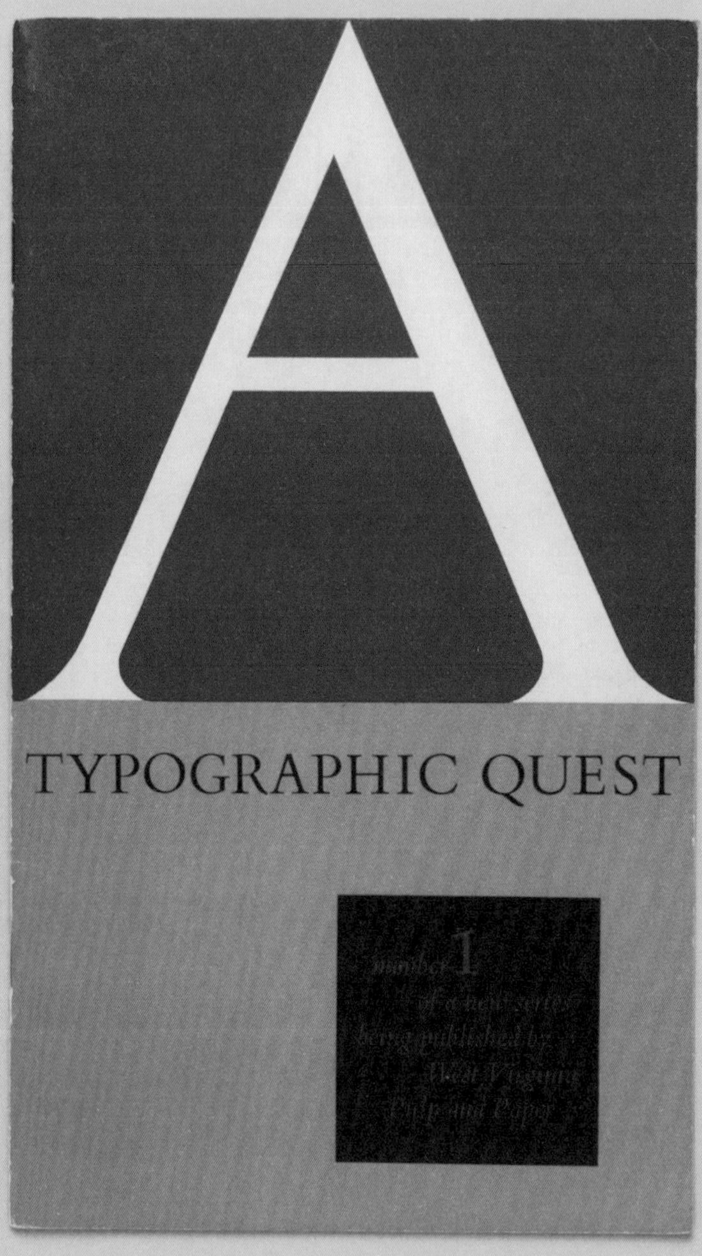

Typographic Quest
Country: USA

Cover Design: Carl Dair

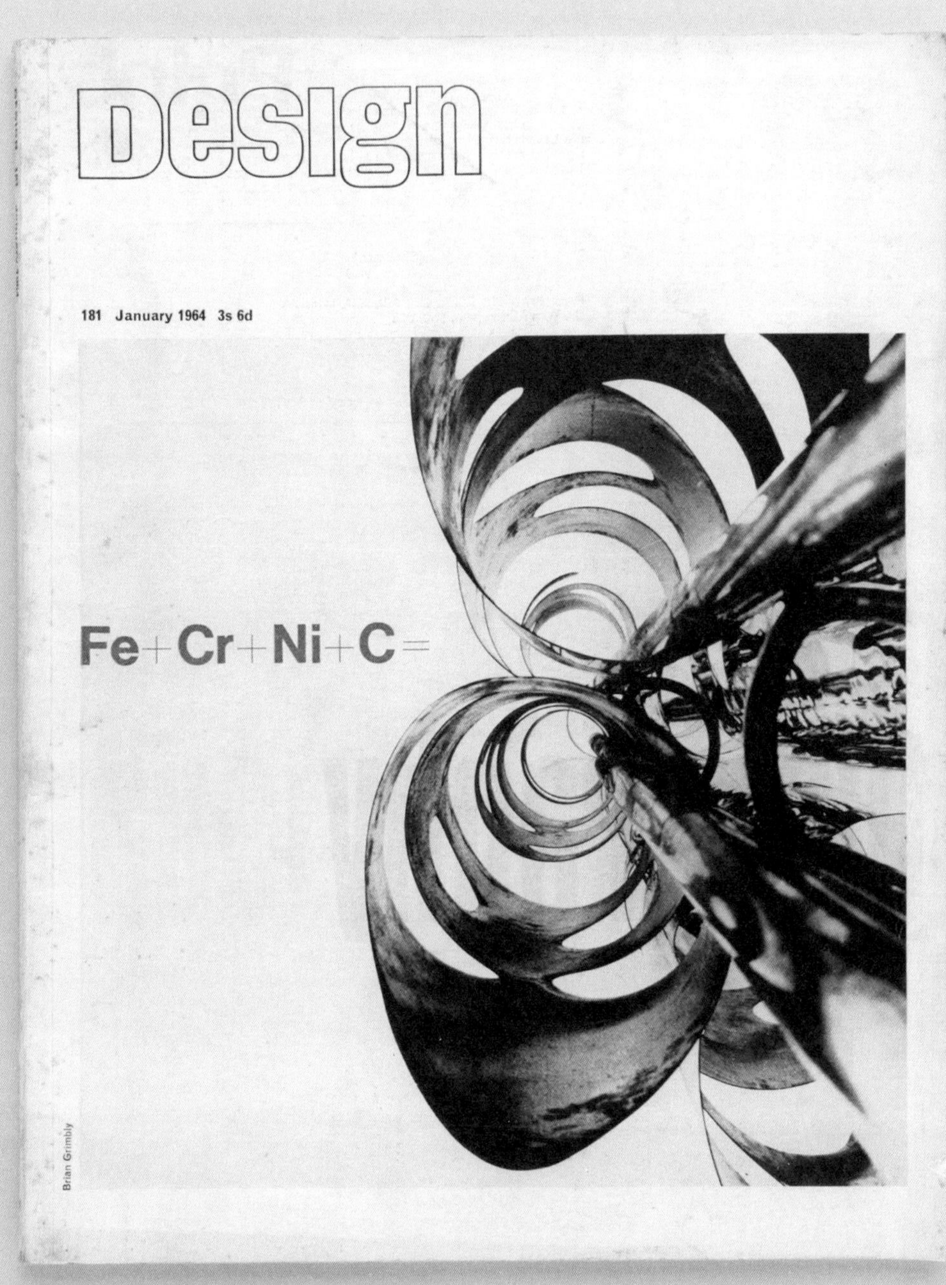

Design
Country: UK

Cover Design: Brian Grimbly

01.1964

AMERICA'S GRAPHIC DESIGN MAGAZINE
JANUARY/FEBRUARY 1964
PRINT XVIII:I

Print

typography 1964 today

Print
Country: USA

Cover Design: Andrew P Kner

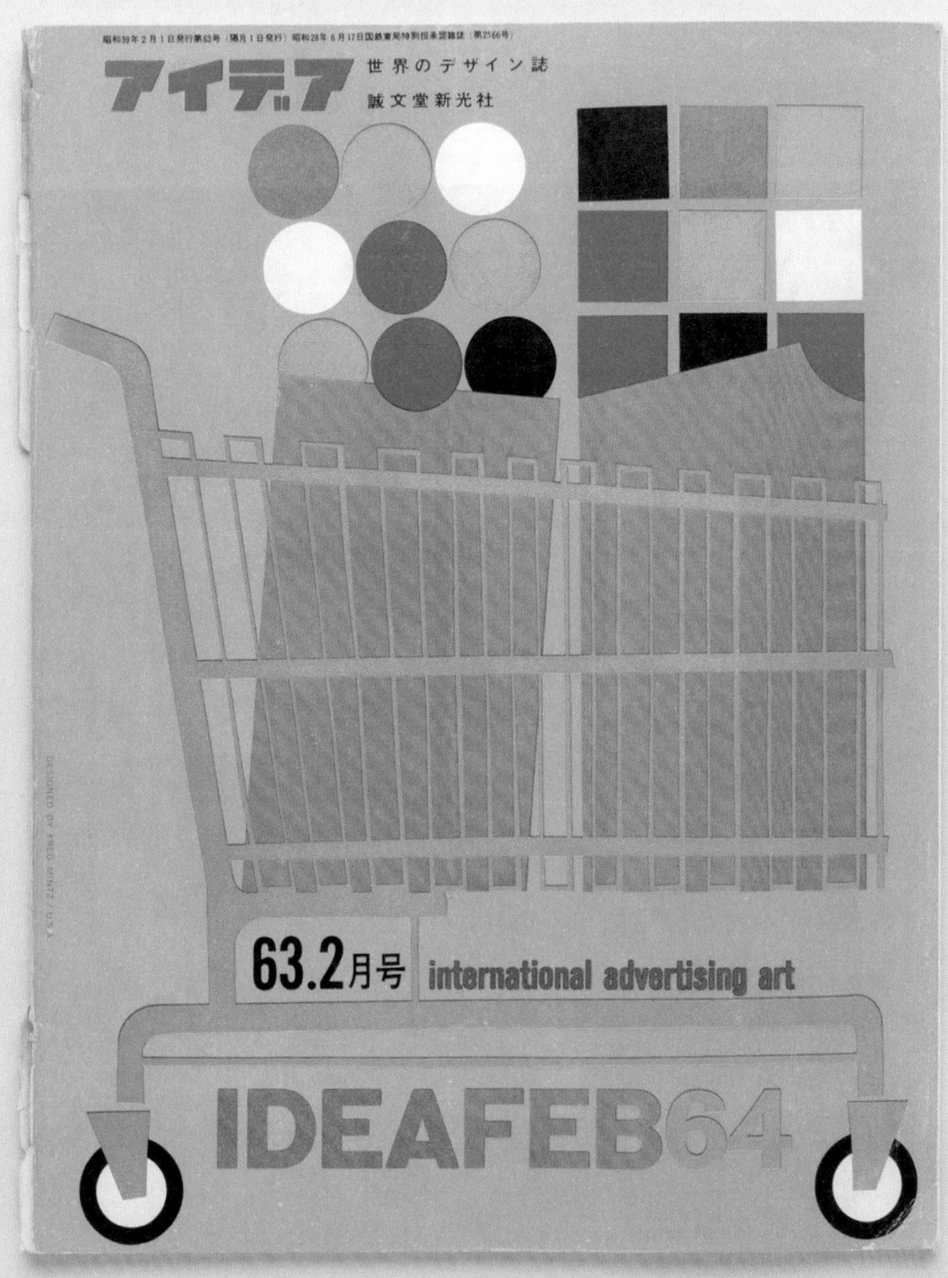

Idea
Country: Japan
Cover Design: Fred Mintz

Idea
Country: Japan

Cover Design: Hiroshi Ohchi

Piet Zwart
P
TM 4
Typographische Monatsblätter Revue suisse de l'imprimerie Schweizer Graphische Mitteilungen

TM (Typographische Monatsblätter)
Country: Switzerland

Cover Design: Fridolin Müller
Courtesy of syndicom

Typographic Quest
Country: USA

Cover Design: Carl Dair

TM	5	Typographische Monatsblätter	Revue suisse de l'Imprimerie	Schweizer Graphische Mitteilungen

Herausgegeben vom Schweizerischen Typographenbund zur Förderung der Berufsbildung
Editée par la Fédération suisse des typographes pour l'éducation professionnelle

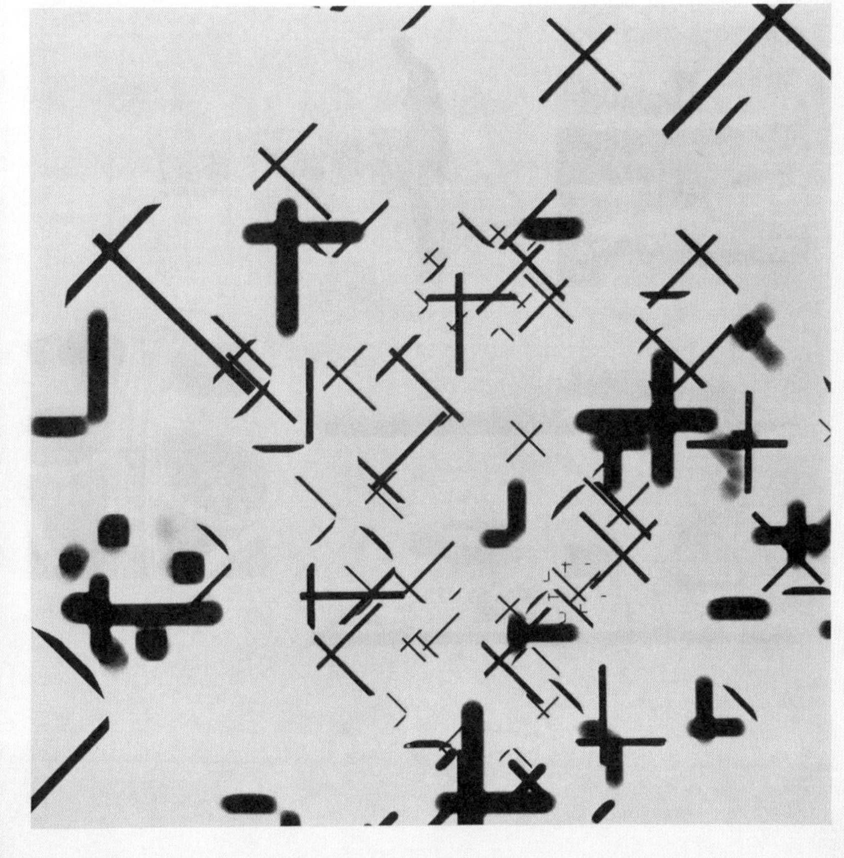

TM (Typographische Monatsblätter)
Country: Switzerland

Cover Design: Felix Berman
Courtesy of syndicom

05.1964

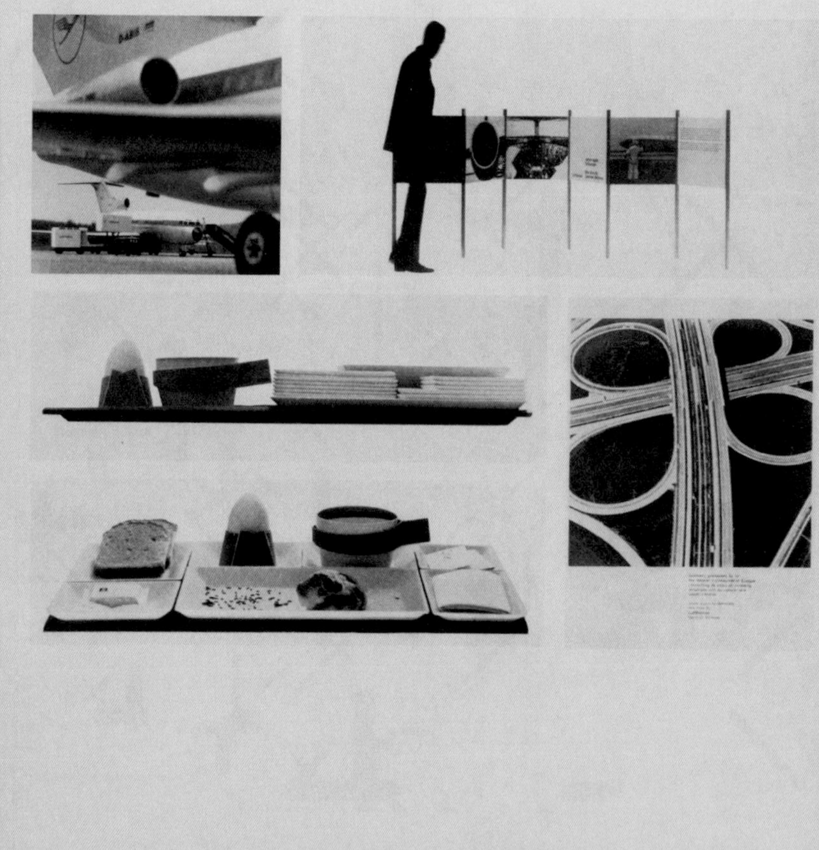

Ulm
Country: Germany

Cover Design: Tomás Gonda

Typographica
Country: UK

Cover Design: Herbert Spencer

PAGINA 5

n. 5 August 1964

Pagina
Country: Italy

Cover Design: Teresa Papetti

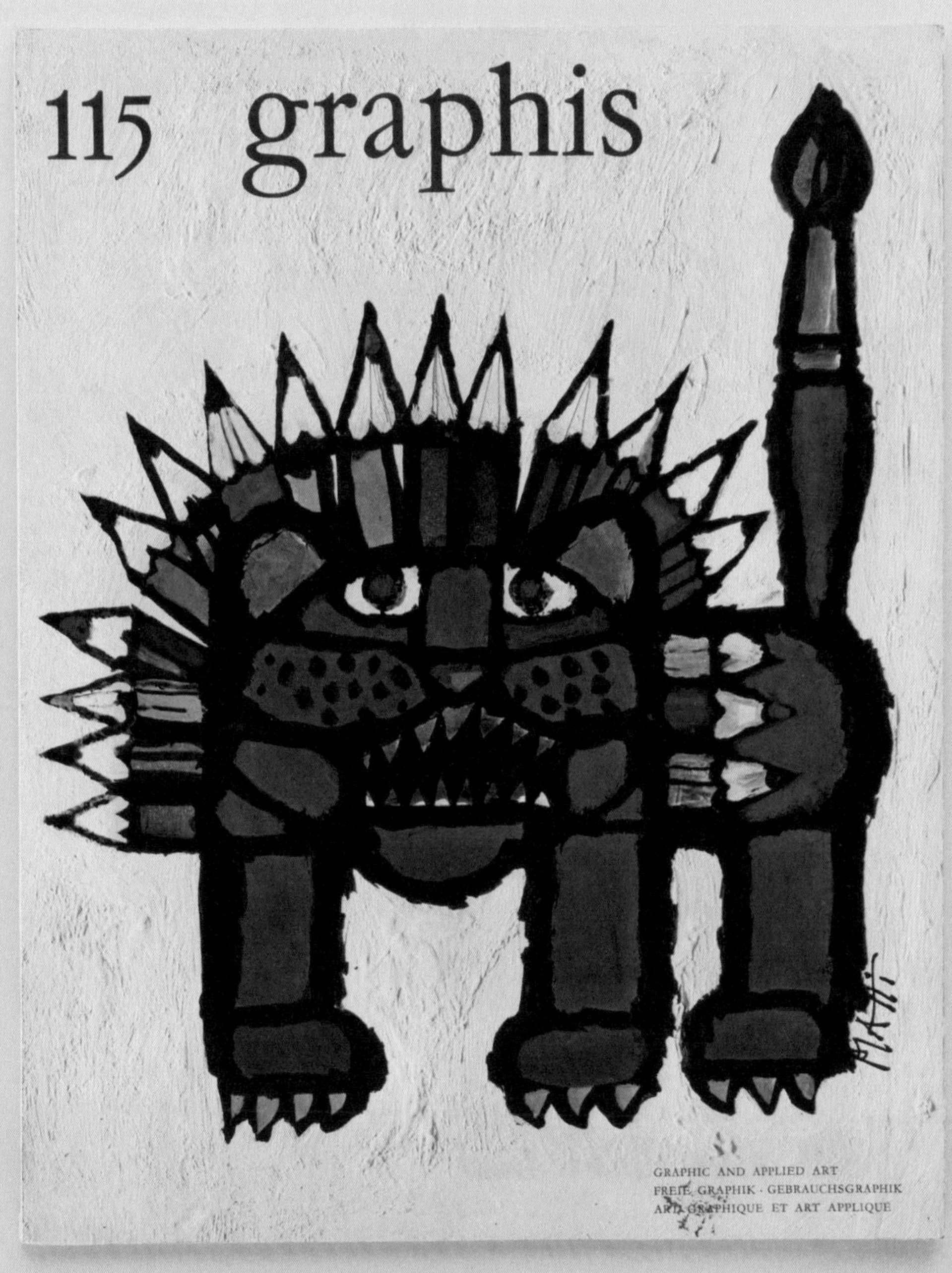

Graphis
Country: Switzerland

Cover Design: Celestino Piatti

11.1964

TM 11 Typographische Monatsblätter Revue suisse de l'Imprimerie Schweizer Graphische Mitteilungen

Herausgegeben vom Schweizerischen Typographenbund zur Förderung der Berufsbildung
Editée par la Fédération suisse des typographes pour l'éducation professionnelle

TM (Typographische Monatsblätter)
Country: Switzerland

Cover Design: Felix Berman
Courtesy of syndicom

Design
Country: UK

Cover Design: Derek Birdsall,
Anthony Froshaug, Brian Grimbly

12.1964

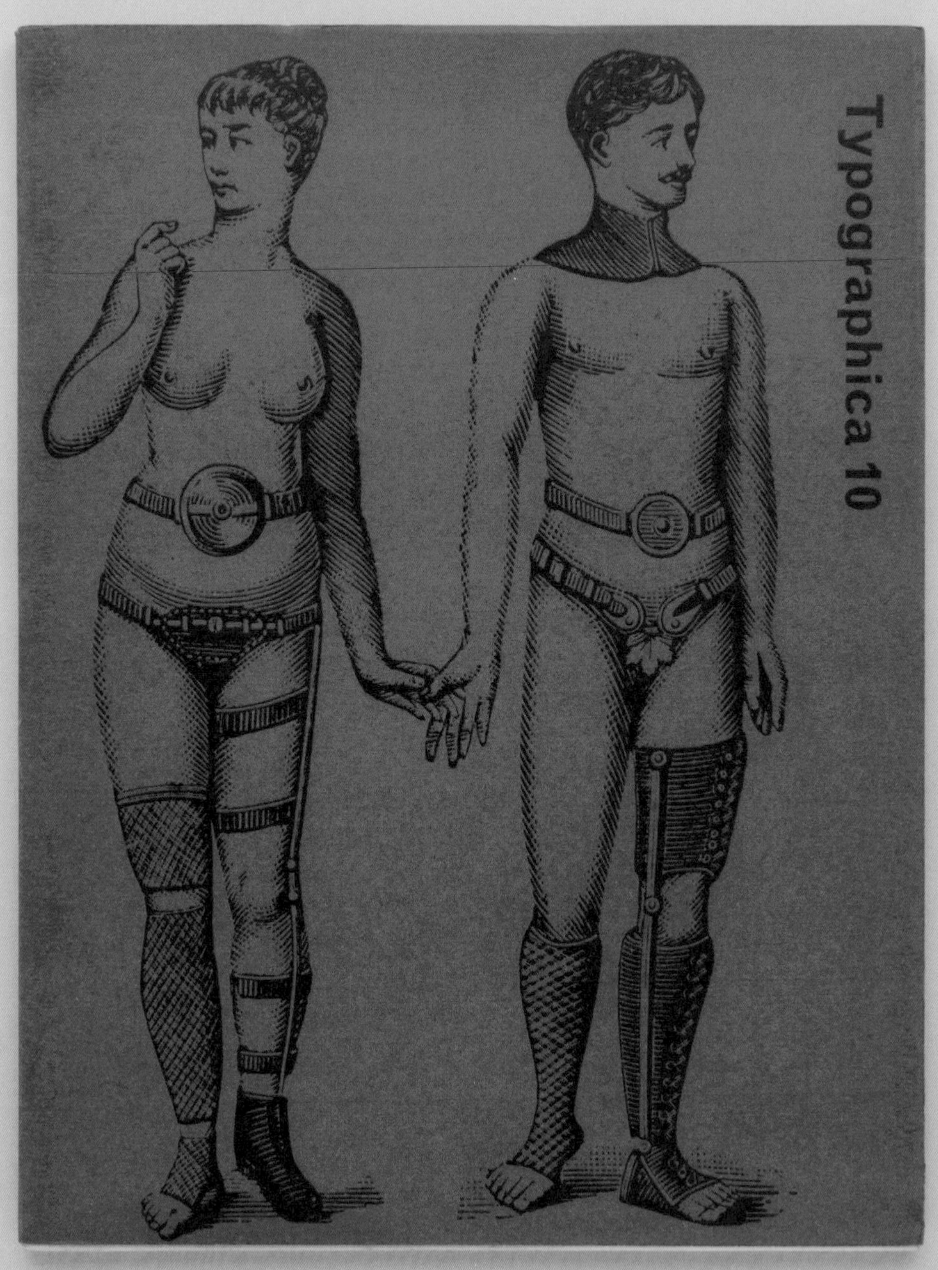

Typographica
Country: UK

Cover Design: Herbert Spencer

TM (Typographische Monatsblätter)
Country: Switzerland

Cover Design: Hans-Rudolf Lutz
Courtesy of syndicom

01.1965

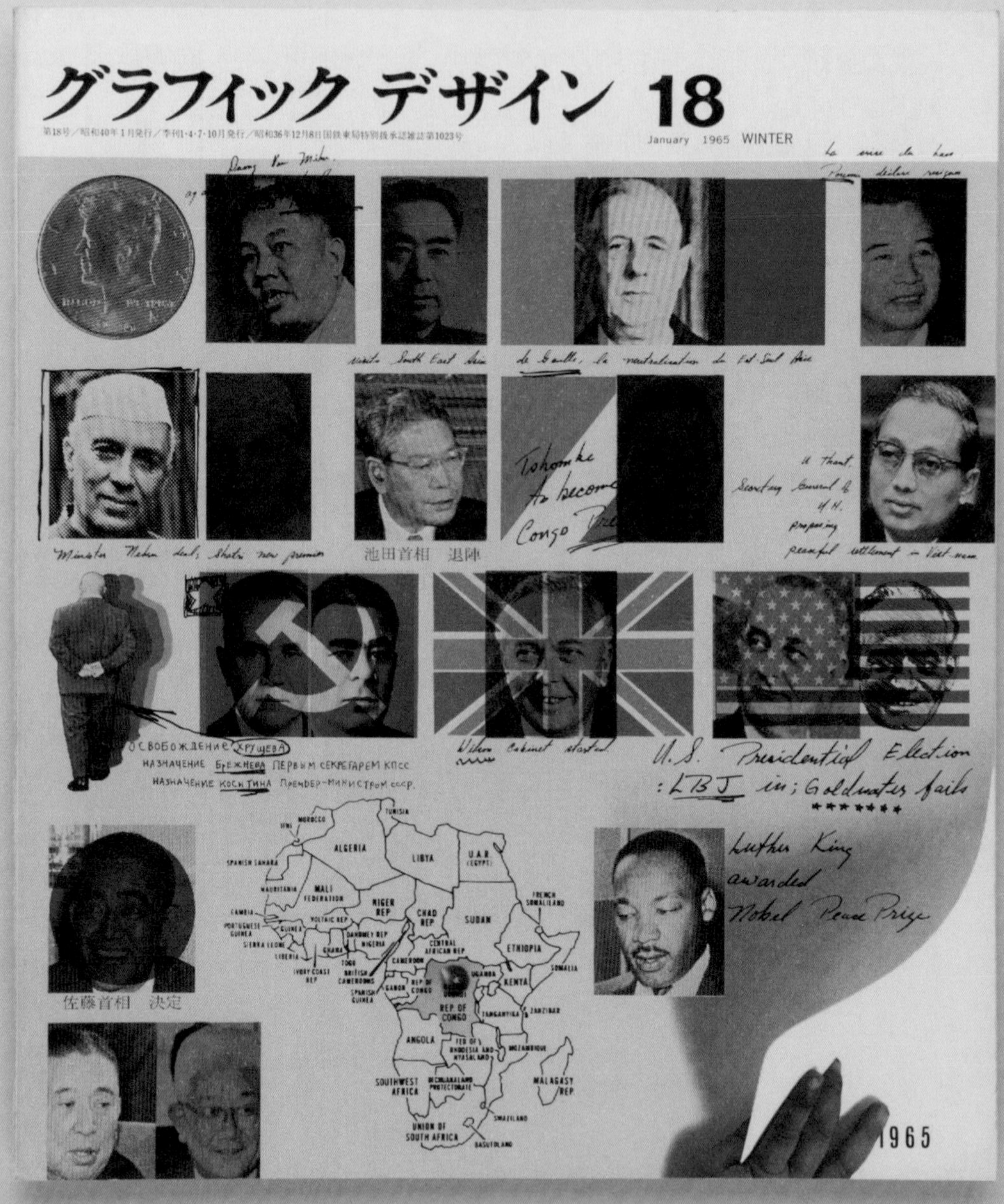

Graphic Design
Country: Japan

Cover Design: Ejima Tamotsu

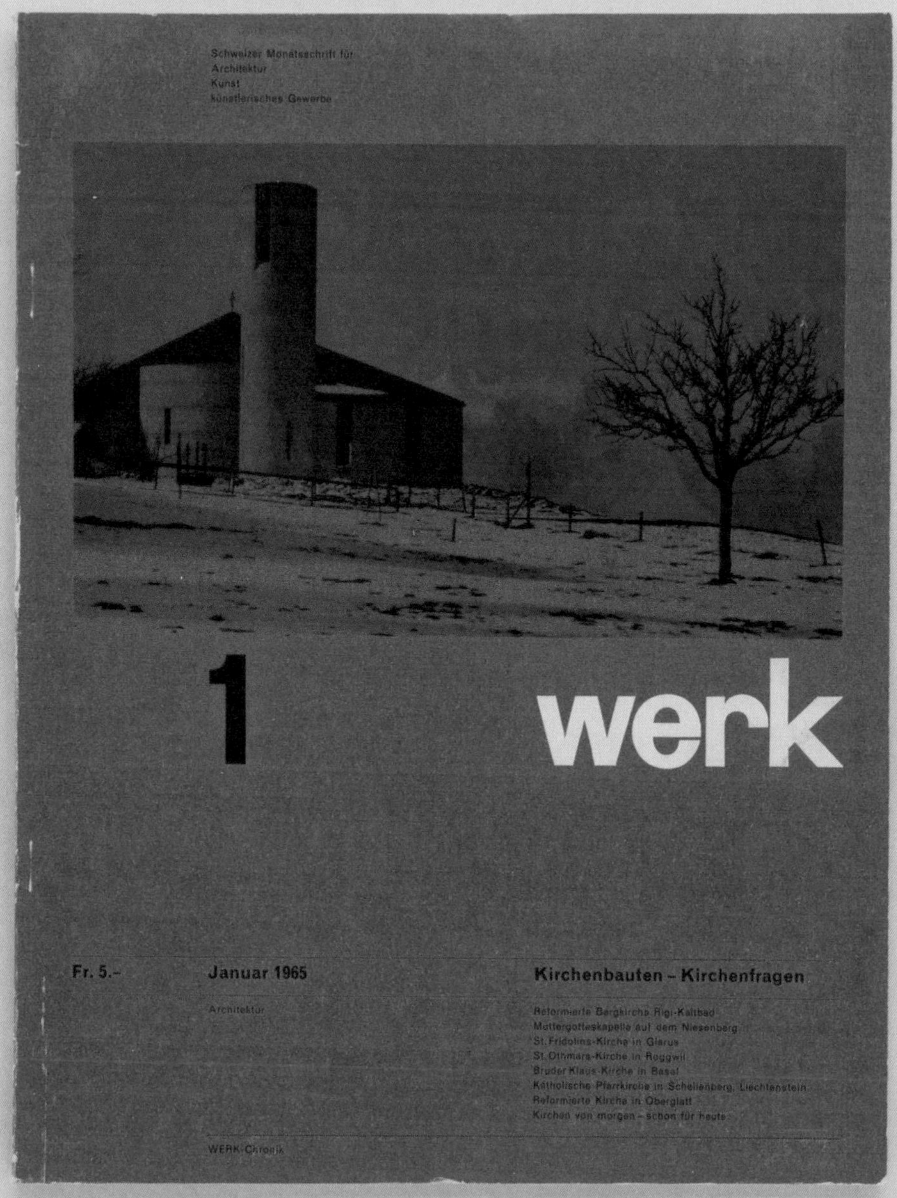

(Das) Werk
Country: Switzerland

Cover Design: Karl Gerstner

Neue Grafik
New Graphic Design
Graphisme actuel

Internationale Zeitschrift für Grafik
und verwandte Gebiete
Text dreisprachig
(deutsch, englisch, französisch)

International Review of Graphic
Design and related subjects
Issued in German, English and French

Revue internationale du graphisme et
des domaines annexes
Parution en langue allemande,
anglaise et française

17
18

Ausgabe Februar 1965

Inhalt

	Inhalt	Contents	Table des matières
Richard P. Lohse, Zürich	Landesflaggen	Flags of the Nations	Drapeaux nationaux
Eckhard Neumann, Frankfurt a. M.	Typografie, Grafik und Werbung am Bauhaus	Typography, Graphic Design and Advertising at the Bauhaus	Art typographique, graphique et publicitaire du «Bauhaus»
Margit Staber, Zürich	Farbe und Linie (Josef Albers)	Colour and Line (Josef Albers)	Couleur et ligne (Josef Albers)
Hans Neuburg, Zürich	Fortschrittliche Fotos der dreißiger Jahre (Anton Stankowski und Hugo Herdeg)	Advanced Photography of the Thirties (Anton Stankowski and Hugo Herdeg)	Photographies progressistes des années trente (Anton Stankowski et Hugo Herdeg)
Hans Neuburg, Zürich	Gestaltung von Packungen	Package Design	La création d'emballages
Fridolin Müller, Zürich	Grafikerausbildung	The Training of the Graphic Designer	Formation de graphiste
Bruno Kammerer, Zürich	Ausstellung ‹Vogelzug›	Exhibition "Vogelzug"	Exposition «Vogelzug»
Richard P. Lohse, Zürich	Produkt und Werbung	Commercial Goods and Graphic Design	Produit et art graphique
LMNV	Katalog in Leporelloform	An Accordion-Folded Catalogue	Un catalogue léporello
Margit Staber, Zürich	3 Sachbücher	3 Text Books	Ouvrages de référence
Hans Neuburg, Zürich	10 neue Plakate	10 New Posters	10 Affiches nouveaux
Edi Doswald, Zürich	Ausstellung Jugend-Festival Helsinki 1962	Helsinki Youth Festival 1962	Festival de la Jeunesse, Helsinki 1962
Josef Müller-Brockmann, Zürich	Japanische Gebrauchsgrafik	Japanese Industrial Design	Art graphique utilitaire au Japon

Issue for February 1965 — Février 1965

Einzelnummer Fr. 30.– / Single number Fr. 30.– / Le numéro Fr. 30.–

Herausgeber und Redaktion
Editors and Managing Editors
Editeurs et rédaction

Richard P. Lohse SWB/VSG, Zürich
J. Müller-Brockmann SWB/VSG, Zürich
Hans Neuburg SWB/VSG, Zürich
Carlo L. Vivarelli SWB/VSG, Zürich

Druck/Verlag
Printing/Publishing
Imprimerie/Edition

Walter-Verlag AG, Olten
Schweiz/Switzerland/Suisse

Neue Grafik
Country: Switzerland

Cover Design: Hans Neuburg

TM (Typographische Monatsblätter)
Country: Switzerland

Cover Design: Hans-Rudolf Lutz
Courtesy of syndicom

03.1965

ulm 12/13
Zeitschrift der Hochschule für Gestaltung
Journal of the Ulm School for Design

Ulm
Country: Germany

Cover Design: Tomás Gonda

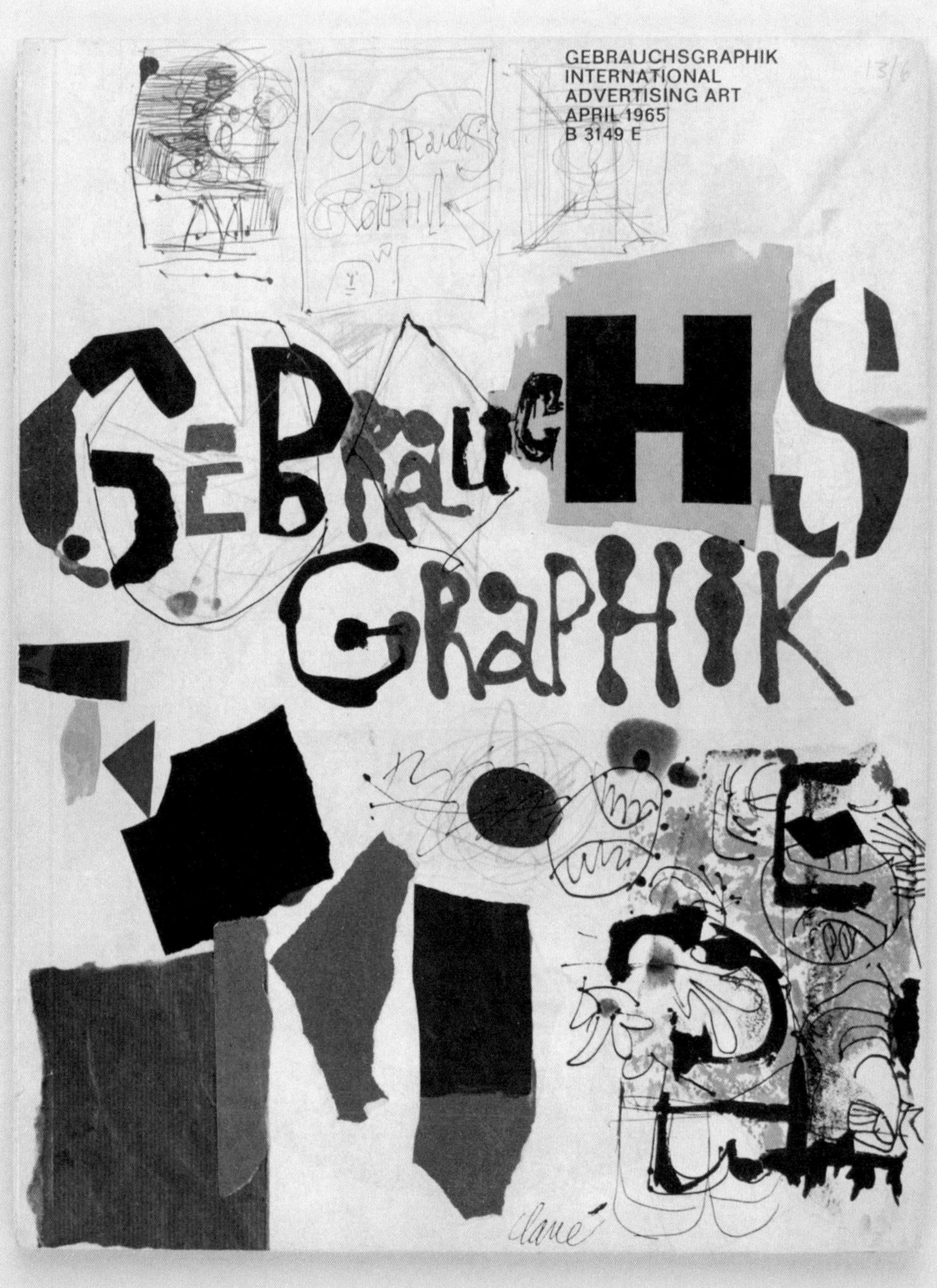

Gebrauchsgraphik
Country: Germany

Cover Design: Antoni Clavé

05.1965

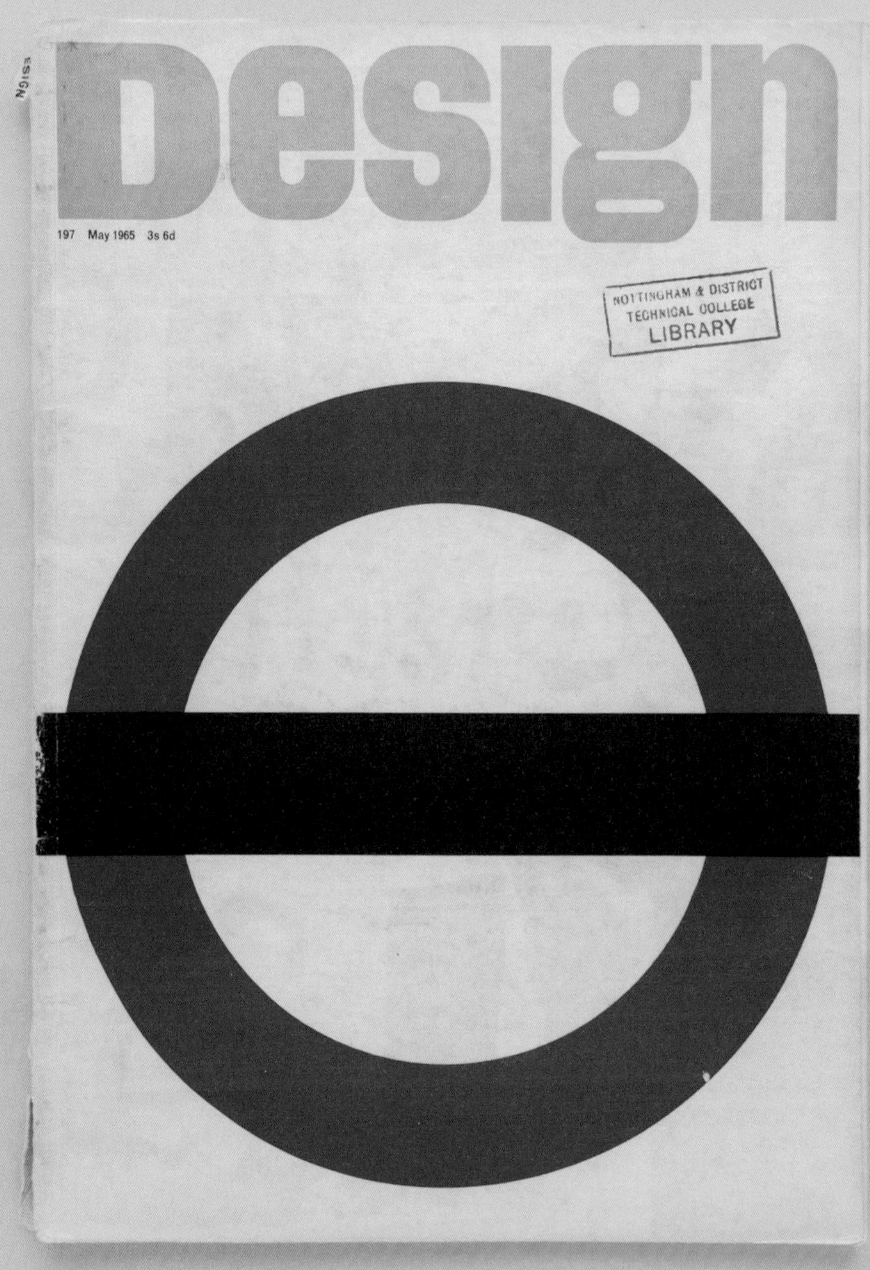

Design
Country: UK

Art Editor: Brian Grimbly

Typographica
Country: UK

Cover Design: Herbert Spencer

08.1965

Design
Country: UK

Art Editor: Brian Grimbly

昭和40年8月1日発行第72号（隔月1日発行）昭和28年6月17日国鉄東局特別扱承認雑誌（第2566号）
INTERNATIONAL ADVERTISING ART
世界のデザイン誌・誠文堂新光社
アイデア
72
ideA
8月号／1965
morillas

Idea
Country: Japan

Cover Design:
Antonio Morillas Verdura

10.1965

Casabella 298

Casabella
Country: Italy

Cover Design: Grafica Milano

10.1965

Graphic Design
Country: Japan

Cover Design: Kimura Tsunehisa

12.1965

Casabella 299

Casabella
Country: Italy

Cover Design: AG Fronzoni

Typographica
Country: UK

Cover Design: Herbert Spencer

12.1965

ulm 14/15/16
Zeitschrift der Hochschule für Gestaltung
Journal of the Ulm School for Design

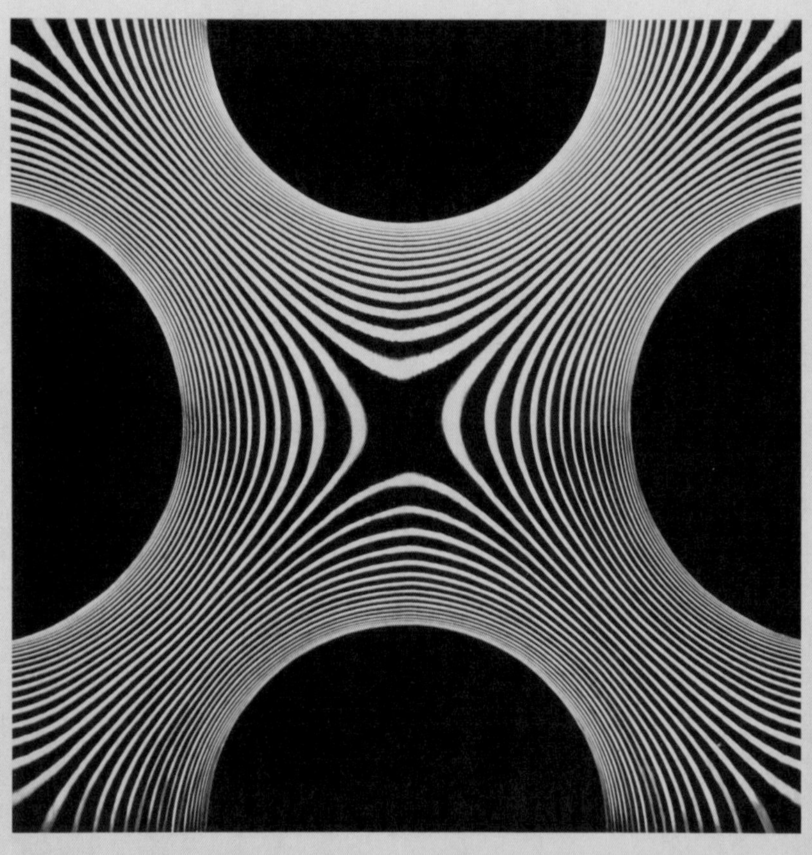

Ulm
Country: Germany

Cover Design:
Eckhard Jung, Herbert Kapitzki

Q Only five issues of *Dot Zero* (USA) were published between 1966 and 1968. Can you say what impact it had on the design scene at the time of its publication?

A In its form, and particularly in its content, *Dot Zero* magazine definitely had an influence on the design scene of its time. Other than a few pioneering magazines, such as Brodovitch's *Portfolio* (1949–51, USA), Josef Müller-Brockmann's *Neue Grafik* (1958–65, Switzerland) and in the popular vein Willy Fleckhaus's *Twen* magazines (1959–70, Germany), insightful and well-designed magazines have been few and far between for the informed professional designer with modernist leanings. Looking back, Pentagram's Michael Bierut, writing in *Design Observer* (2003–present, USA), characterised *Dot Zero* as 'remarkable.' Over forty years after its publication, its designer and creative director Massimo Vignelli remained excited by what the magazine accomplished for Unimark International and for its sponsor Finch Papers. He felt that *Dot Zero* met its objectives of raising the bar for critical discourse about design.

In a personal way, *Dot Zero* magazine has been significant for me. Finch Papers, *Dot Zero*'s sponsor, is located in Glens Falls, New York, which happens to be my home town in upstate New York. Two of my uncles spent over forty years working for Finch Papers, as did I during my college summers. So I have always identified with *Dot Zero*, from my formative beginnings to my connection with Massimo Vignelli, and especially through the visionary form and content of the magazine.

Q By setting all the type in only two weights of Helvetica and printing in black and white on uncoated paper, Vignelli seems to have used the publication as a manifesto for his design philosophy. Is this an accurate assumption?

A The basic visual vocabulary of only two weights of Helvetica, and printing the magazine solely in black and white, was a logical extension of Massimo Vignelli's modernist design canon. Throughout his career he was consistent in this kind of approach. Every project he undertook was a tour de force of this method by which he consistently created graphic design that is timeless.

Q *Dot Zero* had texts by Marshall McLuhan, John Kenneth Galbraith and Umberto Eco. This indicates an ambition beyond mere self-promotion for Unimark, and signals an editorial sophistication that not many design publications can match. In your opinion, did it have any rivals at the time – or since?

A Contrast was always an important idea for Vignelli. In the case of *Dot Zero* he wanted to create a magazine that was modernist in form and substantive in content. In this way *Dot Zero* differed from any of its commercial competition.

Portfolio
1949–51
USA

Dot Zero
1966–68
USA

Q You mentioned Michael Bierut, a former member of the Vignelli studio. He has written that Unimark 'in many ways anticipated the current interest in design thinking in business circles, and expanded the debate on the relationship of good design and good business that continues to this day'. How successful, in your opinion, was *Dot Zero* in achieving this?

A I agree that *Dot Zero* was ahead of its time in form, particularly in content. The interdisciplinary approach so evident in its content did indeed predict today's 'design thinking', and is beginning to be evident in some progressive design education programmes. I always advise my students to look for inspiration anywhere except in design magazines. The further afield they can go the better. Thinkers in theoretical disciplines such as psychology, management science, linguistics and many others can provide ideas and structures that can and should inform the emerging design practitioners of today. As Brodovitch advised his students many years ago, 'keep your fingers on the pulse of the times'.

Q Following on from this idea, what do you think of the current state of design publications?

A Magazines in general today mirror the confusion evident in society, whether it is in business, politics or design education. The effects of Postmodernism have taken their toll on many facets of graphic design. When I teach my design history course about magazines, my students always ask, 'Why are today's magazines so poorly produced and designed? What happened to the elegance of Brodovitch's *Harper's Bazaar* (1867–present, USA) or Liberman's *Vogue* (1892–present, USA)? Why don't we have design journals such as the original *Graphis* magazine (1944–present, Switzerland)?' I see few examples of excellence in today's magazines. *Eye* (1990–present, UK) and *Visible Language* (1967–present, USA) are two excellent publications targeted at designers. Also of note is the Italian product design magazine *Inventario* (2010–present, Italy). Looking back, *Dot Zero* remains as a little-known exemplar of unifying form and content in an excellent magazine.

R Roger Remington is a Vignelli Distinguished Professor of Design at Rochester Institute of Technology. He is an acknowledged and published design historian.

Graphis
1944—present
Switzerland

Visible Language
1967—present
USA

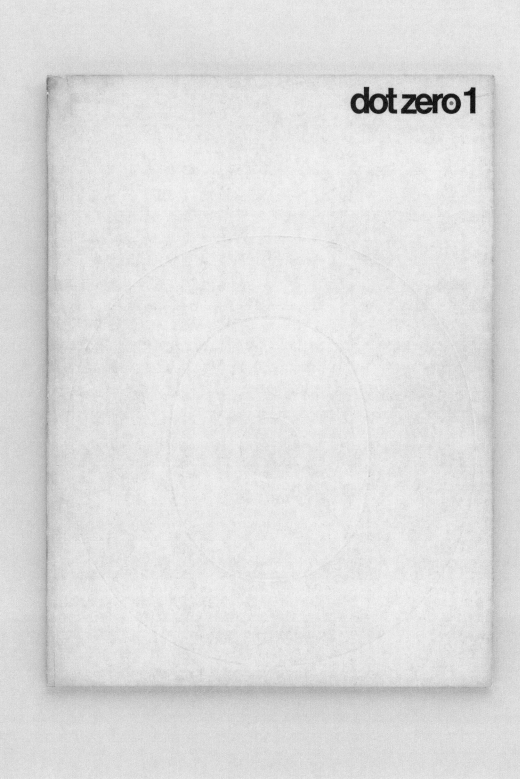

Dot Zero
Country: USA

Cover Design: Massimo Vignelli

01.1966

Print
Country: USA

Cover Design: Gipps & Danne

Casabella
Country: Italy

Cover Design: Grafica Milano

02.1966

Form+Zweck
Country: Germany

Cover Design: Günther Knobloch

Print
Country: USA

Creative Director: Dick Hess

06.1966

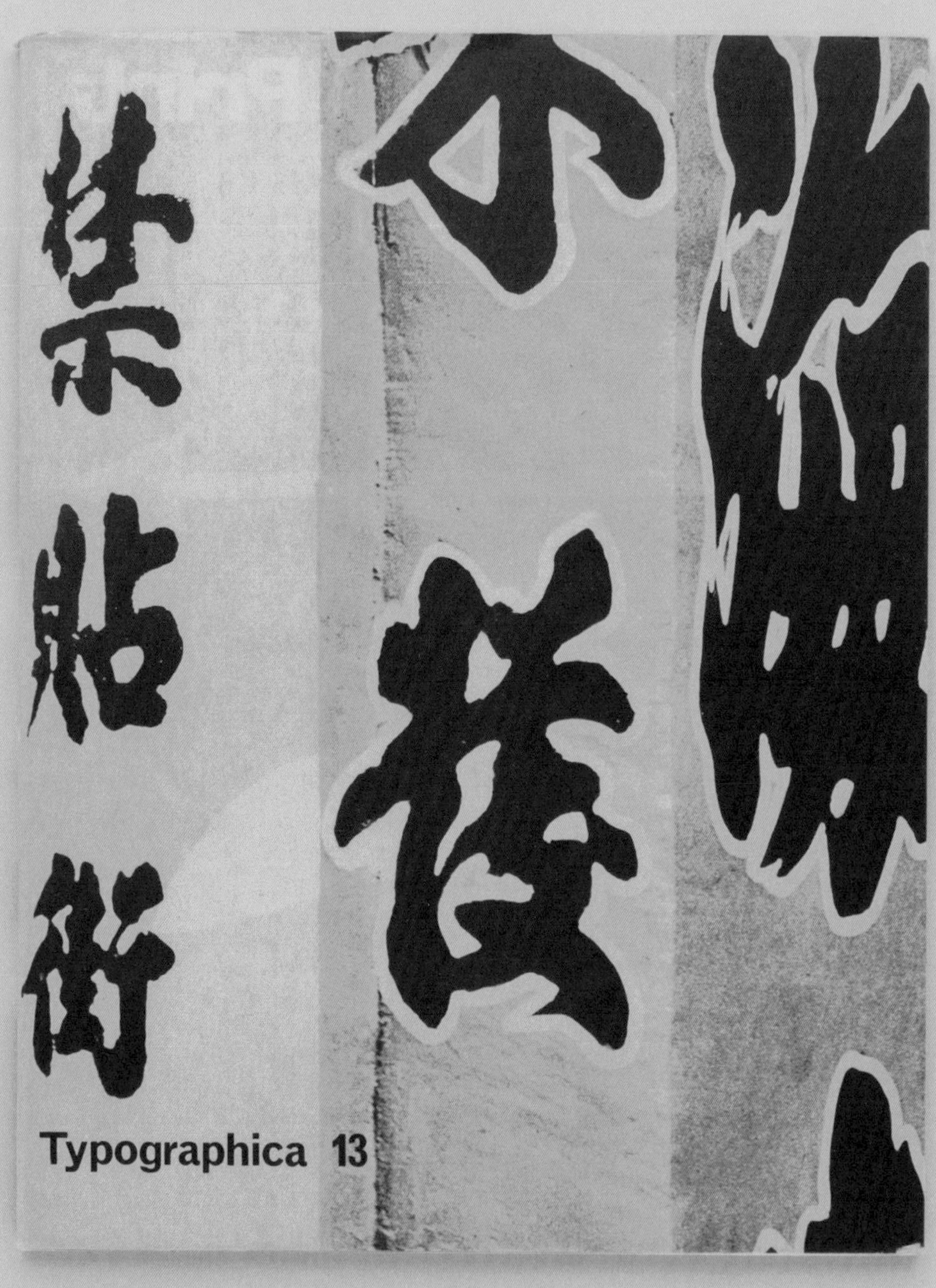

Typographica
Country: UK

Cover Design: Herbert Spencer

Dot Zero
Country: USA

Cover Design: Massimo Vignelli

06.1966

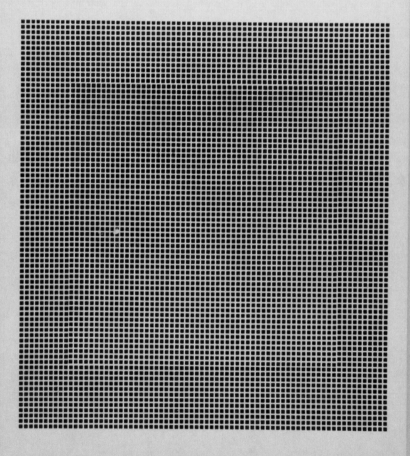

Ulm
Country: Germany

Cover Design: Herbert Kapitzki

Print design and production 4
INCORPORATING 'BOOK DESIGN AND PRODUCTION' JULY/AUGUST 1966 VOLUME 2 3s 6d

Print Design and Production
Country: UK

Design: unidentified

09.1966

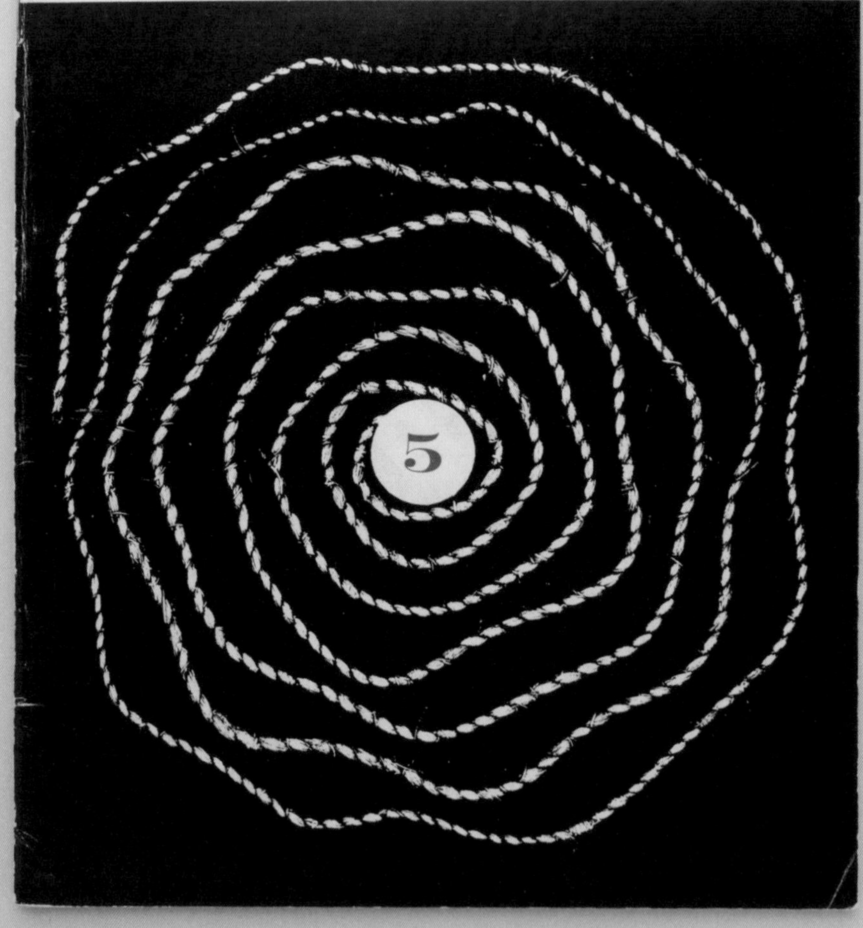

Print Design and Production
Country: UK

Design: unidentified

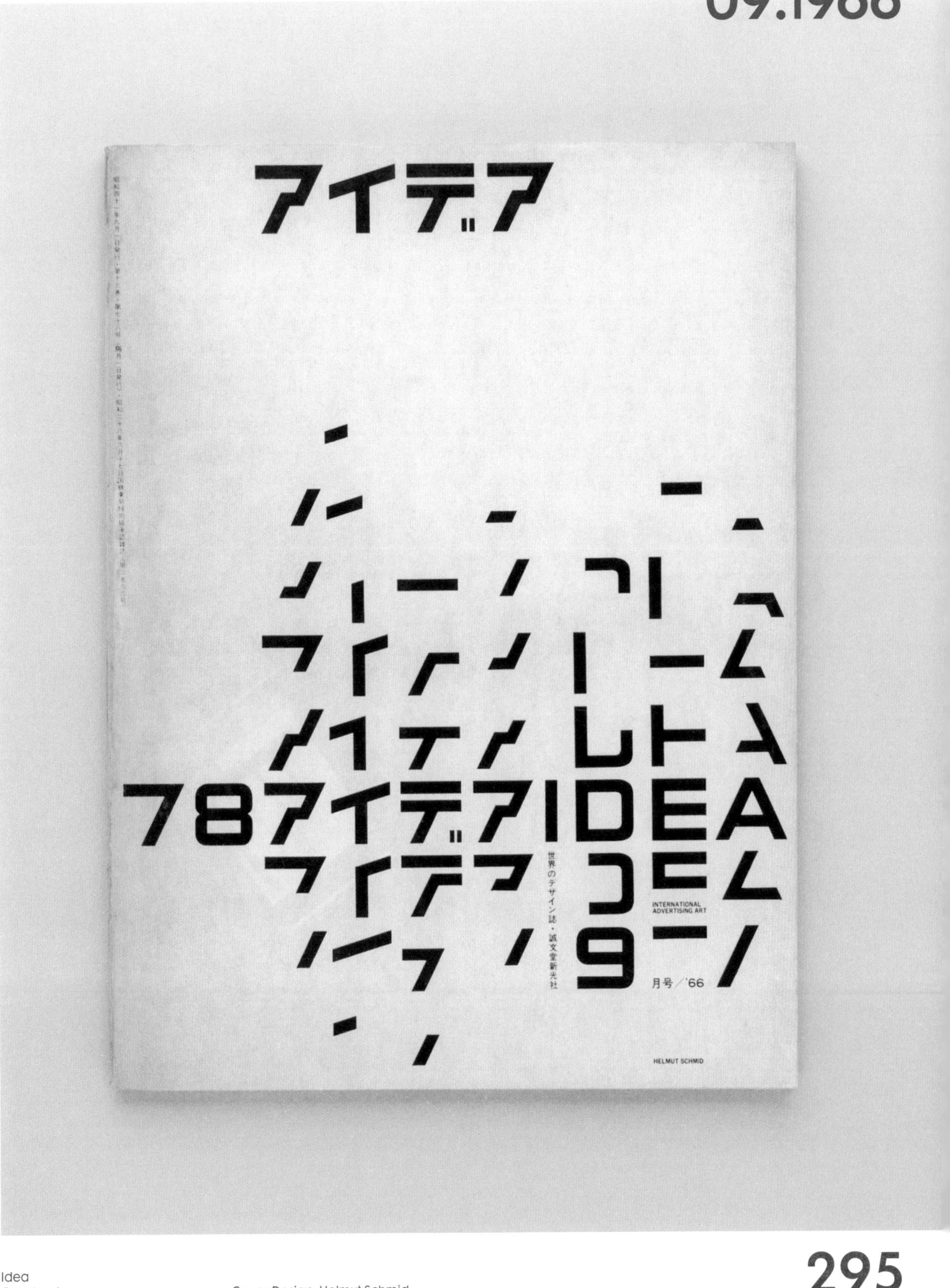

Idea
Country: Japan

Cover Design: Helmut Schmid

12.1966

Typographica
Country: UK

Cover Design:
Crosby/Fletcher/Forbes

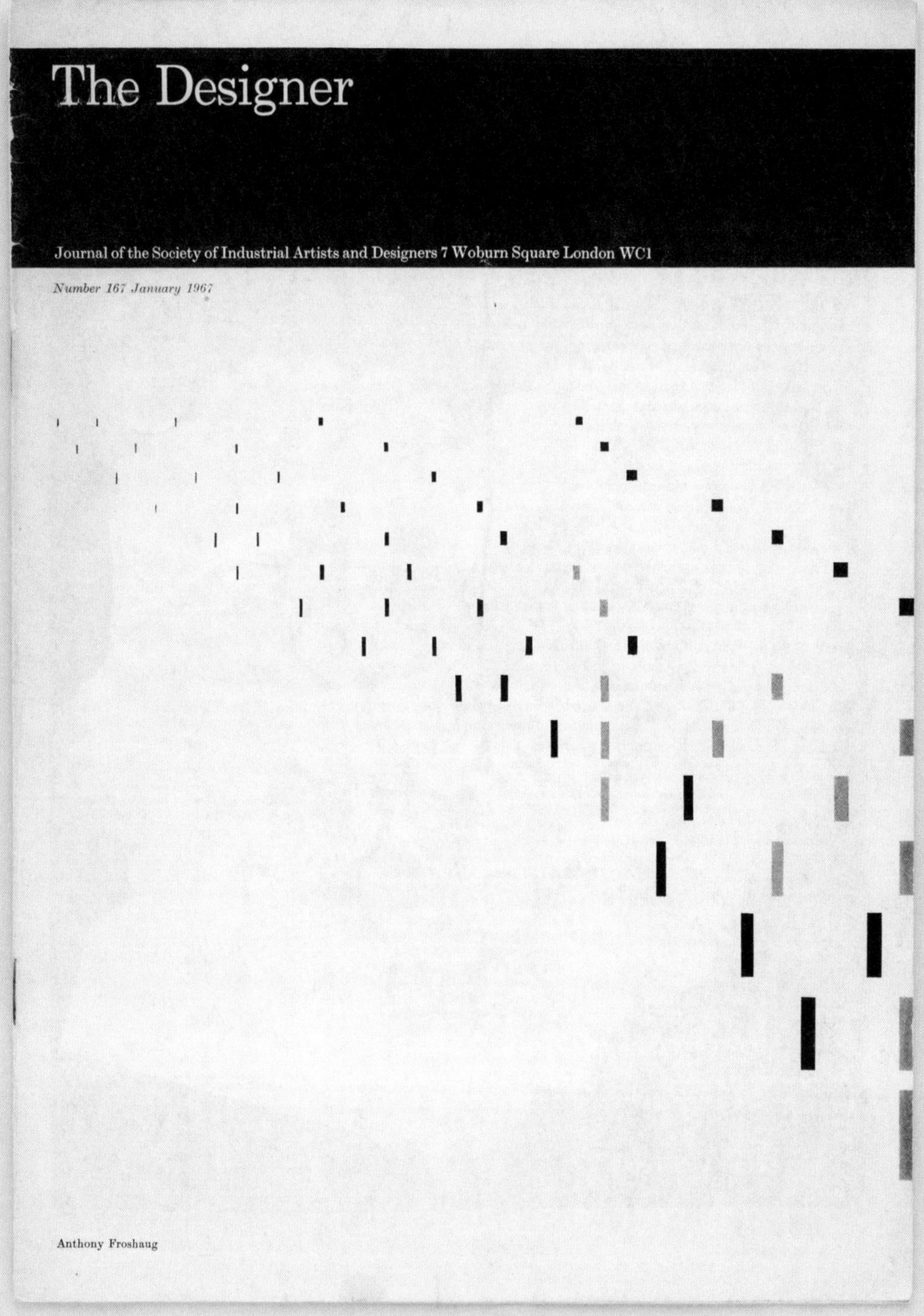

The Designer
Country: UK

Cover Design: Anthony Froshaug

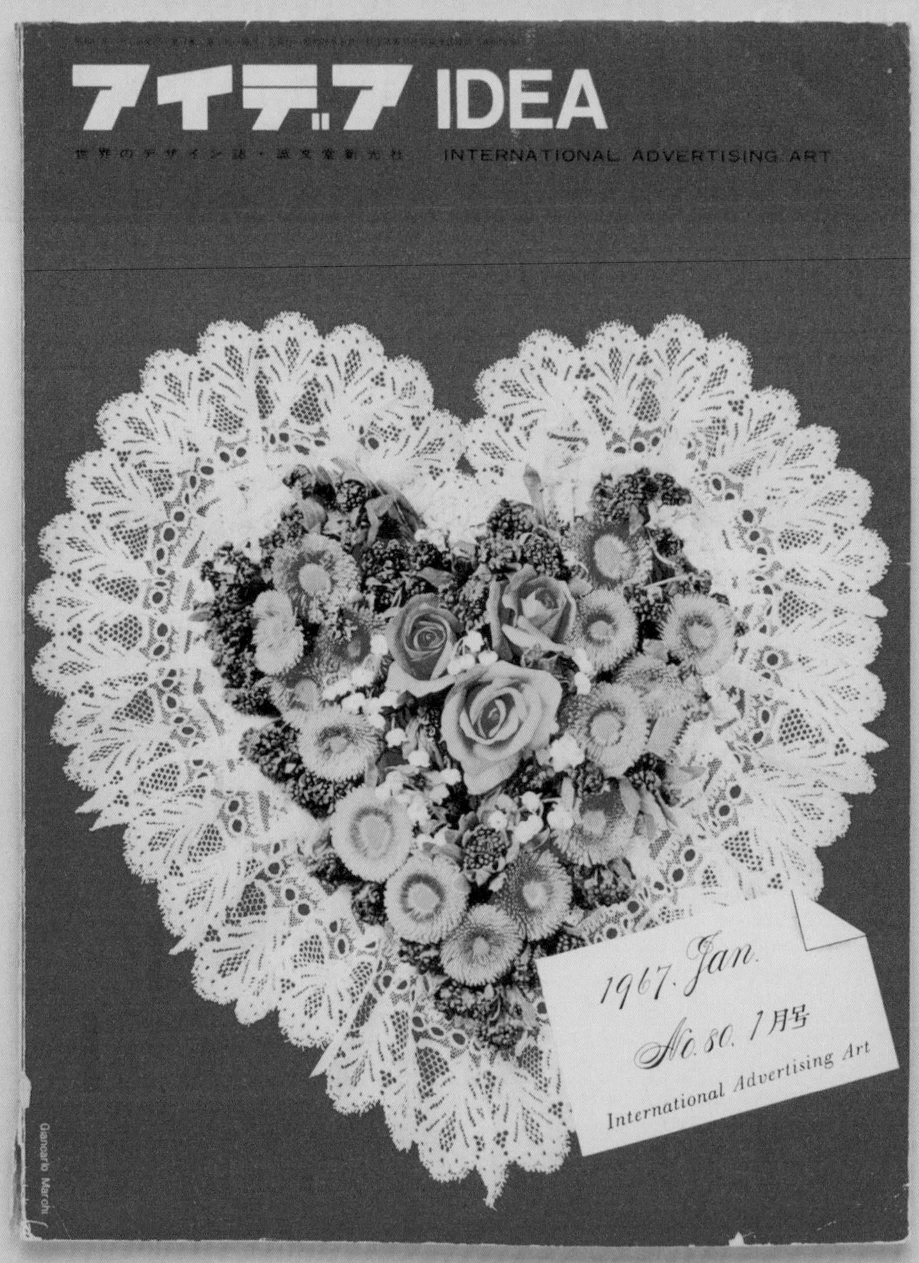

Idea
Country: Japan

Cover Design: Giancarlo Marchi

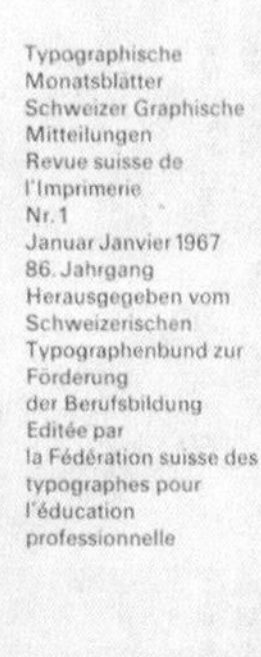

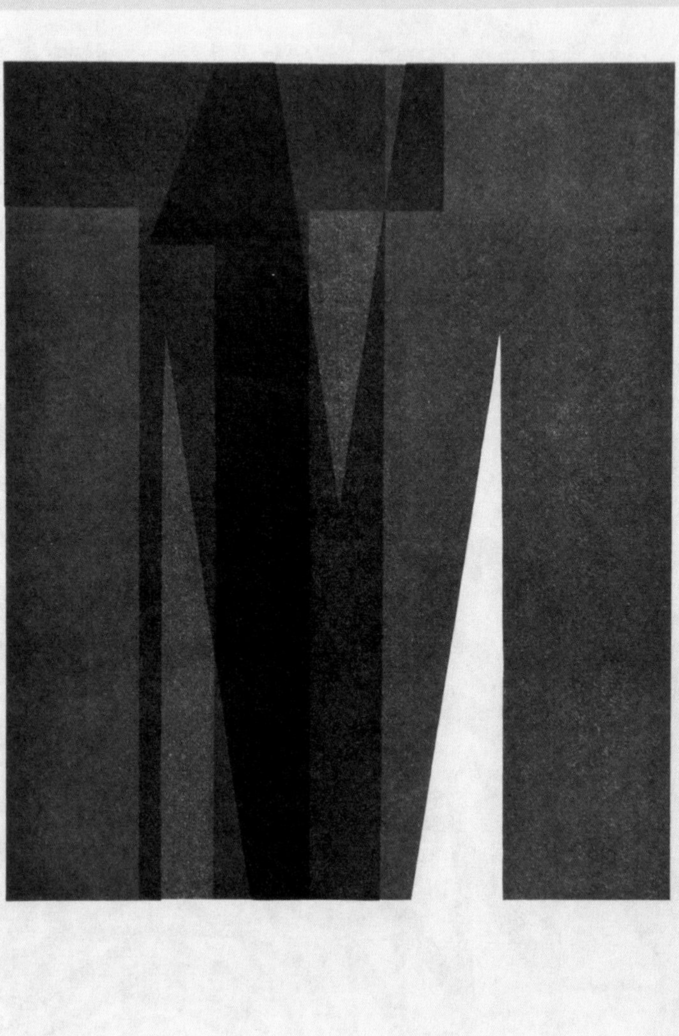

TM (Typographische Monatsblätter)
Country: Switzerland

Cover Design: Horst Hohl
Courtesy of syndicom

03.1967

Print
Country: USA

Art Director: Andrew P Kner

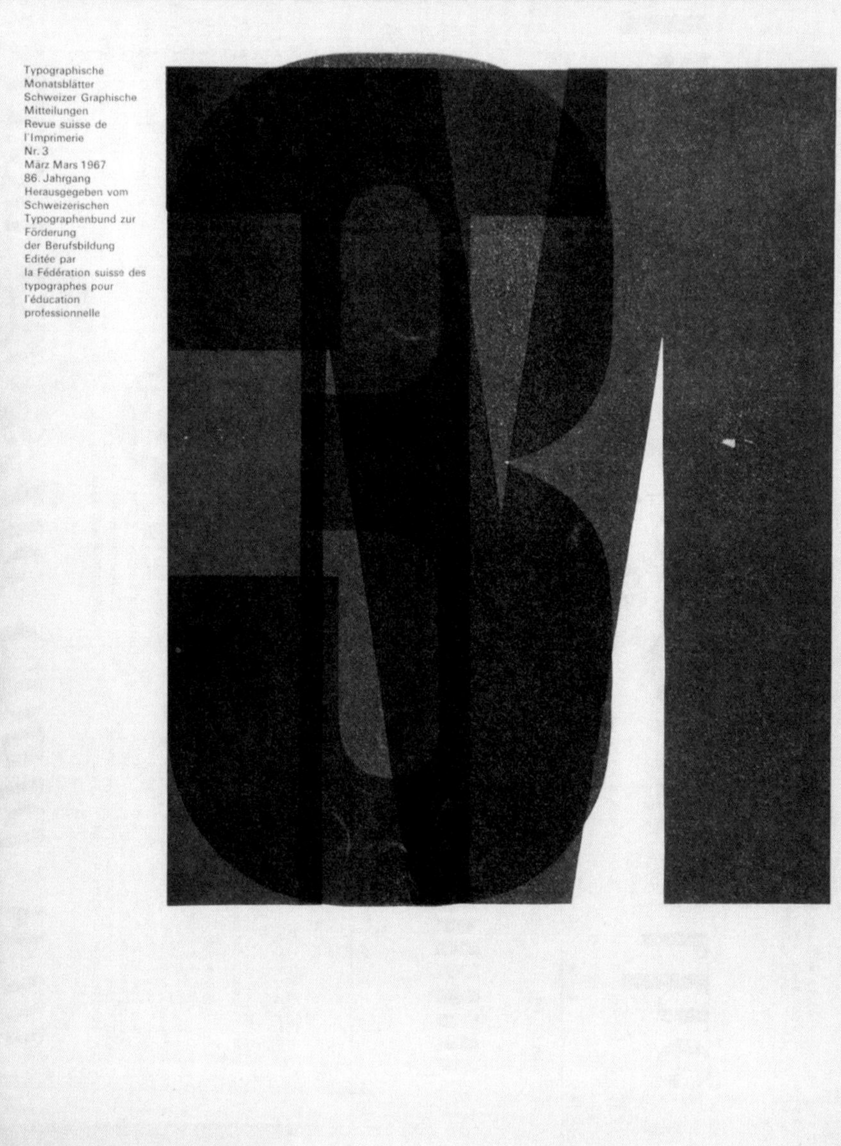

TM (Typographische Monatsblätter)
Country: Switzerland

Cover Design: Horst Hohl
Courtesy of syndicom

03–05.1967

Dot Zero
Country: USA

Cover Design: Massimo Vignelli

LITHOPINION
8
The graphic arts and public affairs journal of Local One, Amalgamated Lithographers of America
Eight American Magazine Covers: A Graphic Exploration

Lithopinion
Country: USA

Art Director: Robert Hallock

05.1967

Print design and production 3

INCORPORATING 'BOOK DESIGN AND PRODUCTION' MAY/JUNE 1967 VOLUME 3 5s

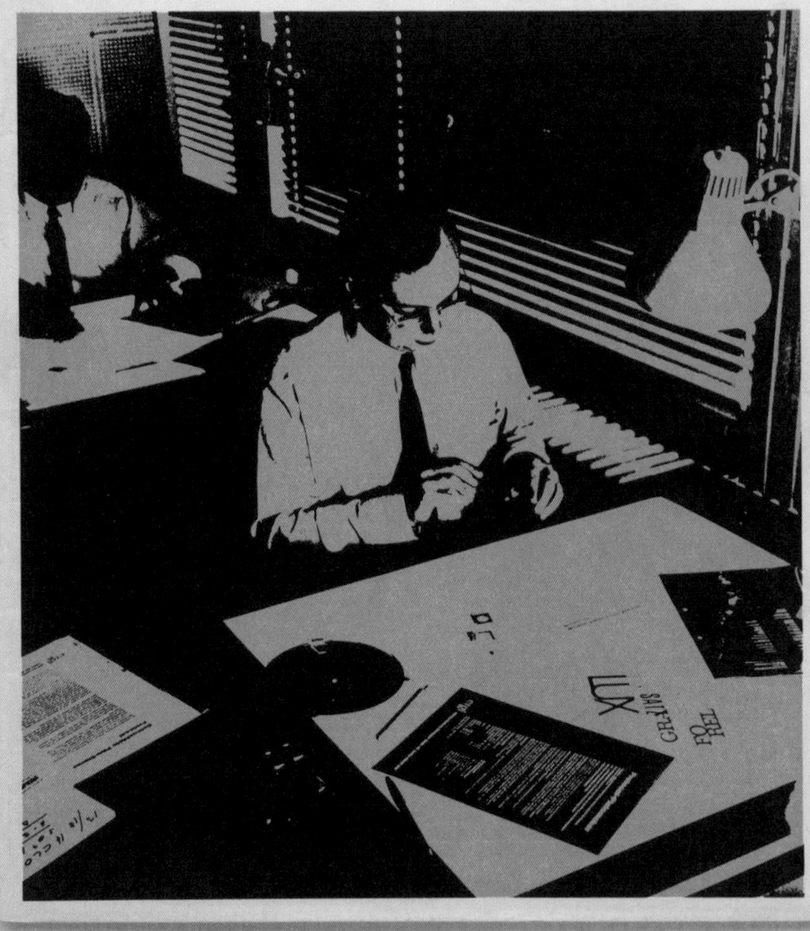

Print Design and Production
Country: UK

Design: unidentified

06.1967

Typographica
Country: UK

Cover Design:
Crosby/Fletcher/Forbes

06–08.1967

Dot Zero
Country: USA

Cover Design: Massimo Vignelli

Ulm
Country: Germany

Cover Design:
H Jacob, Manfred Winter

09.1967

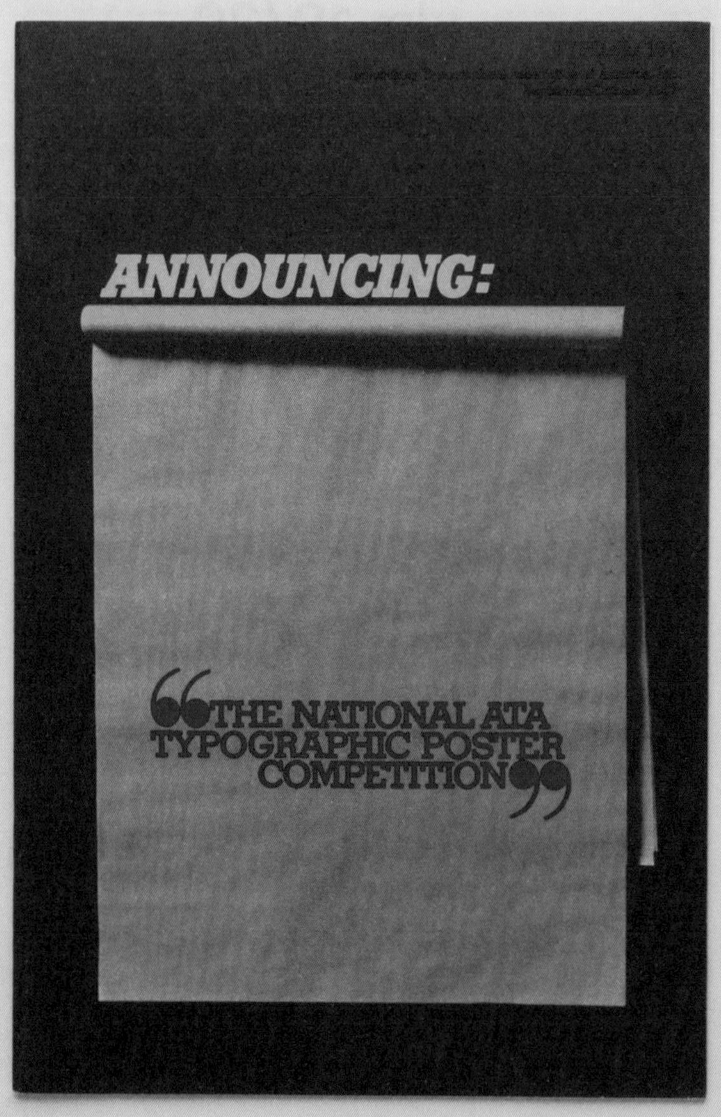

Type Talks
Country: USA

Design: unidentified

Idea
Country: Japan

Cover Design: Tadashi Masuda

11.1967

TYPEtalks

155/November-December 1967
Published by the
Advertising Typographers Association
of America, Inc.

(Printing) created the portable book,
which men could read in privacy and in isolation from others.
Man could now inspire…and conspire. McLUHAN

Type Talks
Country: USA

Design: unidentified

Typographica 16

leave still to paint or to me,
dellbse, and it is time enough
that my pieces go up after
my death. So I lived
on. I was so weak, that I
could not come up into
the bed, when I had to leave
it. A fortnight I was on
top of that blind. But all
goes slowly better. Wantee
has nursed me well.
All my best wishes
Kurt Schwitters.

Cover Design: Herbert Spencer

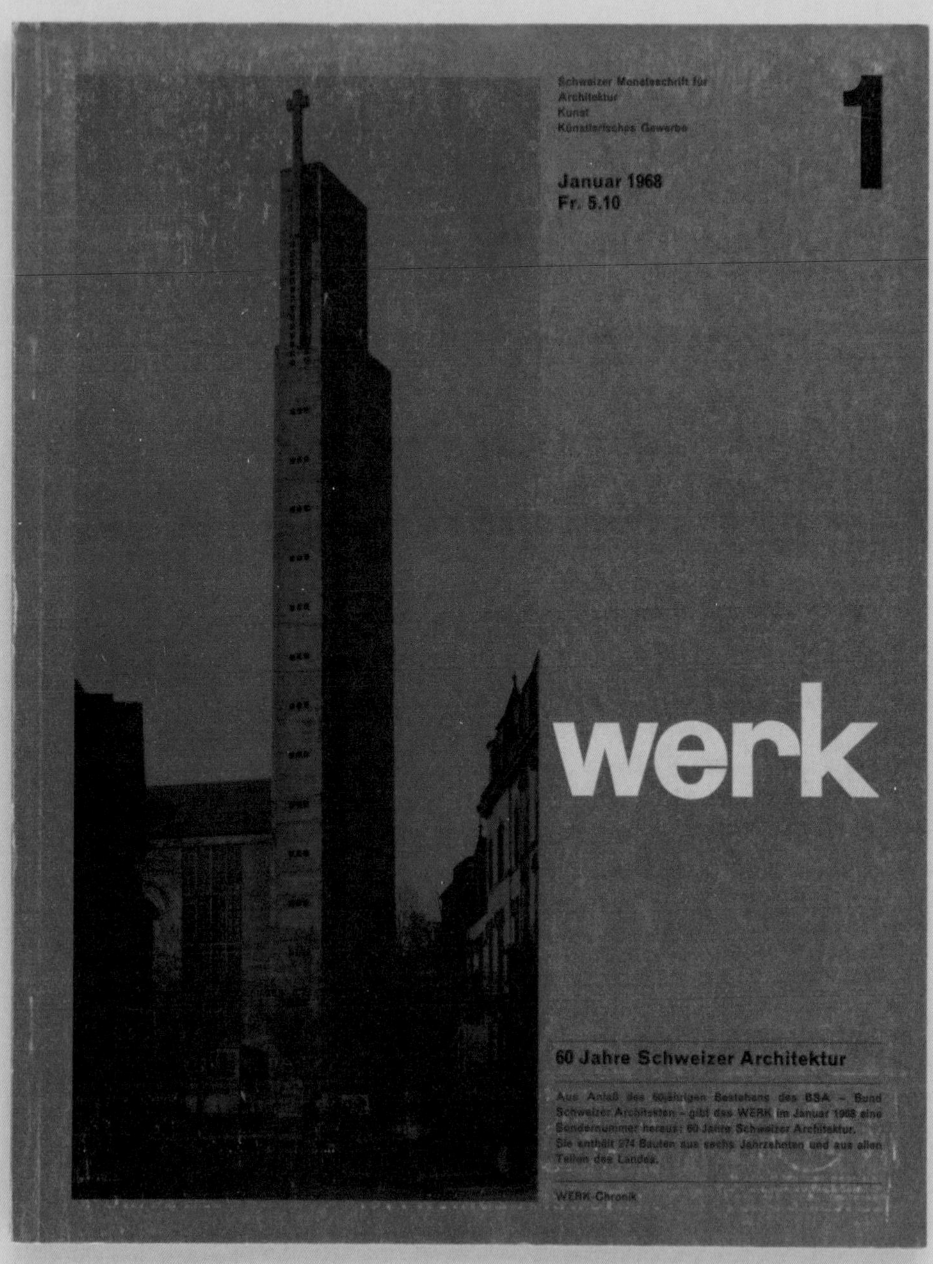

(Das) Werk
Country: Switzerland

Cover Design: Karl Gerstner

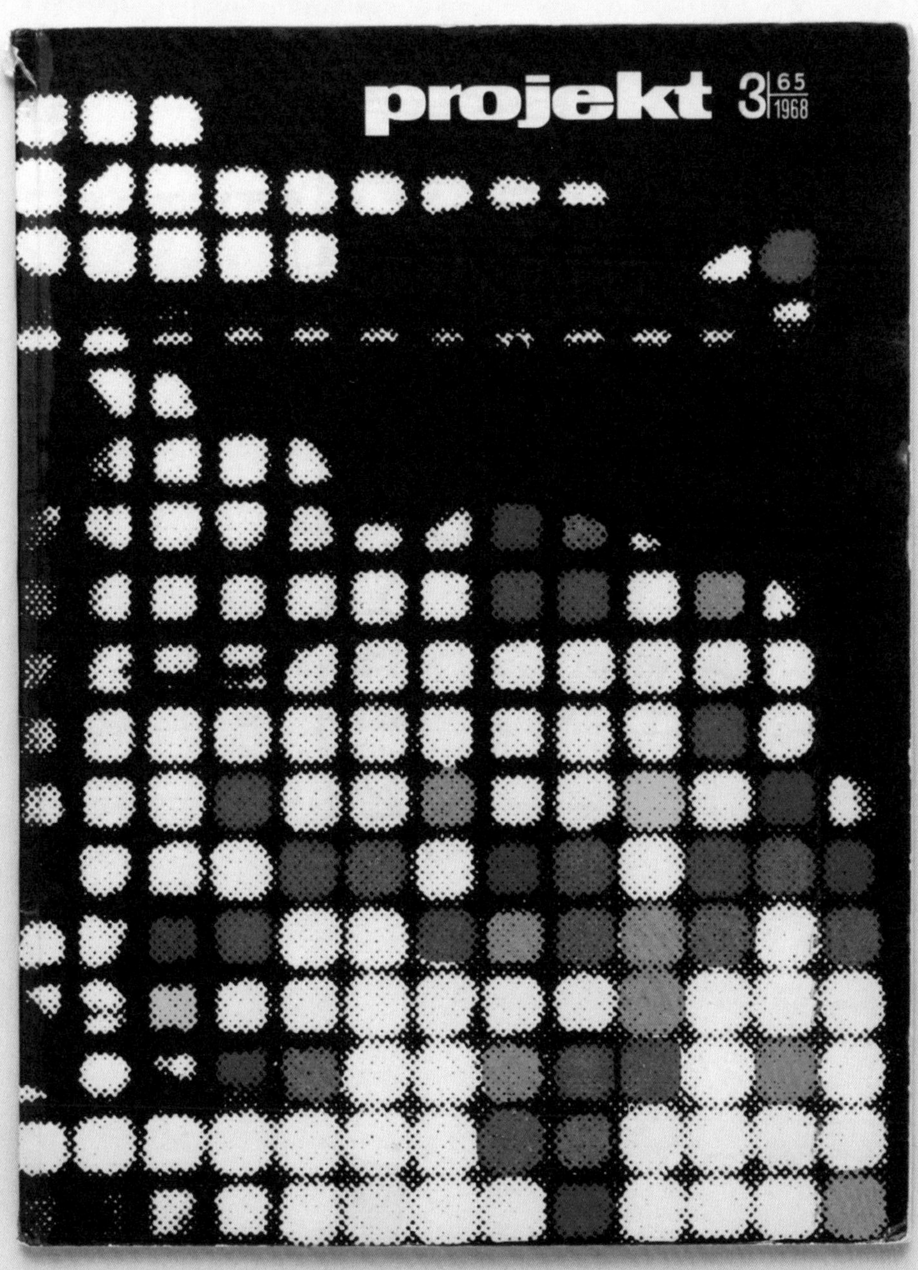

Projekt
Country: Poland

Cover Design: Hubert Hilscher

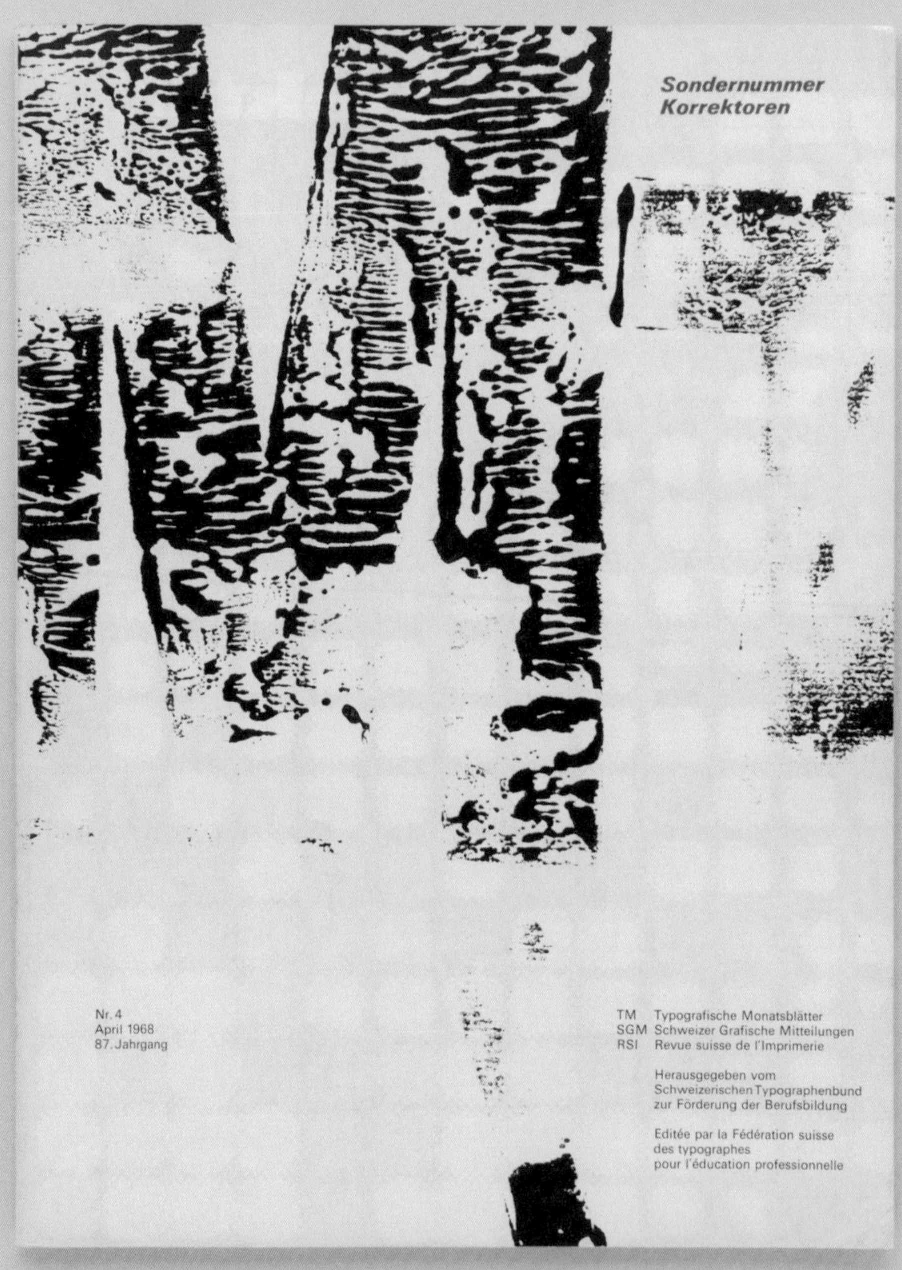

TM (Typographische Monatsblätter)
Country: Switzerland

Cover Design: Hans Ferdinand Egli
Courtesy of syndicom

Ulm
Country: Germany

Cover Design: Manfred Winter

06.1968

18

Format

4. Jg./6-68 E 20638 F

Zeitschrift

verbale
visuelle
Kommunikation

Konkrete Poesie: Texte zum Ansehen

```
elig Selig S
sind sind si
ie die die die die die di
n Armen Armen Armen Armen A
im im im im im im im im im im
ist Geist Geist Geist Geist Geist Geist                          Geist
nn'denn'denn'denn'denn'denn'denn'denn'denn'denn'denn'denn'den
er ihrer ihrer ihrer ihrer ihrer ihrer ihrer ihrer ihrer ihrer
ist ist ist ist ist ist ist ist i                              t ist
as das das das das das das das das das
ch Himmelreich Himmelreich Himmelreich Himmelreich Him
lig Selig Selig Selig Selig Selig Selig Selig Selig Selig Selig Seli
nd sind sind sind sind sind sind sind sind sind sind sind
e die die die die die die die die die die die die die di
ernden Trauernden Trauernden Trauernden Trauernden Tr
'denn'denn'denn'denn'denn'denn'denn'denn'denn'denn'denn'd'
e sie sie sie sie sie sie sie sie sie sie sie sie si
erden werden werden werden werden werden werden werden w
t getröstet getröstet getröstet getröstet getr
rden werden werden werden werden werden werden werden
g Selig Selig Selig Selig Selig Selig Selig S
ind sind sind sind sind sind sind sind
ie die die die die die die die die di
anftmütigen Sanftmütigen Sanftmütigen Sanf
''''''''''''''''''''''''''''''''''''''''

denn denn de
e sie sie sie sie sie
den werden werden werden w
das das das das das das
eich Erdreich Erdreich Erdrei
m zum zum zum zum zum zum zum z                     m zum
be Erbe Erbe Erbe Erbe Erbe Erbe Erbe Erbe Erbe Erbe Erb
n haben haben haben haben haben haben haben haben haben
Selig Selig Selig Selig Selig .....                   ....
d sind sind sind sind si
die die die die die die die die die die die die die die
die'die'die'die'die'die'die'die'die'die'die'die'die'die'die'di
ern hungern hungern hungern hungern hungern hungern hunger
nd und und und und und und und und und und und und und
en dürsten dürsten dürsten dürsten dürsten dürsten dürs
ch nach nach nach nach nach nach nach nach nach nach n
der der der der der der der der der der der de
gkeit Gerechtigkeit Gerechtigkeit Gerechtigkeit Gerechti
denn'denn'denn'denn'denn'denn'denn'denn'denn'denn'den'
sie sie sie sie sie sie sie sie sie sie sie sie
n werden werden werden werden werden werde
ttigt gesättigt gesättigt gesättigt g
werden werden werden werden werden werden wer
..........................................
```


Format
Country: Germany

Cover Design: Peter Hoch

07.1968

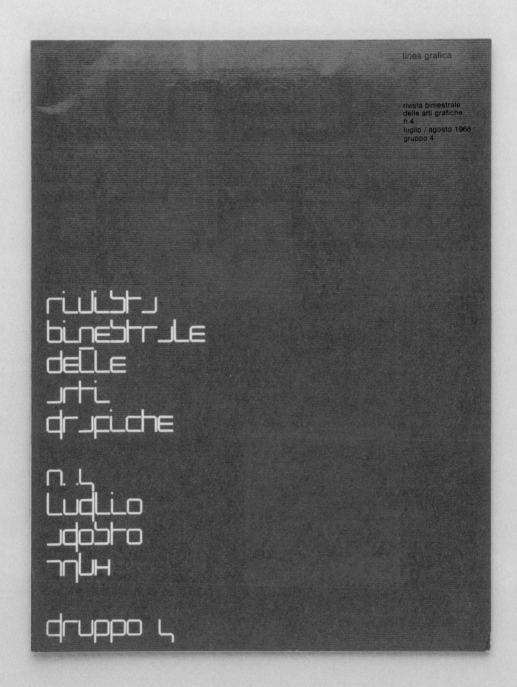

Linea Grafica
Country: Italy

Cover Design: Massimo Dradi
Typeface: New Alphabet by
Wim Crouwel

09.1968

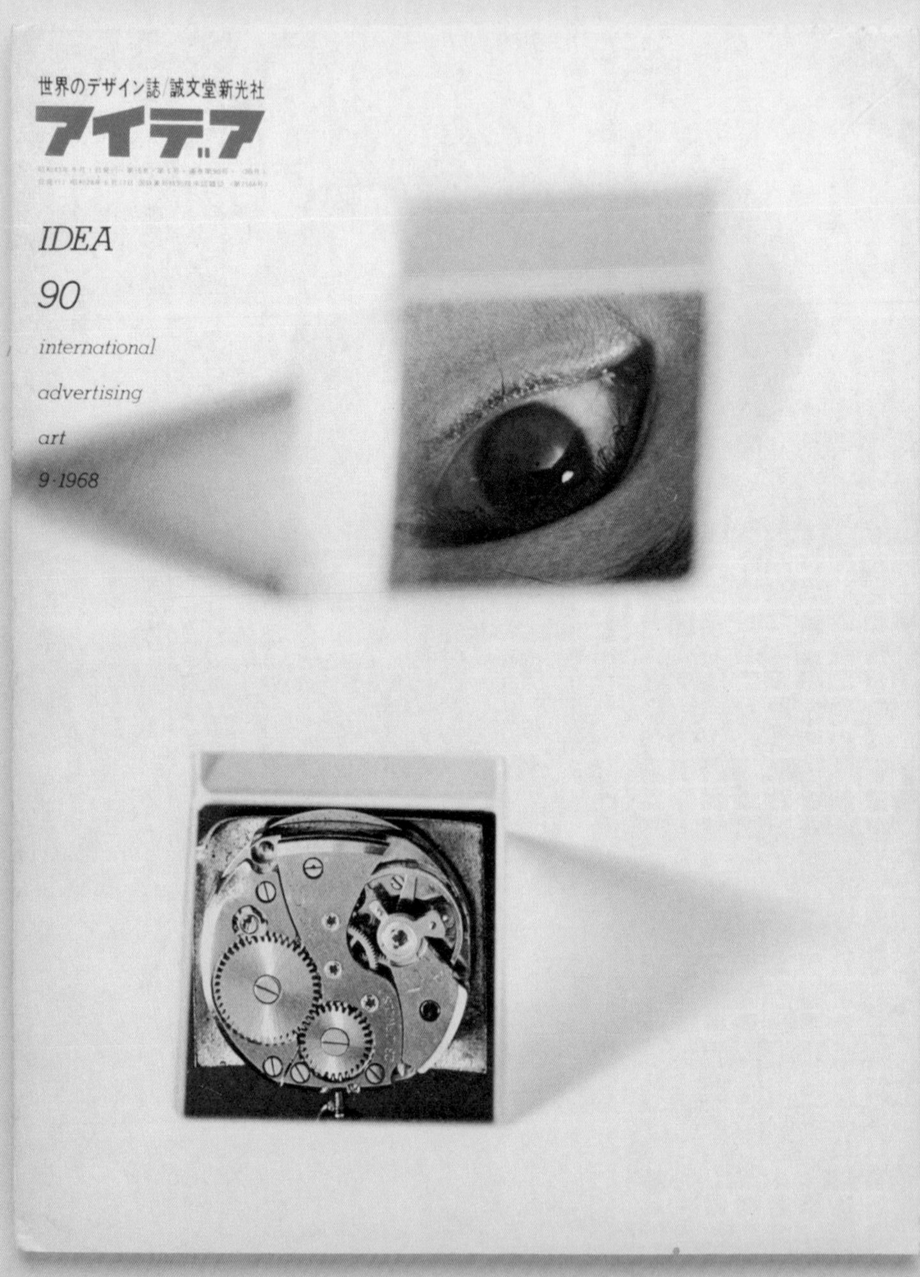

Idea
Country: Japan

Cover Design: Koichiro Inagaki

09–11.1968

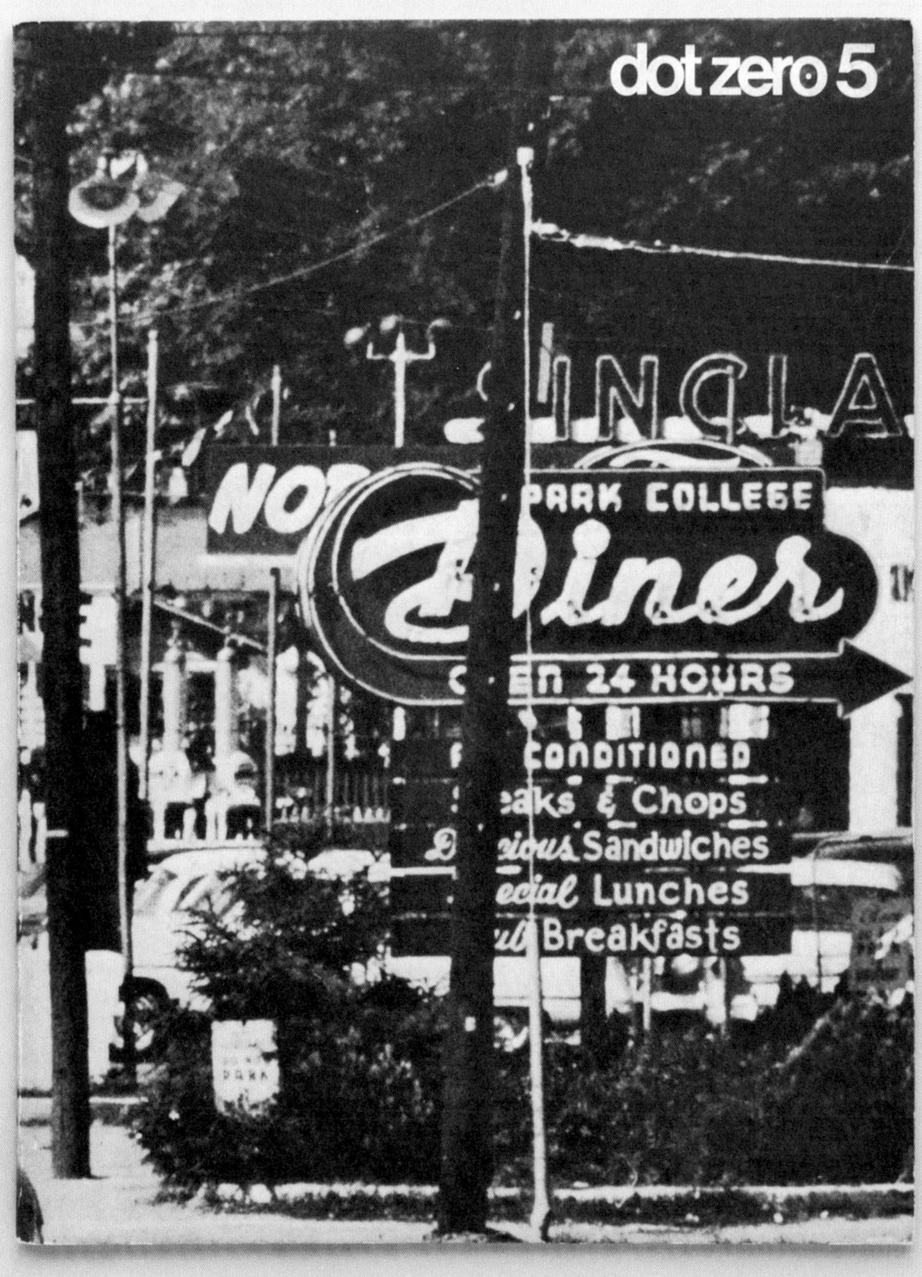

Dot Zero
Country: USA

Cover Design: Massimo Vignelli

Idea
Country: Japan

Cover Design: Kiyoshi Awazu

TYPEtalks/158/1968/Published by the Advertising Typographers Association of America, Inc.
In a mass-producing society, you've got to sell mass goods, and the best way to do it is to advertise by mass advertising.
PAUL RAND DIXON

Type Talks
Country: USA

Design: unidentified

01.1969

Idea
Country: Japan

Cover Design: Tadanori Yokoo

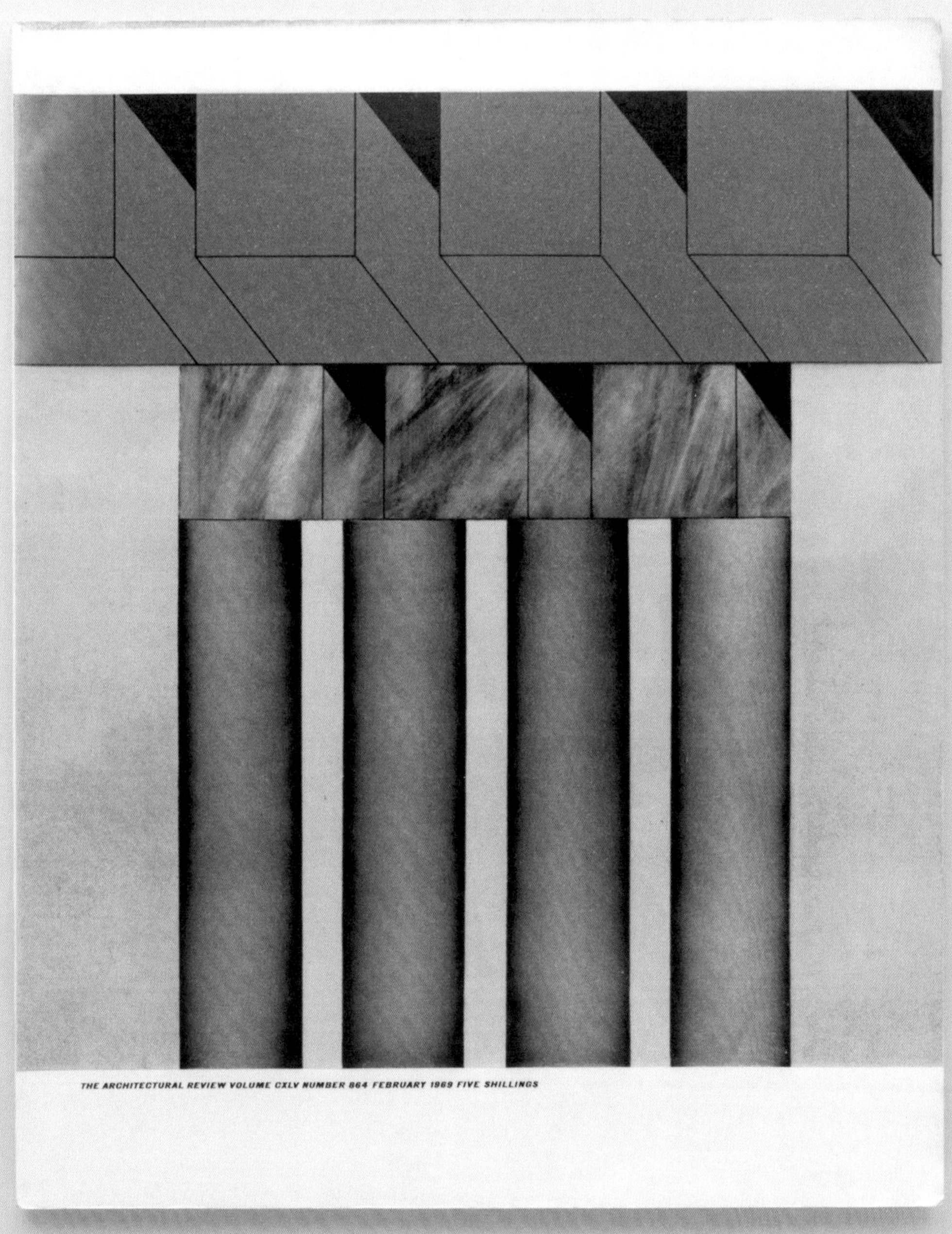

AR (The Architectural Review)
Country: UK

Cover Design: Nicholas Georgiadis

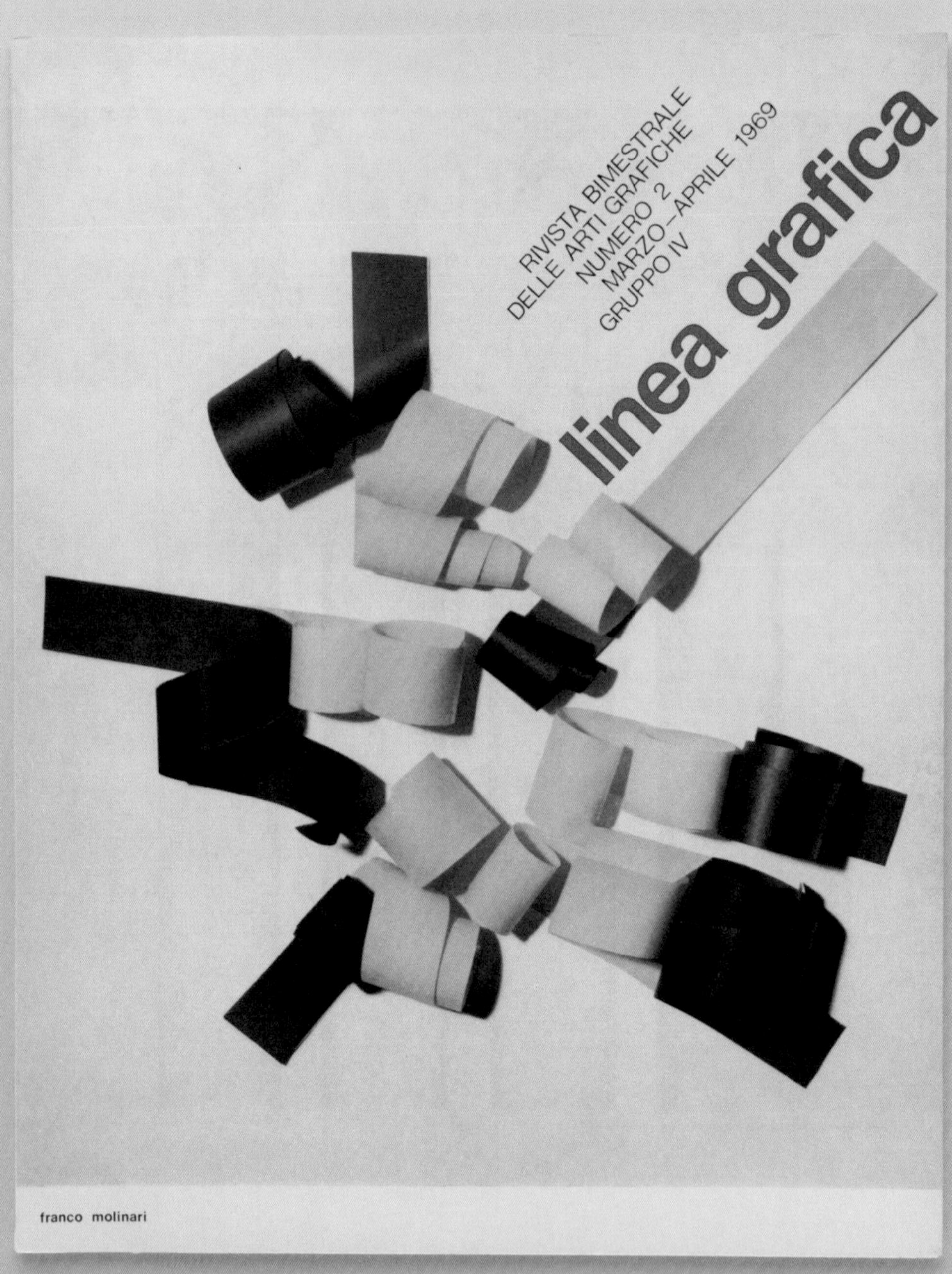

Linea Grafica
Country: Italy

Cover Design: Franco Molinari

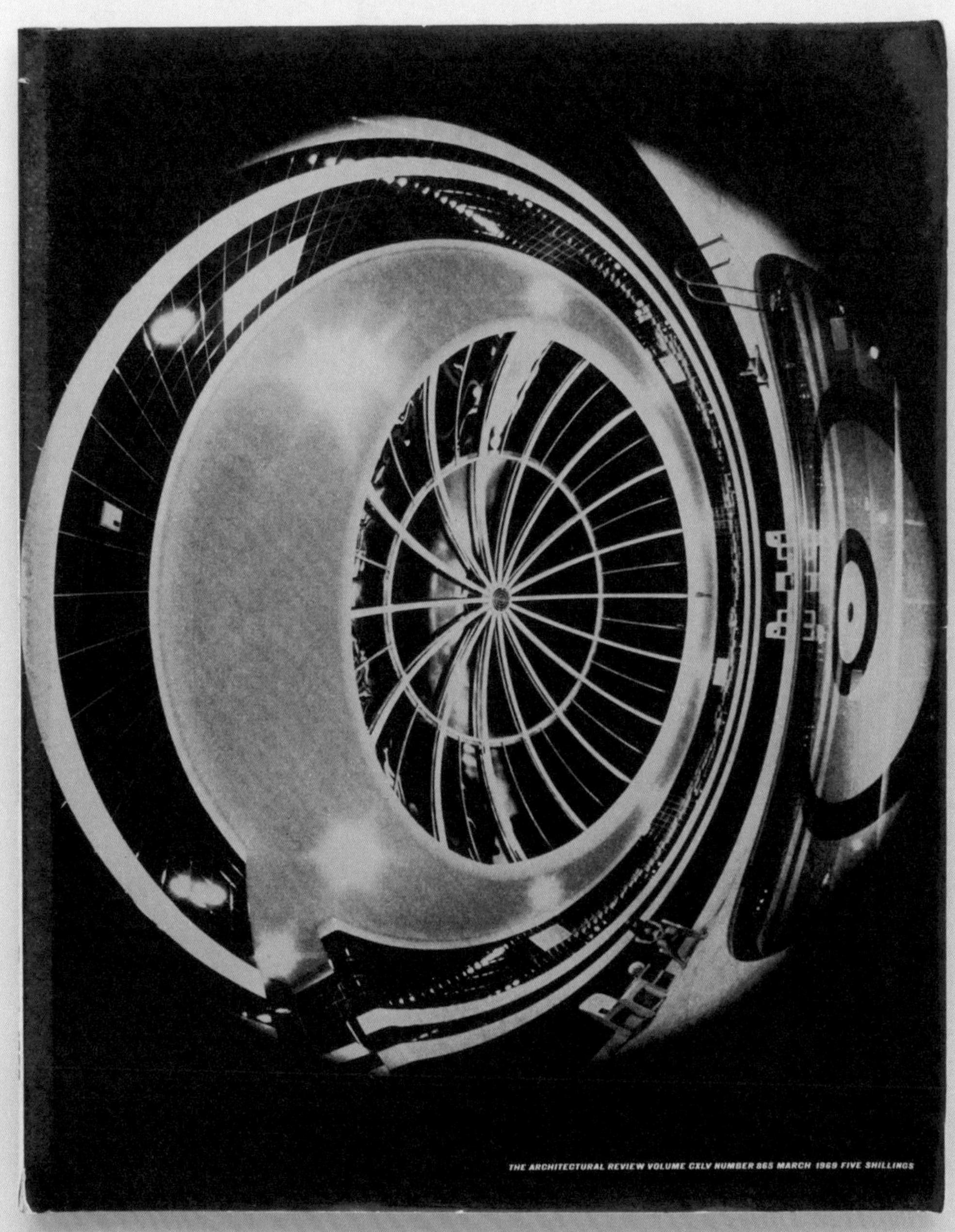

THE ARCHITECTURAL REVIEW VOLUME CXLV NUMBER 865 MARCH 1969 FIVE SHILLINGS

AR (The Architectural Review)
Country: UK

Cover Photography: James Gowan

05.1969

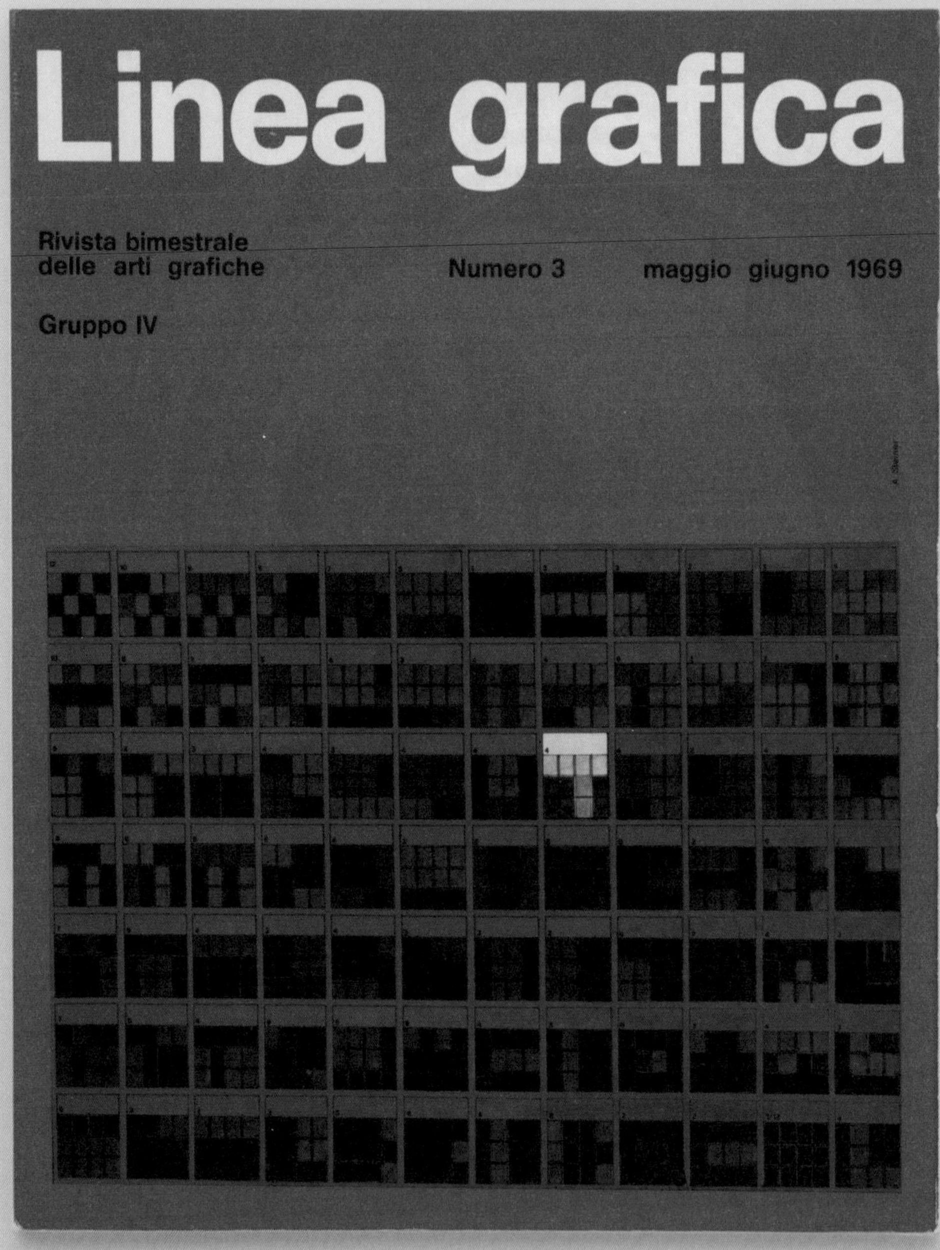

Linea Grafica
Country: Italy

Cover Design: Massimo Dradi

Format
Country: Germany

Design: unidentified

12.1969

GEBRAUCHSGRAPHIK INTERNATIONAL ADVERTISING ART DEZEMBER 12/1969 B3149E

Gebrauchsgraphik
Country: Germany

Art Director: Hans Kuh

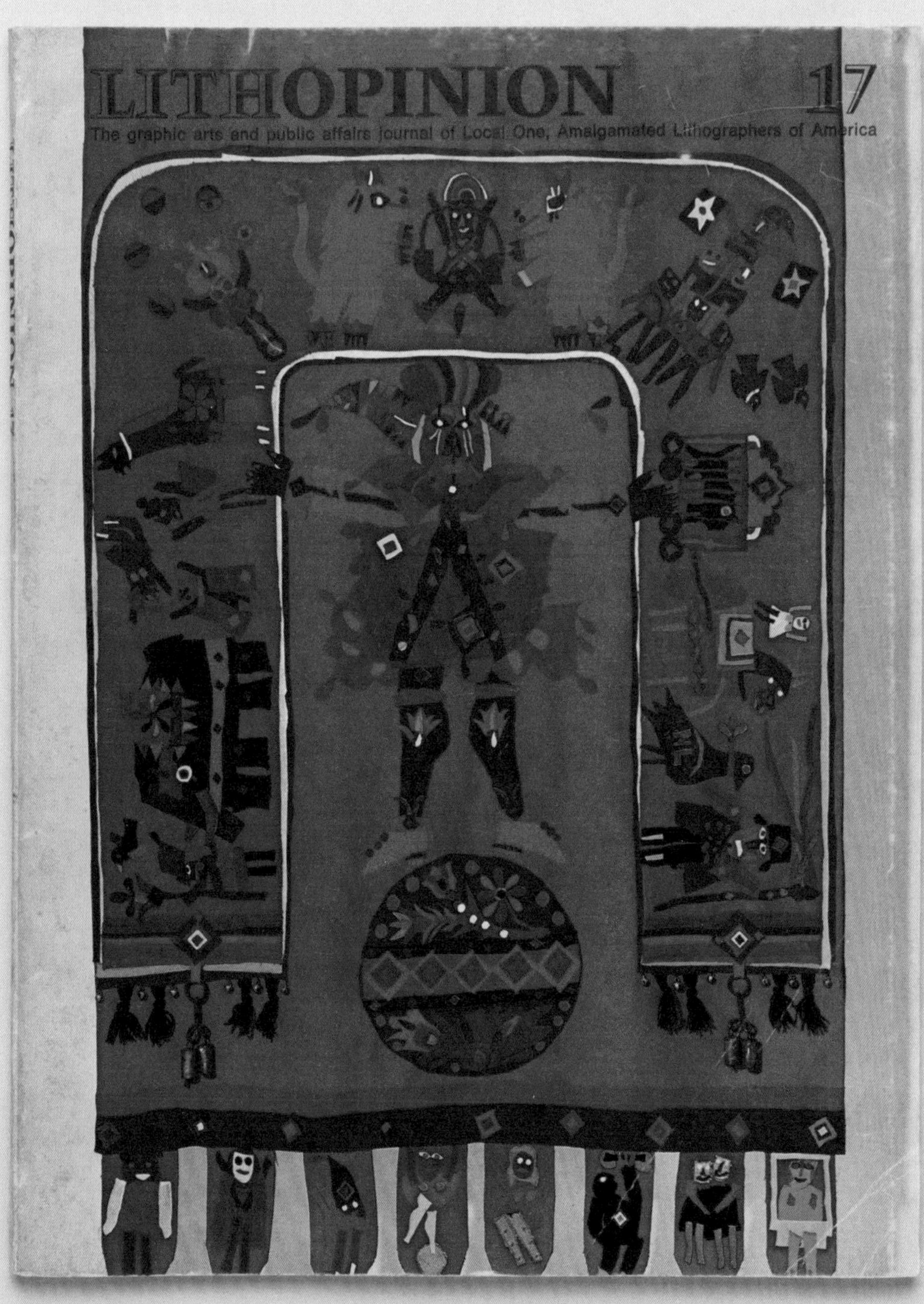

LITHOPINION 17
The graphic arts and public affairs journal of Local One, Amalgamated Lithographers of America

Lithopinion
Country: USA

Cover Design: Robert Hallock

01.1970

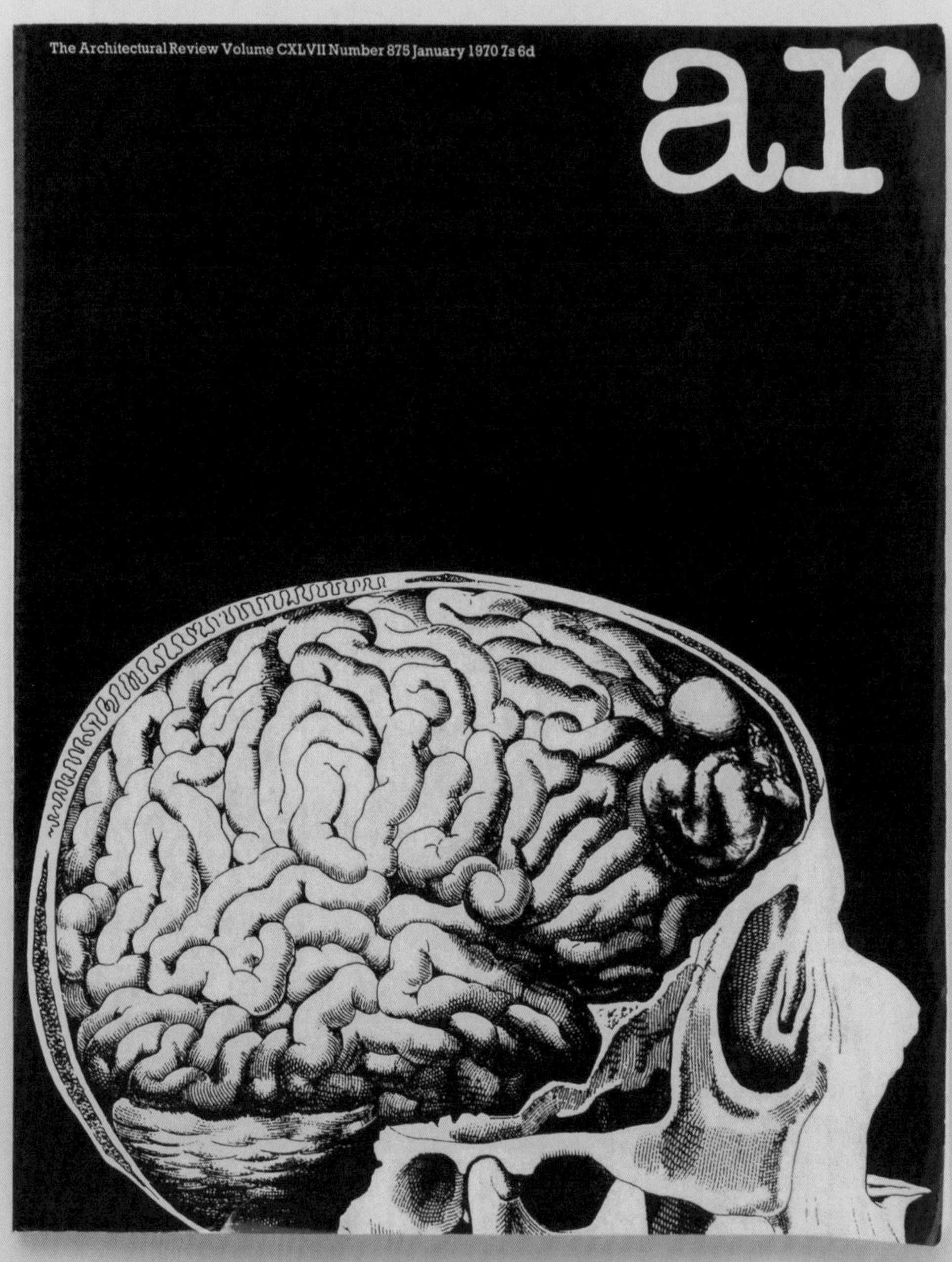

The Architectural Review Volume CXLVII Number 875 January 1970 7s 6d
ar

AR (The Architectural Review)
Country: UK

Cover Design: Wolf Spoerl

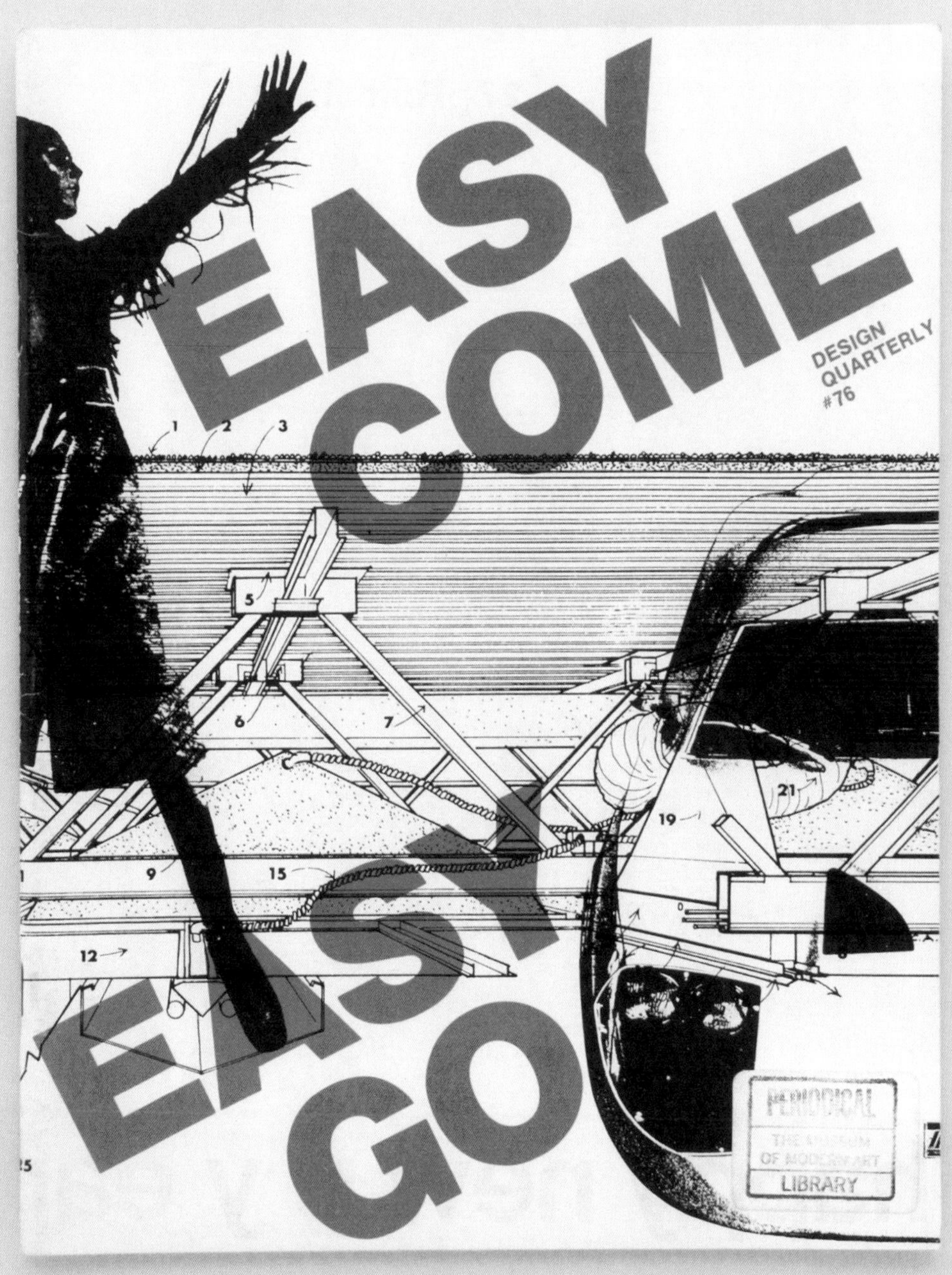

Design Quarterly
Country: USA

Cover Design:
Barbara Stauffacher Solomon
Courtesy of the Walker Art Centre

03.1970

Zeitschrift für verbale und visuelle Kommunikation

6. Jg./3–70 P 20638 F

27 ›Format‹

happy new e y ear

Format
Country: Germany

Cover Design: Manfred Maret

AR (The Architectural Review)
Country: UK

Cover Photography: Courtesy of the Trustees of the British Museum.

04.1970

Projekt
Country: Poland

Design: unidentified

AR (The Architectural Review)
Country: UK

Cover Design: Gerald Nason

06.1970

Gebrauchsgraphik
Country: Germany

Design: unidentified

The Journal
of Typographic Research
Summer 1970

The Journal of
Typographic Research
Country: USA

Cover Design: Jack Stauffacher

09.1970

AR (The Architectural Review)
Country: UK

Cover Design: Michael Reid
Cover Photography: Tim Rock

Graphis
Country: Switzerland

Cover Design: Gottschalk + Ash

The
re-discovery
of the
printed word.
TYPEtalks/The magazine of the printed word/1970, No. 167

Type Talks
Country: USA

Design: unidentified

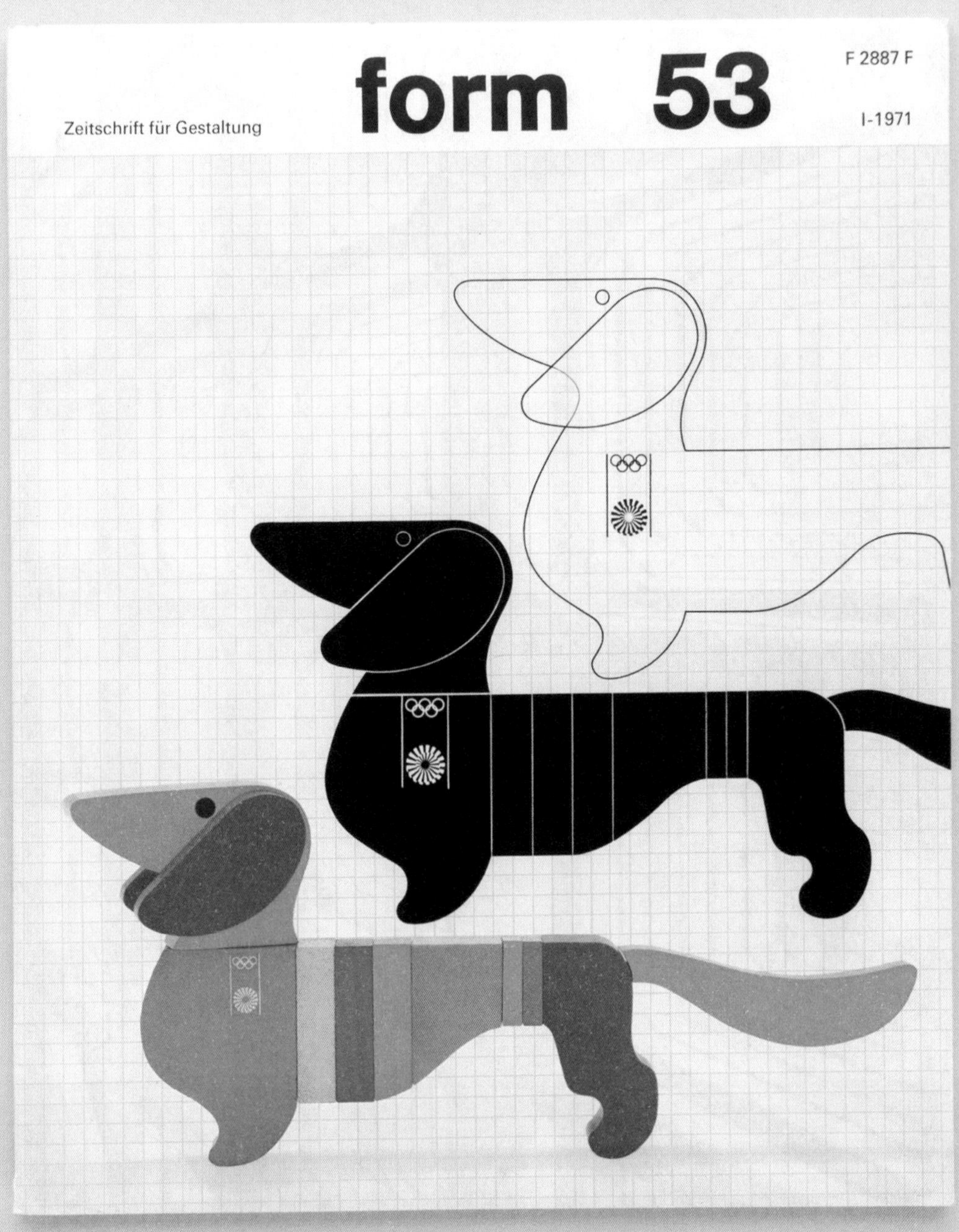

Form
Country: Germany

Cover Design: Hanswerner Klein

02.1971

AR (The Architectural Review)
Country: UK

Design: unidentified

03.1971

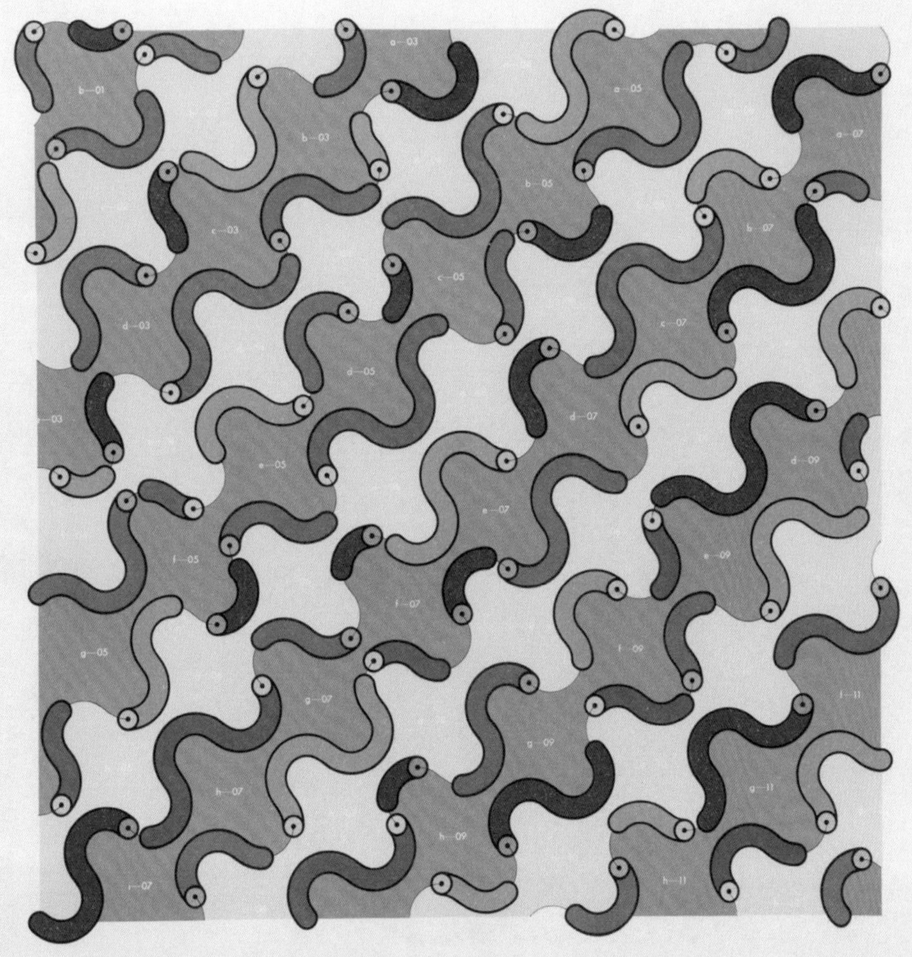

Graphic Design
Country: Japan

Cover Design: Kunito Teruyuki

04.1971

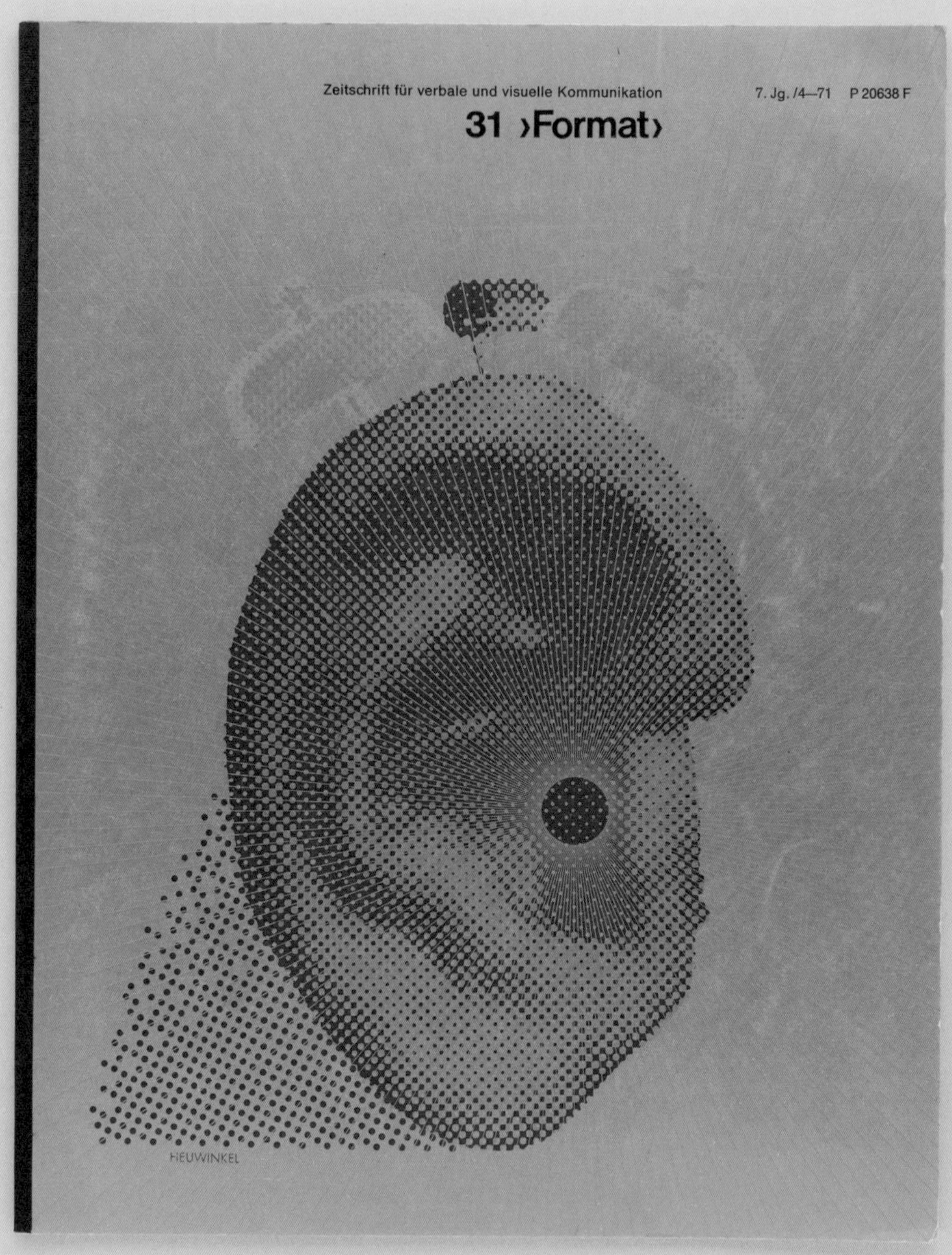

Format
Country: Germany

Cover Design: Wolfgang Heuwinkel

AR (The Architectural Review)
Country: UK

Cover Design: Brian Stapely

Nr. 6/71

Typografische Monatsblätter
Schweizer Grafische Mitteilungen
Revue suisse de l'Imprimerie

Herausgegeben vom Schweizerischen Typographenbund zur Förderung der Berufsbildung.
Editée par la Fédération suisse des typographes pour l'éducation professionnelle.

TM (Typographische Monatsblätter)
Country: Switzerland

Cover Design: Dario Zuffo
Courtesy of syndicom

AR (The Architectural Review)
Country: UK

Design: unidentified

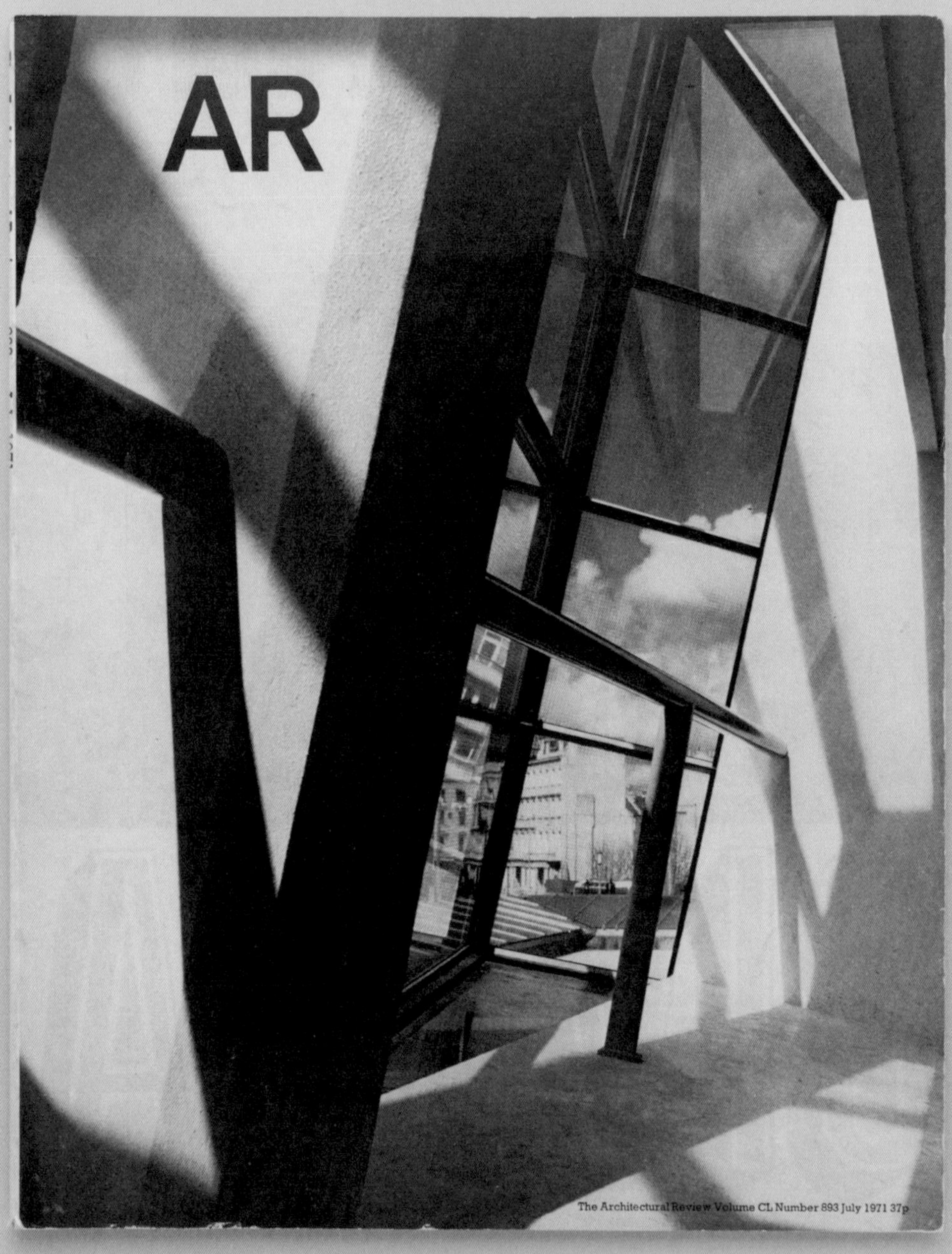

AR
The Architectural Review Volume CL Number 893 July 1971 37p

AR (The Architectural Review)
Country: UK

Cover Design: Richard Einzig

AR (The Architectural Review)
Country: UK

Cover Design: Franco Cisterna

09.1971

Graphis
Country: Switzerland

Cover art: Victor Vasarely

A quarterly Review of International Visual Communication Design

Issue number 2, October 1971

icographic

2

Price per issue 1 US dollar

Published in London by the International Council of Graphic Design Associations

Contents include

Television as universal educator
Defining the goals of education
Laser holography as a new medium for visual communication
Visual study in teaching animation
Research into variability of sign perception in horizontal motion
Audio-visual hardware
The book in an audio-visual world
Visual communication and education
Some views on the recent VisCom 71 congress and exhibition on the learning industry

Icographic
Country: UK

Cover Design:
Patrick Wallis Burke, Geoff White

11.1971

AR
The Architectural Review Volume CL Number 897 November 1971 37p

AR (The Architectural Review)
Country: UK

Cover Design: Philip Thompson

Interview: Teal Triggs

Q What was the first design publication that caught your eye?

A It would have been *Domus* (1928–present, Italy) in the late 1960s when I couldn't have been more than ten years old. My dad was a graphic designer and I distinctly remember the Italian magazine stacked neatly on the living room floor next to his favourite Eames reading chair. The covers attracted my attention – the use of bold graphics, photographic detailing and playful illustrations. By the 1980s, when Ettore Sottsass took over as editor and Postmodernism became *de rigeur*, I was hooked.

Q As an American designer and writer who has lived in the UK for many years, what is the main difference – if any – between USA and UK design publications?

A I guess their editorial emphasis. In recent history, mainstream USA design magazines such as *Communication Arts* (1959–present, USA), *Print* (1940–present, USA), *I.D.* (1954–2009, USA) and *How* (1985–present, USA), have tended to operate as showcases for trade or commercial design. Whereas in the UK, design publications such as *Design* (1949–99, UK), *Blueprint* (1983–present, UK) and *Eye* (1990–present, UK) have traditionally had a strong sense of the historical, cultural and social contexts in which design operates. Trade magazines such *Portfolio* (1949–51, USA) and *Word and Image* (1985–present, UK) were notable exceptions.

Other exceptions, of course, include periodicals that were key to influencing new ways of thinking about graphic design, but also impacted on the visual language of design: in the USA, there was *Wet* (1976–81), *Avant-garde* (1968–71), *Interview* (1969–present), *Spy* (1986–99), *Emigre* (1984–2005), *Beach Culture* (1989–91), *Ray Gun* (1992–2000), and so forth. And in the UK, popular culture and lifestyle magazines such as *i-D* (1980–present) and *The Face* (1980–2004) influenced a generation of designers internationally.

From my experience in both countries, publications that have been mouthpieces for professional design organisations have tended to provide platforms for writing and criticism which encouraged authors to look differently at design and often be more experimental in how they approached their subjects: for example, the AIGA *Journal for Graphic Design* (1947–present, USA), *Icographic* (1971–78, UK), *Circular* (1993–present, UK) and *Typographic* (1969–present, UK), amongst others. Some of the same authors writing in the UK would also write for US publications, providing readers with cross-cultural design perspectives.

Domus
1928–present
Italy

Blueprint
1983–present
UK

Q What is the role of design journalism and critical writing at a time when everything can be seen free online?

A The role of design journalism and critical writing is even more crucial now that content is readily available online. However, the role of the critic as an arbiter of taste has shifted to that of a navigator – leading us through a plethora of information that tells us what to think about design. There is always a space for critical writing to keep the profession from being too introspective. And in order to be critical you need to be informed and alert to what is going on. Today everybody is a critic – but not everybody can be a good critic.

I would suggest that more broadly, the role of the design magazine as a space for debate is losing its position as a place where designers might question and critically engage with the profession. Debates are moving online, either through Twitter or personal blogs and websites, or emerging in hybrid print and digital forms with alternative, independent small press magazines produced and edited by designers. *That New Design Smell* (2011–present, Canada), produced by Michèle Champagne, and *Modes of Criticism* (2015–present, UK/Portugal), by Francisco Laranjo, are cases in point.

Q How have design journals influenced your role as an educator and academic research leader?

A As an educator it's important to help our students engage with current research in the field, but also to be able to position their practice within a historical and theoretical framework. Academic journals are important as forums for inquiry and critical discourse. Journals inform and shape our field professionally and intellectually and, in doing so, help establish a future for the study of design.

Visible Language (1967–present, USA) – edited until recently by Sharon Helmer Poggenpohl – was an early academic design research journal, which influenced my thinking about the potential for design and typographic scholarly research. In particular, an issue from 1978 on the theme 'French Currents of the Letter', designed by four graduate students from Cranbrook Academy of Art – Richard Kerr, Alice Hecht, Jane Kosstrin and Herbert Thompson, with the then co-Chair of Design, Katherine McCoy. This printed issue clearly evidenced the potential for how research and typographic experimentation could be integrated into an academic space.

Whilst academic publishers have tended to become more conservative in their approach to the design of journals (in part fuelled by constraints of online publishing), the introduction of the visual essay has been a regular feature that my co-editors and I have used on the journal *Visual Communication* (2002–present, UK) to encourage alternative formats for disseminating visual research. Equally, in my role as Editor-in-Chief of *Communication Design* (2009–present, UK), we are seeking to provide new and relevant platforms for emerging researchers in graphic and interdisciplinary design practice: for example, the introduction of the specialist archive section and the visual essay format complement more conventional forms of academic writing. My involvement in these and other journals has been important in raising my awareness about new research in the field, which ultimately informs the way that I teach and support students in their learning.

Q You have a strong interest in the role of women in design. How have design journals advanced – or hindered – the cause of a feminist graphic design culture?

A Design journals merely reflect the status quo of its editors and readers. As such, the absence of coverage by the design press of the work of women designers is nothing new. An identifiable male-orientated canon for graphic design is the result of who and how the press has historically covered the field. The cause of a feminist design culture has been hindered by the continual perpetuation of the gaps in raising awareness about women working in the field.

Occasionally, however, it must be said that design magazines address the issues head on. Notable examples include Sheila Levrant de Bretteville's seminal essay published in *Icographic* 6 (1973), which was one of the early essays to raise awareness about a feminist graphic design culture. Later in the 1990s and early 2000s design publications such as *Emigre* and *Eye* gave pages over to an emerging discourse around the canon in design, with key writings by Ellen Lupton, Laurie Haycock Makela, Liz Farrelly, Martha Scotford, Bridget Wilkins and the Women's Design+Research Unit (WD+RU). Yet, even today, most of the awareness-raising is taking place online.

Teal Triggs is Associate Dean in the School of Communication at the Royal College of Art. As an editor, academic and writer, her work focuses on graphic design history, feminism in visual communication and design criticism.

Icographic
1971–78
UK

Visible Language
1967–present
USA

Nr. 1|1972

1

Typographie
realisiert
Sprache

mit Hilfe der gebräuchlichen Schriftzeichen, deren Sinn es ist, Mitteilungen eines Senders einem Empfänger zuzuführen. Wobei unterstellt wird, daß der Sender natürlich zugleich auch Empfänger sein kann.

Manfred Kröplien: 1968

Typographie
ist die Lehre
vom Entwurf von Textdrucksachen,
die für menschliche Wahrnehmung bestimmt
sind und als Kanal im Rahmen einer Kommunikationskette funktionieren.

Kurd Alsleben: 1962

Typografische Monatsblätter Schweizer Grafische Mitteilungen Revue Suisse de l'Imprimerie

TM (Typographische Monatsblätter)
Country: Switzerland

Cover Design: Wolfgang Weingart
Courtesy of syndicom

A quarterly Review of International Visual Communication Design

Issue number 3, 1972

icographic 3

Price per issue 1 US dollar

Published in London by the International Council of Graphic Design Associations

Contents include

On Typos: new Japanese type face
Designing and producing a consumers' association magazine
Designing a periodical for a variety of textual needs
Type designing in the future
Penguin paperbacks
Language and readability
Designing for Nuffield Foundation science teaching projects
A new Hebrew sans serif for bilingual printing
Demise of the point system in sight

Patrick Wallis Burke

Icographic
Country: UK

Cover Design: Patrick Wallis Burke

Sondernummer Februar 1972

TM

Typografische Monatsblätter
Schweizer Grafische Mitteilungen
Revue suisse de l'imprimerie
Herausgegeben vom Schweizerischen Typographenbund
zur Förderung der Berufsbildung
Editée par la Fédération suisse des typographes
pour l'éducation professionnelle

Karl Gerstner:
typographisches Memorandum

typographical memorandum
mémorandum typographique

TM (Typographische Monatsblätter)
Country: Switzerland

Cover Design: Karl Gerstner
Courtesy of syndicom

04.1972

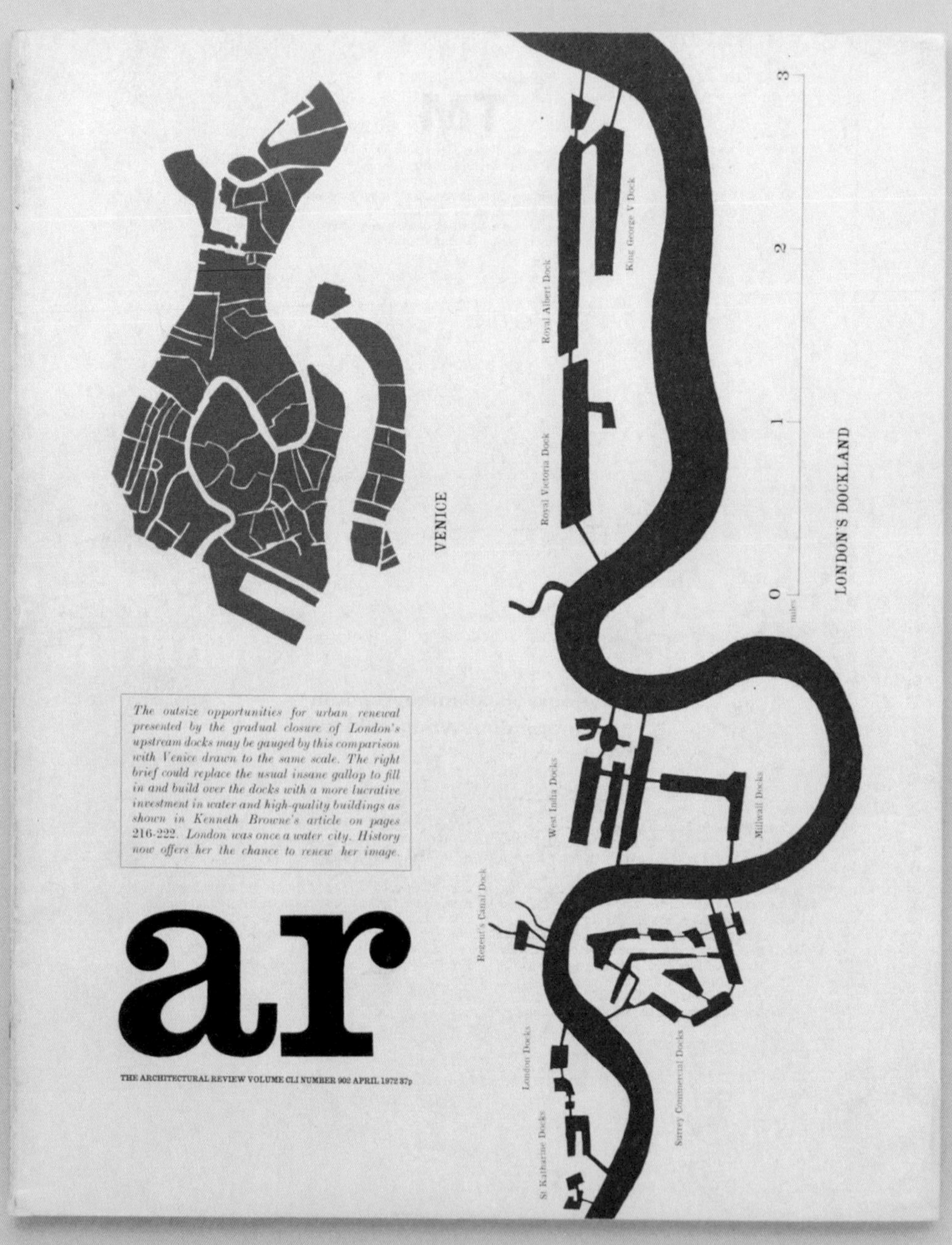
VENICE
LONDON'S DOCKLAND
King George V Dock
Royal Albert Dock
Royal Victoria Dock
West India Docks
Millwall Docks
Regent's Canal Dock
London Docks
Surrey Commercial Docks
St Katharine Docks
0 1 2 3
miles
The outsize opportunities for urban renewal presented by the gradual closure of London's upstream docks may be gauged by this comparison with Venice drawn to the same scale. The right brief could replace the usual insane gallop to fill in and build over the docks with a more lucrative investment in water and high-quality buildings as shown in Kenneth Browne's article on pages 216-222. London was once a water city. History now offers her the chance to renew her image.
ar
THE ARCHITECTURAL REVIEW VOLUME CLI NUMBER 902 APRIL 1972 37p

AR (The Architectural Review)
Country: UK

Design: unidentified

A quarterly Review of International Visual Communication Design

Issue number 4, 1972

icographic

4

Price per issue 1 US dollar

Published in London by the International Council of Graphic Design Associations

Contents include

Relating teaching to what is known about learning
Creativity: a teachable skill?
National Institute of Design, Paldi Ahmedabad, India
An American view of British graphic design education
Problems of adult education
Visual communication in East Africa
Designing books that present a visual argument
The myths of art and science
Our collective knowledge

Icographic
Country: UK

Cover Design:
Herb Gilman, Patrick Wallace Burke

07.1972

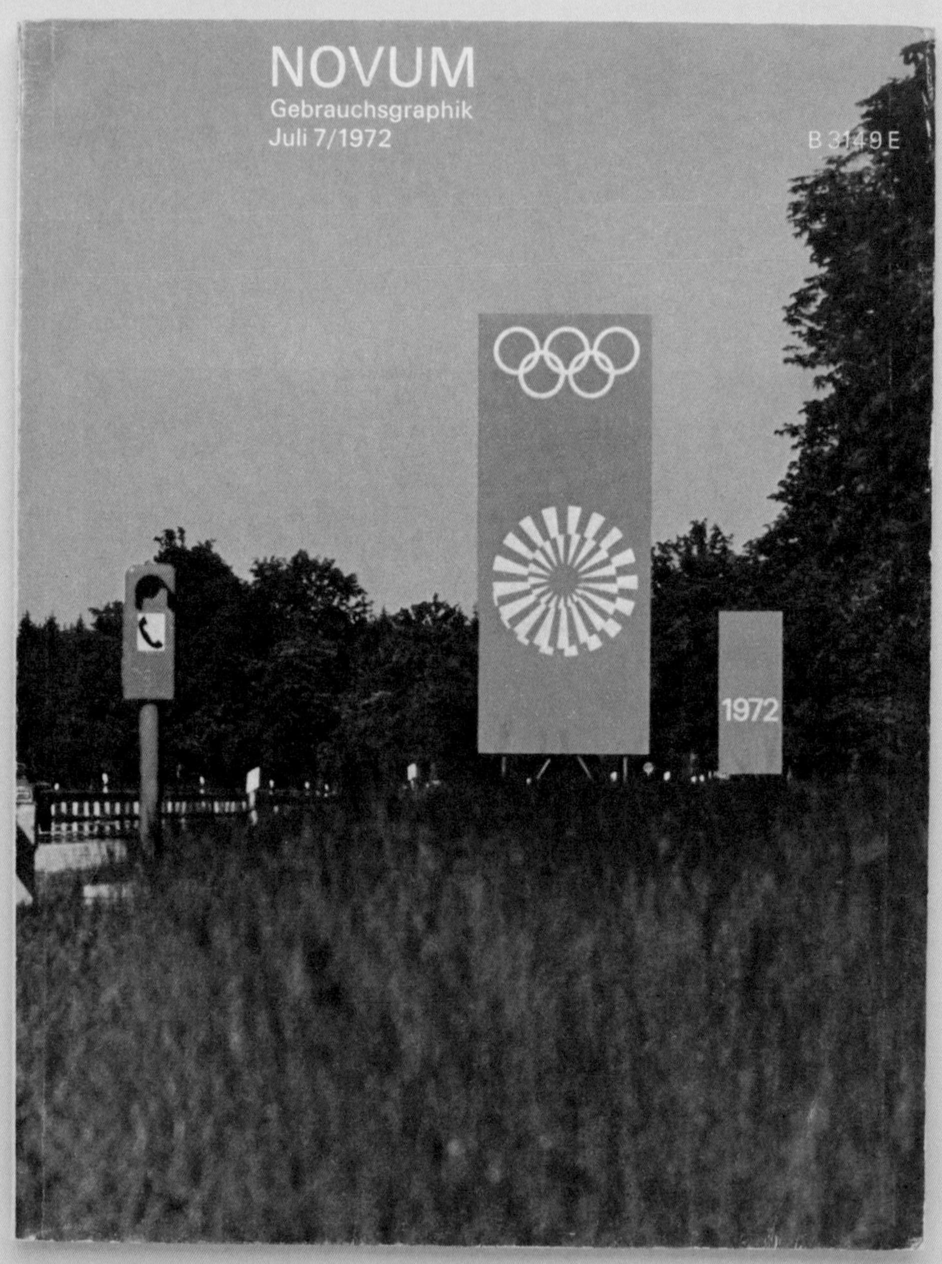

novum
Country: UK

Cover Photo: Gabriele Pée

昭和47年9月1日発行★第20巻★第5号★通巻第114号〈隔月1日発行〉昭和28年6月17日★国鉄東局特別扱承認雑誌〈第2566号〉

アイデア Idea 114

1972-9
International Advertising Art
世界のデザイン誌／誠文堂新光社

Idea
Country: Japan

Cover Design: FHK Henrion

11.1972

Graphis
Country: Switzerland

Cover Design: Otl Aicher

Nr. 12|1972

Sprachencharta :1968

12

Sprechen:
Sprechen ist das dem Menschen eigene Vermogen, Bewußtseinsinhalte in Worte zu fassen und mit der Stimme auszudrucken.

Sprache:
Sprache ist – allgemein gefaßt – ein System von Wörtern, Wort- und Satzfügungen. Alle, die dieses System kennen und anwenden, werden damit befähigt, Bewußtseinsinhalte mitzuteilen und einander zu verstehen.

Schrift:
Schrift ist konventionelle bildliche Darstellung der Wörter einer Sprache. Damit können Aussagen in dieser Sprache festgehalten und weitergegeben werden.

Grammatik:
Grammatik – im weitesten Sinne – faßt die Formen und Fügungen einer gesprochenen oder geschriebenen Sprache auf jeder Stufe ihrer Entwicklung.

Wert der Sprache: **Jede Sprache ist für die menschliche Gemeinschaft, die sich ihrer bedient, und damit für jeden, der zu dieser Gemeinschaft gehört.**

1. sachlich: **Praktisches Werkzeug als Mittel der Aussage und der zwischenmenschlichen Beziehungen.**

2. geistig: Intellektuelles und gemüthaftes Erbe von grundlegender geistiger und sittlicher Bedeutung und als solches ein Bestandteil der Menschheitskultur.

3. künstlerisch: Werkstoff, der literarische Kunstwerke möglich macht.

Unersetzbarkeit: **Diese Merkmale sind allen Sprachen gemein, eignen aber jeder von ihnen auf eine besondere und unverwechselbare Art.**

Aus ‹Dokument Nr. 3› der Sprachencharta des Freiburger Instituts. Freiburg|Schweiz

CONCEPTION & DESIGN WEINGART

Typografische Monatsblätter Schweizer Grafische Mitteilungen Revue Suisse de l'Imprimerie

TM (Typographische Monatsblätter)
Country: Switzerland

Cover Design: Wolfgang Weingart
Courtesy of syndicom

02.1973

441
THE ARCHITECTURAL REVIEW VOLUME CLIII NUMBER 912 FEBRUARY 1973 37p

AR (The Architectural Review)
Country: UK

Cover Design: Philip Thompson

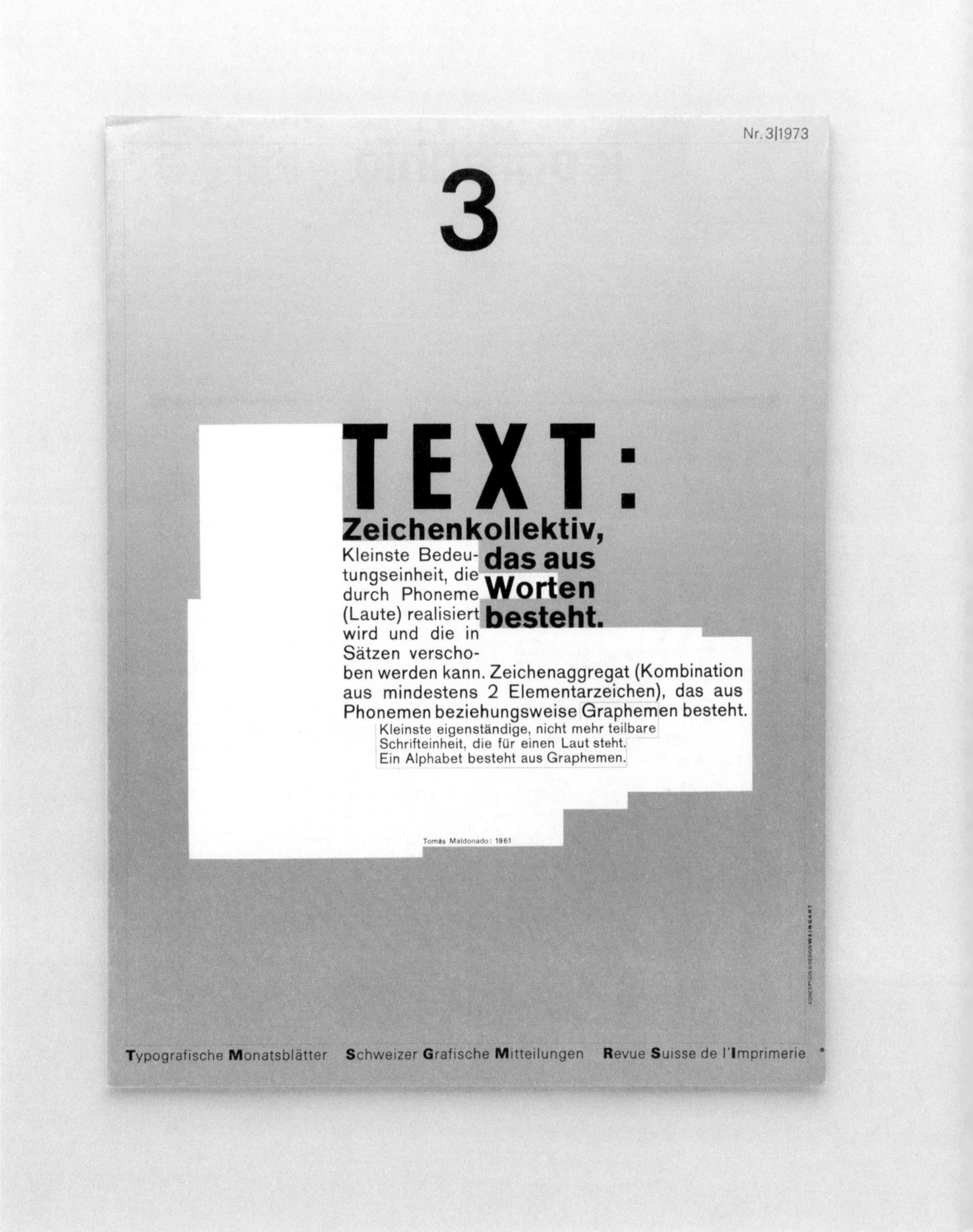

03.1973

Nr. 3|1973

3

TEXT:

Zeichenkollektiv, das aus Worten besteht.

Kleinste Bedeutungseinheit, die durch Phoneme (Laute) realisiert wird und die in Sätzen verschoben werden kann. Zeichenaggregat (Kombination aus mindestens 2 Elementarzeichen), das aus Phonemen beziehungsweise Graphemen besteht.

Kleinste eigenständige, nicht mehr teilbare Schrifteinheit, die für einen Laut steht. Ein Alphabet besteht aus Graphemen.

Tomás Maldonado: 1961

Typografische Monatsblätter Schweizer Grafische Mitteilungen Revue Suisse de l'Imprimerie

TM (Typographische Monatsblätter)
Country: Switzerland

Cover Design: Wolfgang Weingart
Courtesy of syndicom

1973

A quarterly Review of International Visual Communication Design

Issue number 5, 1973

icographic

5

Price per issue 1 US dollar

Published in London by the International Council of Graphic Design Associations

Contents include

Books and barbarity
The role of the book designer
Visual aids
The changing responsibilities of the typographical designer
The book in a changing cultural climate
The essential book
Designing the symbol for International Book Year
Some tasks for future book design
Book review

Patrick Wallis Burke

Icographic
Country: UK

Cover Design:
Patrick Wallis Burke, Herb Gillman

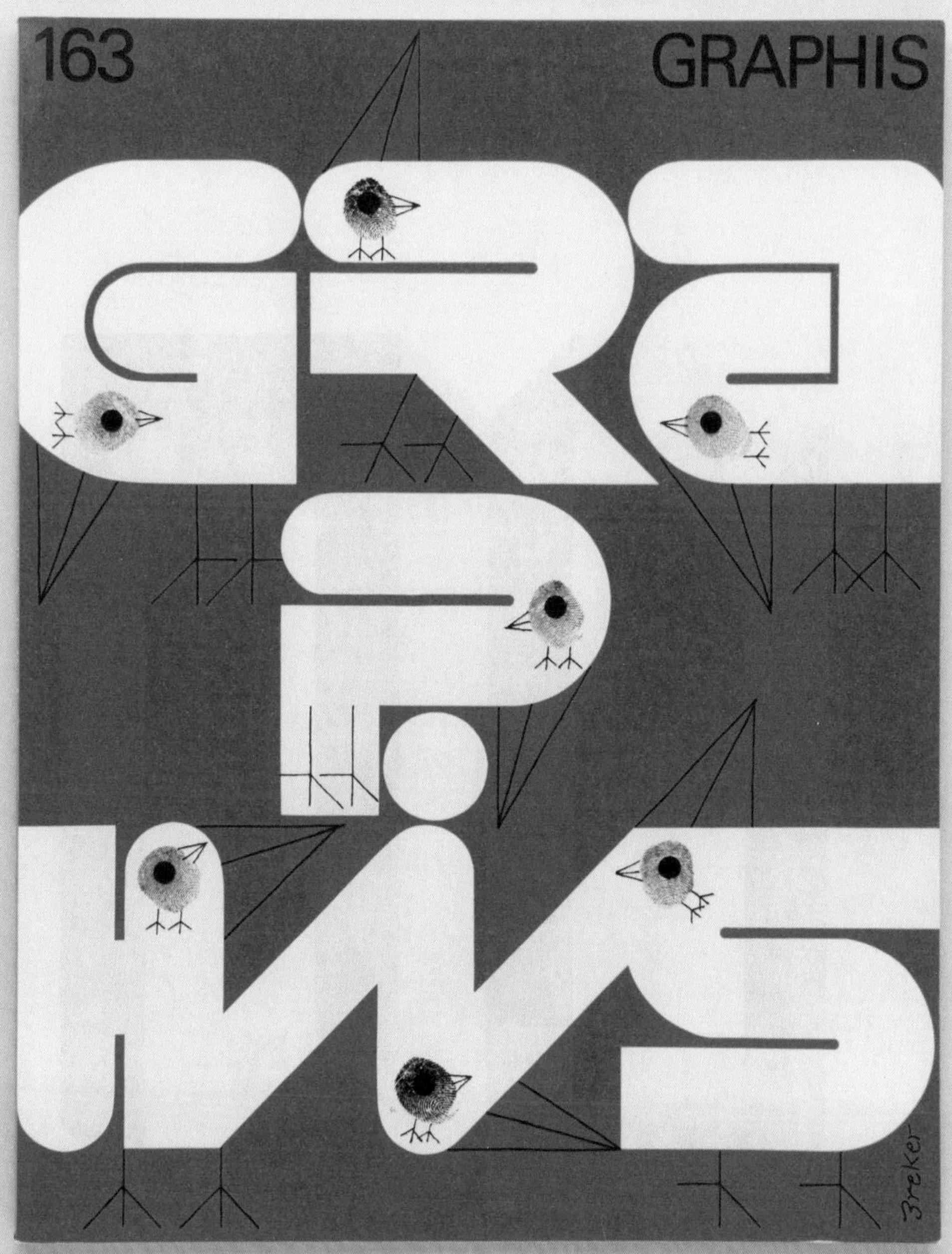

Graphis
Country: Switzerland

Cover Design: Walter Breker

07.1973

Zeitschrift für verbale und visuelle Kommunikation
9. Jg. Heft 4 Juli 73 P 20638 F
44 ›Format‹

Format
Country: Germany

Cover Design: Manfred Glemser

Format
Country: Germany

Cover Design: Klaus Winterhager

Nr.10|1973
GEWIDMET RUDOLF HOSTETTLER
DEDICATED TO RUDOLF HOSTETTLER
DEDIE A RUDOLF HOSTETTLER
Warum und wie
Mit einer Collage von Christa Zelinsky. Und mit einem erklärenden Text zu Idee und Konzeption der Umschläge für die Typographischen Monatsblätter 1972 und 1973.
die TM-Umschläge für 1972 und 1973 entstanden sind.
Why and how TM-covers for 1972 and 1973
came to be
TM 1972 et 1973
créées les couvertures pour les
Comment et pourquoi ont été
With a collage by Christa Zelinsky and text explaining the idea and concept of the covers for the ‹Typographische Monatsblätter› 1972 and 1973.
Avec un collage de Christa Zelinsky. Et un texte qui explique l'idée et la conception des couvertures pour les ‹Typographische Monatsblätter› 1972 et 1972.
Typografische Monatsblätter Schweizer Grafische Mitteilungen Revue Suisse de l'Imprimerie

TM (Typographische Monatsblätter)
Country: Switzerland

Cover Design: Wolfgang Weingart
Courtesy of syndicom

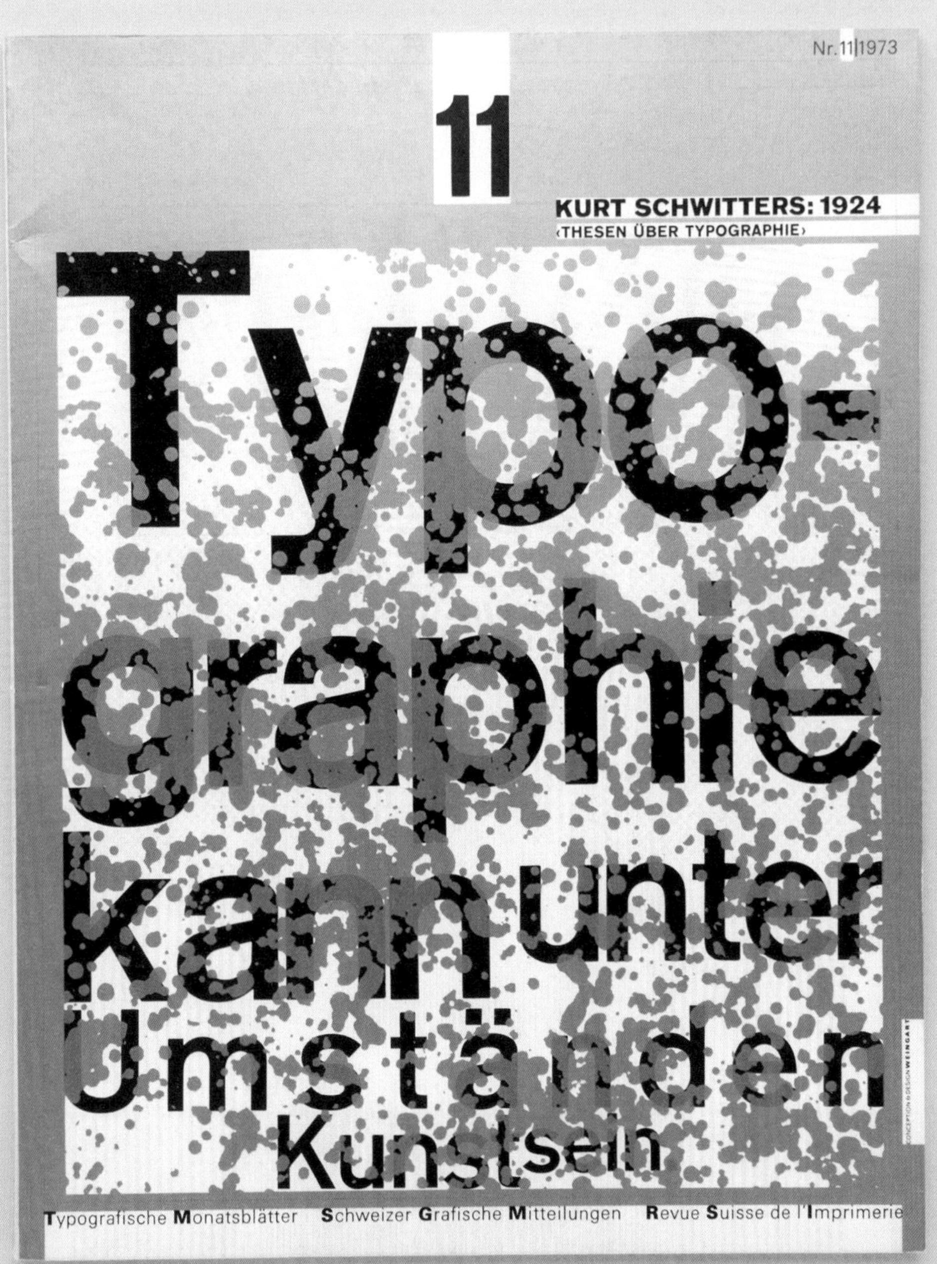

TM (Typographische Monatsblätter)
Country: Switzerland

Cover Design: Wolfgang Weingart
Courtesy of syndicom

12.1973

AR (The Architectural Review)
Country: UK

Cover Design: Enzo Ragazzini

Nr.12|1973

12

Was ist Typographie?

Im Grunde genommen ist Typographie die Anordnung von 26 kleinen abstrakten Zeichen, durch welche die Ideen einer Person, des Autores – einer anderen Person – dem Leser übermittelt werden. Natürlich ist die Voraussetzung, daß jeder weiß, welche Klänge die Zeichen darstellen. Um dieser Tatsache sicher zu sein, hämmern wir diese Klänge unseren Kindern ein, sobald sie fähig sind, sie aufzunehmen. Natürlich wirkt diese Definition, obschon sie grundlegend ist, allzu einfach. Die Typographie kann wohl auf diese Weise erklärt werden, aber sie enthält noch viel mehr. Sie schließt mit ein, daß wir die Buchstaben des Alphabets mit Leichtigkeit erkennen ebenso wie ihre Gruppierung zu Wörtern, Linien und Abschnitten: Die Lesbarkeit soll dadurch vereinfacht werden. Sie bringt die richtige Auslegung der Gedanken mit sich, welche uns die visuelle Verbindung zwischen Verfasser und Leser erleichtert. Die Lesbarkeit enthält die Auswahl der geeigneten Typen für bestimmte Zwecke – die Art der Mitteilung, die Natur des Lesers, das Druckverfahren und das dafür verwendete Papier. Schließlich existiert auch eine ästhetische Seite: Die Typographie, die das Auge anspricht, enthält die gleichen Grundsätze des Gestaltens wie jedes Kunstwerk.

Carl Dair 1964

What is typography?

Come right down to it, it is simply the arrangement of twenty-six little abstract squiggles in such a way that it conveys an idea from one person—the author—to another person—the reader. The assumption is that everybody knows what sounds the squiggles represent; to make sure of that, we hammer it into the heads of our young as soon as they can absorb it. Of course, this definition, while basic, is an over-simplification. Typography is that, but it is much more, too. It involves the ease with which we recognize the letters of the alphabet, their grouping into words and lines and masses—questions of simple legibility. It involves the proper interpretation of the message to facilitate the visual communication between author and reader. It involves the selection of the appropriate types for specific purposes—the nature of the message, the kind of reader, the printing processes and paper employed. And finally, it involves aesthetics, for typography which appeals to the eye will embody the same set of principles of design that goes into any work of art.

CONCEPTION & DESIGN WEINGART

Typografische **M**onatsblätter **S**chweizer **G**rafische **M**itteilungen **R**evue **S**uisse de l'**I**mprimerie

TM (Typographische Monatsblätter)
Country: Switzerland

Cover Design: Wolfgang Weingart
Courtesy of syndicom

AD
1940–42
USA

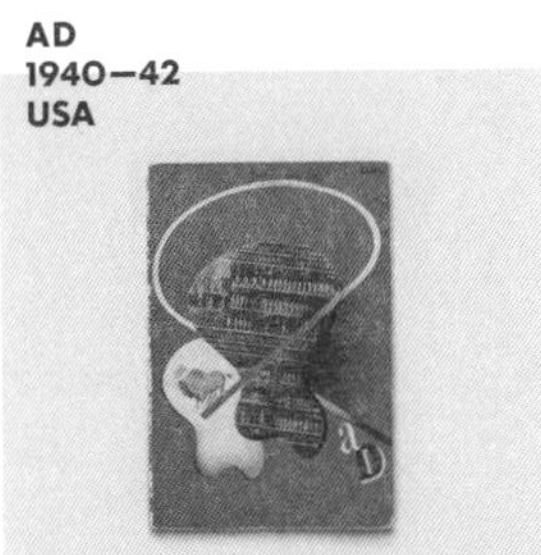

AD (1940–42, USA) was originally known as *PM* magazine. As *AD* (standing for Art Director) it became one of the most influential publications in the USA, showcasing both the best USA-based designers as well as avant-garde practitioners from Europe. As with *PM*, it was founded and edited by Robert L Leslie, and aimed at professionals in the graphic arts. *AD* reflected the rise of the art director, and the role of art direction in the design and advertising industry. Contributors included Herbert Bayer, Lester Beall, Will Burtin, Herbert Matter, Cipe Pineles and Paul Rand. As with *PM*, *AD* did not reappear after World War II.

Alphabet and Image
1946–48
UK

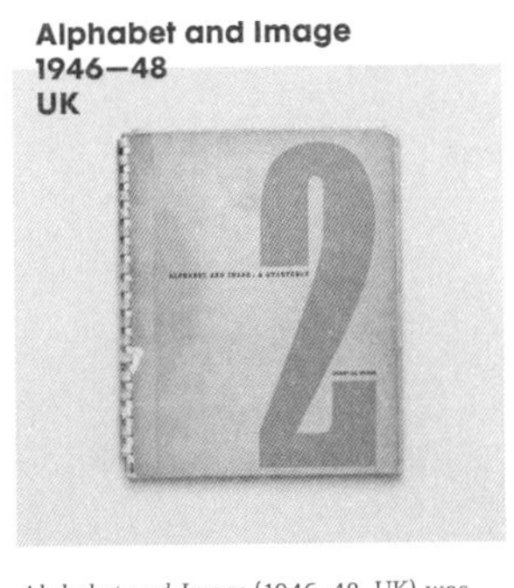

Alphabet and Image (1946–48, UK) was originally published as *Typography* (1936–39). *A&I* was a short-lived, post-war quarterly publication. It was edited and designed by Robert Harlin and focused primarily on illustration. Mike Dempsey, in his blog *Graphic Journey*, called it a 'campaigning publication in its own way. In issue 5 (1947) they accused the master printers and craft unions of "suffering from a mental hardening of the arteries and lack of awareness of some of the greater insistent problems of the day in the allied industries".'

AR (The Architectural Review)
1896–present
UK

AR (*The Architectural Review*) (1896–present, UK) has been published continually since 1896. It is one of the world's leading monthly architecture magazines, and covers topics such as landscaping, interior design and urban planning. Described by architecture critic Deyan Sudjic as 'the grand old lady of architectural publishing', its covers have been designed by many important British graphic designers including Philip Thompson and Brian Stapely.

Architektur Wettbewerbe
1950s–present
Germany

Architektur Wettbewerbe (1950s-present, Germany) is a journal published by Karl Kramer Verlag in Stuttgart. The English translation of the title is 'Architecture Competitions'.

Art Director & Studio News
1953–unknown
USA

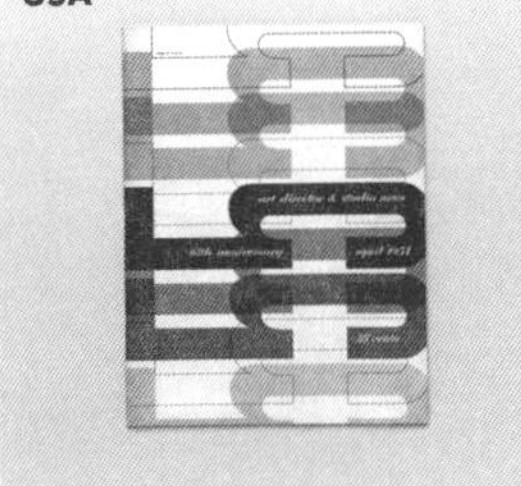

Art Director & Studio News (1953-unknown, USA) was the publication of the National Society of Art Directors. The magazine carried features on subjects ranging from advice on tax for the freelancer, to guidance on designing for the new TV industry. It also carried ads for illustrators offering tuition to those considering a career in art and design. The typographic cover design shown here is by Robert Flynn, a leading designer of jazz record sleeves in the 1960s. Best known today for his work with the jazz label Impulse, he designed covers for John Coltrane, Archie Shepp, Chico Hamilton and others. Flynn died in 1970.

Bauen+Wohnen
1947–79
Switzerland

Bauen+Wohnen (1947–79, Switzerland) was dedicated to architecture and urban development. *Bauen+Wohnen* was published by the Federation of Swiss Architects. Many international architects were featured in its pages including Walter Gropius, Marcel Breuer and Gerrit Rietveld. According to Richard Paul Lohse's website (www.lohse.ch/bio_long_e.html) *Bauen+Wohnen* was designed and co-edited by him from 1947 to 1956. The journal contained photographs, plans and elevations, and featured many of Lohse's signature graphic techniques, including overprinting and a modular grid system based on squares. Shown here are the German editions, which were published from 1952 onwards.

Casabella
1928–present
Italy

Casabella (1928-present, Italy) was founded by Guido Marangoni as a monthly architectural and product design magazine. Initially called *La Casa Bella* (The Beautiful Home) its name changed to *Casa Bella* in 1933 when the architect Giuseppe Pagano became its director. Now named *Casabella*, it has been described as an 'expression of architectural culture', and is widely regarded as an important reference point for architects. The magazine is currently designed by the design studio Tassinari/Vetta.

Creative Art
1983–unknown
USA

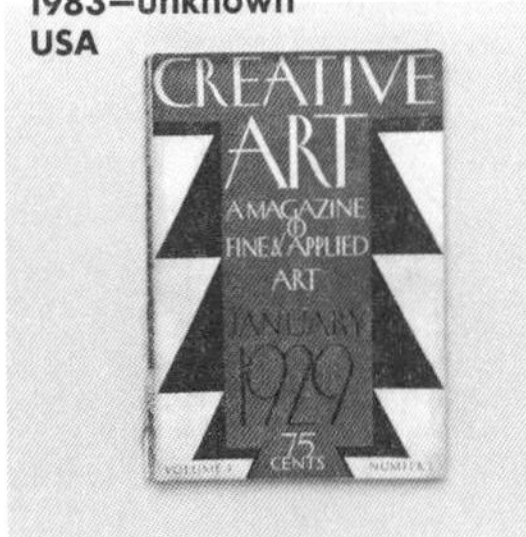

Creative Art (1983-unknown, USA) was for many years an American reprint of the British publication *The Studio*. It featured vintage advertising, design, architecture, fine art and book reviews, with articles by Lewis Mumford and Diego Rivera, photographs by Tina Modotti, and rugs designed by E McKnight Kauffer and Marian Dorn. It was published by Albert & Charles Boni.

Design 1949–99 UK

Design (1949–99, UK) was the magazine of the UK Design Council (formerly the Council of Industrial Design). In an essay on the history of British graphic design journals, the writer David Crowley noted that graphic design rarely featured in the pages of *Design*, and when it did make an appearance, it was usually in relation to 'reports on the systematic techniques behind successful corporate images, road signage or the practical failings of public information campaigns'. Ken Garland was *Design*'s art editor from 1956–62. (Covers reproduced courtesy of Design Council/ University of Brighton Design Archives.)

Design For Industry 1959 UK

Design For Industry (1959, UK) focused on product design and manufacturing in post-war Britain. It was a short-lived publication that had previously existed as *Art & Industry* and *Commercial Art*, both published by *The Studio* in London and New York from 1926 to 1959. In an attempt to address falling sales, the journal was repackaged and renamed *Design For Industry*. The change came too late and *Design For Industry* ceased publication in December 1959. The editor was Robert Downer, and the art editor was Margaret Webb (later to become art editor of *New Scientist*).

Design Quarterly 1954–93 USA

Design Quarterly (1954–93, USA). The first 28 issues of this magazine were published by the Walker Art Center, under the title *Everyday Art Quarterly*. In 1954, the magazine became *Design Quarterly*. With issue 159 (1993), the Walker Art Center ceased its affiliation with the journal, and it was briefly owned by MIT Press. *Design Quarterly* charted the design landscape in America, from contemporary architecture and product design to a more focused look at the social impact of design. Issue 63 (1965) was guest-edited by Reyner Banham. Graphic design did not feature prominently until the editorship of Mildred Freeman (1972–91), when it featured more frequently. In the 1980s issues were guest-edited by, amongst others, Armin Hofmann, Wolfgang Weingart and April Greiman.

The Designer 1960s UK

The Designer (1960s, UK) was an austere, black-and-white periodical produced by the Society of Industrial Artists and Designers. Founded in 1930 as The Society of Industrial Artists (SIA), this was the first professional body for designers in the UK. Founding members Milner Gray, Misha Black and others aimed to establish the professional status of the 'industrial' designer on an equal footing with architects and engineers. The journal covered all forms of applied design (interior design, product design, graphic design, fashion and textile design), with a strong emphasis on professional and ethical matters. Issue 167 (shown here) includes the famous article on grids ('Typography is a grid') by Anthony Froshaug.

Domas 1931–unknown Latvia

Domas (1931–unknown, Latvia), although not strictly a design journal, it is described as a 'monthly magazine of literature, arts and sciences'. It was an influential avant-garde, left-wing cultural publication. It featured cover designs by Niklāvs Strunke (1894–1966), a prominent figure in the 20th-century Latvian avant-garde.

Dot Zero 1966–68 USA

Dot Zero (1966–68, USA) was a partnership between design consultancy Unimark International and paper company Finch, Pruyn. All five issues of *Dot Zero* were designed by Massimo Vignelli, using only two weights of Helvetica, and printed in black and white. The magazine focused on the theory and practice of visual communication. As Steven Heller has noted: 'Articles were uncommonly critical and analytical and raised intellectual themes usually left to scholarly papers, including "A Theory of Expositions", "The Concept of Environmental Management" and "Thoughts on Three-Dimensional Science Communications".' *Dot Zero* stands as a powerful exemplar of Massimo Vignelli's modernist-inspired design ethos.

form 1957–present Germany

form (1957–present, Germany) was founded as *International Revue* by Jupp Ernst, Willem Sandberg, Curt Schweicher and Wilhelm Wagenfeld. *Form* started as a wide-ranging cultural magazine dealing with art, architecture and industrial design, but also discussing ballet, music, poetry and designer manifestos. What began life as the idea of four creative people in 1957 is today a forum offering topics that are intended to 'stimulate the design discourse'.

Form+Zweck 1956–unknown Germany

Form+Zweck (1956–unknown, Germany) translates as Form and Purpose. Originally published as *Form und Zweck* (1956–90), this East German publication was founded by the Institute of Applied Arts to document and develop professional design work. Its editors, as employees of the East German government, could not express ideas that were not government sanctioned, and any articles that supported consumerist or capitalistic leanings were censored. But after the fall of the Berlin Wall the journal was commercially reformulated as *Form+Zweck*.

Format
1968–1980
Germany

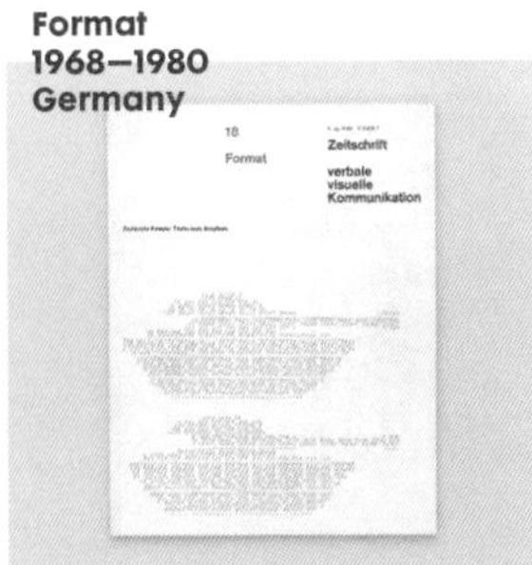

Format (1968–c.1980, Germany) was subtitled Zeitschrift für verbale und visuelle Kommunikation (the magazine of verbal and visual communication). It covered advertising, PR, communication in writing and image, and was published six times a year. It carried articles on typography and photography, and often featured inserts from the paper industry. It was founded by designer and art director Hubertus Carl Frey. Publisher and editor-in-chief for many issues was Dieter Gitzel.

Gebrauchsgraphik
1923–50
Germany

Gebrauchsgraphik (1923–50, Germany) was a professional magazine dedicated to advertising art, and one of the first-generation design journals in Europe. Edited by H. K. Frenzel, and published in English and German, the magazine was utilitarian in its design, showcasing Frenzel's belief that advertising could be a positive force in society. From 1971 to 1996 it was known as *novum-gebrauchsgraphik*, and it remains in print today under the name *novum: World of Graphic Design.*

Graphic Design
1959–86
Japan

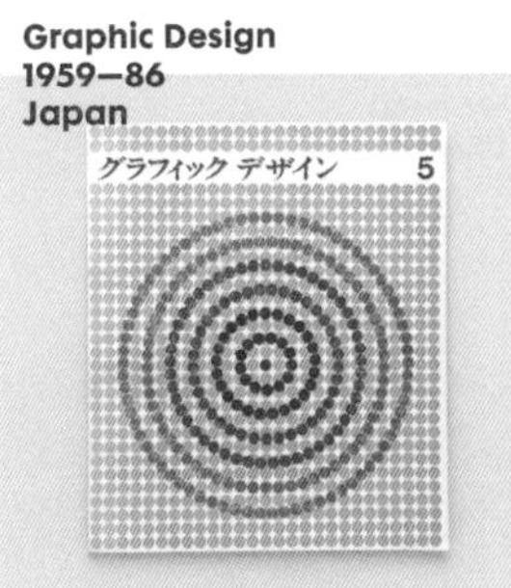

Graphic Design (1959–86, Japan) was edited by designer Masaru Katsumi, *Graphic Design* was one of Japan's most significant design magazines, showcasing both Japanese designers alongside Western counterparts. It lasted for exactly 100 issues. According to *Idea* editor Kiyonori Muroga, 'Masaru was an agent for change, developing the quality and social position of Japanese graphic design. In post-war Japanese society, *Graphic Design* was a vehicle to develop and establish the high cultural standard of graphic design. The content was very curated and academic, compared with other magazines.'

Graphis
1944–present
Switzerland

Graphis (1944-present, Switzerland) was first published in 1944, in Zürich, Switzerland by Walter Herdeg and Walter Amstutz. After a split from Amstutz in 1964, Herdeg became the sole publisher. The company was sold in 1986 to B. Martin Pedersen, and the headquarters were relocated to New York. *Graphis* has been a hugely influential showcase for graphic design, advertising and illustration since its launch. It continues today, with over 350 issues published.

Grafische Revue
1921–1936
Netherlands

Grafische Revue (1921-1936, Netherlands) was a publication produced by the Bond van Typografische Studiegezelschappen (Society of Typographical Studies). It has been described as: 'A periodical that pays much attention to the education of young graphic designers and to the design of the book. Especially interesting is the typographical design of the wrappers of each edition.' Even earlier than *Grafische Revue* was Typefoundry Amsterdam's publication *Typografische mededeelingen* (Typographic announcements). It ran from 1905 to 1934, and afterwards as *Grafische mededeelingen* (Graphic announcements).

Icographic
1971–78
UK

Icographic (1971–78, UK) was edited and designed by Patrick Wallis Burke. The magazine was designed on a four-column grid with headings in Helvetica and body copy in Univers Medium. It was published quarterly by ICOGRADA (International Council of Graphic Design Associations) as an academic journal that attempted to bring visual communication design research to a wider international audience. ICOGRADA was founded in 1963 in London, by Peter Kneebone and Willy de Majo, to create meaningful international dialogue around the future of graphic design. ICOGRADA is known today as ico-D, and publishes the journal *Communication Design*, Interdisciplinary and Graphic Design Research, led by editor-in-chief Teal Triggs.

Idea
1953–present
Japan

Idea (1953–present, Japan) remains one of the most important and longstanding graphic design publications in the world. It has been at the forefront of the international graphic design scene since its inception. Initially the magazine functioned as a shop window for designers around the world. In more recent years, and now under the editorship of Kiyonori Muroga, the magazine has developed a more critical position. *Idea* has always made high-grade reproduction and state-of-the-art printing two of its defining qualities. This is coupled with striking covers and a dynamic non-formatted layout.

Industrial Art News
1932–74
Japan

Industrial Art News (1932–74, Japan). The Industrial Arts Institute (IAI) was originally conceived as an agency for the promotion of mass-production techniques and new products to smaller companies in Japan. It published the influential periodical *Kogei Nyusu* (*Industrial Art News*), a monthly design journal, and held an annual exhibition to showcase new products.

Industrial Design (I.D)
1954–2009
USA

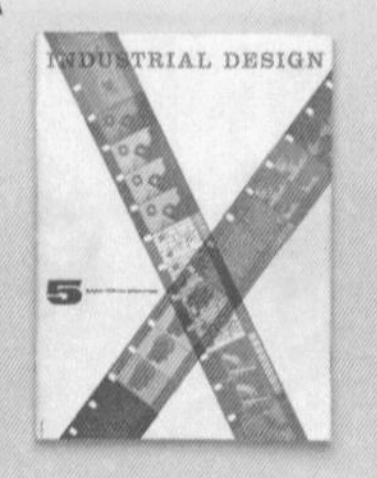

Industrial Design (*I.D.*) (1954–2009, USA) was the invention of publisher Charles Whitney. He was persuaded by his friend the designer George Nelson that a specialised periodical devoted to the growing field of industrial design was needed. Alvin Lustig was the first art director. Many covers in the late 1960s were done by Massimo Vignelli. The print magazine closed in 2009. By this time it was known as *I.D*, whose editors included Ralph Caplan, Chee Pearlman and, lastly, Julie Lasky.

The Journal of Typographic Research
1967–70
USA

The Journal of Typographic Research (1967–70, USA) was founded and edited by Dr. Merald Wrolstad. Wrolstad believed that in order to form a proper understanding of communication design, and in particular the development of typography in its support of reading and writing, it was essential that research and scholarly investigation was employed. After four years he changed the title to *Visible Language*, and in 1987 the journal passed to its second editor, Sharon Poggenpohl, who continued the in-depth investigation into, and interrogation of design.

Linea Grafica
1945–2011
Italy

Linea Grafica (1945–2011, Italy) was a bi-monthly magazine of graphics and visual communication. It ceased publication in 1985 but started up again under a new editor in the same year. It was one of Italy's most influential design publications. In its early days, the magazine promoted the notion of graphic design as a modern profession. According to design historian Carlo Vinti, *Linea Grafica* paved the way for the advancement of a modern, service-oriented, graphic design profession in post-war Italy. The issue shown here features the typeface New Alphabet applied to the journal's logo. New Alphabet was designed by Wim Crouwel.

Lithopinion
1966–75
USA

Lithopinion (1966–75, USA) was subtitled The Graphic Arts Public Affairs Journal of Local One, Amalgamated Lithographers of America, and Lithographic Employees. *Lithopinion* was a quarterly magazine established by Edward Swayduck in 1975, while he was president of Local One, a graphic communication trades union in North America. The magazine ran for thirty-nine issues and showcased high quality graphic design and printing alongside a wide range of articles such as 'Misleading and Dangerous Traffic Signs' and 'Why Children Under 16 Get Hooked on Drugs'. It was well designed, with bold use of illustration and photography.

Magazin DP
1931–37
Czech Republic

Magazin DP (1931–37, Czech Republic). The original title for the first three issues was *Jakzijeme*. It was set up to review Czech cultural life, and was published by the publishing cooperative Družstevní práce. It contained photographs by Josef Sudek and Man Ray featured montages by Karel Teige and Ladislav Sutnar. Its typography and covers were designed by Sutnar.

Motif
1958–67
UK

Motif (1958–67, UK) was part of a series of visual arts magazines published by Shenval Press. It was edited for its thirteen issues by Ruari McLean (1917–2006), the designer, typographer and biographer of Jan Tschichold. It was intended to bring the concept of visual culture to a wider audience by presenting illustrated articles on graphic design, typography and illustration. *Motif* 10 (shown here) has a cover by Peter Blake, and an article by Reyner Banham on Pop Art.

Das Neue Frankfurt
1926–33
Germany

Das Neue Frankfurt (1926–33, Germany) was edited by Ernst May, with covers and design by Hans Lestikow. The magazine focused on metropolitan design, urban planning and architecture. It was a template for publications dedicated to other German cities, and is seen as a key exemplar of Bauhaus design principles.

Neue Grafik
1958–65
Switzerland

Neue Grafik (1958–65, Switzerland) was launched by Josef Müller-Brockmann as part of an editorial collective with Richard Paul Lohse, Hans Neuberg and Carlo Vivarelli. A total of eighteen issues were produced between 1958 and 1965. According to Richard Hollis, in an essay for the book *100 Years of Swiss Graphic Design* (2014), *Neue Grafik* was a trilingual quarterly, 'typeset entirely in grotesque, laid out in a strict grid, representing the orthodoxy of "constructive" design as it had developed in Zürich'.

novum
1971–present
UK

novum (1971–present, UK) has for eighty-five years tracked design activity in Germany and across the world. Between 1971 and 1996 it was known as *novum-gebrauchsgraphik*, and before that as *Gebrauchsgraphik*. The magazine presents articles on contemporary practitioners such as Stefan Sagmeister and Karlssonwilker. Published by Stiebner Verlag in Munich, *novum* has a monthly circulation of 13,500 in over 80 countries.

PM
1934–42
USA

PM (1934–42, USA) was launched by Robert L Leslie, an influential figure in pre-war graphic design and typesetting. The publication was co-edited by Leslie and Percy Seitlin. *PM* (standing for Production Manager) was published in conjunction with the New York-based typographic shop The Composing Room, of which Leslie was a co-founder. The typesetting house also had a gallery space, which was amongst the first places to host graphic design exhibitions in New York. The bi-monthly publication concentrated on print media, with a particular focus on new technologies for printing and production. It ceased publication in 1942 when the United States entered World War II.

Pagina
1962–65
Italy

Pagina (1962–65, Italy) was co-founded by Bruno Alfieri and Pier Carlo Santini, and designed mostly by Heinz Waibl. Published quarterly in English, French and Italian, only seven issues appeared. The magazine focused on the analysis of graphic design and its daily impact. According to design historian Carlo Vinti, *Pagina* 'probably offers the most immediate window into the "golden age" of Italian graphic design ... Bruno Alfieri, founder and editor of the magazine, is a non-designer figure that would deserve more attention in the history of Italian design'. Experimental printing techniques and papers were used, and fold-out pages and items such as posters and booklets were included. Covers were by leading designers, including Max Bill, Eugenio Carmi, Bob Noorda and Pino Tovaglia.

Plan
1943–51
UK

Plan (1943–51, UK) was the spiral bound magazine of the Architectural Students' Association. The first series spanned four issues. The second series from 1945 onwards (shown here is Plan 6, 1949, on the theme of education), continued in the tradition of the *Northern Architectural Students' Magazine* (NASA), until 1948 when the London Architectural Association took over the management.

Portfolio
1949–51
USA

Portfolio (1949–51, USA) was a hugely influential cross-disciplinary publication designed and art-directed by Alexey Brodovitch. *Portfolio* was to become a blueprint for the creative publications of the second half of the 20th century, but due to its extravagance (it was also free of advertising), it only lasted for three issues. Edited by Frank Zachary, the magazine was a large-format publication that drew inspiration from the popular photo journals of the period – principally *Life* and *Look*. It included inserts and foldouts, and was printed on a mixture of paper stocks.

Print
1940–present
USA

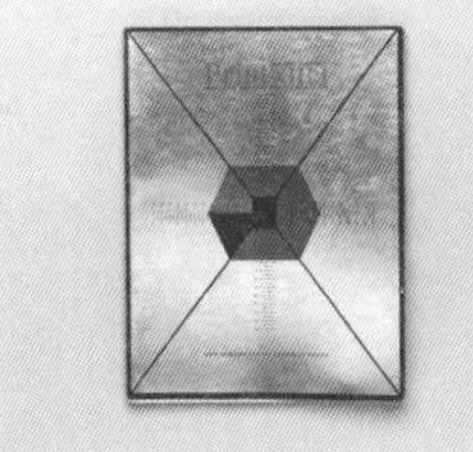

Print (1940–present, USA) started out as a quarterly journal and now appears bi-monthly, covering a wide area of professional, aesthetic and cultural topics. Articles survey and critique the entire spectrum of visual communication, from interactive design to mainstream advertising. Regular contributors have included design writers Rick Poynor, Paul Shaw and Steven Heller. The magazine has a tradition of featuring striking covers created by leading designers. As Steven Heller has noted, *Print* has 'just celebrated 75 years of continuous publishing, a span that makes it the most historically valuable of them all.'

Print Design and Production
1965–67
UK

Print Design and Production (1965–67, UK) was a bi-monthly print trade journal, printed and published by Cox & Sharland. *Print Design and Production* was previously known as *Book Design and Production*. Despite its strong print focus on machinery and the technicalities of printing, the editorial content was surprisingly progressive, with articles on Aubrey Beardsley, prominent graphic designers of the period, and logo design. After 1967 its title was *Print in Britain*.

Projekt
1955–unknown
Poland

Projekt (1955–unknown, Poland) was one of the few publications in the Eastern Bloc to showcase the art and design not only from behind the Iron Curtain, but also from the West. Particularly striking were its covers, many of them created by members of the famous Polish Poster School – among them Henryk Tomaszewski, Józef Mroszczak and Jan Lenica. As a satellite state of the Soviet Union, Poland was subject to censorship and repression, and Polish artists and designers were expected to adhere to the official Soviet style of Socialist Realism. But Poland has a long history of rebellion and opposition, and this contrarian spirit can be seen in the pages and covers of numerous editions of *Projekt*.

De Reclame
1922–36
Netherlands

De Reclame (1922–36, Netherlands) was a Dutch periodical focusing on advertising. *De Reclame* replaced its idealistic predecessor *De Bedrijfsreclame* with a more accepting approach to the fast-growing advertising sector in pre-war Dutch national life. But it also featured avant-garde practitioners such as Piet Zwart, Paul Schuitema and Cassandre. Published monthly, it featured original cover designs, mostly in the fashionable Art Moderne style.

SGM
1947–52
Switzerland

SGM (*Schweitzer Graphische Mitteilungen*) (1947–52, Switzerland) was a trade journal catering for Switzerland's printing and publishing industries, with features on graphic design and new print and production methods. It was published by Verlag Zollikofer in St. Gallen, and its editors were Hermann Strehler and Rudolf Hostettler, both traditional typographers. Later the magazine embraced Swiss Modernism, giving space to the work of Max Bill, Max Huber and Herbert Bayer. In 1952, *SGM* joined forces with *Revue Suisse de l'Imprimerie* and *Typographische Monatsblätter* to form a monthly publication known as *TM* (see below).

Stile Industria
1954–63
Italy

Stile Industria (1954–63, Italy) was Italy's first magazine dedicated to industrial design, graphic art and packaging design. It was a spin-off from Gio Ponti's (1891–1979) *Domus. Stile Industria* promoted design as a cultural force, and gave an international context for Italian graphic design and designers. The covers were designed by many of the leading post-war Italian and international graphic designers, including Michele Provinciali, Pino Tovaglia, Max Huber, Bruno Munari and Franco Grignani.

Type Talks
1945–unknown
USA

Type Talks (1945–unknown, USA) was published by the Advertising Typographers Association of America, for the 'promotion of better graphic communications', with subjects ranging from typography to advertising to print production. The first issue of *Type Talks* appeared in 1945 and well over 100 issues were produced. After a hiatus, publication resumed in 1989 with an issue designed by Paul Rand, and including an interview with Rand.

A Typographic Quest
1964–unknown
USA

A Typographic Quest (1964–unknown, USA) was published by Westvaco (West Virginia Pulp and Paper Co.) It was a short-lived magazine of six issues. The first four in the series were written and designed by Canadian designer Carl Dair, a teacher, type designer and author of the book *Design with Type* (1952). *A Typographic Quest* consisted of six saddle-stitched booklets of about 30 pages, usually printed in two colours. Issue No.1 had as its theme the question 'What is typography?' Issue No.2 was devoted to display typography.

Typographica
1949–67
UK

Typographica (1949–67, UK) was founded and edited by designer, writer, photographer and educator Herbert Spencer, and became a hugely influential journal of typography and visual arts. It was produced in two series: the 'Old Series' and the 'New Series'. Each series was published in sixteen issues. Articles in the journal included 'The integration of photo and type', 'Political typography', 'Recent typography in France', 'Five Polish photographers', 'Road signs in Holland' and 'Avant-garde graphics in Poland between the two world wars'. Spencer was just 25 years old when the first *Typographica* was published.

TM
1932–present
Switzerland

TM (Typographische Monatsblätter) (1932–present, Switzerland). Along with *Neue Grafik*, *TM* was one of Switzerland's two most significant graphic design journals. Published by Der Schweizerische Typographenbund (STB) in Bern, it played a crucial role in advancing modernist graphic design in Switzerland. Jan Tschichold was an important contributor. In the 1990s, *TM* championed the work of Wolfgang Weingart and other radical neo-modernist Swiss typographers. A book was published in 2013 by Lars Muller detailing the history of this important typographic journal.

Typography
1936–39
UK

Typography (1936–39, UK) was founded by Robert Harling a prominent figure in the pre- and post-war British typography scene. He had numerous roles in newspapers, advertising and publishing. He was typographical adviser to *The Sunday Times*, and he designed the Victorian-flavoured typefaces Chisel, Playbill, Keyboard and Tea Chest. *Typography* was the quarterly journal published by James Shand's Shenval Press. It featured articles on children's books, political graphics and ecclesiastical typography. With Shand's support, Harling subsequently launched *Alphabet and Image* (1946–48) a successor to the short-lived *Typography.*

U&lc
1970–99
USA

ulm
1958–68
Germany

Uppercase
1960s–65
Germany

(Das) Werk
1914–present
Switzerland

U&lc (1970–99, USA) was founded by Herb Lubalin and the International Typeface Corporation. *U&lc* (*Upper & Lower Case*) was a magazine for showcasing the graphic arts and typography, and under Lubalin's editorship it became a powerful voice in the phototypesetting world. It featured an eclectic mix of vintage and contemporary subject matter: an article by Norman Mailer on graffiti sits next to one on Spencerian script. Yet, despite the diversity of subject matter, *U&lc* was a commercial enterprise. ITC (of which Lubalin was a founder) used it as a platform to publicise their new typefaces. The tabloid-format publication appeared quarterly and was distributed by direct mail, free to anyone who signed up to receive it. By the end of the 1970s it had a controlled circulation of over 250,000 and an international readership, according to ITC, of one million.

ulm (1958–68, Germany) was a complementary magazine first produced to mark the fifth anniversary of the Ulm School of Design (Hochschule für Gestaltung Ulm), and ran until the school closed a decade later. The publication was founded by Inge Scholl, Otl Aicher and Max Bill, all members of the faculty of the school. The school gained a reputation in the 1950s and 1960s as one of the most progressive institutions for teaching design. The journal was published sporadically over 21 issues. The first issue was a prospectus, with subsequent editions devoted to the school's ever-changing pedagogical philosophy and its industrial connections. The design was by Anthony Froshaug, assisted by Ulm students.

Uppercase (early 1960s–1965, Germany) was a small-format journal produced by the Hochschule für Gestaltung Ulm. Only five issues of this design and typography magazine were published. It was edited by Theo Crosby, a future founding member of Pentagram. Issue 5 (shown here) contained articles on topics such as visual language, the work of Tomás Maldonado, and Roger Mayne's photographic series of London street life. The front and back covers are gatefolds, and open out to form a single geometric composition in blue on white paper.

(Das) Werk (1914–present, Switzerland). The first edition of this magazine appeared in 1914; since then its cover designs have reflected changes in typographic fashion. It began life with a traditional symmetrical layout, but by 1955 it had moved to a modernist, asymmetrical layout (by Karl Gerstner). In 1981, the magazine became known as *Werk, Bauen+Wohnen*. It publishes ten issues per year and is dedicated to current debates on architecture and urbanism. It is the official organ of the Federation of Swiss Architects and the Association of Swiss Interior Designers and Interior Architects, and claims to be the most widely read architecture magazine in Switzerland. It is also available elsewhere in the world, with texts in German, English and French.

Impact 1.0, Design magazines, journals and periodicals [1922–73], and it's sister publication *Impact 2.0, Design magazines, journals and periodicals [1974–2016]*, have been made possible by the generosity and enthusiasm of the following institutions, publishers and individuals:

Archives (both volumes):

Rose Gridneff, the guardian of the University of the Creative Arts archive in Epsom, UK, not only gave us unfettered access to a vast collection of magazines, but also allowed us to draw from her personal collection. Sasha Tochilovsky, a long-standing friend of Unit Editions, gave us freedom to select specimens from the many international titles held at the Herb Lubalin Study Center of Design and Typography in New York, USA. The book was built around the foundation that these two archives provided.

Contributors (both volumes):

We owe a special debt of thanks to the following individuals who contributed magazines and journals from their personal collections: Seymour Chwast and Paula Scher (*Push Pin Graphic*); Rachel Dalton, Jack Grafton, Callin Mackintosh, Sam Stevenson, Tommy Spitters (Spin/Unit Editions); Sarah Douglas (*Wallpaper**); Richard Doust (RCA); Simon Esterson (Esterson Associates and *Eye*); Richard Hollis; Mark Holt (*Octavo*); Domenic Lippa (Pentagram); Matt Lamont (FoxDuo); Quentin Newark (Atelier Works); Richard Spencer Powell (*Monocle*); Hans Dieter Reichert (*Baseline*); Sascha Lobe (L2M3); Mason Wells (Bibliothéque).

Interviewees (both volumes):

James Biber (Biber Architects); Patrick Burgoyne (*Creative Review*); Kirsty Carter and Emma Thomas (A Practise For Everyday Life); Ken Garland; Iker Gil (*Mas Context*); Rose Gridneff (UCA), Richard Hollis; Mark Holt (*Octavo*); Will Hudson (It's Nice That); Jeremy Leslie (magCulture); Kiyonori Muroga (*Idea*); Hans-Dieter Reichardt (*Baseline*); R Roger Remington (Vignelli Centre for Design Studies); Caroline Roberts (*Grafik*); Paul Shaw; Deyan Sudjic (Design Museum); Teal Triggs (RCA); Rudy VanderLans (*Emigre*); Carlo Vinti (Progetto grafico); Mason Wells (Bibliothéque).

Publishers/rights owners (both volumes):

Satoru Yamashita (*+81*); Thomas Weaver (*AA Files*); Kalle Lasn (*Adbusters*); Jon Astbury (*AJ*); Emanuele Piccardo (*Archphoto*); Alexandre Dimos (*Back Cover*); Katrin Zbinden (*Bauen+Wohnen*); Johnny Tucker (*Blueprint*); Mondadori Group (*Casabella*); Sallyanne Theodosiou (*Circular*); Kyle May (*Clog*); Solveig Seuss (*Concrete Flux*); Patrick Burgoyne/Centaur Media (*Creative Review*), Design Council/University of Brighton Design Archives via Chris Finnegan (*Design*); Jo Klatt (*Design+Design*); Ashley Duffalo, Courtesy the Walker Art Centre (*Design Quarterly*); Johanna Agerman Ross (*Disegno*); Domus S.p.A (*Domus*); Peter Bilak, Stuart Bailey (*Dot Dot Dot*).

Rudy Vanderlans (*Emigre*); Michel Chenaux/Isabelle Moisy/Pyramyd (*Etapes*); John L. Walters (*Eye*); Peter Wesner/Stephan Ott (*Form*); Johnathon Vaughn Strebly (*Format*); Christine Moosmann, Hans Peter Copony/Stiebner Verlag GmbH (*Gebrauschgraphik & novum*); B. Martin Pedersen (*Graphis*); Caroline Roberts/Grafik Ltd (*Grafik*); Kim Kwangchul (*Graphic*); Paul van Mameren/Lecturis (*Hard Werken*); Patrick Wallis Burke/The International Council of Graphic Design Associations (*Icographic*); John Jervis/Anja Wohlstrom (*Icon*); Kiyonori Muroga (*Idea*); Laurence Ng/Systems Design Limited (*IdN*); Thierry Häusermann (*IDPURE*); Sam Vallance, F+W (*Industrial Design/I.D.*); Maurizio Corraini Srl. (*Inventario*); Mike Zender (*The Journal of Typographic Research*); Iker Gil (*Mas Context*); © DACS 2016 (*Neue Grafik*); NAi Publishers/Karel Martens (*Oase*); Hamish Muir (*Octavo*).

Erin Cain (*Pamphlet Architecture*); Marcroy Eccleston Smith (*People of Print*); Felix Burrichter/FEBU Publishing (*Pin-Up*); Cody Lee Barbour (*Print Isn't Dead*); Zachary Petit (*Print*); It's Nice That (*Printed Pages*); Thomas Williams (*Process Journal*); Jack Self (*Real Review*); Michel Wlassikoff (*Signes*); Julia Kahl (*Slanted*); Domus S.p.A (*Stile Industria*); Studio (*Studio*), Paul van Mameren/Lecturis (*De maniakken*); Jack Hale (*The Modernist*); Observer Omnimedia LLC (*The Quarterly*); syndicom - Swiss union for media and communication (*TM*); Peter Mertens, Max Kisman (*TYP*); Jonathan Doney, International Society of Typographic Designers (*TypoGraphic*); London College of Communication (*Typos*), International Typeface Corporation, Ltd/fonts.com (*U&lc*); Dr Martin Mäntele (Head of Archive)/Hochschule für Gestaltung, Deutschland (*ulm*); Derek Brazell/AOI (*Varoom*); The MIT Press (*Visible Language*); Jaco Emmen (*de Vorm*); Stichting Industriële Vormgeving/Tel Design (*Vorm*); Freek Kroesbergen (*Vombrichten*); Studio Dumbar (*Zee Zucht*); Vladimir Krichevski, Yelena Chernevich (*Da!*).

Impact 1.0
–
Design magazines, journals and periodicals [1922–73]

Unit 27

Editors:
Tony Brook
Adrian Shaughnessy

Creative Director:
Tony Brook

Writer:
Adrian Shaughnessy

Sub-editor:
Susannah Worth

Design:
Tony Brook
Rachel Dalton
Jack Grafton
Andrea Guccini
Claudia Klat
Callin Mackintosh
Tommy Spitters

Researcher:
Alice Shaughnessy

Proof Reader:
Cathy Johns

Production Manager:
Sam Stevenson

Publishing Director:
Patricia Finegan

Typefaces:
Futura Maxi
Rotis Serif

Paper:
80gsm Multioffset
300gsm Starline creamback

Printer:
Die Keure

ISBN: 978-0-9932316-8-1

Unit Editions
Studio 2
33 Stannary Street
London SE11 4AA
United Kingdom
T +44 (0)20 7793 9555
F +44 (0)20 7793 9666
post@uniteditions.com
www.uniteditions.com